READINGS FOR LEARNING TO TEACH IN THE SECONDARY SCHOOL

Readings for Learning to Teach in the Secondary School brings together key articles to develop and support student teachers' understanding of the theory, research and evidence base that underpins effective practice.

Designed for all students engaging with M level study, each reading is contextualised and includes questions to encourage reflection and help you engage with material critically. Annotated further reading for every section supports your own research and writing.

Readings are structured to make links with the practical guidance in the accompanying core textbook, *Learning to Teach in the Secondary School*. Topics covered include:

- motivation
- troublesome classroom behaviour
- ability grouping
- inclusive education
- personalised learning
- testing
- achievement and underachievement.

Edited by the team that brings us *Learning to Teach in the Secondary School*, this Reader is an indispensible 'one-stop' resource that will support all students studying, researching and writing at M level on PGCE courses, as well as those on all other secondary education courses and masters degrees.

Susan Capel is Professor and Head of the School of Sport and Education at Brunel University, UK.

Marilyn Leask is Professor of Education at Brunel University, UK.

Tony Turner was Senior Lecturer in Education at the Institute of Education, University of London, UK.

LEARNING TO TEACH SUBJECTS IN THE SECONDARY SCHOOL SERIES

Series Editors: Susan Capel, Marilyn Leask and Tony Turner

Designed for all students learning to teach in secondary schools, and particularly those on school-based initial teacher education courses, the books in this series complement *Learning to Teach in the Secondary School* and its companion, *Starting to Teach in the Secondary School*. Each book in the series applies underpinning theory and addresses practical issues to support students in school and in the higher education institution in learning how to teach a particular subject.

READINGS FOR LEARNING TO TEACH IN THE SECONDARY SCHOOL

A companion to M level study

Edited by

**Susan Capel, Marilyn Leask
and Tony Turner**

Routledge
Taylor & Francis Group

LONDON AND NEW YORK

First published 2010
by Routledge
2 Park Square, Milton Park, Abingdon, Oxon OX14 4RN

Simultaneously published in the USA and Canada
by Routledge
270 Madison Ave, New York, NY 10016

Routledge is an imprint of the Taylor & Francis Group, an informa business

Typeset in Times New Roman PS and Helvetica by
Florence Production Ltd, Stoodleigh, Devon

Printed and bound in Great Britain by
TJ International Ltd, Padstow, Cornwall

British Library Cataloguing in Publication Data
A catalogue record for this book is available from the British Library

Library of Congress Cataloging-in-Publication Data
  Readings for learning to teach in the secondary school: a companion
  to M level study/edited by Susan Capel, Marilyn Leask and Tony Turner.
    p. cm.
    Includes bibliographical references and index.
  1. High school teaching.   2. Classroom management.   I. Capel, Susan Anne,
  1953– II. Leask, Marilyn, 1950– III. Turner, Tony, 1935–
  LB1737.A3R35 2009
  373.11–dc22   2009017244

ISBN10: 0–415–55209–5 (hbk)
ISBN10: 0–415–55210–9 (pbk)

ISBN13: 978–0–415–55209–7 (hbk)
ISBN13: 978–0–415–55210–3 (pbk)

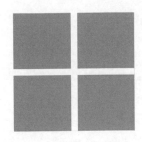

CONTENTS

CONTENTS ■ ■ ■ ■

ILLUSTRATIONS

FIGURES

TABLES

BOX

ACKNOWLEDGEMENTS

1   Emotional preparation for teaching: a case study about trainee teachers in England
    Denis Hayes
    Teacher development, 2003 (Taylor & Francis Ltd, www.informaworld.com, reprint by permission
    of the publisher)
2   Changing contexts: teacher professional development and ICT pedagogy
    Matthew Pearson and Steven Naylor
    With kind permission from Springer Science and Business Media, *Education and Information
    Technologies*, 'Changing contexts: teacher professional development and ICT pedagogy', 2006,
    Vol. 11: 283–291
3   Practice makes perfect? Learning to learn as a teacher
    Hazel Hagger, Katharine Burn, Trevor Mutton and Sue Brindley
    Oxford Review of Education, 2008 (Taylor & Francis Ltd, www.informaworld.com, reprint by
    permission of the publisher)
4   Lesson planning and the student teacher: rethinking the dominant model
    Peter D. John
    Journal of Curriculum Studies, 2006 (Taylor & Francis Ltd, www.informaworld.com, reprinted by
    permission of the publisher)
5   Towards the improvement of learning in secondary school: students' views, their links to theories
    of motivation and to issues of under- and over-achievement
    Keith Postlethwaite and Linda Haggarty
    Research Papers in Education, 2002 (Taylor & Francis Ltd, www.informaworld.com, reprinted by
    permission of the publisher)
6   Recent research on troublesome classroom behaviour: a review
    Robyn Beaman, Kevin Wheldall and Coral Kemp
    Australasian Journal of Special Education, 2007, Vol. 31, No. 1. Reprinted by permission of
    Australian Academic Press.
7   A positive psychology approach to tackling bullying in secondary schools: a comparative evaluation
    Andrew Richards, Ian Rivers and Jacqui Akhurst
    Reproduced with permission from the *British Journal of Educational Psychology* © The British
    Psychological Society
8   The effects of social class and ethnicity on gender differences in GCSE attainment: a secondary
    analysis of the Youth Cohort Study of England and Wales 1997–2001
    Paul Connolly
    British Educational Research Journal, 2006 (Taylor & Francis Ltd, www.informaworld.com, reprint
    by permission of the publisher)

9 Educational psychology and the effectiveness of inclusive education/mainstreaming
   Geoff Lindsay
   Reproduced with permission from the *British Journal of Educational Psychology* © The British Psychological Society

10 Setting or mixed ability? Teachers' views of the organisation of pupils for learning
   Chris M. M. Smith and Margaret J. Sutherland
   Copyright © 2003 nasen. Reproduced with permission of Blackwell Publishing Ltd.

11 Moral education in practice
   Colin Wringe
   With kind permission from Springer Science and Business MediaSpringer, 'Moral education: beyond the teaching of right and wrong', Colin Wringe, *Moral education in practice*, 2006, 159–175

12 Personal understanding and target understanding: mapping influences on the outcomes of learning
   Noel Entwistle and Colin Smith
   Reproduced with permission from the *British Journal of Educational Psychology* © The British Psychological Society

13 Personalised learning: ambiguities in theory and practice
   R.J. Campbell, W. Robinson, J. Neelands, R. Hewston and L. Mazzoli
   Copyright © 2007 Society for Educational Studies (SES). Reproduced with permission of Blackwell Publishing Ltd.

14 Neuroscience and education
   Usha Goswami
   Reproduced with permission from the *British Journal of Educational Psychology* © The British Psychological Society

15 Testing, motivation and learning
   Based on an extensive review by Wynne Harlen and Ruth Deakin-Crick
   (Assessment Reform Group supported by The Nuffield Foundation)

16 'Troublesome boys' and 'compliant girls': gender identity and perceptions of achievement and underachievement
   Susan Jones and Debra Myhill
   British Journal of Sociology of Education, 2004 (Taylor & Francis Ltd, www.informaworld.com, reprint by permission of the publisher)

17 It's not which school but which set you're in that matters: the influence of ability grouping practices on student progress in mathematics
   Dylan Wiliam and Hannah Bartholomew
   British Educational Research Journal, 2004 (Taylor & Francis Ltd, www.informaworld.com, reprint by permission of the publisher

18 Rethinking the school curriculum
   John White
   From: *Rethinking the school curriculum*, edited by J. White, 2004, Routledge. Reproduced by permission of Taylor & Francis Books UK

19 Value-added is of little value
   Stephen Gorard
   Journal of Education Policy, 2006, Vol. 21, No. 2. Reprinted by permission of the publisher (Taylor & Francis Ltd, http://www.tandf.co.uk/journals).

20 The role of teacher research in continuing professional development
   Margaret Kirkwood and Donald Christie
   The Role of Teacher Research in Continuing Professional Development, Margaret Kirkwood and Donald Christie. Copyright © 2006 Society for Educational Studies (SES). Reproduced with permission of Blackwell Publishing Ltd.

INTRODUCTION

Susan Capel, Marilyn Leask and Tony Turner

Teaching is a complex process which draws on many skills, techniques, procedures and abilities. Some skills, techniques, procedures and abilities are learned during an initial teacher education (ITE) course or on the job, such as how to handle groups of young people, present tasks, explain ideas, and so on. Others are already part of you, your personality and include qualities such as empathy, patience, positive outlook, willingness to learn. Yet other aspects of a teacher's repertoire are instinctive, having been learned through experience but not been articulated.

Alongside those skills, techniques, procedures and abilities is the notion of professionalism, the responsibility to teach well and support all pupils. Professionalism requires that you continually strive to improve your teaching, to keep up to date with the changing curriculum, changing views of pedagogy and new resources. In order to improve your teaching you need to review your practice regularly; the notion of a reflective teacher acknowledges that requirement. Structured reflection of your practice allows you to check the quality and impact of your practice and provides a foundation for change and development.

We suggest that there are a number of steps you may take in deciding to change your practice. These steps are:

1   accepting that the effort is worthwhile;
2   appreciating what is working well and what is working less well. This information is gained in part by structured reflection on practice, review of lessons and by being observed by a third party who gives you feedback on your practice; in other words, research into your own practice;
3   using education theories, research and evidence to inform your practice;
4   being prepared to spend time and energy to make the necessary changes.

Your ITE course is designed to start you on this process, but it is merely a start. An ITE course is not designed just to give you a set of skills, techniques and procedures which can be reproduced as needed, but also to enable you to understand the context of classrooms in general and introduce you to a wider set of educational issues. Thus:

> ITE is not an apprenticeship but a step on the journey of personal development in which your teaching skills, techniques and procedures develop alongside an emerging understanding of the teaching and learning process and the education

system in which it operates. This is a journey of discovery that begins on the first day of your course and may stop only when you retire. Teachers are expected to undertake further professional development throughout their career. For this reason we use the term initial teacher *education* rather than initial teacher training throughout this book.

(Capel, Leask and Turner, 2009: 2)

Thus, your ITE course combines the development of your practical teaching, learning to read the classroom and pupils and being able to respond, putting your developing practice into the context of classrooms in general and understanding wider educational issues, underpinned by theory, research and evidence. Thus, developing as an effective teacher requires you to link theory and practice. The focus of the companion book *Learning to teach in the secondary school: a companion to school experience* (currently in its 5th edition) (Capel, Leask and Turner, 2009) is on supporting the development of the skills, techniques and procedures you use in your practical teaching and providing an entry to ways of understanding what you do and see, through introducing underpinning theory, research and evidence which have been synthesised and presented as good practice.

In the schools in which you are placed on your ITE course, you practise your teaching in a specific context with those pupils, in that school, at that time. Your higher education institution (HEI) gives you a broader view, e.g. reflecting on why school 'A' takes one approach and school 'B' has another approach. This enables you to reflect on the strengths of both and how and why you might respond to pupils in different circumstances.

However, in order to develop as a teacher, it is important that you do not only do what the teacher in the classroom does, or what was done to you, nor do it mechanically. Understanding the theory, research and evidence base helps you learn to become a reflective practitioner, enabling you to approach each classroom and respond to the pupils you meet differently. All children are not the same, and children are not the same today as they were when you were a child.

There are a number of different theories about teaching and learning. You need to be aware of what these are, understand them, reflect on them and consider how they help you to explain more fully what you are trying to do and why. Through the process of theorising about what you are doing, reflecting on a range of other theories as well as your own, and drawing on the research and evidence base, you understand your practice better and develop into a reflective practitioner, that is, a teacher who makes conscious decisions about teaching strategies to employ and who modifies their practice in the light of experiences (see Capel, Leask and Turner, 2009: 2).

This takes time. Your ITE course only provides you with a start to developing your own personal understanding of the teaching and learning process. You do not stop learning and developing when you finish your ITE course; rather, you are engaged in continuing professional development (CPD) throughout your life.

Although *Learning to teach in the secondary school* (Capel, Leask and Turner, 2009) and other sources of information you refer to on your ITE course provide underpinning, synthesised information, they may not look at the research itself. This book introduces you to some research which underpins the advice you are given, both in the *Learning to teach in the secondary school* text, by the tutors on your ITE course and by others with whom you work.

It also supports the Masters level component which is included on the Postgraduate Certificate in Education (PGCE) course which many of you are following. Although the readings selected for each section are intended to complement the work you carry out on your course and the literature that your tutors refer to, they are also intended to provide a broader perspective on theories of teaching and learning and give you a sense of the scope of educational thought relevant to your lifelong journey as a teacher.

We encourage you to record a synthesis of each reading in the book (and other papers you read) in your professional development portfolio (PDP). The papers themselves and the information in your PDP may provide the basis for, or support the writing of, assignments for the Masters level component of your ITE course. We provide below some guidance to support your developing ability both to read research and to undertake research in your own educational practice.

As well as using the materials to support the Masters level component of your course, you should also integrate the findings, as appropriate, into your own practical experiences. This requires you to develop your ability to integrate theory and practice, to test out ideas, to identify further papers to support your developing knowledge and understanding and further to broaden your perspective to link with your developing practice throughout your career.

Educational research draws on a range of foundation disciplines, each of which brings different things to education and educational research. Some of these foundation disciplines have underpinned educational research for a long time, including history of education; pedagogy (such as cognitive development, scaffolding); philosophy of education (such as the aims and purposes of education); psychology (including human interactions, motivation, learning theories); and sociology (including diversity, multiculturalism). Other foundation disciplines are relatively new additions to underpinning educational research; for example, neuroscience.

The papers in this reader come from several of the foundation disciplines and therefore provide you with some understanding of the different perspectives and what each brings to our understanding in education.

STRUCTURE OF THE READER

This reader is organised under the same headings as the chapters in the generic book *Learning to teach in the secondary school* (Capel, Leask and Turner, 2009). We have chosen texts to reflect the contents of each original chapter and sometimes to correspond to one or more units in a chapter. Some sections of this book have many readings, e.g. Section 4 has six readings. We have not provided a research paper for every unit, as it is not always possible directly to link a research paper with a particular unit. The further reading section addresses that issue.

As well as reflecting the structure and content of the generic book, we recognise that you, the reader, are in a transitional phase, moving from 'not being a teacher' to the position of 'a qualified teacher' by the end of your ITE year. Thus, we have chosen papers that address, at least in part, some of the concerns of a developing teacher. For example, Reading 1, in Section 1, addresses the emotional aspects that student teachers experience during their ITE year, not just when in school and faced with a range of classes and pupil behaviours, but the emotional roller-coaster ride of success and setbacks that accompany practical teaching in its early stages (Hayes, 2003). Another paper, Reading 10 in Section 4, addresses the issues of pupil grouping by investigating the views of practising teachers on the advantages or otherwise of placing pupils in streamed or mixed ability classes for teaching purposes (Smith and Sutherland, 2003). This topic has exercised teachers, educationalists and policy makers for many years; you are likely to meet this issue during your school experiences, with probably differing practices and opinions across different subject departments in one school. Pupil grouping appears again in Section 6, where the influence of setting on pupil progress and its assessment is investigated in the teaching of mathematics (Wiliam and Bartholomew, 2004).

As the last example shows, we have, on occasions, chosen papers that illustrate a general area of interest, but illuminated through a subject-specific piece of research. The issues raised in such papers have both a general and a specific message and often have important things to say to teachers of other subjects. We hope that you are encouraged by our choice of papers to seek out others across a range of disciplines, as well as in your own teaching subject. We give examples below of where to look further for papers.

We include research conducted outside the UK, as many countries confront similar issues to our own, e.g. Reading 6 in Section 3, by Beaman *et al.* (2007), on troublesome classroom behaviour in Australia and other countries. This is an issue of teaching and learning of importance in many countries.

We have identified papers that are not only relevant to your current circumstance but also are relatively recent and up to date, reflecting some of the current areas of interest both in practical teaching and in longer-term educational research. Although the papers have been published in the twenty-first century, we have included references to some older papers, for example, the paper on moral education is by an outstanding educationalist which we believe is relevant today (Dewey, 1909).

The collection of papers we have assembled reflects also the diversity of educational literature. Most obvious are papers reporting first-hand research (e.g. Reading 4 (John, 2006)). Some of these papers use statistical methods to analyse data and your under-standing of these methods is necessary to understand some educational research (e.g. Reading 7 (Richards *et al.*, 2006)). Other papers report on the secondary analysis of pub-lished research, where an author reworks existing data (e.g. Reading 8 (Connolly, 2006)). Another type of research paper is a review of published research which brings together evidence across a number of studies over a period of time and attempts to summarise current evidence (e.g. Reading 6 (Beaman *et al.*, 2007)). We have also included papers which offer a particular view of an issue, giving opinion and supporting evidence (e.g. Reading 19 (Gorard, 2006)). We have included a paper on neuroscience, where studies in a hitherto unrelated field have been applied to education (Reading 14 (Goswami, 2004)). This is not an exhaustive list of the types of educational publications to which you have access, neither does our selection make a similar claim; nevertheless, the field of educational literature is very wide and worth exploring. We hope this reader provides a start on exploring the educational literature.

ACCESSING RESEARCH

There are many educational journals, the titles of which you can access online through your HEI library or by ordering these from your local library. Alternatively, articles can usually be purchased online. Some journals report first-hand, original research, e.g. the *British Educational Research Journal*, the *British Journal of Educational Psychology*. Other journals offer review papers summarising or commenting on recent research, e.g. *Educational Research Review*, *Oxford Review of Education*. Yet others address specific issues, e.g. the *Journal of Special Educational Needs*; or the concerns of subject teachers, e.g. the *Journal of Research in Science Teaching* (these may contain original research and review papers). Yet broader, general educational issues affecting all teachers are addressed by journals such as, for example, the *Journal of Curriculum Studies* and *Assessment in Education*. In order to select from the wide range of published literature, indexes of current research and their source are published in, e.g. *British Educational Index*, *Educational Research Abstracts* and *Educational Resources Information Centre* (ERIC). There are subject indexes as well as indexes compiled by overseas libraries, e.g. Australia, China, all of which may be accessed on-line through your HEI library system. Your subject association is likely to publish a journal with its own research or reviews of research pertinent to your teaching subject. Finally, your tutor and your course materials provide directions of how to access research for your studies, assignments and wider interest and development.

As well as selecting twenty papers for inclusion, we have identified further readings that move you on from both the main text of the companion book *Learning to teach in the secondary school* (Capel, Leask and Turner, 2009) and the papers in this reader, at times indicating papers covering units in the companion book for which no reading has been provided in this text. To help you select from the further readings, we have provided a short statement illustrating the main thrust of each paper. We encourage you to seek further papers from the research literature to address issues related to your teaching, to better inform your reflective practice.

This is only a start, but we hope it encourages you to read widely around topics, to build up your understanding of the research literature underpinning your work as a teacher and also your understanding of the research process.

Your subject association will have considerable resources and should provide support for you in accessing research evidence about your subject. The Teacher Training Resource Bank was established to make available the evidence you may find helpful in learning to be a teacher (see www.ttrb.ac.uk).

Methodologies have been developed for systematically reviewing the evidence base, in an attempt to make sense of the plethora of research studies through undertaking a meta-analysis of research reports. The Evidence for Policy and Practice Information Centre (EPPI-Centre, www.eppi.ioe.ac.uk) has developed a methodology for systematic reviewing which has been applied to many areas of education, and reports can be found on their website.

INTUTE (www.intute.ac.uk) has a considerable database of resources related to educational research which will help you find information about educational research, and Education-line holds papers from conferences which usually provides access to the most up-to-date source of current research as researchers report their findings to colleagues (www.leeds.ac.uk/bei/).

WHY READ RESEARCH?

> A particular contribution that psychology can make to education is to inform the intellectual tool kits of educationalists and sharpen thinking about the processes of teaching and learning.
>
> (Daniels and Edwards, 2004: 1)

So, reading research, Daniels and Edwards argue, sharpens your thinking about education. This is why, alongside practising the essential skills, techniques and procedures for teaching on your school placements, you can expect, in your university-based work, to have to master the theory and research which provide you with the evidence base about effective practice and which support the rationale for what you do.

You may be surprised to find that the education research community in the UK hotly debates the relevance of research to educational practice. Arguments for the lack of usefulness of educational research to the teacher in the classroom include that education is an art not a science; that knowledge from research undertaken in particular contexts is not transferable because contexts for educational practice vary; that every child is different; that the research undertaken is not relevant; that what research there is, is inaccessible and not in a form that is useful to teachers.

So let's turn this question around. Why would you, as a professional, responsible for the life chances of hundreds of children and, consequently, for the kind of society you will grow old in, not want to find research and evidence which might help you be more effective as a teacher? Well there are good reasons why not.

Educational research relevant to your work may not be easy to find, or has never been undertaken. Research into subject specific pedagogies, for example, is very patchy. You may find the form of publication is inaccessible. The current approach to educational research and its publication in the UK is based on models where the main form of communication of new knowledge is through books or journals to which teachers may not have had easy access. The Internet has made research more accessible, so you should be able to access a large research base from across the world. However, the availability of research papers has revealed the fact that these rarely, of themselves, present knowledge in a way that it can be used in the classroom. One of the editors of this text is currently experimenting with different ways in which technology can be used to present knowledge in more accessible forms, through the project 'Pathways to Learning'.

However, these difficulties do not mean you should give up and not try to access research relevant to your practice. You can expect to see improvements over your time as a teacher. You might also be able to undertake some research yourself where you identify a gap.

READING RESEARCH

Research can often only provide snapshots of the areas being researched, and it is essential, when reading research, that you review the material critically. Box 1.1 suggests a list of questions to consider when you are looking for good quality research and reading

---

Box 1.1 POINTS TO CONSIDER WHEN EVALUATING RESEARCH-BASED PAPERS (ADAPTED FROM NEWMAN, ELBOURNE AND LEASK (2004))

Background: Why was the study undertaken, and who funded it?

Focus: Are the research questions clear?

Research design: Is the design of the research clear? Are the methods used for collecting the data likely to provide reasonable answers to the questions?

Timing: When was the study undertaken? What has changed in the area since this study?

Sampling strategy: What size was the sample? Was the sample representative of the group being studied? Were those participating volunteers?

Analysis of the data: Do you have confidence in the way the data were analysed?

The findings: What weight can you give to the findings, given the points above?

research which is likely to influence your practice. We suggest you use this framework to underpin the synthesis (and inform the notes you include in your PDP) when studying the readings in this book.

UNDERTAKING RESEARCH

> While skilful teachers ensure that their classes learn something worthwhile, unskilful ones may turn off that delicate trip switch in children's psyche which keeps their minds open to lifelong learning.
>
> (Wragg, 2004: 1)

So, how do you ensure that your pupils are learning something worthwhile? As previously mentioned, preparation for becoming a teacher is not training where you are learning a set of skills, techniques and procedures that can be reproduced successfully in any context. Rather, it is an education. An important element of your preparation to become a teacher is learning to read the classroom and the pupils. Action research in your classroom enables you to learn in detail about your impact on the pupils.

Action research, using structured reflection, is a core tool in a teacher's professional toolbox, and the companion text, *Learning to teach in the secondary school* (Capel, Leask and Turner, 2009), and *Starting to teach in the secondary school: a companion for the newly qualified teacher* (Capel, Heilbronn, Leask and Turner, 2004) both provide an overview of action research.

We encourage you to become involved in research projects. The model included in this reader, in the Richards *et al.* (2006) paper (Reading 7), for 9-week interventions provides an example of how you can undertake rigorous research in school within an action research paradigm.

Susan Capel, Marilyn Leask and Tony Turner
June 2009

REFERENCES

Capel, S., Heilbronn, R., Leask, M. and Turner, T. (2004) *Starting to teach in the secondary school: a companion for the newly qualified teacher* (2nd edition), London: Routledge.

Capel, S., Leask, M. and Turner, T. (2009) *Learning to teach in the secondary school: a companion to school experience* (5th edition), London: Routledge.

Daniels, H. and Edwards, A. (2004) *The RoutledgeFalmer Reader in psychology of education*, London: Routledge.

Newman, M., Elbourne, D. and Leask, M. (2004) 'Improving the usability of educational research: guidelines for the reporting of empirical primary research studies in education'. Paper presented at the *5th Annual Conference of the Teaching and Learning Research Programme*, 22–24 November, Cardiff. See also Education-line www.leeds.ac.uk/bei/COLN/COLN_default.html, Reference140679.

Wragg, E.C. (2004) *The RoutledgeFalmer Reader in teaching and learning*, London: Routledge.

BECOMING A TEACHER

INTRODUCTION

Professional development is a lifelong process for the teacher that is aided by regular reflection on practice and continuing education. Professional tools, such as structured action research, that aid you in this process are set out in Units 2.1 and 5.4 in Capel, Leask and Turner (2009), and the Richard, Rivers and Akhurst reading included in this volume (Reading 7) demonstrates how planned interventions over a relatively short period can improve the work of the school.

The different forms of professional knowledge that teachers need are discussed in detail in Unit 1.1 of Capel, Leask and Turner (2009), and the summary of these is reproduced here for you below to consider as you study the readings in this section and in the other sections.

Forms of professional knowledge for teaching (adapted from Shulman, 1987)

1   (Subject) Content knowledge, i.e. the subject material that is to be taught. Schwab (1964) identifies two components of content knowledge:

- substantive: knowing what the important concepts and skills in the subject are;
- syntactic: knowing how the concepts and skills are structured and organised within the subject.

2   General pedagogic knowledge, i.e. the broad principles and strategies of classroom management and organisation that apply irrespective of the subject.

3   Curriculum knowledge, i.e. the materials and programmes that serve as 'tools of the trade' for teachers.

4   Pedagogical content knowledge, i.e. the knowledge of what makes for effective teaching and deep learning that is the basis for the selection, organisation and presentation of the content teachers want their pupils to acquire.

5   Knowledge of learners and their characteristics:

- knowledge of learners of a particular age range (empirical or social knowledge); and
- cognitive knowledge of learners, comprising knowledge of child development and knowledge of a particular group of learners.

6   Knowledge of educational contexts, i.e. including a specific school, catchment area and the wider community.
7   Knowledge of educational ends (aims), purposes, values and philosophical and historical influences: both short- and long-term goals of education and of a subject.

The recommended further readings by Shulman and Grossman provide detailed background to these concepts. However, there is a form of knowledge essential to the teacher that is not covered in this summary of professional knowledge, and this is the focus of the first reading (Hayes, 2003) we have included. This is knowledge about yourself, both as a learner and as a teacher. This type of awareness is sometimes called 'emotional intelligence' or 'emotional literacy', and your emotional preparation for teaching is an important part of your professional development.

READINGS IN THIS SECTION ARE:

Reading 1
Emotional preparation for teaching: a case study about trainee teachers in England
Denis Hayes

Hayes addresses the emotions you face as a student teacher. He examines the concepts of emotional literacy and emotional intelligence raised by Gardner, through his theory of multiple intelligences (1983), and Goleman (1995).
    The experiences of student teachers on school placements form the focus of the study, which seeks to make a contribution to the understanding of emotional literacy and its importance and impact in the workplace in the education sector. A strong argument is made for teachers to be aware of the importance of their emotions and those of their pupils in the learning environment. The experiences of forty-one student teachers were gathered through written accounts that the student teachers provided, knowing they would be used for this reading. They were assured anonymity.

Reading 2
Changing contexts: teachers' professional development and ICT pedagogy
Matthew Pearson and Steven Naylor

The second reading, by Pearson and Naylor (2006), addresses issues teachers are facing as schools adopt pedagogical approaches that integrate ICT into new ways of working to support deep and personalised learning. The increasing use of virtual learning environments (VLEs) or learning platforms is expected of schools to support both pupil learning and staff development. You can expect to find considerable research into the dynamics of changing practice through the introduction of ICT into classrooms, and this may be an interesting focus for small-scale research projects you may be undertaking as part of your ITE and CPD. Involving pupils in this sort of research can be a lot of fun. The reading by Rudduck *et al.* in the further readings provides more information about ways of engaging the pupils' voice in the improvement of the school and ongoing reviews of the effectiveness of pedagogic approaches.

In becoming a teacher you need to evaluate your preconceptions of what schooling is and how teachers teach. You are educating young people some of whom will live into the twenty-second century, so your teaching needs to prepare young people for future challenges society faces, rather than challenges that have already passed. You should expect to use a range of technologies and a range of pedagogic approaches that integrate ICT into the learning experience. Note the focus in one school on 'Learning to Learn' as a precursor to subject-focused lessons. In an information-rich society, being able to find information and evaluate its reliability is a core skill. In the reading, pedagogical approaches to collaborative learning through learning communities and personalised learning are considered.

The research methods used in this reading may be new to you – the inclusion of descriptions of the cases on which the research is based is intended to give you a deeper understanding of the issues reported in the research. Rather than just reporting quantitative or qualitative data, researchers in education often use mixed methods, using qualitative data to convey a sense of the lived experience of the humans involved in the research and quantitative data to indicate a sense of the impact or extent of the issues being reported.

FURTHER READING

Grossman, P.L., Wilson, S.M. and Shulman, L.S. (1989) 'Teachers of substance: subject matter knowledge for teaching', in Reynolds, M.C. (ed.) *Knowledge base for the beginning teacher*, Oxford: Pergamon Press: 23–36.

Banks, F., Leach, J. and Moon, B. (1999) 'New understandings of teachers' pedagogic knowledge', in Leach, J. and Moon, B. (eds) *Learners and pedagogy*, London: Paul Chapman.

You need to be aware of the various forms of professional knowledge that you need to acquire in order to operate effectively as a teacher. Both the above readings explore in depth the different forms of knowledge required for teaching, a summary of which is reproduced in the box in the introduction to Section 1 in this book.

Your self-analysis of the level of your knowledge and understanding in the various forms of professional knowledge for teaching provides a useful guide when planning your professional development.

The further readings above link with Unit 1.1 of the 5th edition of *Learning to teach in the secondary school*.

Rudduck, J. and Flitter, J. (2004) 'Introduction: the case for changing our perceptions of young people' in Rudduck, J. and Flitter, J. (2004) *How to improve your school*, London: Continuum: 1–13.

Jean Rudduck is known for her work on 'pupil voice'. She has worked extensively with teachers and pupils on ways to engage pupils in evaluating how the school is achieving its aims and in contributing to the development of the school. Her work on pupil voice, some of which is reported here, has changed the ways in which pupils are consulted in English schools. Pupil voice is one of the gateways to personalised learning that Professor David Hargreaves identifies (see the Specialist Schools and Academies Trust (SSAT), www.ssat-inet.net/whatwedo/personalisinglearning/personalisinglearninggateway.aspx).

These gateways to personalised learning are listed on the above SSAT site as:

- Assessment for learning
- Learning to learn
- Student voice
- Curriculum
- New technologies
- School design and organisation
- Advice and guidance
- Mentoring and coaching
- Workforce development.

Note that a number of these gateways are addressed in the readings in this book.

The above further reading links with Unit 1.2 of the 5th edition of *Learning to teach in the secondary school*.

Passey, D. (2006) 'Technology enhancing learning: analysing uses of information and communication technologies by primary and secondary school pupils with learning frameworks', *The Curriculum Journal*, Vol. 17, No. 2, June: 139–166.

Austin, R. and Anderson, J. (2008) 'Building bridges online', *International Journal of Information and Communication Technology Education*, Vol. 4, No. 1 (January–March): 86–94.

Both of these readings provide research-based examples of effective use of information and communication technologies (ICT) in classrooms. The first provides examples of how to establish how pupils are learning with technologies, the second provides examples of how the world outside the classroom can be integrated into everyday classroom work. Collaborative projects with schools in other countries, such as the one described by Austin and Anderson, provide a wide range of opportunities for deep learning and for work in all subject contexts.

The above further reading links with Unit 1.4 of the 5th edition of *Learning to teach in the secondary school*.

REFERENCES

Schwab, J.J. (1964) 'The structure of the disciplines: meanings and significance', in Ford, G. and Purgo, L. (eds) *The structure of knowledge and the curriculum,* Chicago: Rand McNally.

Shulman, L. (1987) 'Knowledge and teaching: foundation of a new reform', *Harvard Review*, Vol. 57: 1–22.

EMOTIONAL PREPARATION FOR TEACHING

A case study about trainee teachers in England

Denis Hayes

A NOTE FROM THE EDITORS

This reading contains a succinct description of how the qualitative data from documentary analysis of forty-one student teachers' written reflections on the emotions they experienced on school placements was analysed, which may be helpful for student teachers undertaking small-scale research projects.

This reading links with Units 1.1 and 1.2 of the 5th edition of *Learning to teach in the secondary school*.

QUESTIONS TO CONSIDER

1   Consider the work of Gardner and Goleman alongside the following reading. What emotions are described in the reading that student teachers face in their placements? How do your feelings match with, or differ from, those described? How might an understanding of emotional intelligence and emotional literacy be useful to you in building appropriate relationships with pupils and staff?

2   Duncan (2002) found that successful teachers are able to compartmentalise their lives into 'bounded areas of time, space and place'. What might this mean for you?

This reading was first published as: Hayes, D. (2003) 'Emotional preparation for teaching: a case study about trainee teachers in England', *Teacher Development*, Vol. 7: 153–171.

ABSTRACT

With the attention that has been given in recent years to emotional literacy and its implications for working practices, this article seeks to contribute to a fuller understanding of the impact of emotions on the personal well-being and motivation of 41 primary (elementary) trainee teachers in a university in the southwest of England. Through a process of reflective writing, respondents describe the way that their emotional state affected their confidence and enthusiasm for teaching. These emotions were both edifying (largely associated with the prospect of being back in school) and enervating (largely associated with concerns emanating from previous school experiences and conforming to a new school situation). Findings indicate that a typology of emotional condition consists of anticipatory, anxious, fatalistic and affirming emotions. The research highlights the impact of emotional condition on trainee teachers' ability to function efficiently and suggests that in a time of rapid change and increasing pressure on teachers from every direction, learning to cope with emotions is an important element of training. Consequently, it is proposed that the impact of emotions on trainee teachers deserves considerably more attention than has hitherto been recognised.

BACKGROUND

The significance of emotions in the work and motivation of teachers has long been recognised. The concept of *emotional intelligence*, drawn from the work on multiple intelligences by Gardner (1983), has been made popular by Goleman (1995), who has been instrumental in alerting educationists to the central role played by the emotions in decisions and actions. Research about the demands made on teachers suggests that emotions play a major part (e.g. Helsby, 1998; Shaylock, 1998; Troman and Woods, 2000). Indeed, as Hart (2000) notes, teaching is often 'an emotionally demanding and frequently stressful activity' (p. 61). Golby (1996) rightly reminds us that some emotional experience is integral to all life experiences and argues that emotions in teaching should be viewed *cognitively* because 'anger is always anger at something ... fear is always fear of something' (p. 425). Although Golby's perspective goes some way towards rationalising and ordering emotions, it does little to explain the inexplicable (non-rational) fear commonly felt when people face new situations and where anxiety cannot be linked to a specific cause.

Studies have shown that the emotional demands of teaching are not confined to classroom practitioners but extend throughout the school community. For instance, Duncan (2002) argues that head teachers' emotional intelligence strongly influences the way that they (in this case, women primary (elementary) heads) use their 'professional experience, management knowledge, academic knowledge, intuition, personal qualities and insight to lead their schools' (p. 52). She concludes that successful head teachers have considerable self-confidence, enjoy challenges, are able to compartmentalise their lives 'into bounded areas of time, place and space' (p. 50) and do not allow their professional identity to intrude into the other parts of their lives.

However, it is in the classroom that the impact of a teacher's emotional condition is most readily identified. Lortie (1975) found that 76 per cent of the teachers he interviewed selected 'psychic rewards' as the most significant motivating factor in teaching, compared with 12 per cent who opted for external rewards and 12 per cent who cited the convenience of fitting in with family life. Hargreaves (1999) notes from Lortie's work that, when pupils showed affection towards, and regard for, their teachers and demonstrated that they were enjoying (or had enjoyed) their learning, this was a source of reward for teachers.

Part of the explanation for the intense emotions that teaching engenders is the sort of motivation that drives many practitioners. A variety of other surveys concur that altruism, a love for children, a desire to help pupils learn and the enjoyment associated with 'a job well done' are very significant for the large majority of teachers (e.g. Oberski *et al.*, 1999; Shann, 1998; Tirri, 1999). A comprehensive survey of motivating factors by Spear *et al.* (1999) found that those associated with job satisfaction were (in order of priority) the chance to work with children, relating to colleagues, and developing warm personal relationships with pupils. These and similar studies show that teachers appear to be among the groups of professions that 'identify the goals of their work with the good of humanity at large' (Katz, 1995: 223). Indeed, Nias (1996) argues that, without personal commitment, teaching becomes 'unbalanced, meagre, lacking fire and in the end, therefore, unsuccessful' (p. 306), and to take close account of emotion and its impact on staff is ultimately to safeguard children's education. In similar vein, Acker (1999) comments that 'the unguarded demonstration of a child's affection for the teacher, the emotional attachment between teacher and class, the sense that one is doing a job that counts, give teachers a sense of purpose to sustain them' (p. 4). Woods and Jeffrey (1996) explore the heart of effective teaching and conclude that 'Teaching is a matter of communicating and connecting, through the emotions, through care, trust, respect, rapport. It features a great deal of fun, excitement and enthusiasm' (p. 72). Hargreaves (1998) notes that 'good teaching is charged with positive emotions' (p. 835). With regard to trainee teachers, Wilson and Cameron (1996) argue strongly that trainee teachers' personal commitment is likely to enhance rather than detract from effectiveness.

There are indications that *negative* emotions, with the potential to lead to stress, lower performance and problems with teacher retention, are becoming more widespread (Day and Leitch, 2001; Smithers and Robinson, 1998; Wilhelm *et al.*, 2000). The increase in negative emotions has coincided with a spate of government reforms underpinned by a rational-technicist ideology, in which the emotional dimension of teaching has been neglected and replaced by a 'dominant discourse of pragmatism' (Moore *et al.*, 2002: 563). Woods and Carlyle (2002) note that teachers experience times of uncertainty and worry, fret about trivial things when they are 'down in the dumps' and cope with them when they feel positive about life. They expend nervous energy in adjusting to new situations (such as working with a different age phase of children) and sigh with relief when, for example, inspectors leave the school for the final time. Whereas these emotions are natural and may have little lasting effect upon their sense of well-being, other powerful emotions can disempower and have an adverse effect upon effectiveness and self-identity, referred to by Woods and Jeffrey (2002) as 'the combination of personal identity and self-concept' (p. 90). In similar vein, Woods and Carlyle (2002) argue that, during times of stress, teachers undergo an identity passage as aspects of the 'self' are attacked. This identity passage involves separation from the old identity, transition and eventual realignment within the new boundaries. The authors insist that the identity passage 'is navigated through the emotions' (p. 170) that has implications at a micro-level for individuals which, in extreme cases, can lead to a drastic reduction in self-worth and self-confidence, and change in identity.

These claims raise questions about the relationship between emotional literacy and competence. If emotions are central to teachers' work and lives, they merit a significant place in teacher training. Yet, despite the growing literature about the relationship between a teacher's emotional condition and effective teaching, there has been a dearth of interest about emotions experienced by trainee (student) teachers on school placement. Trainees have little control over where they are placed and enter a school that is largely unknown in respect of the ethos, personalities and patterns of behaviour that characterise it. They have to cope with making an effort to adjust to the prevailing expectations, establish and maintain relationships with staff, learn procedures and adapt to the school's priorities, some of which may be abstruse and difficult to interpret. They are, in effect, teachers in the making, and exposed to similar emotional influences in school as are their qualified colleagues.

THE RESEARCH

The aim of this article is to address the impact of the emotions on trainee teachers using four research questions:

1   What emotions do trainee teachers experience while on school placement?
2   How do they compare with those of practising teachers?
3   What do they tell us about emotional literacy and competence?
4   What are the implications for teacher training?

As an essential component of their training programme, trainee primary teachers ('interns') in England must spend a substantial amount of time on school placement to gain experience of classroom teaching and staff membership. Trainees undertaking an undergraduate degree that leads to Qualified Teacher Status are required to spend 32 weeks in school or similar settings; postgraduate trainees undertaking a one-year course have to spend 18 weeks in school.

The research that forms the basis of this article focuses on the emotional condition of trainee primary teachers prior to, and during the commencement of, their final school placement. In particular, the study tried to identify the extent to which trainee teachers' dispositions before school placement affect their attitudes towards teaching, notably how much practice is influenced by confidence level, self-belief and emotional security.

The research relied principally upon an analysis of forty-one written accounts provided by undergraduate trainee teachers (B.Ed.) as part of a course dissertation that required them to analyse retrospectively their experiences during final school placement. Trainee teachers were asked to write a 2000-word synopsis about their final school experiences based around some or all of the following elements:

■   factors influencing their confidence in the build-up to the placement and during it;
■   adjusting to the new situation;
■   coping with challenges;
■   the impact of school experience upon their motivation for teaching.

In the preparation sessions, trainees were encouraged to reveal their true feelings and not to feel constrained about expressing the full range of emotions they experienced. In the event, assignments gave every impression of being openly and honestly written, and informal comments from trainees afterwards suggested that they valued the opportunity to explore and reflect upon their own experiences, and did not flinch from being forthright.

Respondents composed about one third of the total year cohort, and all of them agreed that their work could be used as data for research. The other two thirds of the year group had selected at an earlier stage to focus on other aspects of school experience than the emotional dimension, such as teaching children with special educational needs and curriculum issues. Participants reflected a representative gender distribution for trainee primary teachers (thirty-four female, seven male), of whom all of the male respondents specialised in the upper primary range (Key Stage 2 (KS2)), and female respondents were almost equally divided between KS1 and KS2. With respect to age profile, approximately one quarter of the respondents was aged over 30 years; of the remainder the majority was 21 or 22 years old. Consequently, the sample was typical of students who undertake undergraduate courses in initial primary teacher education, both from a gender and an age perspective. Respondents were guaranteed anonymity, and the data were not analysed until after the end of the degree course.

The written extracts made public the trainees' emotions that would otherwise have been kept private and provide a rich source of information and insights into their thinking and feelings. The emotions associated with the change of role from student (outside school) to trainee teacher (inside school) and the issues that they encountered are significant in as much as they appear to mirror the sorts of pressures that qualified teachers face when they begin teaching or change schools (e.g. Acker, 1999). Giving the cohort of trainees the opportunity to write about emotionally powerful experiences was important, not only in a cathartic sense to help them come to terms with what had been, in the words of one trainee, 'the most important eight weeks of my life', but also as a preparation for the job of being a teacher during a time of continuous rapid change in schools.

Data were analysed using a qualitative inductive method through open coding and the identification of emerging themes and categories (Strauss and Corbin, 1990). Computer software was not employed in the analysis. Rather, the somewhat laborious but more satisfying process of trawling through the extracts line by line was undertaken. The individual phrases and statements (or 'structural segments' (Wengraf, 2001: 245ff.)) were listed until over 500 had been collected. The structural segments were scrutinised at considerable length until key themes began to emerge. It was quickly apparent that issues relating to respondents' optimism, pessimism and confidence about the forthcoming school placement were threaded throughout most of the respondents' comments, both in terms of the number of entries and the forcefulness with which they were expressed (Kemper, 1993). The fact that emotions played a significant role in shaping the attitude with which trainee teachers approached their placements was confirmed by the common patterns that emerged from data, as decisions were made concerning the inclusion of 'broadbrush detail' from the extracts (Coffey and Atkinson, 1997: 32). The broadbrush analysis indicated that emotions could be edifying (largely associated with the prospect of being back in school) or enervating (largely associated with concerns emanating from previous school experiences and conforming to a new school situation). Subsequently, a typology of emotions was established:

- anticipatory emotions
- anxious emotions
- fatalistic emotions
- affirming emotions.

These categories were gradually 'saturated' using verbatim extracts from respondents' extracts about their feelings prior to undertaking the placement. These 'microcosms' (Scheff, 1997: 48) or 'datum bits' (Wengraf, 2001: 292) were used to illuminate significant issues that respondents were attempting to communicate through their writing. Words and phrases that included terms such as 'anxiety' and 'excitement' and 'felt uncertain about' were used as signals that an emotional response was significant, and the appropriate quotations are offered below as representative of each type.

FINDINGS

Anticipatory emotions

It would be surprising to find a trainee who did not feel excited anticipation prior to a school placement! However, the intensity of some of the emotions described in the accounts was striking. Respondents' accounts of the preplacement period left no doubts that their emotional condition had a significant impact on their preparation for teaching, as expressions of fervour, excitement, agitation, passion and enthusiasm were liberally threaded throughout the accounts. Rita summarised the situation by referring to her belief that the placement was her final opportunity and the ultimate challenge that she had to face and overcome if she wanted to become a qualified teacher:

> Final school experience had arrived. Eleven weeks of placement at a large primary school was to be my destination and I was the only trainee teacher who would be going there. My emotions were running high. This was it! Time to prove myself. A teacher is what I had always wanted to be and it was nearly within my reach.
>
> (Rita)

Louise agonised over the possibility that she might not be able to convince 'significant others' (Stephenson, 1995) that she was up to the job:

> My final school experience was an immense learning curve for my professional development, classroom ability and, most importantly, my confidence. Before commencing the school placement there were the common emotional feelings of excitement and anxiety that are felt before embarking on any new venture. However, the most emotional issue for me was whether I was actually capable of teaching, as this had been questioned by some people previously.
>
> (Louise)

Balbinder explained that going into school involved an 'emotional journey', encompassing excitement and apprehension. She implied that there was no means of avoiding the turmoil that such a voyage would generate. It simply had to be negotiated and coped with in the best way possible:

> There are always mixed feelings initially because no matter how many teaching experiences you have, each one always feels like your first. From day one you begin an emotional journey of excitement as well as apprehension in terms of whether or not you will fit into the school and be able to become an active member within it.
>
> (Balbinder)

Anticipatory emotions were often characterised by a conglomerate of questions and feelings in the minds of trainees. For instance:

> As teaching practice approaches you are filled with a mixture of emotions. Questions spin around in your head: Where will I be placed? What age will the children be? What will the school be like? Will it be anything like last time? This fear of the unknown and uncertainty generates feelings of excitement and anxiety.
>
> (Gemma)

> I had a mixture of emotions. I was looking forward to seeing the school, the class, the facilities, and to assess the general ethos of the place. However, among the excitement there was a genuine feeling of nerves.
>
> (Julia)

Although respondents were keen to become involved again with children in school (a key motivating factor), some of them doubted whether they would be able to cope with the many demands that teaching would make of them. Eve and Ewan were among those who felt this way:

> I looked forward to my final year teaching practice with a mixture of excited anticipation at the prospect of being able to have a 'proper go' and occasional, no, *frequent*, bouts of anxiety brought on by thoughts of 'What if I can't cope with staying up until all hours trying to plan, re-plan and replan again?'
>
> (Eve)

> My mind was filled with conflicting emotions. I tried to be positive yet I was apprehensive. My outward appearance had to be one of confidence yet I felt uneasy and unsure. Indeed, I asked myself many times if I would be hindering the children's learning if I were to teach feeling the way I did.
>
> (Ewan)

For some trainees, the prospect of coping with many weeks of heavy demands erected a psychological barrier that detracted from the positive excitement that came from being involved in children's learning again. These conflicting emotions suggest that, although anticipation could act as a motivator, it could also act as a hindrance when the fears about coping outweighed the trainee's appetite for teaching.

Anxious emotions

For many trainees, anxiety had a major impact upon their attitude in the run-up to the placement. In a minority of cases, the natural anxiety that emerges for most people when they are on the threshold of a new, significant experience seemed to have deteriorated into a more oppressive and even strangulating fear. The use of phrases such as 'distinctly worried' and 'plagued my mind' and descriptors such as 'trepidation' indicated the depth of these feelings. There were particular concerns expressed by respondents in three areas:

■ the need for them to make a good impression on the staff in school;
■ the challenge of adjusting to a new and largely unknown situation and 'finding a place' there;

■ uncertainty about whether their ability and enthusiasm to teach had been lost since the previous placement.

Penny closely contrasted her anxiety about going into school with the most significant and personal event that she had previously experienced. Raj was anxious about being accepted into the social world of the staffroom, and the need to be encultured quickly into school life was a cause of trepidation for Gilly:

It's cold, dark, and this time last year I was six hours away from making my marriage vows. I honestly think I am more nervous now than I was then! It's not the teaching that worries me but making a good impression on the staff.

(Penny)

It was not only the classroom responsibilities that gave rise to my anxieties but also other areas of school life; for example, life in the staffroom. I was distinctly worried that I would find the staffroom to be a 'closed shop' to me as I had in my previous placement. It was, perhaps, this aspect that plagued my mind more than any other, as I understood the importance of forging good working relationships with other members of staff.

(Raj)

One of the biggest challenges facing the trainee teacher is to integrate oneself successfully into the running of a well-established school, with equally established routines and rules. While it obviously feels somewhat alien at first, it can be hard at some placements to ever feel like you have got past that first stage of feeling like an unwelcome invader into other people's workplace. I would be lying if I did not admit to the trepidation I felt going into school experience, almost wholly due to the fact that it was fifteen months since my last period in school, and I found it hard initially to build up my enthusiasm.

(Gilly)

It is significant that none of the respondents referred specifically to the ameliorating impact that talking to tutors had on their fears about the coming challenge. Evidence from the accounts indicates that tutors did not appear to have been aware of the extent to which some trainees were also in need of emotional support and reassurance prior to commencement.

Fatalistic emotions

Around half of the respondents referred to the impact of earlier school placements on the way they viewed the future, and a large number of them described the impact that previous times in school had made on their selfbelief and confidence. Trainees grappled with memories of unsatisfactory situations that had struck at the heart of their emotions, and seemed to be *fatalistic* in the way they perceived their ongoing effect. Some of the trainees' comments suggested that they had a prevailing sense that previous experiences conferred on them a 'win or lose' identity that they would struggle to shake off. Sundhar was haunted by his earlier school placements:

The first lesson that I can draw from my experience is that I hope that I am not so quick as some teachers I have encountered to forget the fear and trepidation experienced by trainee teachers prior to a teaching practice . . . In the preceding days and weeks prior to the practice I became increasingly apprehensive. What would the school be like? Would the staff welcome us? And then the memories of my previous practice mistakes began to haunt me.

(Sundhar)

The reasons for trainees' previous unsatisfactory times in school were varied but were frequently concerned with: (1) the nature of the relationship they had experienced with the class teacher or mentor, (2) the extent of the welcome they felt from staff in the school, and (3) vocational doubts. These feelings resulted in a further lowering of confidence and exacerbated trainees' concerns about their ability to cope with the demands of the coming placement.

Some respondents had been upset by unhappy relationships with teachers in previous placement schools and feared a repeat of the situation. Young-soon's experience was one of the most extreme. The use of words such as 'hated' and 'tyrannical' and 'petrified' indicate the depth of emotion involved for her:

My emotional condition before the placement was shaky for several reasons. First, I did not have an enjoyable third year school experience and although I passed the practice I was worried that I would be in a school that I hated. The reason for not liking my previous school placement was largely down to a tyrannical class teacher who was not approachable and made it perfectly clear that I was not wanted in her classroom. I was petrified that I would be in a similar situation again, but this time for ten weeks.

(Young-soon)

Others referred to the general ethos of poor relationships in the school that had affected their ability to prosper as a trainee and made Kerensa determined that the same thing would not happen again:

My previous school experience highlighted to me the disadvantages of poor relationships and communication between staff. It had affected my teaching because there was a lack of general mutual support. So at the beginning of my new placement, I made an extra special effort to fit into the team and contribute as a member.

(Kerensa)

It is interesting to note that the anxiety that stemmed from unsatisfactory relationships under a previous setting made both respondents grimly determined to do all in their power to avoid the situation recurring. The prospect of being 'isolated' in school by an unfriendly class teacher and therefore unable to undertake the rite of passage from insider to outsider was at the forefront of some respondents' minds. For example:

My second year placement was one in which the class teacher did not make me feel welcome or part of the team. This negative relationship with the teacher made it very difficult for me to progress during that time, due to the feeling that I was an unwelcome intruder into her domain. Since that second year experience I have always worried about going into someone else's classroom for fear of never becoming an 'insider'.

(Louise)

In the most extreme cases, an unsatisfactory experience in school caused a number of respondents to reassess their suitability for teaching. The depth of emotion attached to this fundamental issue of vocation underlines the delicate balance that exists between aspiration and exasperation, as the following selection of extracts clearly shows. The source of their anxiety varies, however; thus, Dave is anxious because of the negative comments he received from a teacher, whereas Lulu had become unsettled by jaundiced remarks made by staff. Paul and Dorothy, on the other hand, seem uncertain whether they want to endure the strains and stresses of teaching and weigh the benefits against the perceived costs:

After my third year practice I questioned for the first time whether I really wanted to be a teacher, as though only five weeks long, it felt like an eternity. Almost from the start I had all the confidence knocked out of me. I did not have a good working relationship with the class teacher.

(Dave)

For me the build-up to the final school experience was not without its problems, even after three successful teaching practices I was still unsure as to whether I really wanted to become a teacher. To me this was an important issue, as on previous school experiences I had encountered a number of teachers who had a severe lack of motivation for their profession.

(Lulu)

The feelings I had at the end of my third school practice were very mixed. Initially I was pleased it was over. Emotionally the pressure was off, so I had time to readjust to normal life. Physically I could catch up on those early mornings and I was nearer the distant goal of becoming a teacher. However, as the Year 4 teaching practice approached, my feelings were that I simply could not be a teacher.

(Paul)

Prior to the final school experience I was still unsure whether I wished to become a teacher. I had made up my mind before going on school visits that if, after two weeks of the practice, I was still unsure, then rather than waste not only my own time but also other people's time, I would give up. This may seem a very pessimistic and defeatist approach. However, having experienced emotional and stressful school practices before, I was not prepared to put myself through such pressure again.

(Dorothy)

A belief that previous experiences would be repeated in the coming placement was strongly represented in the accounts. The trainees had an overriding desire for the placement to be a 'good' one, reflected in factors such as receiving a warm welcome, being given a fair chance to establish a rapport with the class teacher and pupils, and being offered every encouragement to succeed by the host teachers. At the same time, there was a lurking fear that they might find themselves in quite the opposite sort of environment and, just as in their previous experiences, struggle to cope, lose heart and perhaps reject teaching as a suitable career.

Affirming emotions

Not all trainees were haunted by a fear-stricken perspective about their time in school, yet even some of those with positive previous experiences were jittery about their prospects in the new placement. A tension appears to have existed in some trainees' minds between the confidence that had been gained through a rewarding school placement in the past and the uncertainty that arose from a lack of certainty about the future. This conflict is clearly illustrated in the following extract:

> In the build-up to the placement my confidence was quite high as my year 3 practice had been successful and I hoped to build upon this, taking on more responsibility to prepare myself for my own class. I was also a bit apprehensive because I did not know what the school was like, if the staff was supportive and what sorts of backgrounds the children came from.
>
> (Sybil)

Notwithstanding any lingering self-doubt, the contrast was stark between those respondents who had enjoyed their previous placement and those who had not. A positive placement not only liberated trainees to face their new situation with confidence but also confirmed their sense of vocation, as Judy, Grace and Fatima described:

> Before I entered the school I felt very confident about the forthcoming practice. This confidence had manifested itself out of the success of my previous school experience. I was hoping to continue to develop from where I had finished on my third school placement [though] on reflection I realise that this was unrealistic.
>
> (Judy)

> Due to previous good experiences on teaching practice I was looking forward to once again being able to put into practice all that I had learned while in college.
>
> (Grace)

> Having had an extremely successful third year school experience I was left in no doubt that teaching was the job for me. I was confident and raring to get back into the classroom.
>
> (Fatima)

Although previous success in school did not guarantee that respondents would approach their new situation brimming with confidence, it did, for the most part, help them to adopt a positive view of the future and facilitated a smoother rite of passage from outsider to insider.

COPING STRATEGIES

To illustrate the impact that emotional demands placed upon the trainee teachers once in school, and the different ways in which they coped with them, an extended account (Angelina) is presented below. The educational decisions that she was forced to take and the compromises that she made were emotionally painful but essential for survival:

Despite the wide-ranging support for discussion as a tool for enriching learning, it was not widely encouraged by the class teacher. It was made clear to me that she did not approve of my efforts to use discussion as a learning tool and I was chided because I had not conformed to her way of working. For instance, during my lessons in week two, the teacher frequently told me that I spent too much time talking with the children and not enough time dealing with the noise level. Her reaction surprised me greatly, particularly as my lesson plan had identified collaboration as its principal objective and all the children were richly engaged in task-related discussion. The teacher seemed to ignore the distinction between productive noise and misbehaviour. Regardless of my concerns, I wanted to conform to the teacher's expectations of me with the intention of fitting in, so I altered my approach and modified my planning to eliminate collaborative learning. I became very sensitive to the occasions when the children talked to one another, as the teacher and I had a different definition of 'noisy' that made it difficult for me to judge when the volume had reached the limits of her tolerance. This uncertainty caused me further anxiety and an almost obsessive preoccupation with noise. I hate to admit that I even resorted to the ubiquitous 'sshh' technique. I felt that I was shifting from a child-centred philosophy because of the need to conform to the class teacher's wishes.

This uncharacteristic behaviour made me feel very frustrated, particularly as I was consciously denying the children opportunities to scaffold their learning through peer interaction. I was also telling the children to be quiet when I knew that they were talking about things relating to the task, which was something that I had previously been encouraging. As I think back it makes me shudder. Because of my concerns over the class teacher's opinions of me, I feel that I was squandering valuable learning experiences for the children. I felt great relief when I began to share my anxieties with other trainee teachers. They empathised with my desire to conform and one of them compared being a trainee teacher working in another teacher's classroom with wearing someone else's shoes: they just don't fit!

At the end of the placement my practice was deemed by the tutor to be very good. Comments in my final report indicated that I had built an effective working relationship with the class teacher. Of course, I was not going to tell anyone the truth but inwardly I did not get much personal satisfaction from the experience. I will always be left to wonder what would have happened if I had been strong enough to justify and successfully demonstrate my educational principles.

Angelina had clear views about the way in which children learned most effectively but was frustrated by the class teacher's educational philosophy. This clash of learning theory between trainee and teacher meant that maintaining a balance between conformity and innovative teaching proved to be a considerable challenge. Dialogue with the teacher did not resolve the problem and, sensibly, Angelina decided that self-preservation as a trainee teacher outweighed her ideology. Only when she had her own class would Angelina be able to reconcile her preferred theory with classroom practice. Meanwhile she had to grapple with feelings of guilt about not doing what she believed to be the best for the children while under pressure from others to do things differently. Hargreaves (1994) points out that there are many 'guilt traps' awaiting teachers, not least 'depressive guilt' (a term coined by Davies, 1989). Hargreaves interprets depressive guilt as being at its most intense 'when we realise we may be harming or neglecting those for whom we care by not meeting their needs or by not giving them sufficient attention' (p. 144). Carlyle and Woods (2002, drawing on Gottman *et al.*, 1997) remind us that loss of autonomy and a sense of being a puppet with someone else pulling the strings characterise teachers who feel 'emotional dysregulation', defined as 'losses in their ability to control, regulate, and recover from emotional states' (p. 61). Such powerful feelings are exposed through Angelina's account, as she refers to 'squandering valuable learning experiences for the children' and her inward lack of personal satisfaction that the situation imposed. Angelina's admission that she shudders when thinking back is a salutary reminder that guilt strikes deeply at the emotions and is not easily assuaged.

Angelina's anxiety about pleasing the teacher and possibly failing to meet the standards for successful completion of the school placement provided the stimulus to feign enthusiasm for an approach with which she was uncomfortable. At one level, Angelina felt thwarted and upset that she had not been able to exploit her creative potential; on the other hand, the hardships helped to unlock her capacity to persevere and incorporate unfamiliar teaching approaches into her practice. As Robinson (2001) argues, critical evaluation of a situation sometimes necessitates 'a shift in the focus of attention and mode of thinking as we attend to what is working and what is not' (p. 134). For Angelina, her initial teaching approach was 'not working' in the classroom context into which she was placed, and over which she had little control. As a result, Angelina directed her energies towards what Lacey (1977) refers to as 'strategic compliance', in which 'the individual complies with the authority figure's definition of the situation but retains private reservations about them' (p. 72). In such cases the subordinate (in this case, Angelina) benefits by receiving the superior's approval (the class teacher) but suffers emotional turmoil in doing so. Angelina's unwillingness to jeopardise her success on school placement by antagonising the teacher, and a desire to be accepted into the community of practice through conforming to the teacher's theories about learning, involved compromising her own beliefs. Woods (1990) underlines the point that subordinates must be sensitive to the circumstances ('awareness', p. 131), interpret the prevailing orthodoxy, employ compliance strategies and act upon the right issue at the right moment in time. Angelina appears to have been adept in both selecting the issue and the timing.

Angelina managed to navigate the circumstances successfully while safeguarding her emotional well-being. She also gained from the experience in storing up for a later time ways of handling aspects of emotional literacy: notably, understanding and grappling with the demands of her own stress and anxiety, and finding coping strategies. She developed insights into relationships, handling unpromising circumstances and, importantly, about her own strengths and foibles. Consequently, in her preparation for teaching, the negative emotions with which she grappled during her placement proved to be important for the challenges that qualified teachers have to face regularly. Angelina had to adjust her teaching approach and use one favoured by the class teacher, rein in some of her fervour and develop a 'professionalism of conformity' at the school level (Hayes, 2001).

DISCUSSION

Teachers are constantly grappling with powerful emotions, some of which are edifying and others debilitating. The increase in stress-related illness amongst teachers reported by, amongst others, Hart (2000) and Troman and Woods (2000) has been exacerbated by the close scrutiny of performance and the high level of accountability facing every teacher. Rapid changes in government policy, inspections, adjustments to personnel, problematic relations with colleagues, unreasonable parents, mischievous children and excessive paperwork contribute to a sense of being overwhelmed.

Trainee teachers also have to face many of these challenges, but they have less influence upon determining priorities for classroom practice. In addition they grapple with the emotionally exhausting task of enculturation into new school settings. Eisenhart *et al.* (1991) point out that initial teacher trainers invariably emphasise what they refer to as Developing Expertise theory, whereby trainees learn to behave as staff members and handle children in the classroom appropriately. Negotiating a rite of passage, however, relies on attitudes and decisions that are made by the trainee and host teachers, and is thereby highly contextualised. Consequently, the ease with which trainees manage their passage depends partly on their ability to recognise and accept the school's priorities and partly on the host teachers' capacity and willingness to assist the process. Calderhead and Shorrock (1997) insist that contextual factors affect the enculturation in four ways:

1 *sociocultural* (taken-for-granted practices);
2 *personal* (trainees' image of themselves as teachers and their beliefs about teaching);
3 *technical* (the methods and strategies used in teaching);
4 *quality of mentoring* (through coaching, discussion, structuring the context, providing emotional support).

In addition, however, Stephenson (1995) found that the quality of trainee teachers' experience in school depended principally on their emotional condition, which in turn relied on the quality of the mentoring process. Calderhead and Shorrock agree with Zeichner *et al.* (1987) that enculturation (or socialisation) into teaching involves trainee teachers in a considerable amount of manoeuvring and adjustment before they can make headway. These procedures are both wearing and distracting, but mirror to an extent the situation facing a newly qualified teacher, teachers changing school and teachers who are experiencing marked changes in their conditions of work. Bullough (1987) expresses the situation well:

> When a beginning teacher enters school for the first time, s/he enters more than a building; s/he enters a culture of teaching that has evolved in response to school structure and wider cultural values that establishes what is the appropriate teacher role. To function successfully within the school, the beginning teacher must come to terms with this role and the values that sustain it.

(p. 83)

The present study suggests that, in addition to equipping trainee teachers with curriculum knowledge and teaching skills, more attention needs to be paid to their emotional welfare. The imminence of school placement invariably triggers a raft of emotions in trainees, some of whom need to be liberated from irrational fears and helped to identify, and deal with, specific areas of concern. Of particular significance appears to be the impact of previous placements on trainees' attitudes and the concomitant anxieties that they engender about likely failure or success. It is not surprising that trainees who are prone to anxiety are overwhelmed by a sense of inadequacy, fear about what the future holds and their own vulnerability. However, if trainees' emotional battles are viewed as an integral component of preparing for such times, rather than seen as a hindrance to progress, the challenges can be viewed as necessary groundwork in advance of coping with the raft of stressful demands that characterise some aspects of the teacher role.

The typology established through this present research – anticipatory, anxious, fatalistic and affirming emotions – is a useful device for a careful consideration of the emotional challenges facing trainee teachers prior to school experience. However, its limitations as an instrument have also to be acknowledged. For instance, some anticipatory emotions overlapped with the 'anxious' category, and not every fatalistic emotion was negative in character. It would be a mistake to attempt to place trainees into one or other of the four categories without recognising that emotions, by their very nature, are unpredictable, fast-changing and subject to a variety of other pressures (such as health, friendship patterns, family life, etc.). Personality factors are also likely to impinge upon trainees' responses. While an assertive and outgoing character may relish particular challenges, a more timid person may be overwhelmed by them. Again, cultural factors may affect people's reactions to situations, where (for instance) the cultural norms incorporate notions of being steadfast, phlegmatic and generally undemonstrative.

Despite these caveats, greater emphasis on improving the emotional literacy of trainee teachers has a number of potential benefits. First, it improves pedagogic understanding – the impact of teaching, and the conditions for successful teaching and learning. Second, it helps to combat the potentially damaging effects that deep-seated anxiety has on their health and well-being and subsequently on the quality of work. For instance, Claxton (1989) highlights constant noise as being responsible for emotional stress, as 'there are teachers whose daily lives are an eternal battle to contain the unease that noise calls forth in them' (p. 47). Third, it acts as a preparation for the trials and tribulations that characterise the work of teachers, for there are numerous parallels between the experiences of student teachers and those of practising teachers. Carlyle and Woods (2002) refer to this common experience as being 'emotional labour among colleagues' (p. 16), leading to an increase in stress-laden conditions. As a result, performativity is significant both for trainee and qualified teachers. Finally, as guilt traps are a common problem for all teachers (Hargreaves, 1994), so the early identification and recognition of these hazards during training will provide an important constituent of novice teachers' professional armoury. This awareness, in turn, should positively impact upon their willingness to persevere with unpromising situations through the employment of well-rooted emotional fortification, a key dimension of teacher retention.

The successful management of emotions in school is essential if trainees are to avoid the strangulating effect of fear and anxiety. They need to be guided in how to use their emotions in making responsible choices that satisfy them and yet conform to the expectations of the host teachers. The implications for tutors, mentors and host teachers involved in supervision are considerable in recognising and making allowance for the heightened emotions at the start of a placement and in taking practical steps to moderate or avoid their impact once teaching begins (Dunlop, 1984). Strategies include:

■ providing trainee teachers with clear and accurate documentation, free from obfuscation and overpowering detail, as a means of helping them conceptualise the placement requirements;

■ providing opportunity for them to meet key school staff as far in advance of the school experience as possible to placate fears about the 'unseen' and begin the process of establishing sound relationships;

■ clarifying specifically what they will be required to teach, especially during the first week, so that they can begin to prepare lessons and thereby feel more in control of events;

■   stressing that each placement is a fresh opportunity to do well, and success is not dependent on previous experiences in school;

■   emphasising that school experience is intended to be a learning time for trainees, in which mistakes are inevitable and will be used instructively.

Although respondents' extracts later revealed that some of their worst fears were ameliorated once the placement began, the emotional turmoil that some of them experienced beforehand meant that too much of their mental energy was directed towards concerns of the heart rather than practical preparation for the job. Nevertheless, learning to cope with the emotions attached to changing circumstances and stressful situations is, as this research confirms, an integral dimension of teachers' lives. The development and honing of trainee teachers' emotional literacy is an essential element of their preparation for teaching and too important to be left to chance.

REFERENCES

Acker, S. (1999) *The realities of teachers' work*, London: Cassell.

Bullough, R.V. (1987) 'Accommodation and tension: teachers, teacher role and the culture of teaching', in J. Smyth (ed.) *Educating teachers: changing the nature of pedagogical knowledge*, London: Falmer Press.

Calderhead, J. and Shorrock, S. (1997) *Understanding teacher education*, London: Falmer Press.

Carlyle, D. and Woods, P. (2002) *The emotions of teacher stress*, Stoke-on-Trent: Trentham Books.

Claxton, G. (1989) *Being a teacher: a positive approach to change and stress*, London: Cassell.

Coffey, A. and Atkinson, P. (1997) *Making sense of qualitative data*, London: Sage.

Davies, A.F. (1989) *The human element: three essays in political psychology*, Harmondsworth: Penguin.

Day, C. and Leitch, R. (2001) 'Teachers' and teacher educators' lives: the role of emotion', *Teaching and Teacher Education*, Vol. 17, No. 4: 403–415.

Duncan, D. (2002) 'Emotionally intelligent female primary head teachers: the new women of power?', *Education 3–13*, Vol. 30, No. 3: 48–54.

Dunlop, F. (1984) *The education of feeling and emotion*, London: Allen & Unwin.

Eisenhart, M., Behm, L. and Romagno, L. (1991) 'Learning to teach: developing expertise or rite of passage?', *Journal of Education for Teaching*, Vol. 17, No. 1: 51–71.

Gardner, H. (1983) *Frames of mind: the theory of multiple intelligences*, New York: Basic Books.

Golby, M. (1996) 'Teachers' emotions: an illustrated discussion', *Cambridge Journal of Education*, Vol. 26, No. 3: 423–434.

Goleman, D. (1995) *Emotional intelligence*, New York: Bantam.

Gottman, J.M., Katz, L.F. and Hooven, C. (1997) *Meta-emotion: how families communicate emotionally*, Mahwah: Lawrence Erlbaum.

Hargreaves, A. (1994) *Changing teachers, changing times*, New York: Teachers College Press.

Hargreaves, A. (1998) 'The emotional practice of teaching', *Teaching and Teacher Education*, Vol. 14, No. 8: 835–854.

Hargreaves, A. (1999) 'The psychic rewards and annoyances of teaching', in M. Hammersley (ed.) *Researching school experience*, London: Falmer Press.

Hart, S. (2000) *Thinking through teaching*, London: David Fulton.

Hayes, D. (2001) 'The impact of mentoring and tutoring on student primary teachers' achievements: a case study', *Mentoring and Tutoring*, Vol. 9, No. 1: 5–21.

Helsby, G. (1998) *Changing teachers' work*, Buckingham: Open University Press.

Katz, L.G. (1995) *Talks with teachers of young children*, Norwood: Ablex.

Kemper, T.D. (1993) 'Sociological models in the explanation of emotions', in M. Lewis and J.M. Haviland (eds) *Handbook of emotions*, New York: Guilford Press.

Lacey, C. (1977) *The socialization of teachers*, London: Methuen

Lortie, D.C. (1975) *Schoolteacher*, Chicago: University of Chicago Press.

Moore, A., Edwards, G., Halpin, D. and George, R. (2002) 'Compliance, resistance and pragmatism: reconstruction of schoolteacher identities in a period of intensive educational reform', *British Educational Research Journal*, Vol. 28, No.4: 551–565.

Nias, J. (1996) 'Thinking about feeling', *Cambridge Journal of Education*, Vol. 26, No. 3: 296–306.

Oberski, I., Ford, K., Higgins, S. and Fisher, P. (1999) 'The importance of relationships in teacher education', *Journal of Education for Teaching*, Vol. 25, No. 2: 135–150.

Robinson, K. (2001) *Out of our minds: learning to be creative*, Oxford: Capstone.

Scheff, T. (1997) *Emotions, the social bond and human reality*, Cambridge: Cambridge University Press.

Shann, M.H. (1998) 'Professional commitment and satisfaction among teachers in urban middle schools', *Journal of Educational Research*, Vol. 92, No. 2: 67–74.

Shaylock, G. (1998) 'Professionalism and intensification in teaching: a case study of care in teachers' work', *Asia-Pacific Journal of Teacher Education*, Vol. 26, No. 3: 177–190.

Smithers, A. and Robinson, P. (1998) 'Can there ever be enough teachers?', *Times Educational Supplement*, 24 April: 20.

Spear, M., Gould, K. and Lee, B. (1999) *Who would be a teacher?*, Slough: National Foundation for Educational Research.

Stephenson, J. (1995) 'Significant others: the primary trainee view of practice in schools', *Educational Studies*, Vol. 21, No. 3: 309–318.

Strauss, A. and Corbin, J. (1990) *Basics of qualitative research: grounded theory procedures and techniques*, Newbury Park: Sage.

Tirri, K. (1999) 'Teachers' perceptions of moral dilemmas at school', *Journal of Moral Education*, Vol. 28, No. 1: 31–47.

Troman, G. and Woods, P. (2000) *The social construction of teacher stress*, London: RoutledgeFalmer.

Wengraf, T. (2001) *Qualitative research interviewing*, London: Sage.

Wilhelm, K., Dewhurst-Savellis, J. and Parker, G. (2000) 'Teacher stress: an analysis of why teachers leave and why they stay', *Teachers and Teaching: Theory and Practice*, Vol. 6, No. 3: 291–304.

Wilson, S. and Cameron, R. (1996) 'Trainee teacher perceptions of effective teaching: a developmental perspective', *Journal of Education for Teaching*, Vol. 22, No. 2: 181–195.

Woods, P. (1990) *Teacher skills and strategies*, London: Falmer Press.

Woods, P. and Carlyle, D. (2002) 'Teacher identities under stress: the emotions of separation and renewal', *International Studies in Sociology of Education*, Vol. 12, No. 2: 169–189.

Woods, P. and Jeffrey, B. (1996) *Teachable moments: the art of teaching in primary schools*, Buckingham: Open University Press.

Woods, P. and Jeffrey, B. (2002) 'The reconstruction of primary teachers' identities', *British Journal of Sociology*, Vol. 23, No. 1: 89–106.

Zeichner, K.M., Tabachnick, B.R. and Densmore, K. (1987) 'Individual, institutional and cultural influences on the development of teachers' craft knowledge', in J. Calderhead (ed.) *Exploring teachers' thinking*, London: Cassell.

CHANGING CONTEXTS

Teacher professional development and ICT pedagogy

Matthew Pearson and Steven Naylor

A NOTE FROM THE EDITORS

This reading uses a case study approach to explore how the integration of information and communications technologies into lessons might take place, and discusses the knowledge that teachers need to be able to work in this way.

This reading links with Unit 1.4 of the 5th edition of *Learning to teach in the secondary school*.

QUESTIONS TO CONSIDER

1   Read Vignette 1 in the reading, which is about Brinnerton School and the forms of professional knowledge outlined in the box in the introduction to Section 1. What forms of professional knowledge do teachers have to have to implement the Learning to Learn approach? How does this compare with the curriculum you have experienced yourself as a pupil and the curriculum you have come across in schools you have visited? What practices to help pupils learn how to learn would you like to incorporate in your teaching? Having read the three vignettes, what aspects of practice in these schools would you like to see in the school in which you will be teaching?

2   Consider the approach to e-portfolios described in the reading and the forms of professional knowledge outlined in the box in the introduction to Section 1. What skills and knowledge do you need for your pupils to use e-portfolios to record the work they do for you?

This reading was first published as: Pearson, M. and Naylor, S. (2006) 'Changing contexts: teacher professional development and ICT pedagogy', *Education and Information Technologies*, Vol. 11: 283–291.

ABSTRACT

This paper examines data from a series of visits to secondary schools in England that have been identified as doing innovative work with ICT. The paper argues that stable definitions of innovation are difficult in this context and require an understanding of both the technological contexts of innovation and the concept of a school as a dynamic learning community. Data is presented in the form of vignettes to demonstrate how the school visits formed a kind of 'performance' in relation to the schools' own claims about innovations and the enquiries of the research team. Discussion of the data focuses on three key themes that emerge: the changing roles of teachers; new technologies/new pedagogies; and the public face of the school. The paper concludes with the observation that innovation is necessarily complex but pupil agency and creativity should always play a vital part.

INTRODUCTION

This paper draws on data collected as part of a project investigating innovative practice using ICT in English secondary schools. The project, titled Partners in Learning, is sponsored by Microsoft and involves the Teacher Development Agency in England and the National Assembly for Wales. It is gathering evidence of the ways in which ICT can transform pedagogic approaches in certain key areas of secondary schooling in England. English secondary schools face perhaps one of the biggest challenges of any sector of education in terms of introducing innovation and updating teaching and learning practices. The secondary school day is tightly regimented by a timetable which can act as a barrier to extended exploratory sessions, and the division of intellectual labour into subjects, which creates particular epistemological and methodological modes (often called 'subject cultures'), does not encourage the use of ICT as a tool for personal exploration and development. Added to this is the UK government's insistence on using high-stakes test results as the primary vehicle for measuring school performance. These factors ensure that teaching in English secondary schools takes place in a risk averse culture, where teaching 'to the test' is a constant temptation, and innovations using ICT are difficult to enact. Paradoxically, this lack of change to secondary schooling in England is set against a time of rapid social change brought about by the increased availability and uptake of ICT by young people. The ownership of multimedia-capable mobile phones, portable music players and mobile computing devices is increasing rapidly, but pupils in English schools find that many of the skills and the knowledge they acquire informally are not valued within the school setting. Despite this, it is clear that some secondary schools have realised that ICT offers affordances which can transform pedagogic practices and, despite the inherent barriers to change, are pushing ahead with innovative projects. In this paper we examine how schools are challenging the orthodoxies of results-driven teaching and harnessing the potential of ICT to create personalised learning environments for pupils and to change the relationships between the pupils, the teachers and the curriculum.

In this paper we will be interrogating the meaning of the word 'innovative' when applied to education and examining how various meanings are operational. We will argue that clarification of the meaning of innovation as it relates to ICT and schooling is needed in order to identify genuinely new and exciting pedagogic practices. Watson (2002) argues that innovation using ICT for teaching requires the movement from a 'retooling' agenda to a 'reforming' one. In contrast with the retooling implementation that focuses on adapting technology to existing teaching practices, the reforming agenda seeks to rethink the very basis of teaching and what can be achieved with digital technologies. This call for a radical rethink of what technology can do for education is echoed by Lankshear (2003), in his development of digital epistemologies (or digimologies as he punningly neologises), and Pearson and Somekh (2006), who argue for the potential of ICT to transform relationships between teachers, pupils and the knowledge and skills being taught. There is also an acknowledgement that the wide-scale introduction of ICT into a system with the historical rigidity of secondary schooling in the UK will create tensions and fault lines. For instance, John (2004) argues for us to take into account that 'learning in such an environment is often chaotic, messy, may have no tangible beginnings and ends and might breed more confusion before genuine understanding occurs' (p. 104).

It must be acknowledged that understanding an innovative school in terms of its deployment of ICT as a change agent requires us to draw on two bodies of literature. The first is that relating to ICT and schooling [examined elsewhere], the second is work that examines wider school-based innovation and school organisation. Recent work in the UK and US in this area has focused largely on the challenges that an era of standardised reform, centralised policy making and punitive inspections has created for schools attempting to innovate (Coppieters, 2005; Ehren and Visscher, 2006; Taylor Webb, 2006). Giles and Hargreaves (2006) have recently argued that schools need to transform themselves into 'learning organisations' in order to innovate, but this is extremely difficult in the current political climate. Giles and Hargreaves discussed schools in the US, but it can be argued that the pressures of standardised reform are even more acute in the UK, and the space for innovation is reduced even further by a concentration on high-stakes testing and transmissive models of learning.

METHODOLOGY

The main method employed in gathering data for this study was a school visit to sites that had previously been identified as showing innovative practice in relation to the use of ICT. The sites were selected on the basis of recommendations made to the research team and because many of the schools already had a national profile in relation to their work. No attempt was made to create 'scientific' or 'normative' conditions for the sample of case study schools. This was not the focus of the work. The focus instead was on collecting evidence of emerging and cutting-edge practices using ICT in secondary education in the English context. One of the key considerations in collecting the data was expressly not to create the basis for an empirical study, but rather a more informal process the development team called 'mapping the field'. This involved creating a snapshot of current practices and then selecting which elements of these would be more useful in the context of the ongoing study.

The school visit

A total of twelve schools were identified as being suitable for visits and, upon identification, the head teacher was sent a letter requesting a visit to the school which explained that the project was looking for evidence of innovative work with ICT. Although the sample was largely self-selecting and based on recommendations and national profiles rather than a structured relationship with the entire population of secondary schools, the school visits were designed to be standardised as far as possible to ensure that the data collected from each school were amenable to comparison. Detailed planning of the school visits was undertaken to ensure a standard framework. A data collection instrument was designed in order to facilitate a standardised format.

The data collection instrument provided a commonality of focus for the visits and assisted us in organising activity when in the field, but the empirical data collected through this instrument only provide one part of the story. The visit itself needs to be conceived of as an event that is part of the research narrative – not simply an opportunity to collect data. Rather, it should be conceived as an integral part of the ways in which schools presented themselves. The visits therefore had a broadly ethnographic impact. Every aspect of the encounter between researcher and school was invested with some forms of meaning that could be interpreted and layered on to our understanding of that particular case study. A useful way of understanding this is to employ Goffman's (1969) set of concepts related to the presentation of the self in everyday life. Although writing about encounters between individuals, Goffman's work can, with conceptual modification, be applied to an encounter between two types of institution, namely a school and a research organisation. The primary actors in the encounters are still individuals and thus bound by the unwritten rules and rituals of the social bond, but, in representing their particular organisation, they have a further set of obligations which play themselves out in the way the social interactions are organised. Using Goffman's dramaturgical ideas on the social encounter, the school site becomes the stage upon which particular types of scene are played out, using scripts and props selected by the actors. The script of the research team, communicated in advance to the school, needs careful management. On one hand, the school wants to comply with the requests of the research team, but, on the other hand, the school needs to manage the encounters so that it presents its best possible face and directs attention to aspects of its work that are thought to be most innovative. The phrase 'showcase', although heavily connotated with rather flimsy presentational imagery, is apt, as the schools did use the visits to showcase their work. The researchers were happy to play along with this script; after all, we did not have the agenda of another kind of school visitor, the inspectors, who may be seeking to unpick the script and disrupt the scene and plays as much as possible in their search for the unwritten truth lurking behind the school. Presenting the data from each school visit is beyond the limitations of a paper of this length, but, in order to give readers a sense of what happened during the visits, what follows is three vignettes from school visits.

The method of using vignettes has its intellectual roots in the thick descriptions of Geertz (1973) and has also been used by Wenger (1999) to produce a narrative episode that can be used to illuminate particular features of a human activity system. These three vignettes have been chosen because they illustrate themes common to many of the visits. The names of the schools and staff have been fictionalised.

Vignette 1: Brinnerton School

Brinnerton School is located in a flat, open landscape, about 10 miles north of one of the UK's large industrial cities. The school of 1,600 pupils serves a local town and also takes pupils from neighbouring areas. James, a senior teacher at the school, talked me through some of the school's innovations. The 'Learning to Learn' curriculum, taught in a building named the Discovery Zone, is a major focus for the school. Learning to Learn has more curriculum time allocated than that afforded to English, maths or science (8 hours per cycle) and is where a lot of the students also learn their ICT. It is a curriculum that they have bought rather than developed themselves and is based on a number of learning theories, such as those expounded by Claxton (2005) and Gardner (1983). Training has taken place at the school, introducing teachers to learning theories. These have been taken on enthusiastically and form the basis of many lessons.

An 'investigations week' involves a collapsed timetable for the whole year group and allows pupils to work on a single project throughout the week. Last year's was a 'Super Science Week' where they had to 'bring science to the people of Brinnerton'. Investigations weeks are introduced with a video, which often keys into popular television, film or literature. The school's 'in-house' design team develops these videos. They also develop the online resources in collaboration with teachers.

James showed me some of the student portfolios that were being developed and drew a difference between what he described as a 'positivist portfolio', which contained evidence of skills development, and a 'constructivist portfolio', where students use the programs Inspiration (mind-mapping software) and Amazing Me to create their own portfolio with links to a variety of media (video, photographs, diaries). Portfolio construction is something he wants to develop further. The school employs a team of web designers, two of whom showed me some of the work they did at the school. They are both fairly young (in their 20s): one of them graduated in multimedia design, the other in information and library management. They used the *Star Wars* films as a metaphor for their presentation to me, James revealing that 'we are all fans of Star Wars here!'. They work on developing much of the online content for the school and also work on videos that teachers create to enhance their lessons. Their skills in solving problems and creating innovative resources are very high, and they are highly valued in the school. We went to visit some of the 'Learning to Learn' lessons, which were very interesting to see. In one the students were developing a video advert for their town using a series of video clips with Windows Movie Maker. Most notable was the layout of the classrooms, which allowed for group discussion, work on paper or networked laptop PCs when needed. Students were free to move around the central open space and did so. The teacher would also make use of the space, sometimes bringing students around for a group talk and sometimes letting them go off and try things. Two girls who carried on working on the PC during a group discussion were not reprimanded. The atmosphere felt relaxed but very productive. Students in the class talked about the resources they needed for the project: 'I think we need some shots of people', 'We need an introduction'. Talking to the teacher after the lesson revealed some of the philosophy of the Discovery Zone:

■   On the curriculum:

The lesson is working in a context where work skills, dispositions are studied overtly. So as much as we might say this is how you use Movie Maker, you might also say this is resilience.

■   On collaboration:

Similarly James uses a Flash movie that I've made that is about something that I know about that he doesn't. We can have each others' expertise in the classroom, we can team teach when only one of us is in the room.

Vignette 2: Brightsea Language College

Brightsea Language College is set in the inner city of one of England's largest cities. The area has a high level of deprivation. The school works closely with a nearby primary school (of which the college head is executive director). There are many different languages spoken by students at the school, and the school places great emphasis on making links with the various communities that they work with.

Upon arriving at the school I met with the content generation team. They work in an open office area and develop online learning resources for the school's Learning Gateway platform. I talked to them about their views on the technology and its use in the school. A, who also works in the primary school, described some experiences there:

> Children from Year 6 were now emailing work to their teachers. They were also going and doing extra research at home and sending in what they had found. There was a lot of peer support. Children would teach each other what they had learned, even things they had learned in other schools, such as stop-frame animation. They also used video conferencing with Year 3 children between classes where they take to it quite naturally. They can't understand what is actually happening though, they say 'how did those kids get in that screen'.

I talked about how I saw the use of technology moving away from repeating older pedagogies, and J agreed saying that 'a lot of ICT lessons are still chalkboard lessons, where children work on an individual project'. He was critical of the pressure that teachers got from inspections where they would get the computers and the software set up before the lesson. 'They should be able to fire it up themselves to understand how the whole thing works'. Only then did he feel that they could use it independently.

A commented:

> It [the pedagogy/activity] must be done in a way that it can't be done without the ICT. [. . .] Some teachers, still see the computer as a 'budgie cage'. They put a cloth over it in the corner to keep it quiet.

The team also explained how they collaborated with teachers to develop the online content. Some teachers gave very detailed requirements, and others arrived at it through negotiation with the designers. For part of the day I was also given a demonstration of online homework. The teacher, during his free lesson, borrowed two pupils to give them a maths homework exercise, and then took them to an ICT room where they logged on and did the exercise.

I then met the head, who revealed some of his thoughts on the future development of the school. With the Learning Gateway he was planning to develop units of work that could overlay instant messages so that collaboration on a piece of work could be done. In the organisation of the curriculum he really wanted to try out a new approach to teaching subjects that were heavy in content. He recognised that he had some teachers who were passionate about a specific part of their subject but were often expected to be generalists. He wanted to see them deliver a lesson on a theme or part of the subject to several classes at once (up to ninety pupils) as the start of a project that could then be continued by the other teachers. The Learning Gateway would play an important part as it would allow the sharing of resources and foster collaboration throughout the project.

Vignette 3: Roverton School

I had been invited to see the Pyramid at Roverton High school. From my e-mails with the head prior to visiting it seemed I was welcome to come to see this part of the school but they could not be with me all the time. This was fine for me; however, it was not possible to see other lessons taking place outside of this area.

When approaching the school, the Pyramid, a large glass structure about 30 m² at the base, is visible on the horizon. When I arrived at the school I was taken straight to this area. In the Pyramid are about a hundred PCs arranged in four open-plan bays; each bay has a clear table area in the middle. Around the edge of the bays there are desks where various teachers have a work area, and the network manager's desk is also here. The area also links directly with some classrooms. The Pyramid is open from 8 a.m. to 5 p.m. and has been there for ten years. The network manager told me that use of the area out of lessons dropped off when the Internet became popular at home.

An ICT cover lesson was taking place in the bay next to me. The teacher had set cover work for students to practise their typing skills using a tutor program/game that was available on the network. I asked the students what they thought of it: 'It's alright but we've done it before'. A group of girls were going through the exercises and chatting at the same time, while another group (mainly boys) were quieter when going through it. One of the students asked if they could go on the Internet at the end. The teacher replied that they could do so for the last 10 minutes if they worked hard during the lesson. When this time came around I watched the group of boys in the corner first. They had screens with online games pre-minimised at the bottom of the screen that were brought up immediately. They were also more talkative with each other at this time. They showed each other how to get to the games and which ones were the best, and pointed at each other's screens to give advice. One of the games was a car racing game where they could modify and optimise their cars for racing. The group of girls at this time decided to use the free access time to talk to each other. They actually switched off their computers.

During a geography lesson I talked with one of the students about her work, asking her what she thought of her school's Learning Gateway: 'It's good yes, it organises your work for you, you can have checklists of things to do.' She was using websites suggested by her teacher to find information. I asked how she would find other information. 'I don't know – you could go on Google I guess and type it in,' she replied.

I went to talk to the head of ICT, who taught in another area of the school. The rest of the building around the Pyramid was in a bad state of repair, and had suffered a flood the previous week. We talked about the Pyramid, and it was clear that she did not like it: 'I very rarely go in there, I just can't teach in there properly.' She felt that ICT skills should be taught separately from subjects in which they are used, and was concerned over a movement away from this. My discussions with the head of ICT covered many areas, such as her criticism of the National Curriculum, the vision for the school building, and what she saw as a 'movement from classrooms to workspaces'.

DISCUSSION

In what follows, we will discuss the vignettes and draw out three key themes that have emerged from an analysis of the data. The three themes illuminate some key ideas about innovation using ICT in secondary schools. The first theme relates to the way the school presents itself as a public institution and how it 'sells' its innovative practice to a range of stakeholders. The second relates to whether schools are concentrating on the development of new technologies and/or new pedagogies to accompany investment in hardware and software. The final theme relates to the changing role of teachers in schools where ICT is being used to transform teaching and learning.

Public face of the school

As we argued above, any school needs to present a public face and stage-manage the way it presents itself to any audience who visits. We cited Goffman's dramaturgical ideas concerning the presentation of self and suggested that those can be applied at the institutional level as well to describe how schools enact a certain kind of 'performance' to present their innovative work. What emerges from the vignettes is a sense of the tensions and paradoxes that result from this. At Roverton School, the stark contrast between the hi-tech space and the rest of the school demonstrated that it was not always possible to stage-manage a visit so that only the most attractive aspects of the school are showcased. However, at Brinnerton and Brightsea, the visit was managed so other areas of the school were visited, and it was clear that, unlike Roverton, innovation was not associated with a particular location and a specific investment in infrastructure.

New technologies or new pedagogies?

The visits to the schools demonstrated that investment in networks and in software associated with managing, storing and delivering content across these networks is a current area of concentration. This demonstrates that, in many cases, the school is conceiving of technological innovation in terms of improvements to hardware and infrastructure and is seeking ways to upgrade the school network to cope with the increased demands of digital content. In one of the vignettes, a great deal of emphasis was placed on the notion of a 'learning gateway', a particular kind of network configuration (containing both hardware and software) that is conceived of as a way of improving the flow of information between teachers and learners. The ways in which these new networking possibilities are creating pressures for pedagogic change are not immediately apparent, and, invoking Watson's (2002) framework, there will inevitably be tensions between the retooling and reforming agendas in relation to these new technologies.

Changing roles of teachers

One of the key themes to emerge from the schools where innovation had gone beyond the technical phase and was beginning to impact on pedagogical practices was the ways in which teachers' identities and normal work-based activities were being transformed as a result of the school's adoption of new technology. In two of the schools visited, a dedicated team of web designers had been appointed whose task was to take curriculum content and teaching ideas from the teachers and turn them into web-based content. Much of this work was done using techniques that went beyond the creation of static HTML pages using, for instance, Flash animations, digital video and dynamic data-driven applications. What is interesting in these schools is the changing role of the teachers, as defined in relation to a totally new kind of working practice within the secondary school. Traditional models of teaching enshrined the responsibility for producing material at one of two levels. The first level was that of the teacher, whose professional expertise extended to creating worksheets, activities and other artefacts to support learning. The second level was somewhat removed from the school and refers to the entire industry of education content involved in producing textbooks. The creation of a new level of content production, situated between the distanced outputs of the large content manufacturers (who are themselves rapidly adopting digital techniques to widen their portfolios beyond text-based content), is set to change the way a school functions. In both schools, the teams of designers were drawn mostly from art and media backgrounds rather than teaching, as the skills needed for this position are concerned with digital media and design rather than traditional pedagogy. The emergence of these design teams poses a particular challenge to the traditional identity and authority of the teacher. They are no longer the sole proprietor of expert knowledge and need to communicate their pedagogical approaches to others who can help them realise their teaching using digital methods.

CONCLUSION

A secondary school is an extremely complex organisation, and mapping innovative practices is not a straightforward task. Indeed, the notion of a school as a homogenous community has been questioned (Shields, 2000), and it may be the case that it is better to understand innovation at a smaller and more local scale that is within the practices of a particular department or even at the level of the individual teacher. We can conclude that the correspondence between the school's collective efforts at introducing innovative work and the implementation at classroom level is not a particularly straightforward relationship, and more work needs to be done to understand the interface between the two.One reason for these issues in understanding how and why schools are innovating is down to the inherently complex nature of a secondary school, a complexity that works against simple, unified understandings of what innovation could mean in this context. We found that, in the case of at least two vignettes, the schools were using specialised teams to build content for upload into virtual spaces. This adds another layer of complexity into the school structure that did not exist before, and we predict that schools that are innovating in this way may increasingly be adopting these approaches. Where this leads is a matter for speculation, but a trend already seen at Brinnerton and Brightsea for a school to employ in-house e-learning material authors is likely to be adopted in other schools where the logic of dividing labour between content generation (design) and delivery (teaching) will be hard to resist.

The difficulty of the task of understanding innovation is compounded by the multifaceted nature of modern digital technology and the various ways in which it can be used to support educational practices. Schools are currently entering a situation of extreme uncertainty as the pressures created by the information society impact on core activities and create challenges that need creative and innovative responses. Hope (2005) outlines one particular challenge to schools, namely issues concerning the management of student behaviour in relation to networks, but there are other challenges to pedagogy that result from this. We have shown that many schools are producing responses to innovation that rely on investment in larger, faster and more sophisticated networks on which teaching content can be hosted, and subsequent investment in teams with the expertise to produce content to populate these networks. If schools are to make the best use of the opportunities of digital technology, there must be a corresponding emphasis on empowering pupils to take an active part in the production of this content. The tools already exist to do this, particularly blogging and wiki-style interfaces, which allow the creation and customisation of online content. Schools need to develop new pedagogies to enable pupils to move beyond being passive consumers of content.

REFERENCES

Claxton, G. (2005) *Learning to learn* (QCA publication), www.qca.org.uk/downloads/11469_claxton_learning_to_learn.pdf; accessed 6 October 2006.

Coppieters, P. (2005) 'Turning schools into learning organisations', *European Journal of Teacher Education*, Vol. 28, No. 2: 129–139.

Ehren, M.C.M. and Visscher, A.J. (2006) 'Towards a theory on the impact of school inspections', *British Journal of Educational Studies*, Vol. 54, No. 1: 51–72.

Gardner, H. (1983) *Frames of mind: the theory of multiple intelligences*, New York: Basic Books.

Geertz, C. (1973) *The interpretation of cultures*, London: Basic Books.

Giles, C. and Hargreaves, A. (2006) 'The sustainability of innovative schools as learning organisations and professional learning communities during standardized reform', *Educational Administration Quarterly*, Vol. 42, No. 1: 124–156.

Goffman, E. (1969) *The presentation of self in everyday life*, London: Allen Lane.

Hope, A. (2005) 'Panopticism, play and the resistance of surveillance: case studies of the observation of student Internet use in UK schools', *British Journal of Sociology of Education*, Vol. 26, No. 3: 359–373.

John, P. (2004) 'Teaching and learning with ICT: new technology, new pedagogy?', *Education, Communication & Information*, Vol. 4, No. 1: 101–107.

Lankshear, C. (2003) 'The challenge of digital epistemologies', *Education, Communication & Information*, Vol. 3, No. 2: 167–187.

Pearson, M. and Somekh, B. (2006) 'Learning transformation with technology: a question of sociocultural contexts', *International Journal of Qualitative Studies in Education*, Vol. 19, No. 4: 519–539.

Shields, C. M. (2000) 'Learning from difference: considerations for schools as communities', *Curriculum Inquiry*, Vol. 30, No. 3: 275–294.

Taylor Webb, P. (2006) 'The choreography of accountability', *Journal of Education Policy*, Vol. 21, No. 2: 201–214.

Watson, G. (2002) 'Models of information technology teacher professional development that engage with teachers' hearts and minds', *Journal of Information Technology for Teacher Education*, Vol. 10, No. 1: 179–190.

Wenger, E. (1999) *Communities of practice: learning, meaning and identity*, Cambridge: Cambridge University Press.

BEGINNING TO TEACH

INTRODUCTION

Your observation skills are a crucial professional tool that you will need to develop and hone over time; being able to observe pupils' behaviours to understand whether they are learning and managing the work you have set or whether they need your intervention is a basic classroom skill. But you also need to develop your skills at analysing the practice of other teachers, both to learn from them and, as you take on responsibilities through your career, so that you can give professional feedback about how to improve practice.

READINGS IN THIS SECTION ARE:

Reading 3
Practice makes perfect? Learning to learn as a teacher
Hazel Hagger, Katharine Burn, Trevor Mutton and Sue Brindley

The first reading in this section, Hagger *et al.* (2007), addresses the ways in which you learn to teach well. They suggest that the student teacher 'is more able to learn through deliberating about the nature of the expertise that he or she wants to develop than through reflecting on . . . their very limited experience'.

The data were collected over three years from student teachers on their PGCE programme who were then followed through to the first two years of their teaching. Five dimensions affecting the quality of learning were identified: intentionality (whether the learning was planned); frame of reference; response to feedback; attitude to context; and aspirations for their own and pupils' learning.

Reading 4
Lesson planning and the student teacher: rethinking the dominant model
Peter D. John

The second reading in this section, John (2006) discusses traditional and non-traditional approaches to lesson planning and the limitations of practices that imply that planning and delivery of lessons can be managed through adopting a logical, linear approach. Planning lessons effectively so that all pupils learn is a basic professional skill. Being able to set different types of objective, related to different forms of learning, is a skill you need to work on for some time, as is the skill of identifying outcomes from your lessons that demonstrate deep learning.

Figure 4.2 (John, 2006: 491) represents the planning process as a more complex process, drawing on a vast array of knowledge, resources and guidance. The planning undertaken by experienced teachers is typically very brief in comparison with that undertaken by a student teacher, because many components become part of the teacher's professional knowledge, to be drawn on as necessary. For student teachers, without this depth of professional knowledge, the planning process is much more complex and time consuming.

The components of the planning process as set out in Figure 4.2 may provide a useful set of areas to consider when planning your learning as a student teacher, as suggested in the previous section. The importance of planning is acknowledged: 'the practice of planning is as important as the practice of teaching' (John, 2006: 495), but the case is made for a 'dialogic' approach to planning (dialogic meaning 'written as a conversation') rather than a linear approach. The reading also discusses the potential constraints on learning of working towards predetermined lesson outcomes, which linear planning approaches may tend to support.

FURTHER READING

Powell, E. (2005) 'Conceptualising and facilitating active learning: teachers' video-stimulated reflective dialogues', *Reflective Practice,* Vol. 6, No. 3: 407–418.

Your ability to reflect on your own practice is crucial to your progress. However, reflecting on your own practice requires the development of your analytical skills, particularly when you try to look beyond first impressions immediately after you have taught the lesson. This article uses videotaped teaching sequences and the reflective dialogue method to present a detailed analysis of the conceptualisation of active learning of six teachers. This analysis provides a model for articulating your own conceptualisation and a reflective framework for deepening your professional reflection in relation to active learning.

The above further reading links with Unit 2.1 of the 5th edition of *Learning to teach in the secondary school.*

Kyriacou, C., Avramidis, E., Høie, H., Stephens, P. and Hultgren, A. (2007) 'The development of student teachers' views on pupil misbehaviour during an initial teacher education programme in England and Norway', *Journal of Education for Teaching*, Vol. 33, No. 3: 293–307.

A concern of all new teachers is managing a whole group of pupils so that each pupil is actively engaged in learning.In developing your abilities to analyse your practice you will find several tools at your disposal, one of which is questionnaires. This article explores issues around pupil behaviours – types of behaviour and strategies for ensuring positive behaviours in the classroom. This article provides you with a framework for reviewing your own practice in managing behaviour, as well as strategies to test out with your own classes as part of your development as a reflective practitioner.

The above further reading links with Unit 2.1 of the 5th edition of *Learning to teach in the secondary school.*

Myhill, D. and Brackley, M. (2004) 'Making connections: teachers' use of children's prior knowledge in whole class discourse', *British Journal of Educational Studies*, Vol. 52, No. 3: 263–275.

This paper uses data from an ESRC- (Economic and Social Research Council) funded study to investigate teachers' use of prior knowledge in whole-class teaching contexts. How teachers conceptualise prior knowledge is explored. A strong teacher awareness is found of how the teaching under consideration fits with learning previously undertaken by the class, but less awareness of how the learning might build on prior learning outside school was found. The paper considers how teachers make connections between new learning and prior learning, and how those connections can variously support or confound pupils' acquisition of new knowledge and understanding.

The above further reading links with Unit 2.2 of the 5th edition of *Learning to teach in the secondary school*.

Gillard, D. (2005) 'Rescuing teacher professionalism', *Forum*, Vol. 47: 175–180; available online at www.wwwords.co.uk/rss/abstract.asp?j=forum&aid=2566.

Is teaching a profession? If so, what does this mean for you and your practice? The definition of what makes a profession is contested, but two characteristics often cited in definitions are that professions are self-regulating and that there is a body of knowledge that must be acquired. Gillard takes issue with government interventions in teaching that de-professionalise teaching. In a number of articles in the reader and in the future readings, concerns are raised that government interventions are not in the best interests of pupils, and this is where conflict arises between professional values and beliefs held by teachers and what the government requires of educators. From time to time, this conflict surfaces, with concerns usually led by teacher unions.

The above further reading links with Unit 2.2 of the 5th edition of *Learning to teach in the secondary school*.

Barnes, J. (2005) 'You could see it on their faces . . .!', *Health Education*, Vol. 105, No. 5: 392–400.

This article brings together knowledge in neuroscience and the concept of positive psychology (see also the Richards, Rivers and Akhurst article in the reader, Reading 7, which describes the use of positive psychology to improve the ethos of the school).

Through reviewing and discussing research undertaken by the World Health Organisation, Barnes makes the case for re-evaluating what we consider the optimum conditions for pupils' learning and the effect of the learning environment on their mental health.

The happiness of pupils at school is, he argues, something that should be the prime consideration of the school, and he proposes twelve recommendations from the research for schools to consider. You may wish to consider these with respect to the environment and relationships you wish to establish with your own classes.

The above further reading links with Unit 2.3 of the 5th edition of *Learning to teach in the secondary school*.

Wentzel, K. (1997) 'Student motivation in middle school: the role of perceived pedagogical caring', *Journal of Educational Psychology*, Vol. 89, No. 3: 411–417.

This longitudinal study examined adolescents' perceptions of pedagogical caring in relation to their motivation to achieve positive social and academic outcomes in 248 middle school pupils (followed from 6th to 8th grade). Perceived caring by teachers predicted motivational outcomes, even when taking into account levels of psychological distress and beliefs about personal control, as well as previous (6th grade) motivation and performance. Teachers who care were described as demonstrating democratic interaction styles, developing expectations for pupil behaviour in light of individual differences, modelling a 'caring' attitude towards their own work, and providing constructive feedback.

The above further reading links with Unit 2.3 of the 5th edition of *Learning to teach in the secondary school*.

PRACTICE MAKES PERFECT?

Learning to learn as a teacher

Hazel Hagger, Katharine Burn, Trevor Mutton and Sue Brindley

A NOTE FROM THE EDITORS

This reading reports on a study in which data are collected at four stages during an initial teacher education (ITE) year, through a series of post-lesson interviews conducted with twenty-five student teachers to look at the process of professional learning undertaken as student teachers move through their ITE and into their early years as teachers.

This reading links with Chapter 2 of the 5th edition of *Learning to teach in the secondary school*.

QUESTIONS TO CONSIDER

1   How do you expect to learn to become a teacher: passively or proactively? What forms of learning, for yourself, are you planning to undertake? What plans do you need to ensure that the learning experiences you want to have are available to you?

2   Consider the notion of reflective practice described in this reading: see also the Zwozdiak–Myers framework for reflective practice in Unit 5.4 in *Learning to Teach in the Secondary School: A Companion to School Experience* (Capel, Leask and Turner, 2009). What might you do to collect data about how effective you are being as a teacher?

3   Consider the views expressed in Hagger *et al*. about attitudes to receiving
     feedback and the forms of professional knowledge outlined in the introduction
     to Section 1. What is your attitude to feedback about your lessons? How might
     you manage to be proactive about gaining the feedback you want on aspects
     of your practice and pedagogic knowledge that you are specifically focusing
     on developing?

This reading was first published as: Hagger, H., Burn, K., Mutton, K. and Brindley,
S. (2008) 'Practice makes perfect? Learning to learn as a teacher', *Oxford Review
of Education*, Vol. 32: 159–178.

ABSTRACT

The context of this research is one in which teachers are now expected to equip their pupils
with the disposition and skills for life-long learning. It is vital, therefore, that teachers
themselves are learners, not only in developing their practice but also in modelling for
pupils the process of continual learning. This paper is based on a series of post-lesson
interviews, conducted with 25 student teachers following a one-year postgraduate course
within two well-established school-based partnerships of initial teacher training. Its focus
is on the approaches that the student teachers take to their own learning. Four interviews,
conducted with each student teacher over the course of the year, explored their thinking
in relation to planning, conducting and evaluating an observed lesson, and their reflections
on the learning that informed, or resulted from, that lesson. The findings suggest that while
the student teachers all learn from experience, the nature and extent of that learning varies
considerably within a number of different dimensions. We argue that understanding the
range of approaches that student teachers take to professional learning will leave teacher
educators better equipped to help ensure that new entrants to the profession are both
competent teachers and competent professional learners.

INTRODUCTION

In recent years, initial teacher education (ITE) has been a focus of concern in many
countries, with much of the criticism and questioning of established ways of preparing
teachers emanating from governments. This international discontent was based on two
elements. The first was 'a growing belief in the importance of schooling for the civilised
quality of societies and for the success of national economies', while the second has been
'an assumption that the quality of schooling is . . . primarily dependent on the quality of
its teachers and their teaching' (Hagger and McIntyre, 2006: 1).

In those countries where teacher education was the province of higher education
institutions (HEIs), a common criticism was that teacher preparation was overly theoretical
and needed to be more practically based. In England, this desire for greater practicality
found expression in a series of fundamental changes in teacher education carried out in
the 1990s. These included a major shift of responsibilities and resources from higher
education to schools and the introduction of detailed definitions of competences (DfE,
1992, 1993), followed by the introduction of national standards for the award of qualified

teacher status (QTS) (DfEE, 1997). These reforms were accompanied by the introduction of 'a new style of managerialism . . . led jointly by a reformed inspectorate and the newly established Teacher Training Agency' (TTA) (Furlong, 2005: 121). Inspection of teacher education would be carried out by a new-look Office for Standards in Education, while the TTA was given the task of managing the whole system.

The publication of the Green Paper *Teachers: meeting the challenge of change* (DfEE, 1998a) served as a reminder that the New Labour government, like its Conservative predecessor, saw improving the teaching profession as the key to raising standards in schools. Among other things, teachers were reminded that they needed:

■ to take personal and collective responsibility for improving their skills and subject knowledge;
■ to seek to base decisions on evidence of what works in schools in this country and internationally;
■ to anticipate change and promote innovation (DfEE, 1998a: para. 13).

In the same year, another Green Paper, *The learning age: a renaissance for a new Britain,* set out the government's proposals for life-long learning (DfEE, 1998b). In the foreword, the then Secretary of State for Education, David Blunkett, asserted that 'the fostering of an enquiring mind and the love of learning are essential to our future success' (Blunkett, 1998: foreword). While the focus of the proposals was on developing education and skills from post-school to post-retirement, it was teachers in schools who had to enable their pupils to 'learn how to learn', equipping them with the disposition and skills for lifelong learning. It was seen as essential, therefore, that teachers should be learners, not only in developing their practice, but also in modelling for their learners the process of continual learning.

At the heart of these two policy commitments – to raising levels of expertise within the teaching profession, and to creating a society in which adults enter and re-enter learning throughout their lives – lie initial teacher education and training. It is in this earliest stage of a teacher's formation that the foundation for career-long learning is established. It is at this point that beginning teachers need not only to acquire the knowledge, skills and understandings that will enable them to enter the profession as competent classroom practitioners, but also to learn how to evaluate critically and improve their own practice so that they can go on learning.

STUDENT TEACHER LEARNING

The national debates on teacher preparation and subsequent changes to ITE introduced in many countries gave rise to a flurry of research activity and publication, and to a renewed interest in earlier literature, such as the work of Fuller and Bown (1975), focusing on student teacher development. Unsurprisingly, much of the more recent literature has been concerned with new models of partnership (for example, Bullough *et al.*, 2004), the work of teachers as mentors (for example, Wang and Odell, 2002) and the changing role of higher education in teacher education (for example, Furlong and Smith, 1996). There is also, however, a growing and important body of research that identifies the student teachers themselves as the key players in their professional education (see, for example, Bullough *et al.*, 1991; Lacey, 1977; Putnam and Borko, 1997; Sugrue, 1997). This research on student teachers' values, preconceptions, ideals and beliefs and its importance for teacher educators, is summed up by Hagger:

We need then to accept that student teachers embark on their teacher education programmes with varying idiosyncratic ways of thinking about teaching and about learning to teach; that these ways of thinking will powerfully influence both what and how they learn during their programmes; and that those understandings and ideals cannot summarily be dismissed as nave, misleading or unhelpful. We need to take them and their learning very seriously.

(Hagger, 2002: 3–4)

In their study of the reported learning experiences of twenty student teachers, Calderhead and Shorrock (1997) remind us that learning to teach is complex, as there are different kinds of thing to learn and different processes that one needs to engage in:

The use of the term 'learning' itself in describing the professional growth of the student teacher may be misleading since it suggests one generalisable process of development, irrespective of the content to be learned, the context of the learning and the attributes of the learner . . . The important question becomes not 'How do student teachers learn?' but 'How do particular student teachers learn x in context y?'.

(Calderhead and Shorrock, 1997: 193)

In this paper we examine the learning processes in which a group of student teachers engaged during their year of professional preparation. Mindful of the multi-dimensionality of learning to teach, we have adopted a very broad and open view of learning. First, we accept Schoenfield's assertion that 'one has learned when one has developed new understanding or capacity' (Schoenfield, 1999: 6). To that we would add Eraut's point that learning also occurs 'when existing knowledge is used in a new context or in new combinations' (Eraut, 2000: 114).

While learning theories abound, the most popular model of learning to teach remains that of the reflective practitioner. It is often put forward as an antidote to the notion of teachers as technicians, and is a model that most teacher educators in England claim underpins their courses (Furlong et al., 2000). As Parsons and Stephenson (2005) point out, however, the reflective practitioner movement embraces a wide variety of perspectives and positions, and Rodgers (2002) reminds us that there is no consensus as to what constitutes reflective practice, nor as to which components of ITE programmes are likely to produce reflective practitioners.

McIntyre, wary of the rhetoric surrounding reflective practice in pre-service teacher education, has suggested that the 'beginning teacher is more able to learn through deliberating about the nature of the expertise that he or she wants to develop' than through reflecting on what is, after all, their very limited experience (McIntyre, 1993: 43). For McIntyre, reflection is a much more important way of learning for experienced teachers than for beginning teachers. The intuitive nature of experienced teachers' practice means that their learning depends on their bringing to consciousness the taken-for-granted beliefs and considerations embedded in their practice. Novices, on the other hand, are engaged in conscious deliberation and planning, with many aspects of their practice yet to be established. Arguing that novices both need and are well placed to access a range of ideas from a variety of sources, reflection on their experience is seen as having 'the important but limited purpose of enabling them to see the need for these ideas from external sources' (McIntyre, 1993: 44).

Asserting that reflection 'concerns one's present practices, but theorising concerns the whole world of possibilities for the future' (p. 47), he argues for student teachers to be engaged in theorising rather than in reflection. This distinction between reflective practice and practical theorising is developed by Hagger and McIntyre:

> Beginning teachers need primarily to learn in their practice from other people's ideas, both those of experienced practitioners and those of educational researchers and scholars; and they need to submit all these ideas, and of course their own, to a critical examination that goes well beyond commonsense. It is for this much more demanding kind of reflective practice that we use the term 'practical theorising'.
>
> (Hagger and McIntyre, 2006: 58)

Moreover, in view of the paucity of empirical studies of student teachers' learning through reflection, Calderhead's (1989) questioning of whether teaching is best learned through reflection remains pertinent.

THE STUDY

The data discussed were collected as part of a longitudinal study of beginning teachers, following students on a one-year secondary Postgraduate Certificate of Education (PGCE) course through their initial training and subsequently through the first two years of their teaching careers. Thirty-six student teachers from two well-established school/university partnership schemes were originally recruited to the project, twelve from each of the three core subjects of the National Curriculum that operates in all English maintained schools (namely English, mathematics and science). The aim of the study was to examine beginning teachers' developing thinking and practice, and to this end each of the participants was observed teaching and then interviewed to explore his or her thinking in relation to that specific practice. The data presented in this paper relate to the first year of the study, i.e. the initial training year, during which the student teachers were observed and interviewed on four occasions spread throughout the year. It draws on interviews with twenty-five of the student teachers for whom we have full data sets. The interviews were conducted in school, not because we believed this to be the sole site of their learning, but because we considered that questions posed in relation to specific lessons taught by the student teachers would give us the best access to the thinking that informed their practice, rather than to their espoused theories.

The semi-structured interviews focused on the student teachers' perceptions of the lesson and their own learning in relation to their professional practice. The interview schedule was developed with reference to the approach used by Brown and McIntyre (1993) to help experienced teachers articulate their 'craft knowledge', with the aim here of encouraging the student teachers to describe and evaluate their teaching in whatever terms *they* chose. The role of the interviewer was to remain neutral and non-judgemental, probing the student teachers' responses, encouraging them to elaborate on their perceptions of the lesson and to offer explanations for any judgements that they were making. Since the study involved beginning teachers, rather than experienced practitioners, some adaptations were made to the approach adopted by Brown and McIntyre. One significant difference was that the student teachers were also asked to discuss the thinking behind their planning of the lesson, in order to take account of the pre-active phase in the practice of beginning teachers (Clark and Yinger, 1979). As part of this focus, they were invited to discuss the sources of their ideas for teaching. They were also asked to consider what changes to their teaching they might subsequently make as a result of evaluating the lesson in question. The final part of the interview revolved around their learning – first asking what they had learnt from the lesson in question and second inviting them to discuss their wider learning at this stage of the course.

Our original analyses of the student teachers' learning (reported in Burn *et al.*, 2000, 2003) were based on the accounts that they gave of their planning and interactive teaching decisions and the terms in which they evaluated the observed lessons. While this systematic comparison of the student teachers' lesson aims and the conditions that they took into account provided some confirmation of established theories of beginning teachers' development (broadly conceived as a transition from consideration of their own classroom performance to more detailed consideration of the learning processes and achievements of their pupils – see, for example, Fuller and Bown, 1975; Kagan, 1992), it also alerted us to important ways in which this general theory needed to be qualified. The first was the prominence of the pupils and their learning in the student teachers' thinking, even in the very early months of the PGCE year. The second was the extent to which the student teachers continued to focus on issues of classroom management, even as their learning objectives for the pupils became more complex or more clearly defined. Perhaps the most important qualification, however, was the high level of individual variation within the general pattern of development that we were able to describe:

> Although it was certainly possible to discern a number of different types of progression in the aims that they expressed for their lessons over the course of the year, it was equally apparent that there were no common starting points for all of the student teachers. Individuals began at different starting points, seemed to develop at different rates and reached different points along each of a series of separate but inter-related continua.
>
> (Burn *et al.*, 2003: 314)

Since these claims about the student teachers' learning were inferred from accounts of their practice, we were interested to test them against the student teachers' own perceptions of their learning. The research question guiding the next stages of analysis was therefore: 'What claims do the student teachers make about how they are learning to teach?'

DATA ANALYSIS

Answers to this question were sought in two ways, by identifying and analysing first all *specific* references that the student teachers made to aspects of teaching about which they claimed to be learning, and, second, all their more *general* reflections on the processes by which they were learning or on their role as learners. A 'what/how' data grid was completed for every interview, noting each distinctive aspect of teaching identified as a learning focus, along with any details given by the student teachers about the processes by which they had learned this, or by which they believed they would learn it.

Two researchers undertook this stage of the analysis. Each initially coded the same four sets of transcripts, which were then compared to ensure consistent recognition of the aspects of teaching identified by each student teacher as a focus of learning. Analytical categories for the substantive learning foci and processes of learning were developed through an iterative, inductive process. Preliminary categories, derived independently by each researcher from analysis of the first four data sets, were compared and collectively defined, then reviewed and refined in the light of the remaining data sets. All the original discrepancies and any further uncertainties were fully discussed by the research team, and a third colleague coded a sample of the transcripts alongside the two original researchers to confirm the inter-rater reliability of the final coding schedule.

The grids also included all the student teachers' own reflections on the learning process, and each was cross-referenced against the coding schedule used for the original round of analysis, which had captured details of all the sources from which each claimed to have derived ideas for the lesson, any constraints they had mentioned and all the contributions to their learning that they had identified as helpful or unhelpful. Using all these data, a short analytic memo was written recording the researchers' dominant impressions of the changing foci of each student teacher's learning and his or her approach to the learning process.

As we drew up the 'what/how' data grids, it became apparent how much of their learning the student teachers simply attributed to their experiences of planning and teaching. Obviously the format of the interviews, focused on an observed lesson, tended to highlight the importance of the practical experience of planning, teaching and evaluation as the main source of their learning. However, the student teachers were also encouraged to explain why they had planned and taught the lesson in that way, and to consider how this particular lesson related to their ongoing learning, as well as commenting on what they thought they were learning more generally at this stage of the course. As they highlighted aspects of teaching about which they needed to learn, they were also encouraged to suggest how they might anticipate addressing these needs. Overall, eleven different sources of learning were identified by the student teachers (see Table 3.1), including the forms of support built into the ITE programme, such as 'advice' and 'feedback' from their designated mentor, input from the 'university' (either through taught sessions or tutor visits to school), observation of other teachers' lessons, and designated school-based tasks. A further category, 'unspecified', was used to code those instances of learning, or learning needs, about which the student teachers gave no indication as to how the learning had, or would, come about.

As Table 3.1 shows, 'experience' of planning and teaching accounted for 72 per cent of the instances of learning identified by the student teachers. Of the remainder, 7 per cent were not attributed to any source at all, while no other single category accounted for more than 5 per cent of their claims. It is interesting to note that 'learning from experience' encompassed both 'negative' experiences – learning from mistakes – and more 'positive' experiences, including very successful lessons or incidents within them.

The predominance of learning from experience, both in accounting for past learning and as the method by which they expected to address their current learning needs, is unsurprising given the nature of the professional knowledge that they were seeking to acquire. As Eraut has pointed out:

> Although many areas of professional knowledge are dependent on some understanding of relevant public codified knowledge found in books and journals, professional knowledge is constructed through experience and its nature depends on the cumulative acquisition, selection and interpretation of that experience.
>
> (Eraut, 1994: 19–20)

■ **Table 3.1** Sources of learning identified by the student teachers. Total number of instances = 739 (percentage of total given in brackets)

Source	Explanation	Proportion of instances of learning attributed to each	
Experience	Learning attributed to the experience of a specific lesson (usually the one observed)	532	(72.7%)
(a) positive		325	(44.0%)
(b) negative		102	(13.9%)
(c) unspecified		105	(14.3%)
Experimentation	Deliberate trial of a new teaching strategy conceived of as a conscious experiment	20	(2.7%)
Marking	Monitoring or review of pupils' written work after the lesson	4	(0.5%)
Reflection	Conscious review of the student-teacher's practice focused on a specific issue or concern (often conducted some time later, or ranging across several lessons)	25	(3.4%)
Advice	From the mentor (or regular class teacher) given in advance of planning	30	(4.1%)
Feedback	From the mentor or regular class teacher following observation of a lesson taught by the student teacher	36	(4.9%)
Observation	The student teacher's observation of experienced teachers' teaching	19	(2.6%)
Literature	Ideas derived from reading research or professional literature	2	(0.3%)
University input	Advice from the tutor offered either during taught sessions in the university or on visits to school	11	(1.5%)
School-based tasks	Specific teaching or investigative tasks set as part of the jointly planned curriculum programme	6	(0.8%)
Interview	Learning attributed to the process of talking through their teaching in response to the interviewer's questions	3	(0.4%)
Unspecified	No indication as to how the learning had, or would, come about.	51	(7.0%)

Experience is vital since it is in the processes of planning, teaching and evaluation that all the other sources of knowledge on which one might draw come together in action and acquire meaning. As Buchmann (1984) declares, professional knowledge is quite simply knowledge for action.

However, while all the student teachers claimed to learn from experience, the individual analytic memos, which drew both on the specific instances of learning identified in each interview and on each individual's more general reflections, made it clear that 'learning by experience' meant different sorts of things on different occasions or – more obviously – to different student teachers. The simple category 'experience' in fact encompassed a wide variety of learning processes that included, for example:

■ the deliberate trying out and subsequent review of ideas propounded in the university;
■ the implementation of specific teaching tasks outlined in a school's scheme of work, and careful evaluation of their outcomes drawing on a range of evidence;
■ student teachers' instinctive judgements about a plan's effectiveness based on how 'comfortable' they felt with it; and
■ reflections – often emotionally driven – on what they realised they still had to learn about engaging pupils' interest or classroom management.

Using a similar iterative, inductive process to that outlined above, our analysis resulted initially in the identification of seven themes or dimensions according to which the student teachers' approaches or attitudes to learning from experience could be categorised. Following Bullough *et al.* (2004), we found the most effective way of capturing these dimensions was as 'opposable orientations, dichotomous categories, representing aspects of the [student teachers'] development over time (Bullough *et al.*, 2004: 368). We tested the validity of this framework using all four interviews for eight of

■ **Table 3.2** Five dimensions according to which the variation among the student teachers' accounts of their learning from experience were analysed

Dimension	Orientation	
Intentionality *The extent to which learning is planned*	Deliberative	Reactive
Frame of reference *The value ascribed to looking beyond their experience in order to make sense of it*	Drawing on a range of sources to shape and make sense of experience	Exclusive reliance on the experience of classroom teaching
Response to feedback *Disposition towards receiving feedback and the value attributed to it*	Effective use of feedback to further learning	Tendency to be disabled by critical feedback
Attitude to context *Attitude to the positions in which student-teachers find themselves and the approaches they take to the school context*	Acceptance of the context and ability to capitalise on it	Tendency to regard the context as constraining
Aspiration *The extent of their aspirations for their own and their pupils' learning*	Aspirational both as learners and teachers	Satisfaction with current level of achievement

the student teachers. Subsequent refinement led to the identification and elaboration of five distinct dimensions and their associated orientations (see Table 3.2). We were then able to plot the attitudes and approaches to learning from experience of all twenty-five student teachers along a continuum at each interview for each dimension.

FINDINGS

Intentionality

The degree of intentionality in the student teachers' approach to their learning appears as a key issue. By this we mean the extent to which the learning is planned, with one end of the continuum represented by a proactive approach to learning, and the other by an approach that relied on the reaction to each experience of teaching as a guide to development. While both orientations might be characterised by an awareness of there being a 'long way to go' before competence is attained, what distinguishes the latter is that there is little sense of the action that needs to be taken in order to achieve this competence. This approach we call *reactive*, drawing on Eraut's definition of reactive learning as being 'near spontaneous and unplanned, the learner is aware of it but the level of intentionality will vary and often be debatable' (Eraut, 2000: 115).

This end of the continuum is exemplified by one of the science student teachers, whose aspirations appear very high, with an assertion that no one can ever claim to have 'mastered' teaching and that there is always more to be learnt. However, his declaration in the first interview that learning to teach is 'a never-ending tunnel', with 'no Holy Grail' ever to be attained, actually translates into a pragmatic acceptance that there is no point in even striving to reach it. His vague aspirations thus never become specific plans for addressing particular challenges, and his learning is entirely reactive. By the fourth interview he declares.

> I'm not learning through a conscious effort – just through experience . . . which may or may not be useful for the future.
>
> (Science student teacher, interview 4)

This 'reactive' end of the dimension is also characterised by a sense of passivity and an expectation that learning will occur with little intervention on the part of the student teacher. In some cases this appears as a sense almost of helplessness that persists throughout the training year, as in the following example, which is consistent with the student teacher's feelings at each of the four interviews:

> I expect it's quite a steep learning curve and we're just at the bottom really . . . It's just a gradual dawning of things that will work and things that won't.
>
> (English student teacher, interview 2)

While learning to teach is seen by all as an ongoing process, a feature of this particular dimension is the extent to which the process itself – at least for some – becomes the justification as to why they might not be doing well at any given stage. A more 'reactive' orientation is therefore associated with what might be termed an abdication of the responsibility for one's own learning in the face of the amount that needs to be learnt.

Another feature of the more reactive orientation is a failure on the part of the student teachers to consider how they might intervene in their own learning. One example of this is a science student teacher in the early stages of the course. Although she can identify many areas she needs to develop following her own evaluation of her teaching and the feedback from others (for example, her pacing of the lesson and behaviour management strategies), she shows little sign of addressing these issues in planning lessons. Her learning is expressed in terms of what she should have done differently.

There are also occasions when student teachers, while able to describe what has been learnt when looking back over their teaching experience to date, have difficulty in identifying their future learning needs, even during the later stages of the course:

> It's strange. It's all just happening. It's not until I look back at the Standards that I think. 'Gosh, I'm doing this'. This is just happening naturally now . . . I think it's just being in the school environment constantly that is developing my learning.
>
> (Mathematics student teacher, interview 3)

In contrast, the *deliberative* end of the continuum is represented by a commitment to determining what needs to be learnt as well as the means by which the desired learning outcomes could be brought about. This orientation is characterised by a proactive approach to creating opportunities for learning, exemplified by one science student teacher who actively seeks feedback on her teaching at all stages of the course, takes the initiative to observe others in her own and in other subjects and organises a regular after-school discussion meeting of all the student teachers at her school:

> I also feel that my learning is directed by me at this stage. I am the person saying 'I'd like to teach more chemistry' or 'I'd like to teach lower ability groups'. I'm asking for more challenges . . . I'm hoping that I'll be able to work with the other [student teachers] and we can observe each other.
>
> (Science student teacher, interview 4)

Proactivity at this end of the dimension is often associated with an interventionist approach:

> At the moment, because I'm training, I can take a lot of time over working out what I want to be like and what I want to do and try new things and make mistakes . . . I've just this time, and I'm learning, and that's the whole point, the whole reason for me being there isn't it?
>
> (English student teacher, interview 2)

For some, the intentionality is often expressed in the desire to try things out in the classroom. An English teacher, for example, in the later stages of her time in school, adopts an action research approach to developing strategies for working with boys in order to avoid the 'stagnation' in her teaching that she fears might otherwise set in. This enthusiasm to experiment with their teaching in order to promote their own learning is typical of a number of the student teachers who represent a more proactive orientation. This is not just to be found, as one might expect, in the final weeks of the course. In the first interview, one science student teacher is already exemplifying this orientation by deliberately experimenting with role play and drama in the classroom as a means of developing the pupils' understanding of the human immune system.

Frame of reference

While all the student teachers emphasise the value of learning from their own practice, there are clear differences in the extent to which they recognise the value of looking beyond their own experience in order to make sense of it. At one end of this dimension is a tendency to draw on other sources, such as wider reading, discussion with mentors and university tutors and reference to appropriate research findings:

> The analogy I use in teaching is a bit like having all these kind of bubbles in the air, and you're constantly having influences from . . . you know, you've got the school influence here and then you've got the college influence here and the theoretical bit and the core studies and the subject studies bits all mixed in with that, and then you have got your own experience of teaching and your own personal experiences. So you are constantly kind of drawing on all these bubbles and kind of drawing them down, drawing on different elements.
>
> (English student teacher, interview 1)

Between the two extremes of this continuum is a recognition of the need to look beyond one's own teaching, but with a tendency to draw on only a limited range of sources, for example:

> The main way I'm learning is basically through my own experiences and then talking about the lesson afterwards. And also getting ideas. If I've got a class that's difficult, trying to get ideas how to engage them, different approaches to that. Sometimes you want to try something slightly different, but you're not sure how to do it or how they're going to react. And so getting ideas off different teachers and trying them out, or adapting them. That's broadening my repertoire of styles, which is quite useful, rather than always doing what you've done before.
>
> (Mathematics student teacher, interview 3)

The other end of this dimension is represented by a small number of students who seem to restrict the range of sources for their learning as the training year progresses, and focus increasingly on their own experience of teaching in the classroom as the sole source of their learning. This orientation is illustrated by a student teacher who seems to have closed down all the options available to her and wants just to learn from her own experience. Even being observed and given feedback she finds 'quite restrictive', declaring that she has:

> . . . got to the stage now where I'm looking forward to opening my wings and trying to fly away from the nest on my own. I might crash and burn, but I'll pick myself up and try again.
>
> (English student teacher, interview 4)

Further exemplification comes from another student teacher who claims by the final interview that the process of learning to teach has become essentially one of trial and error. She says she is no longer learning by observing others and acknowledges that she is not taking on the responsibility for evaluating her own teaching, even though she is getting less feedback than previously. She also feels that the only way to learn is by being on your own in the classroom and dealing with problems as they arise:

The need to be adaptable is coming through thick and fast now. You're going in and you're doing something. If it doesn't go to plan . . . you've got to do something, rectify it and carry on. And I think that's something you could only learn from being on your own . . . So that's the main way at the moment. Just being on your own and having to do it.

(English student teacher, interview 4)

Response to feedback

The nature of the feedback the student teachers receive, its frequency and the manner in which it is delivered vary significantly and obviously may affect the student teachers' response to it. Notwithstanding this variation, there appear to be different dispositions towards receiving feedback (and critical feedback in particular) and the value that is attributed to it. One orientation is characterised by a commitment to making full use of feedback; to valuing the expertise of the teachers and university tutors providing it; and often to making changes to planning and teaching in the light of the suggestions received:

Taking a tip from the last observed lesson, one of the things was that when I was helping individuals I wasn't positioned in a very vigilant way. So I tried to correct that.

(English student teacher, interview 3)

Among examples of receptivity to criticism are some student teachers who, looking for further challenges, actively seek more critical feedback, wanting to have their thinking and understanding challenged:

I find that sometimes I need somebody to say to me: 'Oh, here is the absolute opposite to what you think. Here is your child centred approach, which is OK, you know, we are not knocking it, but here is the way that I would do it.' And for me to see that absolute opposite and maybe take something in the middle, or find that what I am doing is in the middle of two extremes.

(English student teacher, interview 4)

Furthermore, there can be regret at the fact that feedback is not more frequent, as in the case of a student teacher who finds it 'disappointing' that she doesn't 'get very much feedback' (interview 1) and later feels that she has to rely on her own critical evaluation of the lesson because:

I'm more critical of my teaching than any of the staff that observe me . . . they're far too nice, they never actually tell me really what I know to be wrong.

(Science student teacher, interview 3)

It is important to emphasise that this dimension is concerned with the student teachers' *attitude* to feedback. Whereas some are able to make use of the feedback whatever form it takes, there are others who are unable to cope with it, either because they adopt a defensive stance or because they cannot distinguish between criticism of their teaching and criticism of themselves. The latter is illustrated in the following example:

I've had a few bad ones that have upset me personally because I've spent a lot of time trying to make it interesting, because initially you think 'God, it's you, it's the way you're doing it, it's wrong'.

(Science student teacher, interview 2)

Even in cases where the student teacher has identified that the person giving the feedback has delivered it in a positive way, there are those who still find it difficult not to take it personally. At the extreme end of this continuum is the example of a student teacher who claims to feel 'destroyed' by the feedback, adding:

But I do get upset. I do beat myself up over it and go home in floods of tears about it.

(English student teacher, interview 3)

Attitude to context

Another important dimension in the process of learning from experience concerns the student teachers' attitude to context. Context is broadly conceived and includes the nature of the school, the host subject department, and the role and status of the student teachers themselves.

At one end of this dimension are what one might categorise as acceptance of the context and the desire to use it to further professional learning. For example, a science student teacher, who in the first interview describes the school context as one where student teachers are encouraged to follow a formal approach that she finds constraining, decides very early on that 'there is no point fighting against that'. She uses the framework given to her but keeps thinking about how she can create scope within it to try out 'little bits and pieces that you hope will interest the pupils'. This orientation is further exemplified by another student teacher who uses the context of a potentially difficult lesson on a Friday afternoon both to try out different approaches to developing pupil autonomy through pair and group work and to learn how to monitor such activities effectively.

There is a clear attitudinal difference between those who appreciate the learning opportunities inherent in working with other experienced teachers' classes, and those who see this feature of their course as a serious constraint on their capacity to develop. While some, who are more positively oriented in this respect, feel highly 'privileged', others complain that it makes it difficult to develop their own teaching style because 'when you're taking other people's classes you have to fit in with what they think' (English trainee, interview 1). The tendency to blame the context of being a student teacher within the school characterises the approach of some, such as the student teacher who lays the blame for her not being able to develop a good relationship with the groups she teaches on the simple fact that 'these are not my classes' (Mathematics student teacher, interview 4).

A more negative orientation within the dimension is also characterised by a tendency to hold the mentor, or other colleagues within the school, responsible for the difficulties in making progress. One student teacher complains at length in the final interview about her working relationship with her mentor, and the fact that a colleague has asked her to teach a particular poem that she did not want to teach:

I wish I could just abandon it, but it was their normal class teacher who was excited about it.

(English student teacher, interview 4)

On occasion, lack of progress is attributed to a range of different factors. One student teacher, for example, resents having to teach the prescribed syllabus content to pupils whose level of academic achievement he does not regard as being sufficiently high. Rather than approaching the curriculum and his pupils in a positive way, he instead looks forward to a future context where he could teach interesting things in a school where 'the academic standards are generally higher'. He also complains that there is insufficient support from the science technician in preparing the resources for the lesson, and that he is unprepared for the lessons because of a lack of time to set the classroom up as he would wish. Finally he attributes part of the reason for 'finding [him]self struggling' to the pupils' expectations of him as a teacher.

One interesting point to note, however, is that, whatever orientation individual student teachers may display in relation to this dimension and however much contextual factors may be blamed for any difficulties experienced, it is very rare for the blame to be attributed to the pupils themselves.

Aspiration

An aspirational orientation is one in which boundaries are constantly being pushed out in order to develop professional practice and to avoid the complacency that might set in with the acceptance of a merely satisfactory level of performance. The aspiration may be focused on the strategies that the student teachers are developing or on the ways in which the pupils themselves are learning, as exemplified in the following two quotations from the same student teacher at different stages in the year:

> That's what I've learnt, that's what I believe in – deeply believe – that they have to be part of their own learning, not responsible for it perhaps, but they have to be involved in their own learning in order to learn.
>
> (English student teacher, interview 2)

> I think if you protect their emotional wellbeing in the classroom you will get learning out of them. They will start to learn, they will feel comfortable and confident enough to learn. You have got to build an environment in which they feel safe to learn.
>
> (English student teacher, interview 3)

Even when there is a tension between the aspiration to achieve things in certain ways and the level of competence needed in order to make this feasible, the critical factor is that the desire to improve and develop is expressed in aspirational terms:

> I really wish I could find ways of being more imaginative without confusing the children . . . there's the desire to make the lesson more interesting.
>
> (Mathematics student teacher, interview 3)

Another indication of the more aspirational end of the continuum is an increasing focus on experimentation in the classroom in order to develop both the student teachers' learning and the learning of their pupils. An example is the English student teacher who focuses on his interest in providing multi-sensory input in the classroom and experiments with ways of achieving this.

At the other end of the scale is a tendency to be more easily satisfied with an adequate level of performance. For example, in the first interview, when faced with the complexity thrown up by pupils' investigations of spirals in a mathematics classroom, one student teacher chooses to close down the pupils' options, thereby restricting the range of possible outcomes, in order to make the learning easier for her to manage. Sometimes such a lack of aspiration is acknowledged by the student teachers themselves and is closely related to a perception of their own level of competence. One example is a science student teacher who acknowledges that she has been following the scheme of work very closely and not experimenting in her teaching because she 'wasn't experienced enough to decide what was right or wrong or possible' (interview 3).

Finally, whereas there are instances of some student teachers appearing to become more aspirational as the course progresses and as they gain confidence in their developing skills and expertise in the classroom, there are other examples of those who become less ambitious as learners and teachers, particularly in the final stages of the course. One science student teacher, who described in the second interview how he was experimenting with different teaching approaches with a lower-attaining class of 14–15-year-olds, acknowledges in the final interview that he is no longer trying to develop his own teaching:

> Myself and my teaching partner are looking to the end now, and thinking it's nearly all over, and we're not as focused as we were . . . Last term there was a lot more of experience learning going on, whereas now we're just going through it, going through the motions a bit more I suppose.
>
> (Science student teacher, interview 4)

DISCUSSION AND IMPLICATIONS

As outlined in the introduction, a feature of reformed ITE in many countries has been an increase in the amount of time that prospective teachers spend in schools and classrooms. It could be argued, therefore, that in recent years the practicum, or placement, has assumed even greater importance than before in the professional formation of beginning teachers. Furthermore, Bullough *et al.* remind us that 'for the most part, the case for extending the amount of field experience is supported by a commonsense, conservative view of learning to teach: one learns to teach by doing' (2004: 365). The student teachers in this study spent two thirds of their year of professional preparation in schools, and they were in no doubt about the importance of learning through and from experience. As we argued earlier in this paper, given the nature of the professional knowledge that the student teachers were striving to acquire, it should come as no surprise that they talked predominantly in terms of learning from experience. To acknowledge the importance of experience, however, is not to suggest that accumulated practice is all that beginning teachers need, and we would most certainly want to distance ourselves from those who adopt such a position. Our interest is not so much in the fact that the student teachers claimed to learn from experience, but more in the different approaches to learning to teach that lay beneath this common assertion.

Reminding us of Dewey's (1938) assertion that, while first-hand experience in schools is vital in the preparation of teachers, not all experience is necessarily beneficial, Zeichner argues that:

> Unless the practicum helps to teach prospective teachers how to take control of their own professional development and to learn how to continue learning, it is miseducative, no matter how successful the teacher might be in the short run.
>
> (Zeichner, 1996: 217)

All the student teachers in this study were indeed successful in the short run, in that they passed their respective courses and were recommended for the award of QTS. The questions that need to be asked, however, concern the capacity of student teachers to *continue* learning. What happens to beginning teachers when the support structures and resources of their teacher education programmes are no longer there and they are obliged to function as real teachers? Are they equipped to go on learning in new and diverse contexts?

In this study, there were, in fact, some student teachers whose orientations towards the process of learning from experience meant that the experience could be seen as 'miseducative'. These were the student teachers who assumed that experience would automatically lead to learning and that the more lessons they taught, the better. Their frames of reference tended to be limited, as did their aspirations for their learners and for themselves as teachers. These student teachers evaluated their lessons afterwards and thought about their experience, and to all intents and purposes were engaging in reflective practice. There are limits, however, to what beginning teachers with little accumulated experience of practice can learn from simply looking back on what they have done. While they were able to develop their knowledge and skills and function as competent classroom practitioners, there was no indication that they had learned how to go on learning.

On the other hand, there were some student teachers whose orientations meant that, in addition to looking back on lessons and drawing on their experience of them when planning, they were also looking forward to the 'whole world of possibilities for the future' (McIntyre, 1993: 47) and were working out the first steps they might take towards them. Far from seeing lessons as so 'many miles on the clock', they were aware of the opportunities offered by the teaching of lessons to try out or put to the test their developing thinking and practices. While they regarded experience as important, for them it was but one of a range of sources of learning to which they turned as they continued to draw on the expertise of their tutors and mentors and on research and scholarship. These were the student teachers who would meet with McIntyre's (1993) approval, in that their concerns went beyond their current practice, and their thinking beyond reflection on that practice. They were happy to cast themselves in the role of learners.

One of the challenges facing teacher educators is to design curricula that enable student teachers not only to become competent beginning classroom practitioners but also to build secure foundations for their lifelong learning and professional development. This study serves to remind us of some of the issues around that challenge.

First, in line with earlier studies (e.g. Burn *et al.*, 2003; Calderhead and Robson, 1991; Wideen *et al.*, 1998), the research points to the importance of taking account of the individual learner's agenda about what and how they should learn. If they are to understand the rationale of the course and of the tasks and activities they are expected to undertake, the course must include opportunities to explore and discuss research on the nature, acquisition and development of teaching expertise. Learners tend to learn much more effectively when they have a shared understanding with those teaching them about what they are trying to learn and about the best ways of going about that learning, and student teachers are no different from other learners in this respect. An exploration of individuals' orientations within each dimension and the extent to which they remain stable over time is beyond the scope of this paper and has been reported elsewhere (Hagger *et al.*, 2006). However, it is important to note that, while there were some student teachers whose approaches to learning from experience tended to cluster at the same end of the continuum for each dimension and remained consistent over the length of the ITE course, there were many others whose attitudes and dispositions towards learning varied in relation to specific dimensions and over time. If, as this suggests, student teachers' orientations towards learning from experience are amenable to change, we need to ensure that all student teachers have the space, time and encouragement to articulate, and critically examine, their differing conceptions of the process of learning to teach. As mentors are best placed to provide student teachers with individual attention of this kind, it is important that they too have a developed understanding of the course's rationale. The dimensions and orientations outlined in this paper could prove to be very helpful as a diagnostic tool when exploring student teachers' notions of learning to teach and the role of their own practice in that learning.

The second issue concerns the role of practice and experience in learning to teach. While we do not dispute the central importance of experience in that process, we would take issue with the narrow view of learning from experience summed up in a science student's declaration that 'doing is the best way of learning'. Such a belief – and it is one shared by many teachers and student teachers – leads to an overriding concern with the number of lessons that beginning teachers teach. The logic is straightforward: if one learns through doing, then the more one does, the better. Such a restricted view of learning from experience may well enable student teachers to develop an initial level of competence as classroom teachers, and that of course is to be welcomed. It is unlikely, however, to lead to their developing the commitment, confidence, analytic expertise and habits necessary for critically examining their developing practice and thinking. A restricted view of learning from experience goes hand in hand with a restricted view of the purposes and potential of the school-based component of pre-service teacher education. Of much greater importance than the number of lessons taught are the ways in which student teachers engage in the processes of planning, delivering and evaluating lessons as they develop not only their competence as teachers but also their capacity for continuing development through their own professional learning.

The findings also highlight the tremendous potential and scope for learning that the positive orientations of many of these student teachers opened up. In the light of this capacity for learning, we should perhaps consider spending more time in asking them questions to support their thinking, theorising and developing practice, rather than assuming that our key contribution to their development is to offer answers.

While it is widely accepted that expertise in teaching takes a number of years to develop (Berliner, 1987), the findings of this study lead us to consider Bereiter and Scardamalia's (1993) conception of expertise as a process rather than a state characterised by capabilities that people have. Although it may take years for socially recognised expert performance to develop, the process of acquiring expertise could begin very early. The positions of a number of these student teachers along the dimensions identified suggest that the process of expertise was already underway.

REFERENCES

Bereiter, C. and Scardamalia, M. (1993) *Surpassing ourselves,* Chicago, IL: Open Court.
Berliner, D.C. (1987) 'Ways of thinking about students and classrooms by more and less experienced teachers', in Calderhead, J. (ed.) *Exploring teachers' thinking*, London: Cassell.
Blunkett, D. (1998) 'Foreword', in *The learning age: a renaissance for a new Britain*, London: DfEE.
Brown, S. and McIntyre, D. (1993) *Making sense of teaching*, Buckingham: Open University Press.
Buchmann, M. (1984) 'The priority of knowledge and understanding in teaching', in Katz, L. and Raths, J. (eds) *Advances in teacher education* 1, Norwood: Abley.

Bullough Jr, R.V., Knowles, G.J. and Crow, N.N. (1991) *Emerging as a teacher*, London: Routledge.

Bullough Jr, R.V., Young, J. and Draper, R.J. (2004) 'One-year teaching internships and the dimensions of beginning teacher development', *Teachers and Teaching: Theory and Practice,* Vol. 10, No. 4: 365–394.

Burn, K., Hagger, H., Mutton, T. and Everton, T. (2000) 'Beyond concerns with self: the sophisticated thinking of beginning student teachers', *Journal of Education for Teaching,* Vol. 26, No. 3: 259–278.

Burn, K., Hagger, H., Mutton, T. and Everton, T. (2003) 'The complex development of student teachers' thinking', *Teachers and Teaching: Theory and Practice,* Vol. 9, No. 4: 309–331.

Calderhead, J. (1989) 'Reflective teaching and teacher education', *Teaching and Teacher Education,* Vol. 7, No. 5/6: 531–535.

Calderhead, J. and Robson, M. (1991) 'Images of teaching: student teachers' early conceptions of classroom practice', *Teaching and Teacher Education,* Vol. 17, No. 1: 1–8.

Calderhead, J. and Shorrock, S.B. (1997) *Understanding teacher education: case studies in the professional development of beginning teachers*, London: Falmer Press.

Clark, C.M. and Yinger, R.J. (1979) *Three studies of teaching planning*, East Lansing, MI: Institute for Research on Teaching, Michigan State University.

Department for Education (1992) *Initial teacher training: secondary phase* (Circular 9/92), London: DfE.

Department for Education (1993) *The initial training of primary school teachers: new criteria for courses* (Circular 14/93), London: DfE.

Department for Education and Employment (1997) *Standards for the award of Qualified Teacher Status* (Circular 10/97), London: DfEE.

Department for Education and Employment (1998a) *Teachers meeting the challenge of change,* London: DfEE.

Department for Education and Employment (1998b) *The learning age: a renaissance for a new Britain*, London: DfEE.

Dewey, J. (1938) *Experience and education*, New York: Macmillan.

Eraut, M. (1994) *Developing professional knowledge and competence*, London: Falmer.

Eraut, M. (2000) 'Non formal learning and tacit knowledge in professional work', *British Journal of Educational Psychology,* Vol. 70, No. 1: 13–136.

Fuller, F.F. and Bown, O.H. (1975) 'Becoming a teacher', in Ryan, K. (ed.) *Teacher education: the seventy-fourth yearbook of the National Society for the Study of Education,* Chicago: University of Chicago Press.

Furlong, J. (2005) 'New Labour and teacher education: the end of an era', *Oxford Review of Education,* Vol. 31, No. 1: 119–134.

Furlong, J., Barton, L., Miles, S., Whiting, C. and Whitty, G. (2000) *Teacher education in transition – re-forming professionalism?* Buckingham: Open University Press.

Furlong, J. and Smith, R. (eds) (1996) *The role of higher education in initial teacher training*, London: Kogan Page.

Hagger, H. (2002) 'Professional knowledge and the beginning teacher'. Keynote address given at the *Inaugural UPSI International Teacher Education Conference,* Kuala Lumpur.

Hagger, H., Burn, K. and Mutton, T. (2006) 'Making sense of learning to teach: the interaction of learner identity and context'. Paper presented at *European Educational Research Association Conference,* Geneva.

Hagger, H. and McIntyre, D. (2006) *Learning teaching from teachers: realising the potential of school based teacher education*, Buckingham: Open University Press.

Kagan, D.M. (1992) 'Professional growth among preservice and beginning teachers', *Review of Educational Research,* Vol. 62, No. 2: 129–169.

Lacey, C. (1977) *The socialization of teachers,* London: Methuen.

McIntyre, D. (1993) 'Theory, theorizing and reflection in initial teacher education', in Calderhead, J. and Gates, P. (eds) *Conceptualizing reflection in teacher development,* London: Falmer Press.

Parsons, M. and Stephenson, M. (2005) 'Developing reflective practice in student teachers: collaboration and critical partnerships', *Teachers and Teaching: Theory and Practice,* Vol. 11, No. 1: 95–116.

Putnam, T.R. and Borko, H. (1997) 'Teacher learning: implications of new views of cognition', in Biddle, B., Good, T.L. and Goodson, I.F. (eds) *International handbook of teachers and teaching,* Dordrecht: Kluwer Academic Publishers: 1223–1296.

Rodgers, C. (2002) 'Defining reflection: another look at John Dewey and reflective thinking', *Teachers College Record,* Vol. 104, No. 4: 842–866.

Schoenfield, A.H. (1999) 'Looking towards the twenty-first century: challenges of educational theory and practice', *Educational Researcher,* Vol. 28, No. 7: 4–14.

Sugrue, C. (1997) 'Student teachers' lay theories and teaching identities: their implications for professional development', *European Journal of Teacher Education,* Vol. 20, No. 3: 213–225.

Wang, J. and Odell, S.J. (2002) 'Mentored learning to teach according to standards-based reforms: a critical review', *Review of Educational Research,* Vol. 72, No. 3: 481–546.

Wideen, M., Mayer-Smith, J. and Moon, B. (1998) 'A critical analysis of the research on learning to teach: making the case for an ecological perspective on inquiry', *Review of Educational Research,* Vol. 68, No. 2: 130–178.

Zeichner, K. (1996) 'Designing educative practicum experiences', in Zeichner, K., Melnick, S. and Gomez, M.L. (eds) *Currents of reform in preservice teacher education,* Columbia University, NY: Teachers College Press.

LESSON PLANNING AND THE STUDENT TEACHER

Rethinking the dominant model

Peter D. John

A NOTE FROM THE EDITORS

In this reading, John explores and challenges some accepted notions of how lesson planning is undertaken, describing the current model as 'rationalistic' and 'technical' and proposing a 'dialogic' model.

This reading links with Unit 2.2 of the 5th edition of *Learning to teach in the secondary school*.

QUESTIONS TO CONSIDER

1   John describes the lesson planning process as holding 'creative possibilities' for some student teachers, while for others lesson planning is a 'brick wall of bewilderment and anxiety'. Where is your experience on this spectrum and why? How might your lesson planning be different if you adopt John's advice for a dialogic model?

2   How does John's description of the limitations of the linear model of lesson planning, and of the actual lesson as being guided less by a plan and more by 'broad intentions, intuition, tacit knowledge and lesson images' (John, 2006: 488) fit with your experience of how lessons happen in practice, in spite of careful planning?

This reading was first published as: John, P.D. (2006) 'Lesson planning and the student teacher: rethinking the dominant model', *Journal of Curriculum Studies*, Vol. 38: 483–498.

ABSTRACT

Rationalistic, technical curriculum planning has been the dominant model underpinning student teachers' lesson-planning for a generation or more in England and Wales. In recent years, this process has become embedded in documents that direct initial training. The paper argues that this model leads to a limited view of teaching and learning as well as a restricted approach to learning to teach. Building on recent developments in socio-cultural theory, an alternative, dialogical model of lesson planning is offered which not only emphasizes context-dependency but also sees planning itself as a practice. This process is the key to developing reflective engagement across the different phases of the professional learning cycle.

INTRODUCTION

In virtually every teacher-preparation programme, considerable time is spent teaching novices how to write detailed lesson plans; however, when they begin this process for themselves, their responses are quite diverse. For some, the encounter holds creative possibilities; for others, it is a brick wall of bewilderment and anxiety. Why is developing and constructing lesson plans so difficult to learn as well as teach? Perhaps the answer lies in the fact that the predominant model demands a linearity of thinking that does not necessarily exist. Furthermore, although a variety of lesson-planning formats and approaches are recommended for use, few of the formats are derived empirically. The purpose of this paper is three-fold: first, to stimulate critical thinking about the dominant approach used in teacher preparation in England and Wales; second, to compare the dominant model with research into the lesson planning of both novice and experienced teachers; and, third, to suggest an alternative, dialogical model of lesson planning, where constructing a product (the plan) is seen as secondary to the representation of the planning problem (the process).

THE DOMINANT MODEL

The use of the linear model, which begins with the specification of objectives and ends with a lesson evaluation, pre-dates the current emphasis in the UK on external accountability in teaching and teacher education by more than four decades. The approach has in fact been a pervasive feature of curriculum and lesson planning since the early 1950s, although it gained greater prominence during the curriculum and pedagogical reforms of the 1960s and 1970s. This rational approach to planning owes a great debt to instrumental interpretations of Tyler's (1949) *Basic Principles of Curriculum and Instruction* written in 1949 – amazingly now in its 41st edition – and to other theorists who constructed variants using both extended taxonomies of learning outcomes (Bloom, 1956) and more sophisticated constructs around instruction (Gagn, 1970; Popham and Baker, 1970).

In recent years, the attempts to reform the teaching profession and to restructure formal teacher education in the UK and across the world have meant an increasing emphasis on the importance of competence on the part of student teachers in the skills of curriculum design and lesson planning. In England and Wales, for instance, various official documents from the Department for Education and Employment (DfEE), the new Department for Education and Skills (DfES) and the Teacher Training Agency (TTA) stress the importance of being competent in skills before 'qualified' teacher status can be awarded. *Qualifying to Teach: Professional Standards,* published by the Teacher Training Agency (DfES/TTA, 2001: 9), requires student teachers to demonstrate that they can 'set challenging teaching and learning objectives' and use these 'to plan lessons and sequences of lessons, showing how they will assess pupils' learning'. Additionally, they must show the ability to 'select and prepare resources, and plan for their safe and effective organization, taking account of pupils' interests and their language and cultural backgrounds'. These demands have been embedded in numerous documents issued by the DfES. The KS3 National Strategy for science, for instance, suggests the following format:

■ objective
■ vocabulary
■ resources
■ starter
■ main activity, and
■ plenary.

Institutional templates vary; however, there are common threads, and Figure 4.1 presents a typical, if truncated, example.

It is also worth noting that these admonitions are part of a broader emphasis on outcomes-based education (OBE),[1] and this nexus is part of a thread of ideas stretching back over a century or more. The terminology may change, but the essences remain the same, hence the National Curriculum framework, with its programmes of study, its standards, targets and levels of attainment. Embedded within the TTA and DfES requirements are a series of injunctions that insist that learning outcomes should be the same for all students – operationally defined as exit behaviours and measured against a system of national bench-marking (Elliot, 2001).

The emphasis on OBE has also led to teaching based on a restricted set of aims, which can in turn misrepresent the richer expectations that might emerge from a constructive and creative use of curriculum documents. This, it appears, is more prevalent when assessment is externally mediated. As a result, OBE can de-emphasize the elements of teaching and learning that are not endorsed by the assessment structure. In this sense, OBE runs counter to the rational planning model, which is predicated on the idea of getting greater alignment between objectives, classroom practice and evaluation (Barnes *et al.,* 2000).[1]

However, the endurance of Tyler's (1949) model and its popularity among teacher educators, curriculum consultants, inspectors and classroom teachers suggest a deeper affinity that goes beyond the prevailing political climate. Much of the attraction of this approach to planning lies in its elegant simplicity. Supporters ask questions similar to the ones posed by Tyler (1949): How can we know if we have achieved our aims if we have not specified them clearly in first place? How is it possible to analyse the process of teaching and learning unless we break it down into all its component parts? How can we design, plan or implement anything if we do not go through the rational cycle of formulating objectives, deciding on strategies, selecting resources, organizing activities, implementing delivery and evaluating the results? At root then, Tyler's (1949: 25) framework and numerous copies of it are structuralist in conception – Cherryholmes (1988) contends that they are 'based on a systematic way of thinking about whole processes and institutions whereby each part of a system defines and is defined by the other parts'.

Essential to such a systems approach is the distinction between ends and means, often expressed in planning in the language of aims, objectives and goals on the one hand,

Name: Placement:		Lesson evaluation: Date:
Objectives		
Timing		
Grouping		
Differentiation		
Whole class		
Assessment of outcomes		
Successes		Action plan
Difficulties		

■ **Figure 4.1** A typical lesson-planning template.

and strategies, methods and tactics on the other. Of central importance is the notion that any system is part of a hierarchy of supra-systems and sub-systems, and that such systems can be regulated through constant and meaningful feedback. 'Softened' systems theory, which emerged in the teaching profession in the 1980s (Squires, 1999), introduced new concepts into the then-prevailing educational discourse, terms such as synergy, interaction, equilibrium and 'equi-finality'. The idea of 'feedback', for instance, was seen as more meaningful than the harsher, more behaviourist 'knowledge of results', but they are synonymous. In teaching, the concept of 'system' has found its clearest representation in the emphasis on precise, observable objectives and outcomes in the curriculum, linked by step-by-step approaches to planning and teaching. These sequential steps are outlined below.

Step one involves the selection of the topic or component of the subject to be taught. This subject-matter source and the age and ability-range of the pupils are the major factors in the early consideration of appropriate aims and objectives. These early considerations are also linked to broader social or educational goals, usually in the guise of a National Curriculum (as in England and Wales). *Step two* focuses on the exemplification of aims and objectives, both of which should be linked to wider curriculum considerations. During this step, more precise learning objectives or goals are specified, as pupil learning is operationalized into these objectives, which are often drawn from a combination of cognitive, affective and psychomotor domains and taxonomies. *Step three* involves the preparation of the content to be covered and a consideration of the teaching methods and learning experiences that will best bring about the accomplishment of the set aims and objectives. These usually coalesce into activities or tasks based on the types of method adopted. Here, the lesson plan is broken down into chunks or segments defined by time and activity, with the necessary materials and resources usually prepared together. In *step four*, an assessment process is planned (as is an evaluation sequence), so that the efficacy of the teaching methods and activities can be gauged against the set objectives. Thus, all the steps in the model lead to, or emerge from, the aims and objectives in a linear, rational, ends–means sequence.

Despite the attraction of such a process, much depends on its *use* by student teachers at the various points in their professional learning. Thus, the model does not take into account the contingencies of teaching. Plans constructed according to the rational model may look fine on paper, but classrooms tend to be more uncertain places: time-pressures, organizational issues, attitudes, moods, emotions and serendipity all impinge on the closed structures implied in the model. In fact, the negotiated nature of learning needs to be added to the planning equation if spontaneity and improvisation are to be allowed. Furthermore, means and ends are isolated as successive steps rather than being seen as part of the same situation. This can result in ends being seen as unchanging once their definition is complete, and only open to minor revisions once the teaching and learning process begins.

Finally, while accepting that the systems approach to planning and teaching is a powerful generic idea, it tells us very little about the substance of the particular activity we apply it to. In sum, it does not say enough about the uniqueness of teaching and learning. Used badly, such planning patterns can lead to a progressive disaggregation: teaching and learning are broken down into segments or key elements, which are then subdivided into tasks, which are further broken down into behaviours and assessed by performance criteria. As a result, opportunities for self-conscious reflectiveness (Bruner, 1996) are in danger of being lost, as items of knowledge are parcelled together by well-written objectives.

So, why has the dominant model maintained its popularity? First, it is claimed that student teachers need to know how to plan in a rational way before they can develop more complex lesson structures and become adept at juggling curricular elements. However, it should be remembered that gaining experience and expertise is complex, and interactive teaching requires planning that is flexible and practical from the outset (Calderhead and Shorrock, 1997; John, 2000; Kagan and Tippins, 1992); experienced teachers learn to juggle the classroom variables almost separately from the planning process (Peterson, 1978). Second, it is believed that students *need* to follow the model because the National Curriculum and various standards documents require them to do so (DfES/TTA, 2001). This suggests that students are being prepared for teaching *as it appears to policy makers*; experience tells us that classroom teaching is far more complex and differentiated than policy makers would have us believe.

Third, it is often pointed out that the model and its associated formats can help to overcome the 'loose-coupling' (Weick, 1976) that often exists between schools and HEIs.

A unified, agreed-upon model creates congruence between sites and the personnel involved in delivery of courses, while simultaneously creating greater equity in terms of student teachers' experiences.

Fourth, and most controversially, it can be argued that the use of the rational planning model reinforces a sense of control. It is easier to manage, assess and direct the process of teaching if all student teachers are required to plan according to the same procedure and format. It, therefore, follows that lesson planning is based on prediction and, to some extent, prescription. However, even those with a minimal knowledge of classroom life realize that pupils' responses create an ever-changing dynamic for teaching – one that is in no sense predictable or 'prescribe-able' (Ben-Peretz, 2001).

RESEARCH ON TEACHERS' PLANNING

Despite the apparent ubiquity of the dominant model, there are alternatives. One of the most prominent has been the 'naturalistic' or 'organic' model, based on the work of Stenhouse (1975) and Egan (1992, 1997). They claim that the mismatch between specific objectives and the complexity of classrooms means that teachers need to consider more naturally emerging planning structures. The endemic uncertainty of classrooms (Lortie, 1975) means that statements of objectives can only explain and connect with a small number of the variables that are typical of classroom interaction. Naturalistic planning, therefore, involves starting with activities and the ideas that flow from them *before* assigning objectives. In this way, lesson plans are perceived to be responsive to children's needs, and the teacher can pursue goals that are emergent rather than predetermined. These organic models see objectives as flowing from a cyclical process and are viewed more as symbols – advertisements even – for lessons.

Another approach to planning is the 'interactional method'. This stresses the interactive rather than the discrete character of objectives. Here, learning embedded in the processes of interaction is preferred to the more tightly focused structural approach inherent in the rational model. The emphasis on form is central, which is based less on the outward shape of a lesson and more on a set of graded principles that change during interactive teaching. (This emphasis on form is in contrast to the stress on the mechanics of planning implied in the rational model.) Alexander (2000) likens interactional planning to the structure of a musical performance, where the composition or score is analogous to the lesson plan, and the performance itself shifts according to interpretation and improvization.

These alternative models apart, a number of syntheses of the research literature on the processes of teachers' planning are also available (Clark and Lampert, 1986; Clark and Peterson, 1986; John, 1991). A notable finding relates to teachers' perceptions of the key elements in the curriculum – teacher, learner, context, resources and methodology – and the powerful impact these have on their approaches to planning. Characteristics such as the length and type of experience, the levels of subject and pedagogical knowledge, teaching style, repertoire, and perceptions and knowledge of pupils all influence the planning style adopted (Zahorik, 1970). Most teachers, it appears, also consider the nature of the content and activities before they consider other curricular elements, even though pupils might seem to be their central concern (Clark and Lampert, 1986; Peterson, 1978). Experienced teachers' planning can be best described as a simultaneous consideration of the above elements, rather than a step-by-step or linear progression of decision-making. And planning also occurs during the interactive phases of teaching, as the teacher reflects on situations as they arise and plans ahead accordingly. Some research on student teachers' thinking during their extended practicum shows the emergence of analogous characteristics (John, 2000).

Furthermore, many teachers are guided in their planning and teaching by broad intentions, intuition, tacit knowledge and lesson images (Calderhead, 1989; Doyle, 1990; Eraut, 1994; John, 2000). While these processes are rarely articulated in detail, either verbally or in writing, they nevertheless are geared towards the activity flow of lessons. They elaborate on the material presented in textbooks or other curriculum materials (Feiman-Nemser and Featherstone, 1992; Shulman, 1987) and restructure knowledge for and with pupils during the process of planning and teaching. Time on task and perceived pupil abilities and differentiation often figure prominently in such planning decisions.

Expert–novice studies have also suggested that, whereas experienced teachers engage in long-range planning, the thinking of novices is more short term. Novices describe their planning as time-consuming as they struggle to make sense out of the cornucopia of decisions they have to make regarding content, management, time, pacing and resources. Experts, on the other hand, seem to have a very general plan for lessons, leaving detailed decision-making to the period prior to starting the lesson or to various points in the lesson itself. Novices, particularly early on in their training, have difficulty making predictions about student responses and have problems adjusting their practice according to the exigencies they encounter.

A number of other studies (Kennedy, 1987) have indicated that experienced teachers have a more comprehensive range of teaching skills and are more expert in developing representations of their subject matter than novices, who tend to define learning and teaching more literally. Jones and Vesiland (1996) found that, as student teachers became more experienced, their planning moved from being tightly associated with scripting and the preparation of materials to a larger cluster of concerns that included classroom management, the organization of learning and the need for greater flexibility. It seems that greater exposure to teaching challenged the novices to see planning and preparation less as an unalterable event and more as a concept associated with unpredictability, flexibility and creativity. It was as if the student teachers were seeing planning as the glue that held the various pieces of learning and teaching together, and the linear format, despite being a course requirement, was largely superfluous to their needs as teachers.

Research also indicates that novice teachers have difficulty constructing objectives (both intellectually and semantically), more so if they have to be delineated *before* they have even considered the methods, activities, resources or central idea of the lesson (John, 1992; Kagan and Tippins, 1992). Some studies have shown that many student teachers, particularly early in their training, have difficulty matching goals, objectives and forms of evaluation; many also fail to understand the conceptual (and sometimes semantic) distinctions between aims, objectives and goals (John, 1991; Joyce and Harootunian, 1964). According to Calderhead and Shorrock (1997), Kagan and Tippins (1992) and Lampert (1985), many neophyte teachers have difficulty integrating subject topics, under-standing the concepts or tasks embedded in curriculum materials, and juggling conflicting goals when there is uncertainty about how to achieve multiple desired outcomes. As a result, there is often an elision between aims, goals and objectives on the one hand, and teaching and learning process on the other.

Personality factors and preferences related to teaching style likewise appear to lead teachers to approach their planning differently, and in many cases this has little to do with the amount of experience the teacher has. A number of these predispositions are linked to particular and personal cognitive styles. Research indicates that student teachers enter their programmes with a variety of experiences, preconceptions and models about what constitutes teaching, learning and learning to teach (Calderhead and Shorrock, 1997; Feiman-Nemser and Buchmann, 1985; John, 1996). The literature also points to the diversity of learning styles exhibited by student teachers when planning lessons. Some may be stimulated by creative thinking based around loosely conceived ideas; others may find the seed of a lesson within the content or a particular resource. Whatever approach is taken, the research evidence points to the fact that the end-product – the lesson plan – is often arrived at through a variety of processes, many of which are highly personal, idiosyncratic and embedded in the subject and classroom context of the topic being planned.

CONSIDERING THE ALTERNATIVES

Many of the processes recommended by various authors, agencies and policy makers are mostly derived from information-processing models of learning. As a result, the social processes that influence planning abilities in practical teaching contexts have not gained prominence. Wertsch (1991), for instance, focuses attention on the univocality found in the pervasive conduit metaphor for communication and planning; this, he claims, underpins the transmission model for learning, where the receiver is seen as passive. The model of planning and teaching represented in this minimalist conception develops as follows: aim > input > task > feedback > evaluation. It reflects an approach to teaching and learning wherein reflection and exploration are at worst luxuries, not to be afforded, and at best minor spin-offs, to be accommodated. The emphasis in the system is always on the functions: explaining, questioning, guidance, practice, task-completion, reinforcement and evaluation. All bypass what Eisner (1985) calls the 'educational imagination'. Referring to Bakhtin, Wertsch (1991) goes on to critique the monological assumptions embedded in such communicative acts, preferring instead the concept of dialogality. Lave and Wenger (1991: 76) likewise indicate that any tool or technology must 'always exist with respect to some purpose and is intricately tied to the cultural practice and social organization within which the technology is meant to function'. Viewed from this standpoint, the linear template model lacks the contextual fabric needed to make it a useful cultural tool.

The functionalism embedded in the various schemata or scripts that underpin the dominant model is committed to the creation of de-contextualized modes of action. It is, according to Lave and Wenger (1991), made out of different kinds of 'stuff' from the physical world to which it is to be applied. This static picture of abstract and de-contextualized thinking – where cognitive tools can be pulled out and applied in any context and then returned to the tool kit unchanged – is, in part, a critique of the emerging phenomena of planning templates in ITE. Thus, Linn (2001) argues that a prevailing official lesson-discourse is in fact reflected in the lesson plan.

It may be that a dialogical model of lesson planning, where problem-level processes are emphasized, proves to be a better way forward. Figure 4.2 offers a more balanced approach in that it stresses the importance of representing the planning problem (the process) as a vital precursor to the construction of the product (the plan).

Although the model presented in Figure 4.2 attempts to mimic the natural decision-making of the experienced practitioner, it also recognizes that not all naturalistic decision-making is of the same kind. Lipshitz (1993), after reviewing nine models of decision-making, concluded that real-world decisions are made in a variety of ways, and no single unitary process can fit all situations. The model in Figure 4.2 does not privilege

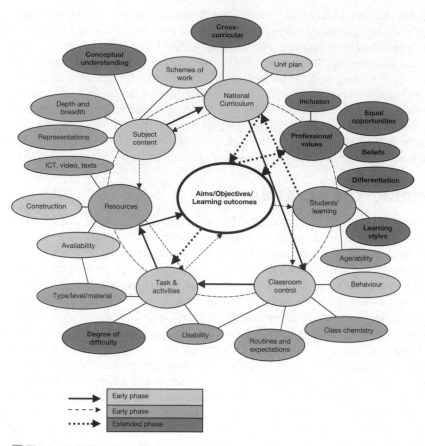

■ **Figure 4.2** The planning process.

a fixed order, and the process of planning it engenders would automatically involve a number of sub-processes. The main core is fixed by the aims, objectives and goals of the plan. However, a number of satellite components rotate around this central element; these represent the foundational aspects of planning, and attached to each are a series of nodes that further subdivide the key aspects. These nodes and satellites are illustrative and can be changed or developed according to context. For instance, the 'scheme-of-work' satellite is specific to the UK, as is the National Curriculum node, while 'students' learning' would be more generic, as would 'classroom management'.

In terms of use, the model may change as a student teacher moves through the various stages of a programme of initial training. The lightly shaded balloons represent some of the core concerns that novice teachers in the early stages of their training might see as significant. Whatever the starting point, there is a constant iterative pattern of shuttling back and forth between each component as the student teacher explores, frames, checks and reframes where appropriate. Gradually, as more and more information becomes available – the size of the class, the ability-range, the time of the day, the availability of resources, etc. – a more concrete plan emerges. This usually occurs only after a creative, yet careful path has been trodden, where each element is visited and revisited in a cyclical fashion, and where, to follow Emerson's dictum, 'the ends pre-exist in the means'. Its advantages are that it encourages a constant interaction with the context and its entities, and underlines the point that teaching, learning, resources, tasks, tools, context and objectives are interconnected rather than separated.

The model can also be applied at different levels of complexity across the various phases associated with student teachers' learning. As Furlong (2000: 13) points out, if novices are to 'deal effectively with complex and changing situations, they need to develop progressively more sophisticated practical theories about how children learn and the knowledge they are trying to teach'. During the *early phase* of their professional learning, student teachers need to know what a lesson plan actually is, as well as understanding the crucial nexus that exists between planning and teaching. Here, the dialogical model can serve as a powerful descriptive tool to acculturate student teachers into the complexities of the planning process. To illustrate this: it is well recognized that, in the early part of their training, student teachers need concrete, even prosaic models of planning to guide their thinking. Here, the model can help them understand the crucial connection between classroom management, subject content and the curriculum (see the lightly shaded balloons in Figure 4.2). It is, therefore, likely that, during this early stage in their learning, student teachers will move between these components in a narrowly drawn fashion. Presenting student teachers with model lesson plans or series of exemplars that exemplify the process could augment this.

As soon as student teachers begin the *practical phase* of their courses, the school-based mentor becomes more prominent, as the novices move through a form of 'legitimate peripheral participation' (Lave and Wenger, 1991). In this sense, they should be scaffolded through a dialogue with real teaching situations. This process is partly mimetic in that various routines and representations are internalized and layered onto their evolving practical theories. However, it is precisely at this point that joint planning can help the novice gain access to the expert knowledge of the experienced teacher. Again, scaffolding should be evident as the novice and the expert move through the process of planning together, jointly informing one another of the process as it evolves. At this point, the model might not only help clarify many of the choices and decisions made by the experienced mentors, but could also lead to a deeper understanding of the craft-knowledge that has been developed through familiarity with the circumstances of their teaching. Such guided reflection may challenge the assumption that framing and designing a lesson simply mean creating concrete recipes or routines interspersed with subject knowledge. This is supported by Bage *et al.* (1999), who discovered that efforts to impose a uniform system of lesson planning on teachers meant that often they did not draw on the full range of their expertise when planning lessons in diverse contexts. They concluded that the uniform system-approach was in fact less sophisticated than what teachers actually did in their classrooms. The model, by challenging this uniformity, could then act as a heuristic, guiding the student teacher to follow the thinking of the experienced teacher as the lesson structure emerges.

This possibility might be further enhanced during structured observation periods, where the model could serve as a tool that might frame an agenda for a post-lesson discussion regarding the 'in-flight' thinking of the teacher. The resulting conversations might reveal the complexity behind the apparent simplicity of experienced teachers' planning. Behind the façade of ease lies a rich and sophisticated appreciation of how children learn, a flexible understanding of the structure and deployment of subject-matter knowledge, and a repertoire of pedagogical skills and strategies (Furlong, 2000). At this point, the novice teachers are likely to want to broaden their repertoire, and further components of the model will be incorporated into their planning practices. They should now have a deeper understanding of classroom management and will begin to see the importance of differentiation, the significance of learning styles, as well as the need to refine their aims, objectives and learning outcomes (see darker shaded balloons in Figure 4.2). It is at this point that they are more likely to return to the central core of the model as they shift their thinking back and forth among a wider range of variables.

As the student teacher becomes more experienced and is 'flying solo' (John and Gilchrist, 1999), the model likewise changes its salience. Rather than guiding, it might now become a creative tool, helping novices clarify and structure their thinking as they engage in the process of preparation. The core of the model should then take on greater significance as the novice begins to ask more complex questions: What do I want the children to learn? What teaching and learning styles might best bring this about? What knowledge and skills are worthwhile and how might they be best learned? How might curricular objectives and learning outcomes best inform my planning? What resources and tools might help me to engage my pupils so that learning might take place? And what are the classroom management implications of my chosen strategy? Such questions require planning and teaching to be more provisional and open to a debate in which issues of value and belief come to the fore. It is during this *extended phase* that the dialogical model can help student teachers develop what Elliott (1998: 51) has called 'that courteous translation of knowledge', by encouraging them to shuttle freely back and forth between the components, examining each according to their emergent professional knowledge, values and expertise.

The model does not, however, neglect product-level planning (see Table 4.1). In fact, it emphasizes the all-important link between the problem-solving processes and the format used to structure the components of the plan. Here, important house-keeping issues need to be noted, such as the booking of equipment, the collecting of assignments, the distribution of texts, the setting of homework, etc. The product also stresses the core elements that have to be followed if a lesson is to be successful, and, thus, pulls together the thinking into a clear, definable classroom guide. Introductions and conclusions, the timing of segments, the setting of activities, seating arrangements, the delineation of objectives and learning outcomes, the classroom management implications, and the teaching and learning styles adopted, all need to be considered and noted within a chronological framework.

Seeing planning in this way helps to establish the understanding that the process of planning is dialogical – a thought-experiment tied to the specifics of the discourse-community in which it is embedded. Hence, the need for adaptation when different subjects and types of teaching are involved. The model also provides more explicit guidance on how to process planning problems by heightening awareness about the crucial interplay of the variety of factors that inform planning – both in terms of individual lessons and in

▪ **Table 4.1** The planning products

Introduction	Subject topic	Booking
Conclusion	Presentation	Equipment
Plenary	Evaluation	Resources
Timings	Homework	Teaching and learning style
Tasks and activities	Administration	Aims and objectives
Classroom layout	Reminders	Key questions

the construction of curricular units. It should also develop a greater metacognitive awareness, whereby the student teachers evaluate and control their own thinking as choices are made. Drawing student teachers' attention to the delineation and choice of objectives by tying them into a range of decisions might also make teaching more responsive to the dynamic and fluid events that can occur during interactive teaching.

The model also allows student teachers to emphasize and de-emphasize certain aspects of planning according to their particular circumstances and needs. Given this, perhaps teacher educators and school-based mentors should encourage student teachers to pay more attention to the integration of knowledge about pupil characteristics, teaching materials and environmental constraints. Student teachers need to know what materials are available and appropriate for particular groups of pupils, be it, for instance, age or ability. Such understandings demand contextual knowledge combined with experience of working with such children. Finally, the model might help students to understand and deal with what Leinhardt (1989) has termed the 'double agenda' of teaching: the tension between an anticipated sequence embedded in the diachronic aspects of lesson planning and the immediacy of the synchronic 'here-and-now' of teaching.

CONCLUSIONS

Enacting the dialogic model outlined in this paper challenges the idea – often embedded in student teachers' implicit theories – that planning is a concrete process involving the enactment of particular routines or recipes (Furlong, 2000). The model also supports an articulation with the emerging concept of 'professional learning teams', where teachers come together to examine specific lessons in order to deepen their understanding of pupils' learning. Such use of 'lesson study' should be encouraged in ITE, thereby challenging the impression, implicit in *Qualifying to Teach: Professional Standards* (DfES/TTA 2001), that teaching is a scripted performance as opposed to a complex engagement with children. Planning, and the teaching of planning models, might then be viewed less as a preparation for practice and more as a practice itself. As Carlgren (1999: 54) points out, the practice of planning is as important as the practice of teaching; the process needs to be treated as 'a simulated practice with reflective backtalk as part of the planning, so that students have experience of naming and framing as well as re-framing'. In this way, language, and in particular the discourse of planning, becomes a reflective tool rather than a pointer to activities in which meanings are hidden.

The ideas presented in this paper remain speculative. They represent a critical commentary on an exceedingly complex area of novice and experienced teachers' professional work. How to plan well remains a knotty but crucial topic for teacher education research and practice. It is a concern too, that the creative, problem-solving, 'intelligent' aspects of planning and teaching become lost as students are encouraged to conform to rigid templates. Wrestling with the technical aspects of lesson-planning will not, in the long-term, encourage pedagogical intelligence. The lesson plan should not be viewed as a blueprint for action, but should also be a record of interaction. Such a definition would help novices view deviation from the lesson plan as a positive act rather than evidence of failure (John, 2000; Kagan and Tippens, 1992). Finally, the so-called Tylerian model, so long in the ascendancy, should be seen as a point of departure rather than a Procrustean bed (Kagan and Tippens, 1992), and student teachers should be encouraged to personalize their plans – as they do to so many other aspects of their classroom practice.

NOTE

1   It has been argued OBE has in fact led to a derogation of many of the fundamentals of rational planning. In particular, it has diminished the central concern for learning, as well as limiting the principles and procedures that teachers might adopt to implement the aims of *their* teaching (Peters, 1964). As Elliot (2001) has contended, the emphasis on goals and targets for learning has led to a reverse linearity, where the curriculum tail wags the teaching dog.

REFERENCES

Alexander, R. (2000) *Culture and pedagogy: international comparisons in primary education*, Blackwell, Oxford.

Bage, G., Grosvenor, I. and Williams, M. (1999) 'Curriculum planning: prediction or response? A case study of teacher planning conducted through partnership action research', *Curriculum Journal*, Vol. 10, No. 1: 49–70.

Barnes, M., Clarke, D. and Stephens, M. (2000) 'Assessment: the engine of systematic curriculum reform', *Journal of Curriculum Studies*, Vol. 32, No. 5: 623–650.

Ben-Peretz, M. (2001) 'The impossible role of teacher educators in a changing world', *Journal of Teacher Education*, Vol. 52, No. 1: 48–56.

Bloom, B.S. (ed.) (1956) *Taxonomy of educational objectives: handbook I: cognitive domain*, New York: McKay.

Bruner, J.S. (1996) *The culture of education*, Cambridge, MA: Harvard University Press.

Calderhead, J. (1989) 'Reflective teaching and teacher education', *Teaching and Teacher Education*, Vol. 5, No. 1: 43–45.

Calderhead, J. and Shorrock, S.B. (1997) *Understanding teacher education: case studies in the professional development of beginning teachers*, London: Falmer Press.

Carlgren, I. (1999) 'Professionalism and teachers as designers', *Journal of Curriculum Studies*, Vol. 31, No. 1: 43–56.

Cherryholmes, C.H. (1988) *Power and criticism: post-structural investigations in education*, New York: Teachers College Press.

Clark, C.M. and Lampert, M. (1986) 'The study of teacher thinking: implications for teacher education', *Journal of Teacher Education*, Vol. 37, No. 5: 27–31.

Clark, C.M. and Peterson, P.L. (1986) 'Teachers' thought processes', in Wittrock, M.C. (ed.) *Handbook of research on teaching* (3rd edition), New York: Macmillan: 255–296.

Department for Education and Employment (1998) *Teaching: high status, high standards* (Circular 4/98), London: DfEE.

Department for Education and Skills and the Teacher Training Agency (2001) *Qualifying to teach: professional standards*, London: (DfES/TTA).

Doyle, W. (1990) 'Classroom knowledge as a foundation for teaching', *Teachers College Record*, Vol. 91, No. 3: 346–359.

Egan, K. (1992) *Imagination in teaching and learning*, Chicago: University of Chicago Press.

Egan, K. (1997) *The educated mind: how cognitive tools shape our understanding*, Chicago: University of Chicago Press.

Eisner, E.W. (1985) *The educational imagination: on the design and evaluation of school programs*, New York: Macmillan.

Elliott, J. (1998) *The curriculum experiment: meeting the challenge of social change*, Buckingham, UK: Open University Press.

Elliot, J. (2001) 'Making evidence-based practice educational', *British Educational Research Journal*, Vol. 27, No. 5: 555–574.

Eraut, M. (1994) *Developing professional knowledge and competence*, London: Falmer Press.

Feiman-Nemser, S. and Buchmann, M. (1985) 'Pitfalls of experience in teacher preparation', *Teachers College Record*, Vol. 87, No. 1: 53–65.

Feiman-Nemser, S. and Featherstone, H. (1992) *Exploring teaching: reinventing an intro-ductory course*, New York: Teachers College Press.

Furlong, J. (2000) 'School mentors and university tutors: lessons from the English experience', *Theory into Practice*, Vol. 39, No. 1: 12–20.

Gagné, R.M. (1970) *The conditions of learning*, New York: Holt, Rinehart, & Winston.

John, P.D. (1991) 'Course, curricular and classroom influences on the development of student teachers' lesson planning perspectives', *Teaching and Teacher Education*, Vol. 7, No. 4: 359–373.

John, P.D. (1992) *Lesson planning for teachers*, London: Cassell.

John, P.D. (1996) 'Understanding the apprenticeship of observation in initial teacher training: exploring student teachers' implicit theories of teaching and learning', in Claxton, G., Atkinson, T., Osborn, M. and Wallace, M. (eds) *Liberating the learner: lessons for professional development in education*, London: Routledge: 90–108.

John, P.D. (2000) 'Awareness and intuition: how student teachers read their own lesson', in Atkinson, T. and Claxton, G. (eds) *The intuitive practitioner*, London: Open University Press: 84–107

John, P.D. and Gilchrist, I. (1999) 'Flying solo: understanding the post-lesson dialogue between student teachers and mentors', *Mentoring and Tutoring*, Vol. 7, No. 2: 101–111.

Jones, M.G. and Vesiland, E.M. (1996) 'Putting practice into theory: changes in the organ-ization of pre-service teachers' pedagogical knowledge', *American Educational Research Journal*, Vol. 33, No. 1: 61–119.

Joyce, B.R. and Harootunian, B. (1964) 'Teaching as problem solving', *Journal of Teacher Education*, Vol. 15, No. 4: 420–427.

Kagan, D.M. and Tippins, D.J. (1992) 'The evolution of functional lesson plans among twelve elementary and secondary school teachers', *Elementary School Journal*, Vol. 92, No. 4: 477–489.

Kennedy, M.M. (1987) 'Inexact sciences: professional education and the development of expertise', in Rothkopf, E.Z. (ed.) *Review of research in education*, Vol. 14, Washington, DC: American Educational Research Association: 133–167.

Lampert, M. (1985) 'How do teachers manage to teach? Perspectives on problems in practice', *Harvard Educational Review*, Vol. 55, No. 2: 178–194.

Lave, J. and Wenger, E. (1991) *Situated learning: legitimate peripheral participation*, Cambridge: Cambridge University Press.

Leinhardt, G. (1989) 'Math lessons: a contrast of novice and expert competence', *Journal for Research in Mathematics Education*, Vol. 20, No. 1: 52–75.

Linné, A. (2001) 'The lesson as a pedagogic text: a case study of pedagogic designs', *Journal of Curriculum Studies*, Vol. 33, No. 2: 129–156.

Lipshitz, R. (1993) 'Converging themes in the study of decision making in realistic settings', in Klein, G.A., Orasanu, J., Calderwood, R. and Zsambok, C.E. (eds) *Decision making in action: models and methods*, Norwood, NJ: Ablex: 124–146.

Lortie, D.C. (1975) *Schoolteacher: a sociological study*, Chicago: University of Chicago Press.

Peters, R.S. (1964) 'Education as initiation'. An inaugural lecture delivered at the University of London Institute of Education, 9 December 1963, London: Evans Brothers.

Peterson, P.L. (1978) 'Teacher planning, teacher behavior, and student achievement', *American Educational Research Journal*, Vol. 15, No. 3: 417–432.

Popham, W.J. and Baker, E.L. (1970) *Systematic instruction*, Englewood Cliffs, NJ: Prentice-Hall.

Shulman, L.S. (1987) 'Knowledge and teaching: foundations of the new reform', *Harvard Educational Review*, Vol. 57, No. 1: 1–22.

Squires, G. (1999) *Teaching as a professional discipline*, Brighton, UK: Falmer.

Stenhouse, L.A. (1975) *An introduction to curriculum research and development*, London: Heinemann.

Tyler, R.W. (1949) *Basic principles of curriculum and instruction*, Chicago: University of Chicago Press.

Weick, K.E. (1976) 'Educational organizations as loosely-coupled systems', *Administrative Science Quarterly*, Vol. 21, No. 1: 1–19.

Wertsch, J.V. (1991) *Voices of the mind: a sociocultural approach to mediated action*, Cambridge, MA: Harvard University Press.

Zahorik, J. (1970) 'The effects of planning on teaching', *Elementary School Journal*, Vol. 3, No. 1: 143–151.

CLASSROOM INTERACTIONS AND MANAGING PUPILS

INTRODUCTION

Effective classroom management, those arrangements made by teachers to establish and maintain an environment in which learning can occur, is an essential prerequisite for effective learning to take place. Part of those arrangements are related to interactions with pupils. Relationships between teachers and pupils are complex. Teachers need well-developed skills and techniques to communicate with, and to motivate, pupils, which they can adapt according to the particular class and individual pupils. Understanding the theoretical and research underpinnings of communication, motivation and classroom management is therefore essential.

Three readings are included in this section: the first on research on motivating pupils; the second on research into pupils' behaviour; and the third on bullying. However, there is a large amount of research on classroom interactions and managing pupils to which you are encouraged to refer.

READINGS IN THIS SECTION ARE:

Reading 5
Towards the improvement of learning in secondary school: students' views, their links to theories of motivation and to issues of under- and over-achievement
Keith Postlethwaite and Linda Haggarty

This reading, by Postlethwaite and Haggarty (2002), reports on secondary pupils' views of what made them want to learn, what made it difficult for them to learn and what teachers could do to help them learn. It then relates these views to some psychological views of motivation and models developed from attribution theory. The research is in three parts: the first part used semi-structured individual and group interviews with pupils, the second and third a questionnaire developed from the results of the interviews with pupils. The second part reported on questionnaire results with two groups of Year 11 pupils, and the third on comparisons between Year 11 pupils who were identified as under-achieving and those who were identified as over-achieving. Results showed that pupils had a clear view about what supports or hinders their learning and these could be understood in terms of theories of motivation. Under- and over-achieving pupils differed in the extent to which they engaged in behaviours supportive of their learning (conformity to the work and social norms of the classroom and communication with teachers), but not in the way in which they perceived teacher behaviour. This paper is an example of research using more than one method of data collection.

Reading 6

Recent research on troublesome classroom behaviour: a review
Robyn Beaman, Kevin Wheldall and Coral Kemp

The second reading in this section, by Beaman *et al.* (2007), reviews fifteen research articles, published over the previous ten years, on troublesome behaviour in the classroom. Nine of the studies included were conducted in Australia and seven in the USA, Hong Kong, Jordan, Greece and Malta. The research reviewed includes research in early years, primary and secondary schools, using a range of research methodologies. The main themes which form the focus of this review of research are: the prevalence of pupils who are behaviourally troublesome (although teachers can expect between two and nine pupils in any class with some level of behaviour problems, the number rises from early years to adolescence); the time spent managing troublesome behaviour (many teachers believe they spend too much time on behaviour management, this being between 10 and 25 per cent of lesson time); gender differences (boys are consistently perceived to exhibit more troublesome behaviour than girls); types of (mis)behaviour in classrooms, their severity and frequency (talking out of turn is consistently identified as causing most problems in the classroom). This paper is an example of research which has been undertaken in a context different to that in which you, the reader, are working (e.g. outside the UK; in primary or special schools; in another subject).

Reading 7

A positive psychology approach to tackling bullying in secondary schools: a comparative evaluation
Andrew Richards, Ian Rivers and Jacqui Akhurst

The third reading in this section, by Richards, Rivers and Akhurst (2006), reports on an intervention programme which adopts a positive psychology (PP) approach to tackle bullying. This approach focuses on the individual strengths of pupils rather than on their behaviours. It involves pupils in problem-solving the issue of bullying and promotes the development of socially and individually valued personal qualities. The researchers gave pre- and post-intervention measurements (self-report questionnaires which included items on bullying behaviour, general well-being and mental health) to an experimental and control group. Results indicated that those pupils who experienced the PP intervention programme showed reduced levels of bullying and slightly better general well-being scores, but not mental health scores. This paper is included because it is an example of quasi-experimental research, which is less common in educational research than other types of research.

FURTHER READING

Burnett, P. (2002) 'Teacher praise and feedback and students; perception of the classroom environment', *Educational Psychology*, Vol. 22, No. 1: 5–16.

The relationship between praise and feedback given by teachers and the perceptions of pupils of the classroom environment was investigated in six rural elementary schools (n = 5,747). A hypothesised model was tested using structural equation modelling. Results showed that negative teacher feedback and effort feedback were both related to pupils' relationships with their teachers, while ability feedback was related to perceptions of the classroom environment. Praise was not related to teacher–pupil relationships nor to classroom environment. Significant age and gender differences were found. In addition, satisfied pupils received more general praise, general ability feedback, effort feedback and less negative teacher feedback when compared with dissatisfied pupils.

The above further reading links with Unit 3.1 of the 5th edition of *Learning to teach in the secondary school*.

Swinson, J. and Knight, R. (2007) 'Teacher verbal feedback directed towards secondary pupils with challenging behaviour and its relationship to their behaviour', *Educational Psychology in Practice,* Vol. 23, No. 3: 241–255.

Teachers' verbal feedback to pupils has been linked with pupil behaviour. This study examined teacher verbal behaviour that was directed towards those pupils the teachers had identified as being especially difficult to teach. Observations of a series of lessons in a secondary school showed that those pupils identified as especially difficult to teach were less on-task and more likely to 'shout out' in lessons than their peers. However, they were found to behave appropriately in well-run lessons, where on-task rates were high for all pupils. Teachers tended to give more attention to the identified pupils in the form of positive feedback directed towards their work, but also negative feedback directed towards their behaviour. A positive relationship was found between teachers' use of positive feedback and the identified pupils' on-task rates.

The above further reading links with Units 3.1 and 3.3 of the 5th edition of *Learning to teach in the secondary school*.

Hufton, N.R., Elliott, J.G. and Illushin, L. (2002) 'Educational motivation and engagement: qualitative accounts from three countries', *British Educational Research Journal*, Vol. 28, No. 2: 265–289.

This paper reports on a study which used detailed interviews with secondary aged pupils in Sunderland, Kentucky and St Petersburg to examine a number of key factors underpinning educational motivation and engagement, in particular, attitudes about schooling, self-evaluations of academic performance, patterns and rate of work at home and at school, reasons why education may be valuable and aspirations for the future. Results showed high levels of self-satisfaction for English and American pupils and lower self-evaluations for Russian pupils. Effort appeared to be emphasised more than ability in explaining differential performance. The paper also explores the influence of peers and teacher–pupil relationships upon classroom behaviour and work rates and differing perceptions as to the intrinsic and extrinsic value of education.

The above further reading links with Unit 3.2 of the 5th edition of *Learning to teach in the secondary school*.

Mclellan, R. (2006) 'The impact of motivational "worldview" on engagement in a cognitive acceleration programme', *International Journal of Science Education*, Vol. 28, No. 7: 781–819.

Cognitive Acceleration through Science Education (CASE) is an intervention programme which has reported remarkable success in enhancing cognitive development and in raising academic achievement in Years 7 and 8 (aged 11–13 years) in the United Kingdom. Critics, however, have questioned whether the differential cognitive gains made by participants can be explained by a purely cognitive mechanism. This paper presents findings from a longitudinal study that looks at whether differences in motivational style might provide an explanation. A goal theory approach to motivation was utilised. The motivational orientation, related beliefs and self-concepts of approximately 1,600 secondary pupils attending nine schools, five of whom were delivering the CASE intervention, were assessed before and at the end of the programme, which took place over the first two years of secondary schooling. Results suggested that pupils exhibit six different motivational styles or world-views. Change in motivation can be gauged by examining changes in world-view over the time-span of the research. The paper also looks at differences in the change of motivation of pupils attending CASE and control schools and the complex relationship between motivation and cognitive gain. The discussion looks at the implications of these findings, including whether world-view can explain differential cognitive acceleration effects.

The above further reading links with Unit 3.2 of the 5th edition of *Learning to teach in the secondary school*.

Papaioannou, A.G., Tsigilis, N., Kosmidou, E. and Milosis, D. (2007) 'Measuring perceived motivational climate in physical education', *Journal of Teaching in Physical Education*, Vol. 26, No. 3: 236–259.

This paper presents a new instrument to measure motivational climate in physical education in order to measure pupils' perceptions of teachers' emphasis on mastery, performance-approach, performance-avoidance and social approval goals. The instrument was based on the principle of compatibility, according to which perceptions of climate and achievement goals should be compatible in terms of target, action domain, life context and time. Nine hundred and twenty-eight middle school pupils completed the instrument plus instrument which measured intrinsic motivation, amotivation and satisfaction. These were analysed statistically using structural equation modelling, investigation of factor correlations, correlation of this measure with intrinsic motivation, satisfaction and amotivation in physical education and investigation of intra-class correlations. Results show evidence that the new instrument has construct validity and suggest that mastery and social approval goals can facilitate intrinsic motivation of pupils.

The above further reading links with Unit 3.2 of the 5th edition of *Learning to teach in the secondary school*.

Bromfield, C. (2006) 'PGCE secondary trainee teachers and effective behaviour management: an evaluation and commentary', *Support for Learning*, Vol. 21, No. 4: 188–193.

This article addresses classroom management in ITE. Data were gathered from student teachers both by interview and by questionnaire to ascertain their ongoing concerns during a one-year PGCE course and to identify key issues for teacher education providers. The key finding for teacher education providers is the need to move student teachers' thinking from a traditional behaviourist approach to one that highlights the relationship between behaviour and learning.

The above further reading links with Unit 3.3 of the 5th edition of *Learning to teach in the secondary school*.

Ellis, A.A. and Shute, R. (2007) 'Teacher responses to bullying in relation to moral orientation and seriousness of bullying', *British Journal of Educational Psychology*, Vol. 77, No. 3: 649–663.

The aims of this study were to examine: (a) whether moral orientation predicts teachers' responses to bullying; (b) the role of perceived seriousness of an incident in moderating responses to bullying; and (c) factors that are important to teachers when deciding whether to intervene. One hundred and twenty-seven primary, middle and high school teachers were recruited during staff meetings at five schools. Data were analysed using correlational and hierarchical multiple regression analyses examining how moral orientation and seriousness predict teachers' responses to bullying. Care moral orientation predicted a problem-solving response, while justice orientation predicted a rules–sanctions response. Care and justice orientations also interacted to predict rules–sanctions, but not problem-solving responses. However, seriousness of an incident accounted for the majority of variance (46 per cent for rules–sanctions and 40 per cent for problem-solving responses). Seriousness did not moderate the relationship between moral orientation and responses to bullying. Thus, although teachers' moral orientation impacts on the response to bullying they choose, this is not as important as the seriousness of the incident.

The above further reading links with Unit 3.3 of the 6th edition of *Learning to teach in the secondary school***.**

TOWARDS THE IMPROVEMENT OF LEARNING IN SECONDARY SCHOOL

Students' views, their links to theories of motivation and to issues of under- and over-achievement

Keith Postlethwaite and Linda Haggarty

A NOTE FROM THE EDITORS

This reading reports on research based on the attribution theory of motivation using three methods of data collection: semi-structured individual interviews with pupils, group interviews with pupils, and questionnaires.

This reading links with Unit 3.2 of the 5th edition of *Learning to teach in the secondary school*.

QUESTIONS TO CONSIDER

1   Often researchers and teachers look at an issue from a teacher perspective. Why is it important to gain a pupil perspective on teaching and learning?

2   Motivation is important in effective teaching and learning, but how do we know what makes an individual pupil want to learn; what makes it difficult for an individual pupil to learn; what teachers do or do not do that helps or hinders an individual pupil's learning?

3   What are the main features of attribution theory; why is this a valuable theory to use to motivate pupils in the classroom; and what impact will its use have on what occurs in the classroom? There are many other theories of motivation that can be used; what differences would result from the use of one of these other theories and why?

This reading was first published as: Postlethwaite, K. and Haggarty, L. (2002) 'Towards the improvement of learning in secondary school: students' views, their links to theories of motivation and to issues of under- and over-achievement', *Research Papers in Education*, Vol. 17: 185–209.

ABSTRACT

This paper reports the views of students in a secondary comprehensive school on what made them want to learn, what made it difficult for them to learn, and what teachers could do to help them learn. It relates these reported views to some established psychological views of motivation and to models derived from attribution theory. It investigates the views of students identified as under- and over-achievers through the comparison of CAT scores in Year 7 and GCSE performance, and reveals that 'conformity to the work and social norms of the classroom', and 'communication with teachers', were two key factors which distinguished under- and over-achievers. However, the differences were not always in directions which might have been predicted.

INTRODUCTION

The work reported here was undertaken as part of a long-term study which attempted further to improve learning in a secondary comprehensive school in Oxfordshire. The project as a whole began with a focus on differentiation and transfer of learning (Postlethwaite and Haggarty, 1998), issues which had been identified by *teachers* as worthy of attention. The work reported here was based on a commitment to gain a *student* perspective on effective teaching and learning and was undertaken in three phases.

First, a research officer interviewed a sample of students aged 11–18, using individual and group interviews to provide an initial exploration of students' thinking about effective teaching and learning. The general thrust of students' comments is reported below and related to relevant literature.

Second, key ideas from this set of interviews were assembled into a questionnaire which was then completed by all students in one Year 11 year group, and by a sample of over- and under-achieving students in another Year 11 year group. The results of this questionnaire were subjected to factor analysis to explore any possible structure in the students' responses. The seven factors that emerged were labelled by a group of teachers and researchers. These labels were found to match ideas from some of the literature on motivation.

Third, we investigated the views of under- and over-achieving students. Under- and over-achieving students differed significantly in terms of their perceptions of some aspects of their experiences of teaching and learning. These differences may give useful clues to areas of school practice that are worthy of further development.

The three phases are reported separately below, with reference to methodology and literature in each section. A brief discussion of specific results is provided in each section, with an overall discussion in Section 5.

We recognize that there may be subject-specific aspects of this issue that would be worthy of investigation, but these were not explored in the present study, which took a more general view.

PHASE 1: AN INITIAL EXPLORATION OF STUDENTS' THINKING ABOUT EFFECTIVE TEACHING

Our intention in this phase was to focus on issues which students throughout the 11–18 age range in the school identified as significant for them when thinking about their own learning. We collected data through semi-structured interviews in which we took a very open approach, designed to encourage students to say what was of importance to them, rather than to respond to questions of our own (Powney and Watts, 1987: 18). The meetings between the students and the research officer took the form of individual interviews, small group discussions, form group discussions and meetings with representatives of whole year groups. This was in recognition of the fact that individual and group interviews both have advantages and disadvantages (Powney and Watts, 1987: 25) and in particular to gather as wide a range of views as possible. For example, the individual interviews might allow students to express views which they saw as unpopular among their peers, while the group interviews might give students the confidence to say critical things which they may have been too anxious to say in the one-to-one interview situation. The circumstances of the interviews with respect to privacy and openness to public scrutiny were consistent with ideas from Hazel (no date). We were explicit with the students that, as the overall goal of the research programme was the improvement of learning in the school, results from the interviews *would* be communicated to teachers, but took care to reassure them that anonymity would be preserved and no student would be identified as the source of any given idea.

The interviews were based on questions which had been generated by the Effective Learning Group (ELG). This is a group comprised of teachers in the school and two collaborating university lecturers. ELG is engaged in a long-standing action research programme in the school (Haggarty and Postlethwaite, 1995). The questions were:

- ■   What makes you want to learn?
- ■   What, in the world around you, makes it difficult for you to learn?
- ■   What, within yourself, makes it difficult for you to learn?
- ■   What kinds of thing do teachers do that help you to want to learn?
- ■   What kinds of activities help you to learn best?

The questions were thought likely to encourage consideration of factors internal to the student, and external factors of context and culture both within the school and more broadly.

The research officer reported that, in the responses to these questions, there was substantial agreement 'across all the years (7–13) and, as far as it is possible to judge, abilities'. The general thrust of students' comments is recorded below.

Many students spoke of motivation being high when teachers 'make the lesson fun', and are themselves enthusiastic about the work. However, one student warned against unremitting, over the top enthusiasm, which, although it could be recognized as genuine, was nevertheless, tiring! In general, students wanted variety within lessons.

Many students said that their interest in lessons was maintained when there was a match between the work and their own abilities. They wanted to work at their own pace, and to have some say about what and how they learnt. They wanted to be involved in lessons. As one student put it, they did not want 'just to copy from books'. They wanted teachers to see them as individuals and to know where they had got to in their learning. Many of the students saw this, rather than any sense of '(the) teacher being a friend or buddy', as the basis for creating a good relationship with the teacher, and this 'good relationship' was seen as essential for good motivation – especially by girls. Many students said that it was important that the teacher knew their work well. For example, one student said that teachers should 'assess your work in relation to your previous efforts so that praise could be accepted and constructive criticism used'.

Many references were made to the importance of praise and encouragement, students stressing that these enhanced their self confidence. Formal systems of praise such as commendations were not cited with particular enthusiasm, and unfair distribution of praise was seen as having a very negative influence on motivation. Many Year 11 girls were clear that praise should be specific and should help them to understand what was good about their work (so that the good things could be repeated) and where improvements might be made (so that they could continue to progress).

Some references were made to the importance of regular marking of work. Many student responses indicated that they really valued marking which included specific comments on good or bad points in the work. Although they recognized that teachers were under time pressure, they pointed out some of their teachers achieved this standard of marking. The implication was, 'Why not all?'. Views were varied about whether every error (e.g. of spelling) should be corrected in every piece of work.

Most students wanted the physical conditions within which they worked to be pleasant and stressed the demotivating effect of 'tatty classrooms'.

Many students were critical of those of their peers who disrupted lessons. They expected teachers to 'be firm with any student making nasty, mocking, cutting down comments in the classroom'. They also wanted teachers to tackle students who were 'dossing about'. Without the security that comes from this approach from teachers, students argued that at best they would be unwilling to show that they were motivated, and at worst might become unmotivated.

The students were specifically asked about their own responsibilities for creating the conditions that would improve motivation. Some accepted that they should 'take a positive attitude, listen to what is said, try to learn', but others were very conscious of the limits to student control.

Some students recognized that the financial circumstances of some of their peers made it difficult for them to provide personal resources, even something as simple as a pen. They were therefore scornful of the fuss which some teachers made when students came without equipment. Several students were also clear about the broader influence that a traumatic home situation could have. One student whose own home circumstances were not problematic said, 'a hard life at home might lead to a hard life at school'.

Many students wanted teachers to be approachable so that they felt able to ask questions and make mistakes without fear of the consequences. They also wanted teachers to provide clear explanations that took account of where they were actually starting from. Lessons that began 'You've done this in Year 7' were often seen as flawed: as one student said, 'Maybe you haven't, and if you have, but have forgotten, it is hard to ask questions about it'.

These student comments are entirely consistent with ideas that can be identified in the literature on pupils and schooling (e.g. Beynon, 1985; Cooper and McIntyre, 1996; Harris and Rudduck, 1993; Measor and Woods, 1984). They can also be readily related to attribution theory (Hewstone, 1983; Hewstone *et al.*, 1996). For example, students seem to have made external attributions for successful learning (e.g. 'learning follows from a supportive home situation'), as well as comments that related to factors internal to themselves (e.g. 'learning follows from taking a positive attitude to work'). Jones and Davis (1965) developed an attributional model in which effects are linked to actions, then to knowledge and abilities, then to intentions and finally to dispositions. Students discussed the *effects* produced by teachers (e.g. 'After a teacher has said that it's hard to ask questions') and the *actions* those teachers took (e.g. providing detailed feedback on work), but usually said little about teachers' *knowledge, ability, intentions or dispositions*. Some of their comments could be seen as self-serving (Miller and Ross, 1975), relieving students of individual responsibility for failure. Some might be seen as group-serving (Hewstone *et al.*, 1982), maintaining the interests of the student group against those of other groups such as teachers.

As well as being of intrinsic interest, the findings confirm that students have well-formulated opinions about their learning, and about the things which teachers need to do to help them learn. Since the very open questions that were used to structure the interviews did nothing to prompt responses about particular aspects of motivation, it is interesting that the responses could be understood in terms of detailed elements of motivational theory.

PHASE 2: YEAR 11 STUDENTS' RESPONSES TO A QUESTIONNAIRE DERIVED FROM PHASE 1

These individual and group interviews gave valuable insights into student thinking. Comments made by an individual student would doubtless have an impact on that individual's engagement in the school. However, such comments may have little validity for the majority of her or his peers. We therefore wanted more widely to assess student opinion on some of these issues. Since our ultimate goal was to produce insights which might guide the development of effective teaching and learning, we designed a questionnaire for this second phase of the work on items from the interview data over which teachers and/or students could be considered to have some control. We therefore omitted items related to such things as the economic circumstances of students' families. The questionnaire was designed by the university lecturers. The draft was discussed and modified by the whole ELG. The final version of the questionnaire is presented at the end of the paper.

Two samples of Year 11 students were invited to complete the questionnaire. Because of the focus on under- and over-achieving students in phase 3 of the work, one sample consisted of those fifty-six Year 11 students whose GCSE achievement was one standard deviation above or below their predicted achievement. Further details of the selection of this sample are given in Section 4. The other sample was the whole

Year 11 year group of 180 students in the subsequent year. For both samples, students were assured that their completed questionnaires would be read only by the university lecturers involved in the research, with only anonymous general findings being fed back to school staff.

Students' responses to the questionnaire items

Overall, there was a somewhat disappointing 41 per cent return rate for the questionnaire. Table 5.1 shows, for each item, the numbers of responses made by students in each questionnaire category. A response in Category 1 meant that the student reported that s/he 'always' behaved in the way described in the item; a response in Category 5 meant that s/he 'never' behaved in this way. Throughout the paper, therefore, low scores correspond to more favourable views and behaviours.

It is interesting that, even though the items about the students as learners were derived from statements made by students during the interviews described above, there were several items on which more than 20 per cent of students reported that they 'rarely' or 'never' behaved in the way described in the item. These items are listed in Table 5.2. (The 20 per cent groups in relation to each item were not always made up from the same individual students.)

Five of these seven items are about communication with teachers. These findings suggest that some students engaged in this communication and discussed it at interview as an important factor in their learning. However, a small yet substantial proportion of students did not engage in it. It is fascinating to speculate on reasons for this mismatch. It could be a simple difference in perception between different students – perhaps some did not see communication as important; it could be that all students saw communication as important, but some did not act on this perception. If the second speculation is correct, did this sub-group lack appropriate skills to initiate or engage in such communication; did they initially make the effort but then find conversations with teachers unrewarding; was there a climate in which talking to teachers was unacceptable within the peer group; was everyone too busy getting through the day (or the curriculum) to find time for such conversations; were there no appropriate places in which such conversations could be had?

Similar points can be made in relation to the questions about teaching. Students at interview identified all the teacher activities in this part of the questionnaire and argued that the activities supported their learning, yet more than 20 per cent of the respondents reported that teachers 'rarely' or 'never':

- showed their own enthusiasm and excitement about the work (Item 3: 23 per cent);
- displayed the student's work in the classroom (Item 8: 44 per cent);
- helped the student to feel OK about mistakes that s/he had made (Item 15: 22 per cent) (figures show the percentage of students responding 'rarely' or 'never' to the item).

This does not, of course, mean that these things rarely or never went on for any student, simply that more than 20 per cent of students felt that each of these things rarely or never went on for *them* personally. Again it is fascinating to ask:

- Would an external observer agree with the perceptions of these students?
- Would the teachers involved agree?
- Why did these substantial groups of students feel as they did?

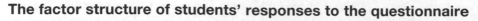

The factor structure of students' responses to the questionnaire

In addition to the analysis of individual questions, we wished to establish the underlying factorial structure of students' responses to the questionnaire. The questions relating to behaviours for which the students were responsible, and those relating to behaviours for which the teacher was responsible, were analysed separately.

THE FACTOR STRUCTURE OF STUDENTS' RESPONSES TO QUESTIONS ABOUT STUDENT BEHAVIOUR

A principal components analysis was carried out using SPSS. The number of extracted factors was determined by the criterion that each factor eigenvalue should be greater than 1. Through this, seven orthogonal factors were extracted. Together these explained 66.2 per cent of the variance in scores. The loadings of the separate variables on the factors (after varimax rotation) are shown in Table 5.3. Loadings greater than 0.50 are shown. There was no negative loading less than –0.50.

The subject:variable ratio in this analysis was roughly 4. This might be regarded as somewhat low. However, Arrindell and van der Ende (1985) demonstrated that factor solutions were not greatly influenced by the subject:variable ratio, so we felt justified in continuing with the analysis (see also Kline, 1994).

The following interpretation of these factors was developed during a meeting of the ELG, which decided that the factors could be labelled as follows:

- Factor 1: I conform to the work and social norms of the classroom.
- Factor 2: I am analytical about my learning.
- Factor 3: I communicate with my teachers about my learning.
- Factor 4: I prepare myself for learning.
- Factor 5: I organize my work.
- Factor 6: I accept that I can influence my learning.
- Factor 7: I make sure I have enough to eat.

The fact that these factors were empirically extracted as orthogonal encourages one to be thoughtful about the independence of analysing learning (Factor 2), preparing for learning (Factor 4) and organizing work (Factor 5). This is thought provoking as these aspects of the learning process might, at first sight, appear to be inter-related.

The nature of these factors reinforces what might be inferred from scrutiny of the students' responses to the individual items on the questionnaire: namely that, when they were asked to identify and then rate items that affected their learning, they largely identified issues that could be understood in terms of student motivation. This is hardly surprising: for example, Galloway *et al.* (1998: 19), writing of the variation in performance of students with different teachers, and in different schools, argues that 'motivation is unlikely to be the only factor in these differences, but it would be odd to deny its potential importance'.

One might immediately notice that the factors that emerged in our study were related to models of motivation that stressed issues internal to the students, rather than issues such as their perception of the relevance of education to the world of work, or the likelihood of being able to gain employment when they left the education system. This was, however, an inevitable consequence of our decision to select from the whole range of students' interview comments, items for the questionnaire that were within the control of teachers

■ **Table 5.1** Student responses: frequencies

Question		1 (always)	2	3	4	5 (never)
Q.1 KS3 motivation		7	41	40	8	1
Q.2 KS4 motivation		17	39	21	18	2
Q. about you as a learner	1a	8	35	38	15	1
	1b	30	32	26	7	1
	1c	36	32	18	9	2
	2	44	39	13	2	0
	3	29	42	18	7	0
	4	26	56	14	2	1
	5	16	25	24	24	9
	6	4	16	27	32	19
	7	14	34	40	6	3
	8	18	50	25	2	1
	9	27	44	22	5	0
	10	4	15	31	29	19
	11	18	21	34	10	5
	12	14	21	47	11	4
	13	19	36	33	6	3
	14	27	46	17	5	1
	15	23	29	25	16	5
	16	11	22	39	18	7
	17	17	40	35	4	1
	18	38	47	11	1	1
	19	24	41	30	2	1
	20	27	35	23	11	1
	21	42	37	13	5	0
	22	15	14	34	23	11
	23	67	19	9	1	1
	24	11	20	32	26	9
Q. about teaching	1	7	37	44	8	1
	2	9	43	35	7	4
	3	7	29	40	19	3
	4	10	40	39	8	1
	5	17	39	21	15	4
	6*	15	30	25	9	0
	7	15	31	27	4	1
	8	2	20	22	25	10
	9	18	21	28	10	2
	10	13	27	24	13	0
	11	4	25	39	9	1
	12	14	19	39	7	0
	13	15	29	29	6	0
	14	9	29	29	7	4
	15	9	21	31	17	0
	16	11	33	26	5	1
	17	18	30	24	4	1
	18	10	23	34	10	1
	19	18	25	21	14	1

* Because of a printing error some respondents could not answer questions 6–19 in this second section. The individual items are identified in the full questionnaire, which is appended to this paper.

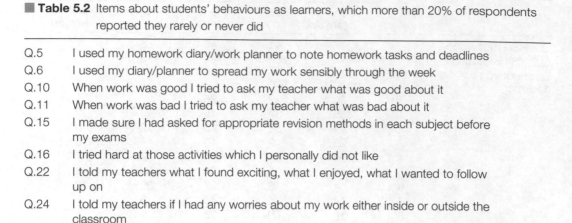

■ **Table 5.2** Items about students' behaviours as learners, which more than 20% of respondents reported they rarely or never did

Q.5	I used my homework diary/work planner to note homework tasks and deadlines
Q.6	I used my diary/planner to spread my work sensibly through the week
Q.10	When work was good I tried to ask my teacher what was good about it
Q.11	When work was bad I tried to ask my teacher what was bad about it
Q.15	I made sure I had asked for appropriate revision methods in each subject before my exams
Q.16	I tried hard at those activities which I personally did not like
Q.22	I told my teachers what I found exciting, what I enjoyed, what I wanted to follow up on
Q.24	I told my teachers if I had any worries about my work either inside or outside the classroom

or students – a decision in turn based on our long-term goal for enhancing effective learning in the school. This 'internal' emphasis cannot, therefore, be used as evidence for the relative importance (even for this student sample) of internal and broader socially related influences on motivation. The detailed nature of the factors derived from the questionnaire does, however, repay more thorough scrutiny.

The students' views seemed quite closely to match several specific psychological theories of motivation.

Factor 1 seems to be related to the notion of fitting in to the classroom group and may therefore be to do with feelings of affiliation with that group. Maslow (1970) includes the need for affiliation and affection as part of the basic needs hierarchy in his model of motivation.

Factor 2 is concerned with reflection upon one's own performance – i.e. it relates to metacognition. Brophy (1986) lists several ways of capitalizing on students' intrinsic motivation. Developing metacognitive awareness is one of them. This in turn is consistent with a wide range of research in the field of learning difficulties (see Postlethwaite (1993) for a summary) which indicates the importance of metacognition in learning. Factor 2 suggests that students have consistent views about elements of metacognition and therefore that the concept may have some meaning for them.

Factor 3 is clearly concerned with wide-ranging conversations with the teacher about one's learning – students who engage in such conversation would clearly be taking some responsibility for their own performance. The importance of such responsibility is entirely consistent with ideas from attribution theory developed by Kelley (1972). He outlined four basic attributions of success or failure (ability, effort, task difficulty and luck) and indicated that effort is the one which provides the students with the sense of having some control over, and therefore responsibility for, their future performance. As such, effort-based attributions could provide an escape from Galloway *et al.*'s notion (1998) of 'learned helplessness' as a maladaptive motivational style.

Factor 4 is concerned with meeting basic physiological needs and relates to the base level of Maslow's (1970) needs hierarchy.

Factor 5 is a different aspect of taking responsibility for one's own learning: it is more concerned with planning and organizing than learning. Like the issue of talking to teachers, it is consistent with ideas from attribution theory.

■ **Table 5.3** Rotated factor structure of student replies about student behaviours

Variable		Factors						
		F1	F2	F3	F4	F5	F6	F7
V1	I make sure I have enough sleep				.67			
V2	I make sure I have enough to eat							.72
V3	I make sure I'm appropriately dressed				.66			
V4	I make sure I arrive on time				.61			
V5	I make sure I have the necessary equipment	.66						
V6	I will do as asked	.58				.51		
V7	I use my homework diary to plan for deadlines					.73		
V8	I use my homework diary to spread work					.62		
V9	I recognize my successes		.71					
V10	I recognize my mistakes		.71					
V11	I see that learning is for my benefit							
V12	When my work is good I ask teachers what was good			.71				
V13	When my work is bad I ask teachers what was bad			.72				
V14	I see that getting stuck is OK							
V15	To keep trying with difficult work is OK		.64					
V16	I see that increased effort improves learning						.56	
V17	I ask about revision methods					.54		
V18	I try hard at things I don't like	.63						
V19	I accept responsibility for good atmosphere in class							
V20	I am sensitive to others	.60						
V21	I listen to others						.70	
V22	I ask teachers when something is difficult			.53				
V23	I am polite to teachers	.70						
V24	I told my teachers what I enjoyed			.67				
V25	I attend lessons regularly	.67						
V26	I share worries with my teachers			.52				

Factor 6 is about seeing the need to make an effort (attribution theory again) and to learn from the ideas of others.

Factor 7 is another aspect of attending to physiological needs (Maslow, 1970).

Further exploration of the factor structure of the data was carried out. We noted that Factors 7 and 6 were 'made up' of only one and two variables, respectively. Kline (1994) argues that this is unsatisfactory. By reducing the number of extracted factors to four, we were able to remove factors of this kind. The explained variance in this alternative solution was reduced to 53 per cent, and the minimum eigenvalue was 1.42. The four factors that were extracted were very similar to the first four factors discussed above and could certainly still be related to the same four theoretical models. The only new insight was that Factor 2 now also included the variables 'I accept responsibility for a good atmosphere in class' and 'I listen to others' suggesting an awareness of the social context of learning as well as the internal processes.

This description of the factors in terms of psychological theories of motivation is inevitably an interpretation of the data analysis provided by the authors and other members of ELG. However, it is of especial interest as the items from which the factors were derived came from the students themselves during interviews, and were not written by the researchers on the basis of any theoretical framework. It is also important to note that the questions used to prompt students in the interviews were very broad (see Section 3 of this paper) and were therefore unlikely to influence the students to generate items that fitted any particular theoretical ideas.

It seems therefore that, not only did students in interview choose to mention individual items which might be seen to relate to one of a range of motivational theories, but that their views on the whole range of items were inter-related in ways that were consistent with these theories. We suggest that the formal theoretical ideas in the field of motivation to which we have made reference above had some clear 'working meaning' for the students, even though they would almost certainly have been unable to give a formal description of any of those theories.

FACTOR STRUCTURE OF STUDENTS' RESPONSES TO QUESTIONS RELATING TO TEACHER BEHAVIOUR

A similar process was completed for the questions relating to behaviours for which the teacher was responsible. A principal components analysis extracted four orthogonal factors with eigenvalues greater than 1. Together, these explained 61.4 per cent of the variance in scores. The loadings of the separate variables on the factors (after varimax rotation) are shown in Table 5.4. All loadings greater than 0.50 are shown. There was no negative loading that was less than –0.50.

The interpretations offered for these factors were:

■ Factor 1: The teacher values my work.
■ Factor 2: The teacher values me as a learner.
■ Factor 3: The teacher actively helps me with work.
■ Factor 4: The teacher respects my personal intellectual space.

These factors also make good sense in terms of the research literature on motivation. However, they are less tightly linked to that structure than was the case for the factors related to student behaviour. Given the source of these factors, this is not, perhaps, surprising.

■ **Table 5.4** Rotated factor structure of student replies about teacher behaviours

Variable		Factors			
		F1	F2	F3	F4
V27	There were established routines at the start and end of lessons and at points of change within lessons			.50	
V28	I could see the point of each of my lessons	.79			
V29	Teachers showed enthusiasm and excitement	.58			
V30	Work was at the right level	.76			
V31	Teachers could judge how much effort I made			.63	
V32	Teachers valued it when I made an effort			.55	
V33	Teachers tried to sort out my difficulties			.59	
V34	Teachers displayed my work in classrooms	.62			
V35	Teachers valued me as a person		.71		
V36	Teachers stopped students ridiculing each others' ideas				
V37	Teachers responded well to my ideas		.77		
V38	Teachers tried to keep me actively involved in lessons		.62	.51	
V39	Teachers tried to give me responsibility for my learning				
V40	Teachers encouraged me to use my own methods				.79
V41	Teachers tried to make me feel OK about my mistakes			.60	
V42	Teachers encouraged me to puzzle things out for myself				.83
V43	Teachers did not tolerate students who messed around				.53
V44	Teachers gave me praise when I deserved it		.76		
V45	Teachers wrote comments on my work that helped my learning			.65	

Factor 1 suggests that students recognized several elements of teaching that gave high status to the work agenda in the classroom. If they thought their teachers did one of these elements, they tended to think they did all of them. The elements included care in planning (communicating clear objectives and setting work at the right level), in delivery (showing enthusiasm and excitement) and in display of students' work.

Factor 2 might indicate that students saw consistency in the different ways in which their teachers responded positively to students' work (e.g. students who thought teachers were responding well to their ideas also thought they were giving praise when it was deserved). In a similar way, Factor 3 might indicate that students saw consistency in the ways in which teachers responded to work that needed correction or development (students who thought teachers tried to sort out students' difficulties also thought they made students feel OK about their mistakes). What is particularly interesting is that the extraction method forced Factors 2 and 3 to be orthogonal. The fact that students' perceptions of how teachers handled positive responses were loaded on one of these factors, and their perceptions of how teachers handled negative responses were loaded on the other, suggests that students viewed these two aspects of teachers' behaviour independently. Students could, for example, feel that teachers responded well to ideas and that they gave appropriate praise, but also say that they did not 'make me feel OK about my mistakes' or 'write comments that helped my learning'.

Factor 4 seemed to be about students' perceptions of the ways in which teachers respected (and required other students to respect) individuality in students' work styles in the subject.

PHASE 3: DIFFERENCES IN THE QUESTIONNAIRE RESPONSES OF UNDER- AND OVER-ACHIEVING STUDENTS

The study grew out of an interest in what teachers could do to raise the levels of the educational performance of their students, and in what students could, themselves, do to contribute to this improvement. In the first two phases of the work, we have identified teacher and student behaviours which the students felt were related to the effectiveness of their learning. It is possible that students who over-perform in relation to their measured ability are those who were able to capitalize on these behaviours, whereas those who under-perform are those for whom the behaviours were especially problematic. We therefore carried out comparisons of under- and overachievers, as we felt these might reveal the factors on which either the students themselves, or their teachers, or both, could most profitably focus attention.

Identification of the under- and over-achievers

Identification of the two sub-groups was based on a mismatch between students' actual performance at the age of 16 in GCSE examinations, and their predicted performance based on their score on the Cognitive Abilities Test (CAT) (Thorndike *et al.*, 1986) at the age of 11.

The work was done with students who were in Year 11 in two consecutive years. CAT scores had been obtained for these students when they were in Year 7, and average GCSE scores for each student were calculated on the basis of their performance in that examination in Year 11. (Students whose Year 7 CAT scores were missing were excluded from this part of the analysis.) *Average* GCSE scores were used, partly because this is the measure of prior performance that is used in national prediction of A-level results, and partly because of the examination entry pattern at the school. Most students were entered for nine or ten GCSEs, the variation being mainly the result of decisions to take examinations (such as typing) which lie outside the GCSE framework. Use of *total* GCSE scores would therefore disadvantage students who happened to take such examinations, for their total GCSE score would inevitably be depressed.

For each year group, CAT and average GCSE scores from the whole cohort were entered into a regression analysis to generate an equation from which predicted GCSE scores could be calculated from the CAT scores. This was done separately for boys and for girls so that students who did better or worse than expected in relation to others of their own gender would be identified, even if there were significant differences in the relationships between CAT score and GCSE result for the two genders.

Once the regression equations were known, the difference between each student's predicted GCSE score and actual GCSE score (known as the residual) was calculated.

■ **Table 5.5** Numbers of 'under-' and 'over-' achievers

Cohort	Boys		Girls	
	Under-	Over-	Under-	Over-
1	17	12	16	11
2	11	7	7	9

■ **Table 5.6** Numbers of 'under-' and 'over-' achievers returning questionnaires

Cohort	Boys		Girls	
	Under-	Over-	Under-	Over-
1	1	7	7	6
2	1	3	3	4

Within each cohort, the standard deviations for these residuals were then found for the boys and girls separately.

Again for each cohort, and for boys and girls separately within that cohort, standardized residuals were calculated by dividing the residual for each student by the standard deviation of residuals for the appropriate cohort and gender. Where the standardized residual was greater than 1, the student was designated as 'over-achiever'; where it was less than –1, the student was designated an 'under-achiever'. The numbers of students identified in this way as doing better or worse than expected are shown in Table 5.5.

For the sub-group of under- and over-achievers defined in this way, the number of questionnaire responses that were returned was as shown in Table 5.6.

There were two extra responses in which the gender of the student was not stated. The 38 per cent overall return rate was somewhat disappointing; the 7 per cent rate for the underachieving boys was especially unsatisfactory and rendered further division of boys and girls impossible.

It could be argued that the least well-motivated students will be the ones who failed to return data. This would reduce differences between the two sub-groups. Differences which *were* detected may therefore be those which were especially marked.

The analysis which follows takes both cohorts and both genders together because of the small numbers. On each of the questionnaire items, it compares the responses of under- and overachievers.

Students' estimates of their own motivation during KS3 and KS4

Students' own estimates of their motivation during KS3 and KS4 were not significantly correlated (Pearson correlation = 0.17, n = 32, ns). This suggested that their reported levels of motivation changed between the two key stages and that these changes were not

■ **Table 5.7** Students' estimates of their motivation at KS3 and KS4

Under-/over-achievers	KS3		KS4	
	μ	sd	μ	sd
under	2.83	0.72	2.58	1.08
over	2.25	0.91	2.10	0.97
t value, df, p	1.89, 30, 0.07		1.31, 30, 0.21	

predictable, or, of course, that the self-estimates of motivation were not reliable. The mean scores for the students' estimates are shown in Table 5.7, together with comparisons between the under- and over-achieving groups.

The table suggests that the mean perceived motivation of both under- and over-achievers changed towards the more positive end of the scale (1 was described as 'extremely motivated'; 5 as 'not at all motivated') as the focus for the self-report changed from KS3 to KS4. The standard deviations suggest that the range of motivation within each sub-group, but particularly within the under-achieving group, increased – perhaps indicating that some students were not caught up in the general improvement in perceived motivation at KS4. The t-test results show that there were no significant differences between students who did better or worse than expected in their perceptions of their own motivation at KS3 and at KS4, though the differences approach significance in KS3. This overall lack of difference was surprising, but perhaps indicates that one of the problems that faced teachers was that students who did worse than expected did not necessarily see themselves as having poor motivation for their work in school. It is also possible that those who did better than expected may have been judging themselves quite harshly.

The results were also examined using the chi-squared test. The whole range of responses (1–5) led to small numbers in some of the cells of the chi-squared table. Recoding was therefore carried out, placing students who responded 1 or 2 into one group and the remainder into a second group. This additional analysis revealed significant differences at KS3 between under- and over-achieving students (chi-squared = 6.53, df = 1, p < 0.01 chi-squared corrected for continuity), but this was not repeated at KS4 (chi-squared = 0.57, df = 1, ns). When reflecting on KS3, the levels of motivation reported by under-achievers were lower than those reported by over-achievers. If this is the stage at which students recognize that they are not fully engaged, this may be the most effective point on which to focus teacher effort to address the issue of motivation with the students. (There is, of course, the possibility that students who did worse than expected were only willing to recognize their lack of motivation in retrospect: perhaps, had they been asked about their personal level of motivation during KS3, they would, at that point too, have claimed that they were working hard.)

Students' estimates of aspects of behaviour for which they held responsibility

The variables under consideration in this section are those derived from Section 3, Questions 1–24 of the questionnaire. On most of the variables under this sub-heading, there

■ **Table 5.8** Differences in the views of under- and over-achievers on behaviours for which students have responsibility

Behaviour	Under-achievers		Over-achievers		F	sig of F	t	sig of t
	μ	sd	μ	sd				
I saw that learning was for my benefit and satisfaction	2.41	1.00	1.76	0.70	2.02	ns	2.21	<0.05
I treated other students with sensitivity and respect	2.25	0.96	1.62	0.67	2.08	ns	2.22	<0.05
I listened to the ideas of other students and considered how they might influence my ideas	2.50	0.90	2.00	0.59	2.73	<.05	1.74	ns
I worked with my teachers in a polite way, e.g. when asking questions or talking to them	2.08	0.90	1.45	0.76	1.41	ns	2.13	<0.05
I attended all my lessons regularly	1.67	0.78	1.14	0.36	4.71	<.01	2.20	<0.05

When F was significant, the SPSS approximate t-test (unequal variances) was used.

was no significant difference between the scores of under- and over-achieving students, when the two groups were compared using the independent samples t-test. The only variables for which significant differences were detected are listed in Table 5.8.

On these five variables, under-achievers returned higher scores than over-achievers, indicating that they felt that they less often behaved in the way described. On four of the variables, the differences in the means of the two groups were significant according to the t-test. (Pooled variance t was used where the F test showed no significant difference in variance; separate variance t was used where the F test was significant.) For one variable ('I listened to the ideas of other students . . .') the means were not significantly different, but the F test demonstrated that there was significantly more *variation* in the scores of under-achievers. Since these were variables on which the students appeared to recognize differences in their behaviour, they may indicate issues which teachers could work on with the underachieving group to raise the effectiveness of their learning.

Students' estimates of aspects of behaviour for which their teachers held responsibility

The remaining items on the questionnaire (Section 5, Questions 1–19 of the questionnaire) covered aspects of work for which the *teacher* had responsibility, but which were mentioned by students in the interviews. Items covered issues such as the enthusiasm shown for the lesson by the teacher, and the teacher's use of praise. It was interesting that

■ **Table 5.9** Differences in the factor scores of under- and over-achievers: pupil behaviour factors

Factor	Under-achievers		Over-achievers		F	sig of F	t	sig of t
	μ	sd	μ	sd				
Factor 1: I conform to the work and social norms of the classroom	0.39	0.80	−0.44	0.81	1.03	ns	2.77	<0.01
Factor 2: I am analytical about my learning	0.38	0.92	0.06	0.63	2.17	ns	1.17	ns
Factor 3: I communicate with my teachers about my learning	−0.46	0.93	0.25	0.95	1.05	ns	−2.03	<0.05
Factor 4: I prepare myself for learning	−0.66	0.61	−0.33	1.02	2.73	ns	−1.01	ns
Factor 5: I organize my work	−0.07	0.85	−0.34	1.07	1.58	ns	0.73	ns
Factor 6: I accept that I can influence my learning	0.38	0.79	−0.04	0.67	1.42	ns	1.58	ns
Factor 7: I make sure I have enough to eat	0.28	1.12	−0.29	0.67	2.78	ns	1.74	ns

none of these items showed a significant difference between under- and over-achieving groups. Our results therefore offer no support for a view that under-achieving students perceived their teachers' actions very differently from over-achievers.

Differences between under- and over-achievers in terms of factor scores

Once the factors had been established, scores for each student on each factor were calculated by SPSS. Under- and over-achieving students were then compared in terms of these factor scores. The results of these comparisons for the pupil behaviour factors are shown in Table 5.9.

All of the scores contributing to Factor 1 were such that a high score implies lower degrees of conformity. In terms of conformity, students who did worse than expected had a significantly higher mean factor score (i.e. lower level of conformity) than those who did better than expected.

Since three of the variables which individually showed significant differences between the under- and over-achieving groups (see Table 5.8) were components of Factor 1, it is not surprising that this factor emerged as significantly different through overall analysis of the factor score.

For Factor 3 (communication with teachers), students who did worse than expected had a lower mean factor score than those who did better than expected, implying that the first group did *more* talking to their teachers. This is a surprising finding to which we will return in Section 5.

On the remaining five factors, there were no significant differences between the two sub groups. There were also no significant differences between the two sub groups in terms of their scores on the factors related to teacher behaviour.

DISCUSSION

This paper has shown that students had clear views about things which support or hinder their learning. In the light of our data analysis, we will now discuss each phase of the research in turn and offer ideas (eight in all) which we think may be promising in leading to improved learning.

Students' views could be understood in terms of well-established theories of motivation. Under-achieving and over-achieving students differed in some respects, especially in the extent to which they engaged in behaviours supportive of their learning. They did not differ in the ways in which they perceived teacher behaviour.

From the perspective of attribution theory, the interview results in *Phase 1* suggest that, *in seeking ways to improve teaching and learning, teachers might*:

1   draw students' attention to the distinction between internal and external attributions. They might then discuss how internal attributions can provide a means of escape from Galloway *et al.*'s (1998) notion of 'learned helplessness' as a maladaptive motivational style, by recognizing that individuals have (at least some) responsibility for, and scope for influence over, the situations in which they are participants;

2   help students to understand the intentions behind teacher actions, in order to help them come to better informed opinions about the wide range of teacher actions to which they will be exposed; and

3   help students and teachers to recognize that their perceptions of situations will often differ from those of the others involved. They might explain that individuals and groups may well have self-serving and group-serving motives behind the ways in which they look at things. Greater recognition of this point may support students and teachers in an understanding that 'things look different from over there' and generate a greater willingness to question their own explanation of situations.

From a more general perspective, one might note the importance that students gave to the appropriate use of praise, and the significance they placed on teachers knowing them as individuals (especially in terms of what they already knew and could do, and in terms of where they were likely to have difficulties).

In Phase 2, the analysis of the individual questionnaire items was based on identifying items which a fifth or more of students felt rarely happened for them. This analysis suggests that greater attention might be paid to encouraging effective communication between teachers and students, and that teachers should show enthusiasm for the lessons they teach, should display students' work, and should help students to feel OK about making mistakes.

Two factor analyses were conducted to explore the structure of the students' thinking about (a) their own responsibilities for learning and (b) the teachers' responsibilities for their learning. The first factor analysis revealed that their views could be understood in terms of:

■   students' need for affiliation;
■   the importance of metacognition;
■   the importance of communication with teachers; and
■   the need to develop effort-based attributions for success.

In seeking ways to improve teaching and learning, teachers might give increased attention to these issues by:

4   valuing emotionally supportive classroom atmospheres (Watts and Bentley, 1987) e.g. by accepting partial answers in a positive way and refusing to allow peers to ridicule one another's ideas;
5   providing the tools for improved metacognition (Feuerstein *et al.*, 1980), e.g. by encouraging discussion of how students solved problems; what they did when they got stuck; which, of a range of solutions, was the most effective and why;
6   ensuring that communication is encouraged and is effective for the student; and
7   ensuring that effort is rewarded so that students are able to develop a notion that effort leads to success, e.g. by taking explicit steps to elicit information about the effort expended on a piece of work rather than inferring this from such things as the appearance or quality of the work (Postlethwaite, 1993).

The second factor analysis revealed that teachers showing enthusiasm for the lessons they teach, displaying students' work and helping students to feel OK about making mistakes were linked in students' minds. All these teacher behaviours loaded on to the same factor. The cluster of behaviours could be seen as indicating that teachers 'wanted to be in classrooms to support students' learning', rather than 'had to be there to deliver a curriculum'. Maybe, without shared understanding between teachers and students of this sense of the *purpose* of teaching, significant improvement in students' perceptions of the detailed practice of teachers will be hard to achieve. In a climate of reductionist lists of teaching competencies, such as those provided to those involved in initial teacher education by Circular 4/98, this is perhaps an important issue to consider.

Further teaching behaviours, identified through the second factor analysis as issues to which attention might be given, were: how teachers respond to good work; how they respond to work that needs correction or development; and how they value individuality in students' working methods. These emerged as separate factors, suggesting that the students may have seen these behaviours as only loosely related. For example, students may have said that a teacher always responded well to good work but rarely responded effectively to weaker work. The results remind us that identifying the positive so that students can build on it, and identifying problems that students can address, may be two different skills. Each may need to be given separate attention if teaching behaviours are to be further improved.

Phase 3 concentrated on differences between under- and over-achieving students.

Under- and over-achievers did not show any significant differences on the individual items related to teacher behaviours, nor did they differ in terms of the factor scores related to teacher behaviours. The differences between the groups were all related to student behaviours.

Since under-achieving students perceived their motivation in KS3 (but not KS4) to be lower than those who subsequently did better than expected, actions to improve learning might sensibly be targeted at KS3. However, achieving improved learning at that stage will not necessarily be easy, and getting the timing of any interventions right may well be critical. For example, Harris and Rudduck (1993: 333) comment that, for pupils in Year 8:

> Quite simply, where teachers – and researchers – may anticipate that what goes on in the classroom will constitute the foreground experience of schooling, with the personal and interpersonal explorations providing the background, for the students the relationship may . . . be the other way round.

However, Year 9 might provide a formalised opportunity for students to re-engage (Harris *et al.*, 1995), with option choices providing a focal point for discussion about learning.

Whenever actions are taken, it is likely to be useful to focus on key issues relating to the ways in which increasing effort improves learning. Linked to this, students need to be encouraged to judge their own efforts, since they reported that teachers did not always do this well.

In seeking ways to improve teaching and learning, a final 'teacher action' might therefore be:

8   to attend particularly to KS3 when targeting action to improve learning for potential under-achievers.

In addition to differences between under- and over-achievers on individual items about student behaviour as learners, there were also two significant differences on factor scores for the two groups: under-achievers conformed less to the work and social norms of the classroom, and under-achievers communicated *more* with their teachers than did over-achievers.

This last, surprising result calls for further comment, though at this stage what follows is merely speculation on our part. The items that made up the communication factor (Factor 3) were mainly about student-initiated conversation with teachers. It is therefore unlikely that the more extensive communication that the students reported themselves as having with teachers was at the teachers' request (e.g. had come about as a result of doing work which was judged to be inadequate). It could well be that under-achieving students needed, and so initiated, more conversation with teachers in order to ask them about work with which they are having difficulty. One might expect such additional conversation to lead to improved learning and therefore to move the students from the under-achieving group. The fact that this had not happened suggests that this additional conversation was not productive. The main idea that this raises for us is that, in dealings with under-achieving students, teachers should take care to monitor the *effectiveness* of their communication with these students (and not be satisfied simply because of the amount). This in turn raises questions about how such communication could be made as effective as possible. Maybe the other pointers offered in this paper are relevant again here: communication should be well planned to address good and bad points in the work under discussion; well matched to the individual; respectful of students' different working methods; supportive of an individual student's membership of groups within the class; attentive to the development of metacognition; and planned to support the development of effort-based attributions.

The issue of communication between teachers and students has been flagged at various points in this paper. It is clearly important and is part of further work that we have conducted in the school. This will be reported separately in due course.

ACKNOWLEDGEMENTS

The authors would like to thank all members of the Effective Learning Group at the school. The work reported in this paper is essentially the work of that group as a whole. It indicates what can be achieved by school staff who are committed to improving on an already high standard of professional practice, collaborating with Higher Education lecturers through careful research and serious debate. We would like to thank all students of the school who contributed to the initial discussions, to the questionnaire exercise and to the interviews. We would particularly like to thank Ros Collins, who was research officer, and whose skill in talking to youngsters enabled us to establish the baseline views on which everything else was based. Finally, we would like to thank the TTA for financial support for part of this research which was undertaken as part of a teacher researcher project.

REFERENCES

Arrindell, W. and Van Der Ende, J. (1985) 'An empirical test of the utility of the observer-to-variables ratio in factor and components analysis', *Applied Psychological Measurement*, Vol. 9, No. 2: 165–178.

Beynon, J. (1985) *Initial encounters in the secondary school*, Lewes: Falmer Press.

Brophy, J. (1986) 'Motivating students to learn mathematics', *Journal for Research in Mathematics Education*, Vol. 17, No. 5: 341–346.

Cooper, P. and McIntyre, D. (1995) *Effective teaching and learning: teachers' and pupils' perspectives*, Buckingham: Open University Press.

Feuerstein, R., Rand, Y., Hoffman, M.B. and Miller, R. (1980) *Instrumental enrichment: an intervention program for cognitive modifiability*, Baltimore: University Park Press.

Galloway, D., Rogers, C., Armstrong, D. and Leo, E. (1998) *Motivating the difficult to teach*, London: Longman.

Haggarty, L. and Postlethwaite, K. (1995) 'Working as consultants on school-based teacher-identified problems', *Educational Action Research*, Vol. 3, No. 2: 169–181.

Harris, S. and Rudduck, J. (1993) 'Establishing the seriousness of learning in the early years of secondary schooling', *British Journal of Educational Psychology*, Vol. 63, No. 2: 322–336.

Harris, S., Wallace, G. and Rudduck, J. (1995) '"It's not that I haven't learnt much. It's just that I don't really understand what I'm doing": metacognition and secondary-school students', *Research Papers in Education*, Vol. 10, No. 2: 253–271.

Hazel, N. (no date) 'Elicitation techniques with young people', *Social Research Update Issue 12*; available online at http://131.227.9.250/sru/SRU12.html; accessed 14 June 1999.

Hewstone, M. (ed.) (1983) *Attribution theory, social and functional extensions*, Oxford: Blackwell.

Hewstone, M., Jaspars, J. and Lalljee, M. (1982) 'Social representations, social attribution and social identity: the intergroup images of "public" and "comprehensive" schoolboys', *European Journal of Social Psychology*, Vol. 12: 241–269.

Hewstone, M., Stroebe, W., Codol, J.-P. and Stephenson, G. (1996) *Introduction to social psychology – a European perspective*, Oxford: Blackwell.

Jones, E. and Davis, K. (1965) 'From acts to dispositions: the attribution process in person perception', in Berkowitz, L. (ed.) *Advances in experimental social psychology*, Vol. 2, New York: Academic Press.

Kelley, H. (1972) 'Causal schemata and the attribution process', in Jones, E., Kanhouse, D., Kelley, H., Nisbett, R. *et al.* (eds) *Attribution: perceiving the causes of behaviour*, Morristown, NJ: General Learning Press.

Kline, P. (1994) *An easy guide to factor analysis*. London: Routledge.

Maslow, A. (1970) *Motivation and personality*, New York: Harper & Row.

Measor, L. and Woods, P. (1984) *Changing schools*, Buckingham: Open University Press.

Miller, D. and Ross, M. (1975) 'Self-serving biases in the attribution of causality: fact or fiction?', *Psychological Bulletin*, Vol. 82: 213–225.

Postlethwaite, K. (1993) *Differentiated science teaching*, Buckingham: Open University Press.

Postlethwaite, K. and Haggarty, L. (1998) 'Towards effective and transferable learning in secondary school: the development of an approach based on Mastery Learning', *British Educational Research Journal*, Vol. 24, No. 3: 333–353.

Powney, J. and Watts, M. (1987) *Interviewing in educational research*, London: Routledge & Kegan Paul.

Thorndike, R., Hagen, E. and France, N. (1986) *Cognitive abilities test* (2nd edition), Slough: NFER-Nelson.

Watts, M. and Bentley, D. (1987) 'Constructivism in the classroom: enabling conceptual change by words and deeds', *British Educational Research Journal*, Vol. 13, No. 2: 121–135.

APPENDIX

Improving school learning: student questionnaire

Name: ....

1 Think back to years 7, 8 and 9.

How would you rate your motivation to learn in school? ....
(put a number from 1 to 5: 1 means extremely motivated; 5 means not at all motivated; 2, 3 and 4 are somewhere between the two)

2 Think back to years 10 and 11.

How would you rate your motivation in school then? ....
(1 means extremely motivated; 5 means not at all motivated)

3 **Questions about you as a learner**

Think about how you helped your own learning and think in general about each of the following statements. Put a tick in the column which best describes you.

		always	often	sometimes	rarely	never
1	I made sure that I was ready to learn by ■ having enough sleep ■ having enough to eat ■ being dressed appropriately					
2	I made sure I arrived to lessons on time					
3	I made sure I brought equipment required for each lesson					
4	I tried to do what I had been asked in each lesson					
5	I used my homework diary/work planner to note homework tasks and deadlines					
6	I used my diary/planner to help me spread my work sensibly through the week					
7	I managed to recognize success in the progress and improvements I made					
8	I managed to recognize my mistakes					
9	I saw that learning was for *my* benefit and satisfaction					
10	When work was good I tried to ask the teacher what was good about it					
11	When work was bad I tried to ask the teacher what was bad about it					
12	I didn't mind getting stuck over work occasionally because I could see this was an essential part of learning					
13	I recognized that keeping on trying with a difficult task was good for my learning					
14	I could see that increasing the efforts I made could improve my learning considerably					
15	I made sure I had asked for appropriate revision methods in each subject before my exams					
16	I tried hard at those activities which I, personally, did not like					
17	I accepted some responsibility for helping to maintain a good working atmosphere in lessons					

		always	often	sometimes	rarely	never
18	I treated other students with sensitivity and respect					
19	I listened to the ideas of other students and considered how they might influence my ideas					
20	I told the teacher when I was finding something difficult or when I had not understood the task I had been set					
21	I worked with my teachers in a polite way, for example, when asking questions or talking to them					
22	I told my teachers what I found exciting, what I enjoyed, what I wanted to follow up on my own					
23	I attended all my lessons regularly					
24	I told my teachers if I had any worries about my work either inside or outside the classroom					

5 Questions about teaching

Think about the teachers who taught you in the school and think in general about each of the following statements. Put a tick in the column which best describes your experiences.

		always	often	sometimes	rarely	never
1	There were established routines at the start and end of lessons and at points of change within my lessons					
2	I could see the point of each of my lessons					
3	Teachers showed their own enthusiasm and excitement about the work					
4	Work was pitched at the right level – not too easy and not too difficult					
5	Teachers seemed to be able to judge how much effort I had made					

		always	often	sometimes	rarely	never
6	Teachers valued it when I made an effort with my work					
7	Teachers tried hard to help me sort out any difficulties I had with the work					
8	Teachers displayed my work in classrooms					
9	Teachers valued me as a person					
10	Teachers stopped students from making fun of each others' ideas					
11	Teachers responded well to my ideas					
12	Teachers tried to keep me actively involved in lessons					
13	Teachers tried to give me some responsibility for my own learning					
14	Teachers encouraged me to use my own methods to work things out					
15	Teachers tried to help me feel OK about mistakes I made					
16	Teachers encouraged me to puzzle things out for myself					
17	Teachers did not tolerate students who messed around					
18	Teachers gave me praise when I deserved it					
19	Teachers wrote comments on my work which helped my learning					

If you feel you would like to add any other information which you think would be helpful, please do so below.

RECENT RESEARCH ON TROUBLESOME CLASSROOM BEHAVIOUR

A review

Robyn Beaman, Kevin Wheldall and Coral Kemp

A NOTE FROM THE EDITORS

This reading reviews fifteen research articles on troublesome behaviour in the classroom using a range of research methodologies and undertaken in a range of contexts, many of which are likely to be different to that in which the reader is working (e.g. outside the UK; in primary or special schools; in another subject).

This reading links with Unit 3.3 of the 5th edition of *Learning to teach in the secondary school*.

QUESTIONS TO CONSIDER

1   Beaman and Wheldall (1997) concluded that prevalence rates of troublesome classroom behaviour from studies around the world are somewhat equivocal. Why might the rates be equivocal?

2   Why would teachers be more concerned about troublesome behaviour that affects them in the course of their teaching than troublesome behaviour that causes difficulties for other pupils in the classroom?

3   What strategies have been identified from research to reduce the incidence of troublesome behaviour in the classroom and, hence, reduce the amount of time teachers spend on managing classroom behaviour?

4   The most troublesome classroom behaviours identified by teachers were those that were most frequent, but generally low level but irritating, e.g. talking out of turn and hindering other pupils. Why might this be?

This reading was first published as: Beaman, R., Wheldall, K. and Kemp, C. (2007) 'Recent research on troublesome classroom behaviour: a review', *Australasian Journal of Special Education*, Vol. 31: 45–60.

ABSTRACT

A review is provided of recent research literature on the topic of troublesome classroom behaviour, published over the past decade or so with particular reference to research carried out in Australian schools. Nine Australian studies are reviewed, as well as a further seven from the USA, Hong Kong, Jordan, Greece and Malta. Seven of the studies deal with the early years and primary level of schooling, with six studies at the secondary level, and three that span primary and secondary levels of schooling. The following main themes are elucidated: the prevalence of behaviourally troublesome students; time spent managing troublesome behaviour; gender differences; and types of classroom (mis)behaviours, their severity and their frequency. Recent research confirms earlier findings that classroom misbehaviour is of widespread concern to teachers but that the main causes of disruption, while being frequent, are often relatively trivial in nature ('talking out of turn' behaviours in particular). While prevalence rates for troublesome students across classes are variable, boys are consistently identified as being more troublesome than girls.

INTRODUCTION

Effective classroom behaviour management is probably even more crucial today than in the past, given contemporary commitment to educating students with a diverse range of special educational needs within the least restrictive environment. The inclusion of students with disabilities within regular classrooms requires teachers to have high-level classroom management skills, as well as the necessary skills to programme effectively for all students in the class. Teachers engaged in such a complex instructional mission need highly effective behaviour management techniques in order to meet the needs of all the students in their classrooms.

Moreover, while students with severe behaviour and/or emotional disorders are relatively easily identified (and, as a consequence, typically receive special education provision and placement), a substantial proportion of children who experience serious behavioural and emotional difficulties attend regular schools (Harris *et al.,* 1993; Swinson *et al.,* 2003). Chazan (1994) argued that the vast majority of children with emotional and behavioural difficulties are educated in their usual classes in mainstream schools, and 'the question of removing them does not arise' (p. 261). These students, as well as typically developing students with more commonplace disruptive behaviours, may well present management challenges to their teachers.

Conway (2005) has pointed out that one of the most pressing concerns of teachers, when students with 'additional needs' (p. 213) are included in their classrooms, are the emotional and behavioural needs of these students. But he also successfully argues that behavioural issues are not restricted to students with special educational needs, but are 'common across both students with additional needs and their regular class peers' (p. 214). Clearly, some behavioural problems are likely to be a feature of nearly every classroom. It is not surprising, then, that problems of classroom order and discipline frequently stimulate public interest and debate. The role of the media in building and shaping public perception must be continually assessed. In the Australian context, Jacob (2005) has argued that 'well publicised violent events in recent years have exaggerated the public's perception of the level of disruptive behaviour in schools, and created the impression that mis-behaviour is more pervasive than is the case' (p. 6). Inaccurate perceptions about what occurs in classrooms can seriously damage education systems, demoralising staff and students, and making the teaching profession an unattractive option for a future workforce. Researchers have an important role to play in informing with data the debate about matters such as school and classroom discipline. This is particularly the case when topics attract such media and public interest. Researchers can provide the evidence whereby widely held perceptions can be challenged or confirmed.

Interest in behaviour in classrooms is not limited to public debate. Given the impact of inappropriate or disruptive classroom behaviour on the effective use of instructional time in classrooms, it is not surprising that the study of troublesome classroom behaviour has long been evident in the educational research literature, as noted by Beaman and Wheldall (1997) in their review of the literature relating to troublesome classroom behaviour. It is the purpose of the present review to update the findings of Beaman and Wheldall in the light of more recent research completed over the past decade or so.

Beaman and Wheldall (1997) focused on three major themes: that is, the prevalence of troublesome classroom behaviour; gender differences in troublesome classroom behaviour; and the types of classroom behaviour teachers found to be the most troublesome and the most frequent. They found that prevalence rates of troublesome classroom behaviour from studies around the world were somewhat equivocal; that there were clear gender differences in relation to the most troublesome students in the class, with boys being consistently nominated as the most troublesome students; and, that the classroom misbehaviours that teachers found most troublesome were relatively innocuous, but occurred so frequently as to be a recurrent cause for concern. Beaman and Wheldall also emphasised that reports of classroom violence had been overstated, and that the most persistent and irritating classroom misbehaviours that concerned teachers appeared to be *talking out of turn* and *hindering other students*.

At the outset, it may be useful to reiterate what is meant by the terms troublesome, inappropriate or disruptive classroom behaviour. Merrett and Wheldall (1984) defined disruptive classroom behaviour as activity that interferes significantly with a student's own learning; interferes with another student's learning or responses; interferes with the teacher's ability to operate effectively, or any combination of these. This definition remains appropriate for the purposes of this review.

The focus of this review is not on diagnosed emotional disturbance and behaviour disorder per se, as the vast majority of students nominated by teachers as being problematic could not be considered as having a diagnosed or diagnosable condition. Problematic behaviours are, however, on a continuum, and inevitably some of what occurs to distress teachers in classrooms will be the result of some students who manifest behaviours that are consonant with emotional disturbance and behaviour disorder.

Context has always been an important consideration when it comes to defining or describing troublesome or disruptive behaviour. When troublesome classroom behaviour from the perspective of teachers is the focus, it would appear that teachers are most concerned with those behaviours that affect them in the course of their teaching, more so than the behaviour problems that cause difficulties for the students they teach. Mertin and Wasyluk (1994) have gone so far as to say that teachers perceive different problems from others involved in the care of children, observing that much depends on the nature of the problem and who defines it. They argue that teachers' determination of a problem is based more on the practical issues such as classroom management and the more obvious and evident indicators of behavioural and emotional disturbance, with teachers more likely to define as a problem a behaviour directly related to the classroom or playground environments (Mertin and Wasyluk, 1994). It is classroom behaviour that is the focus of the present review.

In order to allow comparison with Beaman and Wheldall (1997), this review is similarly structured, considering, in turn, the prevalence of behaviourally troublesome students; time spent managing troublesome behaviour; gender differences; and types of classroom (mis)behaviour, their severity and their frequency. Table 6.1 comprises a summary of recent studies relevant to this review, including details of the samples involved.

PREVALENCE OF BEHAVIOURALLY TROUBLESOME STUDENTS

Beaman and Wheldall (1997) concluded that, while findings were equivocal as to estimated prevalence rates of behaviourally troublesome students in classes, 'the average classroom teacher could typically expect to find from two to nine students with some level of behaviour problem in his/her class of thirty students at any one time' (p. 50). Mertin and Wasyluk (1994) reported that the number of children with emotional and/or behavioural problems in the general population is generally regarded to be in the order of 10 per cent. Those with more severe forms of problematic behaviour, for example, conduct disorder, are estimated to represent between approximately 2 and 6 per cent of the population when considering children aged 4–18 years (Kazdin, 1995).

Similarly, Jenson *et al.* (2004) estimated that students with externalising disorders (such as non-compliance, aggression, impulsivity, arguing and rule breaking) make up 3–5 per cent of the students in public school classrooms, and 'are some of the most difficult students to manage in an educational setting' (p. 67). When less serious forms of disruptive behaviour are also considered, the proportion of students who have the potential for disruptive behaviour in the classroom is much higher. In a large study of elementary school students in the USA (see Table 6.1 for details), Kamphaus *et al.* (1997) found that 20 per cent of the sample were classified within two of seven clusters they identified, namely, *Disruptive Behaviour Disorder*, which accounted for 8 per cent of the sample, and a sub-clinical form of disruptive behaviour problem which the researchers labelled *Mildly Disruptive*, which accounted for a further 12 per cent, amounting to a total of 20 per cent of the sample for these two clusters. (The other clusters identified were *Well Adapted* and *Average* (together accounting for 53 per cent of the sample), *Learning Disorder* (17 per cent), *Physical Complaints/Worry* (6 per cent) and *Severe Psychopathology* (4 per cent) Kamphaus *et al.* (1997).) While significant behavioural disorders occur relatively infrequently, when combined with the less disruptive behaviours, it is clear that a significant minority of a class may present as behaviourally troublesome to classroom teachers.

Behaviour management challenges are evident from the early years of schooling. Stephenson *et al.* (2000) explored the behaviours of concern to teachers in the early years of school in an Australian study involving teachers of Kindergarten to Year 2 students (see Table 6.1 for more details). They found additional management strategies were considered necessary for 5 per cent of male students and 2 per cent of female students. In another Australian study, Herrera and Little (2005) found that 9 per cent of Kindergarten teachers reported behaviour problems in their students (see Table 6.1). These trends continue in the primary school years and beyond. Little *et al.* (2000) reported that about 10 per cent of teachers in their study of Australian primary to early secondary school students (see Table 6.1) also experienced difficulties dealing with student behaviour.

As detailed in Table 6.1, in Hong Kong, Leung and Ho (2001) have found that 15 per cent of the class are behaviourally troublesome to primary teachers. In a parallel study involving Hong Kong secondary school teachers, Ho and Leung (2002) again found 15 per cent of the class to be behaviourally troublesome (see Table 6.1). While these Hong Kong data indicate a similar level of disruptiveness at both the primary and secondary school levels, other studies show an increasing proportion of the class as being troublesome as students move through the school system.

Oswald (1995) showed a progressive rise in the percentage of students who were considered to have failed to respond to student discipline strategies, in a large Australian study dealing with the number of difficult primary children by school year (see Table 6.1). Comprising 6 per cent of the sample at Reception (or Kindergarten), the proportion of troublesome students rose appreciably and steadily to 16 per cent in Year 7 (with the exception of Year 6, when a small decline from the figures for Year 5 was evident). Consistent gender differences, with boys being identified much more frequently as being difficult to manage, were also evident in this study, an issue to be reconsidered later.

Arbuckle and Little (2004) similarly reported gender differences and increased incidence in behaviour management challenges as students progressed from primary to secondary schooling in their Australian study. As detailed in Table 6.1, about 18 per cent of male students and 7 per cent of female students required additional management support for disruptive behaviour. Moreover, the incidence of disruptive behaviour increased from primary school to lower secondary school, particularly in the case of boys (Arbuckle and Little, 2004). The rise in the number of difficult to manage students with increasing age (and the preponderance of boys being troublesome) demonstrated by Oswald (1995) and Arbuckle and Little (2004) supports the statement by Kazdin (1995) that, 'In general, antisocial behaviors are of the externalising type and are much more evident in boys and adolescents' (p. 10). A similar phenomenon had been observed in the UK in the earlier studies of troublesome classroom behaviour, where Wheldall and Merrett (1988) found 16 per cent of students in primary classes to be troublesome, rising to 20 per cent in the secondary school study (Houghton *et al.*, 1988).

The emotive issue of the apparently increased prevalence and severity of behaviour problems over time has recently been addressed by Jacob (2005). Jacob has provided interesting detail of education department reports over a twenty-year period. Jacob cited a 1984 Departmental Review entitled, 'The incidence and management of alienated, disturbed and/or disruptive students in high and district high schools', as indicating that 'there had been a substantial increase in the number of difficult students that secondary schools were dealing with and that the situation was now bordering on a crisis' (Jacob, 2005: 6).

■ **Table 6.1** Summary of studies relating to troublesome classroom behaviour

Study	Date	Country	Participants	Relevant findings
Early years and primary studies (including lower secondary)				
Herrera and Little	2005	Australia	63 Kindergarten teachers	9% of teachers reported problems with student behaviour
Kamphaus *et al.*	1997	USA	1,227 elementary school children (6–11 years)	20% of the sample classified within two of seven clusters, *Disruptive Behaviour Disorder* (8%) or *Mildly Disruptive* (12%)
Leung and Ho	2001	Hong Kong	144 teachers from 10 primary schools	1. 15% of the class behaviourally troublesome 2. 93% of teachers nominated a boy as the most troublesome student in the class 3. Only 24% of primary teachers use less than 10% of their time managing student behaviour
Little *et al.*	2000	Victoria, Australia	189 5–14 year-olds	10.5% of teachers reported difficulties with student behaviour
Oswald	1995	South Australia	2,354 students in Reception (K)-7	1. Progressive rise in behaviour management challenges with increasing age: 6% in Reception to 16% in Year 7 2. Boys identified much more frequently as troublesome
Poulou and Norwich	2000	Greece	170 primary teachers	1. *Work avoidance*, *depressive mood* and *negativism* as the top three most serious misbehaviours 2. *Lack of concentration*, *talking without permission*, and *untidiness* the top three most frequent misbehaviours
Stephenson *et al.*	2000	Western Sydney, NSW, Australia	130 teachers K-2 teachers (5–8-year-olds)	1. 5% of males and 2% of females require additional behaviour management strategies 2. *Distractability/attention span/ does not listen* caused the most concern to teachers at the K-2 level
Secondary school studies				
Borg	1998	Malta	605 teachers from 16 (single-sex) state secondary schools	*Drug abuse*, *cruelty/bullying*, and *destroying* top three most serious behaviours. *Stealing* also a problem

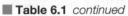

Table 6.1 *continued*

Study	Date	Country	Participants	Relevant findings
Ho and Leung	2002	Hong Kong	187 teachers from 14 secondary schools	1. 15% of the class behaviourally troublesome 2. 71% of teachers nominated a boy as the most troublesome student in the class
Little	2005	Victoria, Australia	148 secondary school teachers	1. 68% of teachers thought they spent too much time on classroom behaviour problems 2. Found 5.3 troublesome students in an average class: 3.5 of these are boys (66%) 3. *Talking out of turn* nominated as the most troublesome (35%) and most frequent (37%) misbehaviour, followed by *idleness*
Infantino and Little	2005	Victoria, Australia	350 secondary school students	*Talking out of turn* was the only behaviour perceived by both students and teachers as being the most troublesome and most frequent classroom misbehaviour of concern
Haroun and O'Hanlon	1997	Jordan	28 male secondary	*Talking out of turn, inattention* and *lack of motivation* were the top three disruptive behaviours nominated by teachers
Stuart	1994	NSW, Australia	105 secondary teachers	*Stealing, destroying school property* and *cruelty/bullying* the three most serious behaviours faced by teachers

Other studies across primary and secondary school levels

Study	Date	Country	Participants	Relevant findings
Arbuckle and Little	2004	Australia	96 primary to lower secondary students	1. Progressive rise in behaviour management problems from primary school to lower secondary 2. 18.2% of male students and 7.25% of females required additional behaviour management support
Langdon	1997	USA	714 elementary and high school teachers	58% of respondents reported that lessons were regularly disrupted by student misbehaviour
Hart *et al.*	1995	Victoria, Australia	Primary and secondary teachers	Teachers, on average, spent 24.5% of their time managing behaviour

Figures in the 1984 report indicated that an average of 3.8 per cent of the secondary school population (with a variation of 1–12 per cent between schools) presented with difficult or challenging behaviours.

Nearly twenty years on, Jacob chaired a working group dealing with the policy statement on students with challenging behaviour in Tasmania, Australia. Again, teachers considered that the number of difficult students had 'increased substantially' (Jacob, 2005: 6) in recent years. But, in 2002, teachers estimated around the *same* proportion of students with extreme behaviour difficulties, around 2–4 per cent, with similar wide-ranging estimates from school to school, as had been found in 1984 (Jacob, 2005). As Jacob observed: 'In both cases, 20 years apart, teachers reported that there had been a significant increase, yet the estimated percentage of children with difficult behaviour was approx-imately the same' (2005: 6).

Notwithstanding the fact that the variation in prevalence rates reported in the various research studies probably reflects the variations in students' age, location and behaviour problem identification techniques (as noted by McGee *et al.*, 1984), it still holds that the average classroom teacher could typically expect to find at least two, and perhaps up to nine, students with some level of behaviour problem to be present in a class of thirty students at any one time (Beaman and Wheldall, 1997). Prevalence rates for disruptive behaviour may vary, but what is apparent from the research presented in this review is more evidence of a rising percentage of behavioural difficulties in classrooms as students move from the early years to adolescence. This suggests a pattern of increasing disruption as students move into the secondary school system.

TIME SPENT MANAGING CLASSROOM BEHAVIOUR

Research has consistently shown that around 50 per cent of teachers, at all levels, typically claim to spend more time on problems of order and control than they believe they should (reviewed by Beaman and Wheldall, 1997). In a recent Australian secondary school study, Little (2005) also found a relatively high percentage of teachers (68 per cent) who considered that they spent too much time on order and control in the classroom (see Table 6.1). In line with the generally large amounts of time spent on classroom management in the UK and in Australia cited above, Langdon (1997) reported that, in a national survey of teachers in the USA, 58 per cent of respondents reported that their lessons were regularly disrupted by student misbehaviour.

The issue of how much time spent on order and control is too much time appears to be an arguable point. In a Victorian study in Australia, Hart *et al.* (1995) argued that classroom behaviour management was not a major source of stress for teachers, given that teachers, on average, spent around 25 per cent of their time managing behaviour. Losing nearly a quarter of available time on classroom management, however, represents a very significant loss of instructional opportunities. In their Hong Kong studies, Leung and Ho (2001) and Ho and Leung (2002) found that only 24 per cent of primary teachers used less than 10 per cent of their time in class managing behaviour, leaving three quarters of teachers spending more than 10 per cent of their time on classroom management. At the secondary level, teachers reported spending less time managing classroom behaviour than their primary teacher colleagues (with 46 per cent of secondary teachers spending less than 10 per cent of their time), a finding contrary to the secondary studies referred to above (in terms of perceptions of time spent at least). Suffice to say, and as Leung and Ho (2001) pointed out:

If we consider spending 20 per cent or more time on classroom management had reached the level of concern, then 39.3 per cent of the teachers we surveyed were confronted with discipline problems. If the criterion was lowered to 10 per cent or more, then almost 76 per cent of teachers could be considered spending excessive time on problems of order and control.

(Leung and Ho, 2001: 230)

GENDER DIFFERENCES

Boys have long been the focus of attention when it comes to troublesome or disruptive behaviours, and research has consistently confirmed that boys appear to be perceived as more troublesome than girls, as Beaman and Wheldall (1997) made clear. The more recent classroom behaviour research literature also supports such a finding. As detailed in Table 6.1, Little (2005) found that, of the 5.3 troublesome students in an average Australian secondary class, 3.5 of these students were boys (66 per cent) (see also Arbuckle and Little, 2004). Moreover, in the Hong Kong studies of primary (Leung and Ho, 2001) and secondary (Ho and Leung, 2002) teachers' perceptions of disruptive classroom behaviours, styled after the Wheldall and Merrett studies, boys were found to be the most troublesome students by 93 per cent of primary teachers and 71 per cent of secondary teachers.

Kann and Hanna (2000) have noted that there is a primary difference in the way boys and girls present symptoms of disruptive behaviour disorders and as a consequence are likely to come to the attention of the teacher. They summarised this as follows:

Externally directed behaviours generally associated with boys are acts that are harmful to others or the environment, such as stealing, lying, fighting, and destructiveness. Behaviours that are internally focused are more common in girls and include anxiety, shyness, withdrawal, hypersensitivity and physical complaints.

(Kann and Hanna, 2000: 268)

The findings on this issue, then, are unequivocal: boys are consistently perceived as more behaviourally troublesome than girls at both primary and secondary levels. The more externalising nature of boys' behaviour identifies them more readily to teachers as being problematic in the classroom. Moreover, the range of behaviours boys typically engage in are more likely to have an impact on those around them, including the teacher.

TYPES OF CLASSROOM BEHAVIOUR, THEIR SEVERITY, AND THEIR FREQUENCY

Turning to the types of classroom behaviours teachers find most problematic, the earlier research found a consensus of opinion among teachers that the most common and the most troublesome classroom behaviours were relatively trivial, a finding that was subsequently to be frequently (and almost universally) replicated (Beaman and Wheldall, 1997). Rather than identifying serious and threatening behaviours, the earlier research consistently identified talking out of turn as the most troublesome, and the most frequent, misbehaviour in primary and high school classrooms. This was also true even for the most troublesome behaviours of the particularly troublesome individual children in the class.

Studies carried out over the course of the last decade or so have largely come to very similar conclusions. In Australia, Little (2005) explored teachers' perceptions of students' problem behaviour in secondary schools in Victoria (see Table 6.1). Seeking to replicate aspects of the UK secondary school study of Houghton *et al.* (1988) in an Australian context, Little surveyed 148 secondary teachers using a modified version of the questionnaire used in the UK study. Little found that talking out of turn was both the most troublesome (35 per cent of teacher responses) and the most frequent (37 per cent of teacher responses) troublesome behaviour selected by secondary teachers out of the ten behaviours itemised on the questionnaire. *Idleness* followed talking out of turn as the most troublesome (22 per cent) and the most frequent (21 per cent) misbehaviour, followed by *hindering others* at 17 per cent and 13 per cent, respectively, for the most troublesome behaviour and most frequent troublesome behaviour. While *disobedience* (13 per cent) was another behaviour category that attracted more than 10 per cent of responses for the most troublesome behaviour, no other behaviour registered above 10 per cent for most frequent troublesome behaviour. *Aggression*, which arguably causes some considerable concern for teachers, attracted only 2 per cent of responses for most troublesome behaviour and less than 1 per cent for most frequent troublesome behaviour. Clearly, it is the relatively trivial but frequent misbehaviours that cause teachers the most concern in Australian schools, as well as in UK schools and elsewhere.

Little (2005) also asked teachers to consider the questions regarding the most troublesome and most frequent misbehaviours across years they taught. Analysed by year levels (Years 7 and 8; Years 9 and 10; and Years 11 and 12), some differences in the responses of teachers were apparent. While talking out of turn was the first choice of teachers of Years 7 and 8 (48 per cent) and Years 9 and 10 (33 per cent) students for the most troublesome behaviour, for teachers of Years 11 and 12 students, the most trouble-some behaviour was idleness (41 per cent), followed by talking out of turn (23 per cent). These data suggest that, in the senior years of secondary school, teachers were finding the lack of application on the part of their students more problematic than inappropriate class-room talk. Moreover, in a recent secondary school study by Infantino and Little (2005), talking out of turn behaviour (including talking back) was the only behaviour perceived by both students and teachers as being the most troublesome and most frequent classroom misbehaviour of concern (see Table 6.1).

Further evidence of the dominance of talking out of turn as the principal irritant for teachers was found in a study conducted in a single-sex Jordanian secondary school. Haroun and O'Hanlon (1997) elicited information about the kinds of student misbehaviour teachers had to deal with in the course of their classroom teaching (see Table 6.1). They were also asked which of the behaviours they nominated were the most frequently occurring and why they thought these behaviours occurred. Seeking the behaviours from the teachers themselves resulted in very similar types of behaviour to those found by earlier researchers, as noted by Haroun and O'Hanlon. Teachers identified eight misbehaviours with the following frequency (listed here from most frequent to least frequent): talking out of turn; inattention; lack of motivation; out of seat; inappropriate banter; non-verbal noise; asking to leave classroom; and bullying. Haroun and O'Hanlon drew attention to the fact that the first seven of these behaviours were similar in that they all 'interrupt the planned teaching and learning process in classrooms' (1997: 34). This phenomenon is similar to that found by Wickman (1928) in his early study, that teachers identify those things as problematic in the classroom that are active disturbances; that is, those things that stop them from getting on with what they think they should be doing. In other words, teachers are troubled by those behaviours that are a problem 'not so much related to learning outcomes as to teaching intentions' (Haroun and O'Hanlon, 1997: 34).

More recent studies in Hong Kong building on the work of Wheldall and Merrett (1988) and Houghton *et al*. (1988) have been completed at the primary and secondary school levels (Ho and Leung, 2002; Leung and Ho, 2001). Using a modified version (using fifteen behaviour categories rather than ten) of the questionnaire used in Wheldall and Merrett (1988), primary school teachers rated talking out of turn as the most disruptive (42 per cent of teacher responses) and most frequent (54 per cent), followed by *non-attentiveness* as the next most disruptive (14 per cent) and the next most frequent (13 per cent) behaviour. While *forgetfulness* attracted 10 per cent of teacher responses for both most disruptive and most frequent misbehaviour, no other behaviours scored above 10 per cent.

In the parallel secondary school study, Ho and Leung (2002) found that disruptive behaviours in secondary school were a continuation of those found at primary school level. Talking out of turn was again the most disruptive (30 per cent) and most frequent misbehaviour (39 per cent), followed by non-attentiveness for the next most disruptive and next most frequent (both at 19 per cent). As can been seen by the relative percentages, however, the problem with non-attentiveness did increase in the secondary years (if not overtaking talking out of turn) as a problematic behaviour, a similar finding to that of Little (2005) in Australia. Forgetfulness was also quite common, with 15 per cent of teacher responses indicating that it was a frequent problem (as well as being considered as most disruptive by 11 per cent of secondary teachers). Other more prominent behaviour problems at the secondary level were idleness/slowness, again similar to recent Australian research (Little, 2005) (scoring nearly 10 per cent for both most disruptive and most frequent), and *verbal abuse*, which also scored nearly 10 per cent for the most disruptive behaviour in secondary classes, with secondary teachers reporting a wider variety of behaviours than their primary school colleagues.

In the Hong Kong studies, talking out of turn was perceived as the most disruptive and the most frequent behaviour by the majority of teachers at both primary and secondary school levels. As others had found, disruptiveness and the likelihood of occurrence of the behaviour (frequency) were 'very much related' (Ho and Leung, 2002: 225). These findings add further weight to the considerable and accumulating evidence from around the world that behaviours that cause the most problems for teachers are of a mild, but constant, nature.

In summary, talking out of turn has been shown to be the consistent first choice of teachers in terms of what causes most disruption in the classroom. Irrespective of geographic location or level of schooling, talking out of turn is clearly the behaviour at the core of classroom disorder. This has been reported in the research literature for over twenty years.

OTHER PERSPECTIVES

Some researchers have chosen to focus on the seriousness of student misbehaviour, rather than its troublesomeness or frequency in investigations of what causes difficulties for teachers.

Poulou and Norwich (2000) reported that Greek primary school teachers (see Table 6.1) rated as most serious '"work avoidance", "depressive mood", "negativism", "school phobia" and "lack of concentration"' (p. 184). While these more internalising behaviours caused the most concern to teachers, it was, however, '"lack of concentration", "talking without permission", "untidiness" and "fidgeting"' (p. 181) that were the most frequent behaviour problems encountered by these teachers.

Following earlier studies by Borg and Falzon (1989, 1990), Borg (1998) investigated secondary school teachers' perceptions of the seriousness of students' undesirable behaviour. This large study, involving 605 randomly selected teachers (302 female teachers and 303 male teachers) from sixteen state secondary schools (all secondary schools in Malta are single-sex schools), comprised roughly equal numbers of teachers drawn from girls' and boys' schools (47 per cent from girls' schools, 53 per cent from boys' schools). At the secondary level, Borg found *drug abuse*, *cruelty/bullying* (in common with the primary study) and *destroying* to be the top three ranked most serious behaviours. *Stealing*, which had ranked as the most serious behaviour problem in the primary school study, was again ranked highly (fourth of out forty-nine behaviours), thereby still considered to be a problem at the secondary level. (Stuart (1994) had found similar findings in her Australian study, i.e. stealing, destroying school property, and cruelty and bullying being the three most serious or undesirable behaviours faced by New South Wales secondary teachers, to be discussed below.)

Borg (1998) also found significant grade-level differences in perceived seriousness of behaviour, as well as a number of significant pupil sex and teacher sex differences. He argued that certain teacher, pupil and school characteristics acted as 'moderators' of the perceived seriousness of problem behaviours, adding further evidence to the effect of certain variables on teacher perceptions of problematic behaviour found in the earlier primary school studies in Malta (Borg and Falzon, 1989, 1990). In contrast to the findings of other researchers at both the primary and secondary levels (e.g. Conway *et al.*, 1990; Houghton *et al.*, 1988; Little, 2005; Merrett and Wheldall, 1984; Wheldall and Merrett, 1988), *interrupting* and *talkative/tattling* (both of which could be considered as talking out of turn behaviours) were *not* considered serious for these Maltese teachers and were ranked a long way down the list in terms of perceived seriousness, ranking 37/49 and 43/49, respectively, in this secondary school study (Borg, 1998).

Moreover, in an Australian study seeking to determine if the findings of Wickman's seminal study (1928) were stable over time and culture, Stuart (1994) surveyed teachers utilising the fifty items from Wickman's list (1928). Stuart asked teachers how serious or undesirable each of the behaviours was in any Year 8 boy or girl. She found stealing (ranked second on Wickman's list), destroying school property (ranked tenth on Wickman's list), and cruelty and bullying (ranked eighth on Wickman's list) to be the three most serious or undesirable behaviours faced by teachers.

These findings may appear to be somewhat at odds with the general pattern of findings from the UK, Australian and other studies in the area. The framing of the question focusing on seriousness should be borne in mind here, however. It could be argued that the terminology used by researchers such as Wheldall, Merrett and Houghton, in terms of signifying the degree or severity of the problem behaviour (most troublesome) (as opposed to frequency – most frequent), may well be interpreted differently by teachers from a request to consider what is the most serious problem behaviour of the student or class. Interestingly, Stuart (1994) commented that teachers' responses were similar, regardless of whether they were asked to rate the behaviour of a particular student or to consider student behaviours more generally, a finding consistent with those found by Wheldall, Merrett and Houghton in their studies, where the troublesome behaviour of the most troublesome individual students was invariably the same as those nominated for the class as a whole (Houghton *et al.*, 1988; Merrett and Wheldall, 1984; Wheldall and Merrett, 1988).

In Australia, Stephenson *et al.* (2000) surveyed K-2 teachers about which child behaviours concerned them, as well as their needs for support in dealing with such behaviours (see Table 6.1). They found that the cluster of behaviours described as *distractibility or attention span a problem/does not listen* caused the most concern. This was followed by, in equal proportions, the four behaviours described as *physically aggressive with others/bullies*; *excessive demands for teacher's attention/does not work independently*; *does not remain on-task for a reasonable time*; and *disrupts the activities of others*.

Stephenson *et al*. (2000) noted that their results may have reflected some high levels of concern about relatively infrequent behaviour. Again, the manner in which a research question is framed may influence the findings. For instance, if one asks a teacher what might be the *serious* classroom behaviours with which they have to deal, the more dramatic, even dangerous, behaviours might be provided. The frequency of these types of behaviour, however, may be extremely low. In terms of the everyday impact on the teacher with regard to 'getting on with the job', it might be quite small. This is not to say that incidents of serious classroom behaviour are not a cause for concern; they clearly are. What is of concern here, however, is the behaviour that causes day-to-day disruption in the classroom.

Without seeking to diminish the impact of isolated and infrequent serious events in schools, it could be argued that it is the daily, high-frequency, trivial classroom behaviours that are wearing for teachers over time. It is likely that it is these troublesome, but not serious, behaviours that are responsible for the stress related to classroom teaching.

CONCLUSION

What is clear from the literature reviewed above is that, while the evidence concerning estimates of the prevalence rates of behaviourally troublesome students remains somewhat equivocal, there is further evidence that disruptive classroom behaviour appears to increase as students move from the early years into the secondary years of schooling. There is also further, consistent evidence to show that teachers continue to perceive boys as more behaviourally troublesome than girls. Similarly, there is also convincing and mounting evidence to suggest that the classroom misbehaviours that teachers find most troublesome are relatively innocuous but occur so frequently as to be a recurrent cause for concern. This does not mean, however, that such misbehaviour does not affect teachers and their ability to do their job.

The findings from the present review point to the need to redouble our efforts in imparting sound, behaviourally inspired management skills in the preparation programmes for new teachers and in professional development programmes for existing teachers. It is perplexing that so few advances have been made in the successful management of disruptive classroom behaviour over the period of this and the previous review. Equipping teachers with the knowledge and skills to deal more positively with the inevitable challenges of classroom teaching is an essential element in improving the educational environment for students and teachers alike.

It would be a travesty if, as quickly as students with intellectual, physical and sensory impairments were being included in regular classrooms, increasing numbers of students with behaviour problems were being excluded from the mainstream and moved into segregated educational settings. The push, often politically motivated, to remove turbulent students from the educational mainstream arguably has potentially dangerous outcomes, not only for the students themselves, but also for the community as a whole. Devoid of good role models, these students may not be best served by being thrust together in an environment in which aberrant behaviour is the norm. Parallels with the prison system should not go unnoticed. It must surely be a priority for education systems that as many students as possible are educated in the least restrictive educational environment, and we must collectively guard against students with disruptive or troublesome behaviour becoming 'the new excluded'.

REFERENCES

Arbuckle, C. and Little, E. (2004) 'Teachers' perceptions and management of disruptive classroom behaviour during the middle years (years five to nine)', *Australian Journal of Educational and Developmental Psychology*, Vol. 4: 59–70.

Beaman, R. and Wheldall, K. (1997) 'Teacher perceptions of troublesome classroom behaviour', *Special Education Perspectives*, Vol. 6, No. 2: 49–53.

Borg, M. (1998) 'Secondary school teachers' perception of pupils' undesirable behaviours', *British Journal of Educational Psychology*, Vol. 68: 67–79.

Borg, M. and Falzon, J. (1989) 'Primary school teachers' perception of pupils' undesirable behaviours', *Education Studies*, Vol. 15: 251–260.

Borg, M. and Falzon, J. (1990) 'Primary school teachers' perceptions of pupils' undesirable behaviours: the effects of teaching experience, pupils' age, sex and ability stream', *British Journal of Educational Psychology*, Vol. 60: 220–226.

Chazan, M. (1994) 'The attitudes of mainstream teachers towards pupils with emotional and behavioural difficulties', *European Journal of Special Needs Education*, Vol. 9: 261–274.

Conway, R. (2005) 'Encouraging positive interactions', in Foreman, P. (ed.) *Inclusion in action* (3rd edition), Southbank, Victoria, Australia: Thomson Learning.

Conway, R., Tierney, J. and Schofield, N. (1990) 'Coping with behaviour problems in NSW high schools', in Richardson, S. and Tizard, J. (eds) *Practical approaches to resolving behaviour problems*, Hawthorn, Australia: ACER.

Haroun, R. and O'Hanlon, C. (1997) 'Teachers' perceptions of discipline problems in a Jordanian secondary school', *Pastoral Care*, June: 29–36.

Harris, J., Tyre, C. and Wilkinson, C. (1993) 'Using the child behaviour checklist in ordinary primary schools', *British Journal of Educational Psychology*, Vol. 63: 245–260.

Hart, P., Wearing, A. and Conn, M. (1995) 'Conventional wisdom is a poor predictor of the relationship between discipline policy, student misbehaviour and teacher stress', *British Journal of Educational Psychology*, Vol. 65: 27–48.

Herrera, M. and Little, E. (2005) 'Behaviour problems across home and kindergarten in an Australian sample', *Australian Journal of Educational and Developmental Psychology*, Vol. 5: 77–90.

Ho, C. and Leung, J. (2002) 'Disruptive classroom behaviours of secondary and primary school students', *Educational Research Journal* Vol. 17: 219–233.

Houghton, S., Wheldall, K. and Merrett, F. (1988) 'Classroom behaviour problems which secondary school teachers say they find most troublesome', *British Educational Research Journal*, Vol. 14: 297–312.

Infantino, J. and Little, E. (2005) 'Students' perceptions of classroom behaviour problems and the effectiveness of different disciplinary methods', *Educational Psychology*, Vol. 25: 491–508.

Jacob, A. (2005) 'Behaviour – whose choice?', *Australasian Journal of Special Education*, Vol. 29, No. 1: 4–20.

Jenson, W., Olympia, D., Farley, M. and Clark, E. (2004) 'Positive psychology and externalising students in a sea of negativity', *Psychology in the Schools*, Vol. 41, No. 1: 67–79.

Kann, R. and Hanna, F. (2000) 'Disruptive behaviour disorders in children and adolescents: how do girls differ from boys?', *Journal of Counselling and Development*, Vol. 78: 267–274.

Kamphaus, R., Huberty, C., Distefano, C. and Petoskey, M. (1997) 'A typology of teacher-rated child behavior for a national US sample', *Journal of Abnormal Child Psychology*, Vol. 25: 453–463.

Kazdin, A. (1995) *Conduct disorders in childhood and adolescence* (2nd edition), Thousand Oaks, CA: Sage.

Langdon, C. (1997) 'The fourth Phi Delta Kappa poll of teachers' attitudes towards the public schools', *Phi Delta Kappan*, Vol. 78, November: 212–220.

Leung, J. and Ho, C. (2001) 'Disruptive behaviour perceived by Hong Kong primary school teachers', *Educational Research Journal*, 16: 223–237.

Little, E. (2005) 'Secondary school teachers' perceptions of students' problem behaviours', *Educational Psychology*, Vol. 25: 369–377.

Little, E., Hudson, A. and Wilks, R. (2000) 'Conduct problems across home and school', *Behaviour Change*, Vol. 17: 69–77.

McGee, R., Sylva, P. and Williams, S. (1984) 'Behaviour problems in a population of seven year old children: prevalence, stability and types of disorder: a research report', *Journal of Child Psychiatry*, Vol. 25: 251–259.

Merrett, F. and Wheldall, K. (1984) 'Classroom behaviour problems which junior primary school teachers find most troublesome', *Educational Studies*, Vol. 10: 87–92.

Mertin, P. and Wasyluk, G. (1994) 'Behaviour problems in the school: incidence and interpretation', *Australian Educational and Developmental Psychologist*, Vol. 11, No. 2: 32–39.

Oswald, M. (1995) 'Difficult to manage students: a survey of children who fail to respond to student discipline strategies in government school', *Educational Studies*, Vol. 21: 265–276.

Poulou, M. and Norwich, B. (2000) 'Teachers' perceptions of students with emotional and behavioural difficulties: severity and prevalence', *European Journal of Special Needs Education*, Vol. 15, No. 2: 171–187.

Stephenson, J., Linfoot, K. and Martin, A. (2000) 'Behaviours of concern to teachers in the early years of school', *International Journal of Disability, Development and Education*, Vol. 47: 225–235.

Stuart, H. (1994) 'Teacher perceptions of student behaviours: a study of NSW secondary teachers' attitudes', *Educational Psychology*, Vol. 14: 217–230.

Swinson, J., Woof, C. and Melling, R. (2003) 'Including emotional and behavioural difficulties pupils in a mainstream comprehensive: a study of the behaviour of pupils and classes', *Educational Psychology in Practice*, Vol. 19, No. 1: 65–75.

Wheldall, K. and Merrett, F. (1988) 'Which classroom behaviours do primary school teachers say they find most troublesome?', *Educational Review*, Vol. 40: 13–27.

Wickman, E. K. (1928) 'Teachers' list of undesirable forms of behaviour', in Williams, P. (ed.) (1974) *Behaviour problems in school*, London: University of London Press: 6–15, reprinted from *Children's behaviour and teachers' attitudes*, New York: Commonwealth Fund.

A POSITIVE PSYCHOLOGY APPROACH TO TACKLING BULLYING IN SECONDARY SCHOOLS

A comparative evaluation

Andrew Richards,
Ian Rivers and
Jacqui Akhurst

A NOTE FROM THE EDITORS

This reading, which adopts a positive psychology (PP) approach to tackle bullying, reports on a study in which pre- and post-intervention self-report questionnaires are given to an experimental and control group.

This reading links with Unit 3.3 of the 5th edition of *Learning to teach in the secondary school*.

QUESTIONS TO CONSIDER

1   There are different definitions of bullying – why might this be? Are there any generally accepted features of bullying and what is its impact – both on the bullied and the bully?

2   The research in this paper is using a quasi-experimental design – using a control and experimental group with a pre-and post-test self-report questionnaire. Why is it classed as quasi-experimental? What is a true experimental design, and why are both of these relatively little used in educational research?

3   How does the Every Child Matters agenda (DfES, 2005) relate to the type of research that is conducted in education?

4   How would the main findings from this research impact on what occurs in classrooms?

This reading was first published as: Richards, A., Rivers, I. and Akhurst, J. (2006) 'A positive psychology approach to tackling bullying in secondary schools: a comparative evaluation', *Educational & Child Psychology*, Vol. 25, No. 2: 72–81.

ABSTRACT

Anti-bullying interventions in schools favour approaches that practically tackle the problems in the classroom as well as the playground. However, the effectiveness of curriculum-based interventions is often context specific. A Positive Psychology (PP) approach to tackle bullying focuses upon the individual strengths of pupils rather than behaviours. It foregrounds the greater involvement of pupils in problem-solving the issue of bullying, and promotes development of personal qualities that are valued both socially and individually. In this study, a positive psychology intervention programme was designed for implementation in a school's year seven Personal, Social & Health Education (PSHE) lessons, with a control group recruited from another school. The effectiveness of the programme was measured both pre- and post-intervention using self-report questionnaires which included items on bullying behaviour, general well-being and mental health. Results indicated that, among those pupils who experienced the PP intervention programme, levels of bullying reduced and they scored marginally better in terms of general well-being but not mental health. Further developments in the programme are underway.

INTRODUCTION

Pupil consultation within the school environment often prioritises the understanding of social or practical issues (e.g. lockers, school dinners, playground facilities) rather than academic ones. However, within the past few years, educationalists have recognised the value of pupils' input into pastoral systems and structures. Fullan (2001) emphasised the need to hear students' voices, noting that students were often perceived more as beneficiaries of programmes rather than as participants in the process of negotiating change. This realisation of the potential role pupils can play in bringing about change is reflected within the priorities set out in the *Every Child Matters* agenda (DfES, 2005). Given the emphasis placed upon pupil engagement, there is likely to be a continued growth in the literature evaluating this and other such approaches in the coming years. In this paper, we will explore how a programme drawing from positive psychology (PP) led to a change in reports of bullying among secondary school pupils in an English school.

Over the past two decades, the nature and prevalence of bullying in schools, together with an assessment of psycho-social factors, have been of increasing interest to those interested in educational psychology and child development. Current definitions of 'bullying' include references to forms of harassment that include repeated overt aggression (physical and verbal) and psychological distress (Galloway, 1994; Haynie *et al.*, 2001; Olweus, 1999). Actions such as the intent to cause physical or emotional harm to another, or to deprive an individual or group of social relationships or possessions are also included in definitions (Olweus, 1993; Tattum, 1993).

In the UK, in their study of pupils' experiences of bullying in six primary and six secondary schools, Oliver and Candappa (2003) found that 51 per cent of Year 5, and 28 per cent of Year 8, pupils reported being victimised in some way by their peers. Particularly vulnerable pupils include those who may be singled out because of their actual or perceived minority status, being labelled 'lesbian' or 'gay', or those who have special educational needs (Eslea and Mukhtar, 2000; Nabuzoka and Smith, 1993; Rivers and Duncan, 2002). It is interesting to note that, since the early work on anti-bullying interventions conducted in the 1990s by Smith and colleagues, rates of bullying seem to be at an all-time high when compared to figures such as 25 per cent for primary schools and 10 per cent for secondary schools in the mid 1990s (see Smith *et al.*, 2004).

Bullying has also been shown to have significant negative effects on the physical and emotional health of both bullies and their victims (Weinhold, 2000), with exposure to repeated acts of bullying having more marked impact on victims (Due *et al.*, 2005). Recent research has highlighted outcomes of bullying within schools such as poor attitude to school, substance abuse, absenteeism and even suicide (Feinberg, 2003; OFSTED, 2003). Previous exposure to trauma (including victimisation), duration and frequency of events, and the personal meaning for the individual are involved in predicting the onset of mental health problems (Yule, 1999). Additionally, among minority groups, self-selected coping strategies may result in further problems and have been linked to the onset of substance abuse (Due *et al.*, 2005).

Salmivalli *et al.* (1999) noted that, among victims, a lack of a sense of having control, together with a perceived lack of social support, significantly impacts upon the well-being of these pupils. Indeed, Demaray and Malecki (2003) have emphasised the role of social support as a protective factor, acting as a buffer against stress.

With the increasing interest in bullying issues in schools, numerous intervention programmes have been developed, aimed at reducing bullying behaviour. One of the first substantial evaluations of an anti-bullying intervention was that conducted in Bergen by Olweus in the 1980s. Olweus reported a 50 per cent attrition in bullying, utilising his step-by-step approach to whole school training and intervention. Differing anti-bullying approaches have been trialled, and some, it has been argued, are counter-productive, resulting in a change of behaviour of victims rather than that of pupils who bully (Olweus, 2004). Yet, many of these programmes have not been empirically evaluated and, as a result, their efficacy may only be context specific, and thus do not fulfil the claims of general efficacy (Rappaport, 2000).

The application of positive psychology

PP is primarily concerned with the empirical study of human happiness and strengths. It is also concerned with individuals' resilience to negative life events, including bullying. Simply speaking, PP represents an attempt to unite research and theory about what makes life worth living (Peterson and Park, 2003). It has emerged as a reaction to the pathology-focused nature of much research and intervention work conducted in psychology.

The concept of *happiness* is somewhat vague and many researchers have dissolved the term into different categories. Seligman (2003) began by identifying three different paths to attaining 'happiness':

1   positive emotion (the pleasant life)
2   engagement (the engaged life)
3   meaning (the meaningful life).

Positive emotion represents a transient state of happiness which is mostly situation specific. *Engagement*, although reliant on the situation also, represents an activity where an individual can 'lose oneself'. *The meaningful life* represents purpose and the fulfilment of personal potential (Peterson, *et al.*, 2005). Researchers have noted that those who are most satisfied with life are those who aim towards all three states, but with greater weight on *engagement* and *meaning* rather than *positive emotion*. Studies have shown the positive effect happiness can have on social relationships (see Seligman *et al.*, 2005), and, therefore, any intervention aiming to develop or encourage positive social relationships must consider the extent to which it is both *engaging* and *meaningful* to the individual.

Seligman *et al.* (2005) developed one of the first large-scale intervention studies in PP. This Internet-based study aimed to identify the impact of five different happiness exercises on overall reports of happiness (N = 577 adults). After doing the exercises, a depression scale and the Steen happiness index (SHI, developed for use in the study) were completed. The distinctive intervention exercises included 'three good things in life', a 'gratitude visit', an account of 'you at your best', identification of 'signature strengths', and 'use of these strengths' in a new way. A placebo control exercise was also employed which required some participants to write about their early memories each night for one week. Participants in the control group showed an immediate boost in reports of happiness (SHI) and a decline in reports of depressive symptoms. However, this effect was short-lived, and participants returned to baseline levels shortly after. This was also true for those who participated in the 'you at your best' intervention, the 'gratitude visit' and 'identifying signature strengths'. However, writing about three good things that happened each day and using signature strengths in a new way led to people reporting being happier and less depressed up to six months later. Seligman and his colleagues did not discount some of the short-lived interventions entirely. They argued that such interventions should not be undertaken in isolation, but rather as a component of a multi-exercise programme. Furthermore, they suggested that a multi-exercise programme may exceed the beneficial effects of any single exercise.

Drawing from a variety of sources, a number of interpersonal qualities have been identified as playing a central role in PP: for example, character strengths and virtues (Seligman, 2003) and positive emotions (Snyder and Lopez, 2002). Personality traits such as agreeability and conscientiousness can often have a positive impact on social situations, such as group or classroom activities (Seligman, 2004). The following interpersonal qualities are said to be largely situation specific but can be nurtured amongst pupils: altruism (Costa and McCrae, 1992), optimism (Seligman, 1998), empathy (Eisenberg *et al.*, 1996), being good natured or amiable and the ability to work with others on group tasks or towards a collective goal (Carr, 2004), social acceptance (Keyes, 1998) and patience and fairness (Vandiver, 2001). These interpersonal qualities inform the programme developed in this study.

Because PP seeks to adopt preventative measures by building from a baseline of mentally healthy individuals, a focus on positive interpersonal qualities (such as those mentioned above) could prove valuable in an anti-bullying intervention, if they could be systematically identified in each pupil and built upon. Indeed, pupils already exhibit many of these qualities, to varying degrees, in social situations. However, taking Seligman's hypothesis a step further, it would seem that it is the extent and manner in which these interpersonal qualities are exhibited that may help to reduce bullying. For example, some pupils may think of themselves as an accepting person, but still tease another if they are perceived as different. In that situation, they were not accepting at that time and might want to think about why they were not. Indeed, pupils could be encouraged to think about how they could use these qualities in a new way (to tackle bullying in this instance). This would represent a similar approach to Seligman and his colleagues, as mentioned above. By providing examples such as these and engaging pupils in activities that were meaningful to them, it was hypothesised that the prevalence of bullying would be lessened.

Background and aims of the present study

In conjunction with a Local Education Authority's Curriculum and Management Advisory Service, the first author (Andrew Richards) undertook a pilot investigation, where a PP approach was designed to guide anti-bullying interventions for pupils in Year 7 of a secondary school in a sub-region, with an additional school participating as a control. The purpose of the study was to determine whether or not a PP intervention would not only reduce bullying in schools post-intervention, but that it would also impact upon reports of general well-being and mental health.

METHOD

Design

This study employed a quasi-experimental, non-related groups design. A target sampling method was used, where schools with similar bullying prevalence rates from a previous audit were approached. Two schools agreed that pupils in their Year 7 groups could complete three pre-intervention measures and then nine weeks later repeat the exercise. In the PP intervention school, eight Personal, Social and Health Education (PSHE) lessons were delivered using materials designed by the authors. The second (control) school completed the questionnaires at a nine week interval; however, during the interim it followed the normal PSHE curriculum and did not include lessons on bullying issues.

Participants

In the PP intervention school, 258 pupils participated in the pre-test and 206 in the post-test. The sample comprised 51.8 per cent males and 48.2 per cent females (mean age 11.6 years). The majority described themselves as White British (88.4 per cent) or White other (5.2 per cent). The control school was from the same region, with pupils of both sexes from similar socio-economic backgrounds and ethnic origins. A total of 162 pupils completed the pre- and post-intervention measures (mean age of 11.3 years). 46 per cent were males and 54 per cent females, with 91.4 per cent describing themselves as White British.

Instruments

The effectiveness of the programmes was measured using a pre- and post-intervention self-report questionnaire. Questions about the nature and prevalence of bullying and substance abuse were based on the questionnaire developed by Olweus (1991). The KINDL-R questionnaire for measuring health-related quality of life in children and adolescents (Ravens-Sieberer and Bullinger, 1998) was utilised. The KINDL-R has six sub-scales, each with four items measured on a five-point Likert scale. The sub-scales measure quality of physical health, feelings in general, personal worth, feelings about family, feelings about friends and feelings about school life. The instrument has a high degree of reliability (coefficient alpha ≥ 0.70; Ravens-Sieberer and Bullinger, 1998).

The Brief Symptom Inventory (BSI) (Derogatis, 1975) is a 53-item inventory. Participants were asked how much a specific problem (e.g. 'feeling fearful') had distressed them in the past week, with responses on a five-point Likert scale. Six of the nine symptom dimensions were selected for use, based on the known association between experiences of bullying/victimisation and the onset of somatization disorders, interpersonal sensitivity, depression, anxiety, hostility and phobic anxiety. The BSI has high internal consistency (coefficient alphas range from 0.71 to 0.85), with good test–retest reliability, and convergent, discriminant and construct validity.

The PP intervention programme

The PP intervention programme lasted nine weeks in total, with teachers receiving lesson plan guidelines from the first author. The guidelines contained directions on objectives, outcomes and recommendations relating to the time spent on each task (referring to associated resources that were also provided). As teachers were not always familiar with PP concepts, explanations were included to highlight the purposes behind the sessions. Each session focused on the development and application of individual strengths and qualities within a social context and were based upon the development and expansion of eight interpersonal qualities: empathy, altruism, optimism, team spirit, amiability, fairness, social acceptance, patience. Below we will provide a summary of each lesson. As we are only able to give an outline in this paper, please contact the first author (Andrew Richards) for a full description of each lesson plan and the resources used.

SESSION 1: DEFINING INTERPERSONAL QUALITIES

During this session, the term 'interpersonal quality' was introduced to each class. The definitions for each of the eight qualities were also discussed, with support from an overhead transparency (OHT). Pupils were then provided with a worksheet with three of the qualities listed. These differed to allow pupils to work with different interpersonal qualities and share in a discussion afterwards. They were then asked to define those qualities and give examples of how they might apply them in a social setting such as school.

SESSION 2: DEFINITIONS OF BULLYING – APPLICATION OF QUALITIES

Teachers were asked to discuss definitions of bullying and to list different types of behaviour, asking the class whether or not the behaviour was a type of bullying. Pupils were then given a worksheet with two accounts from victims of bullying and answered questions relating to helping behaviour and the interpersonal qualities, victims' feelings and forms of bullying. Teachers were then advised to emphasise that bullying is not always clearly obvious and to discuss the pupils' responses to the questions.

SESSION 3: POSTER DESIGN USING ICT – DEPICTING INDIVIDUAL STRENGTHS

Pupils were asked to design a poster depicting one of their selected interpersonal qualities/strengths. The posters had to include a statement using the quality they chose, e.g. 'Fairness includes everybody'. It was suggested that some posters were chosen for display in the Year 7 areas.

SESSION 4: ROLE PLAY – APPLYING INTERPERSONAL QUALITIES

This session involved pupils working in small groups. The groups were asked to think of a scenario where one member is going through a difficult time and in need of some support. Examples were given (e.g. new to school, being bullied). Pupils were asked to portray a supportive role using one of the eight interpersonal qualities. Pupils were then asked to 'act out' their scenarios, and other groups were to attempt to guess which interpersonal quality was being demonstrated. This aimed to give pupils an opportunity to think about how they might apply their strengths in a social setting.

SESSION 5: PUPILS MANAGING SCHOOL – PERSONAL REFLECTION

Using either an OHT or worksheets, pupils were asked to complete a number of statements relating to the past year at school. The questions related to personal feelings about the past in school, both pleasant and unpleasant. Pupils were then asked to list five things that had happened in the past week for which they were grateful (see Seligman *et al.*, 2005). In small groups, pupils were asked to imagine they were managing the school. Using the answers they had provided, they compiled an action plan to improve interpersonal/ supportive relationships between pupils and reduce bullying in school. At the end of this session, a homework assignment was set which involved listing three things each pupil was grateful for at the end of each day, for a total of one week.

SESSION 6: OPTIMISM VERSUS PESSIMISM

Definitions of optimism and pessimism were discussed. Pupils were then given a worksheet with questions on optimism and pessimism that related to them. The last question listed eleven words, and pupils were asked to identify them as optimistic or pessimistic, e.g. 'distrust', 'cheerful', 'hope'. Teachers were then asked to discuss responses with the class. Teachers were advised that studies have shown that optimism can act as a 'buffer' against depression when people experience negative life events (Carr, 2004) and that the pupils should understand that the outcome of a situation can depend on the outlook of the individual concerned.

SESSION 7: DEVELOPING AND APPLYING INTERPERSONAL QUALITIES

This session was developed to give pupils a greater insight into the meanings and applications of the eight interpersonal qualities. A worksheet was distributed which was designed to provoke deep thought on the subject. Definitions of the qualities were included to help them answer the questions. The questions related to second parties who lacked specific qualities, second parties who have employed their qualities to succeed, pupils employing their qualities to succeed, developing interpersonal qualities and helping behaviour.

SESSION 8: RECAP AND REFLECTION

This final session involved recapping and reflecting on the past seven sessions. Pupils were given a worksheet to complete, with seven questions asking them to recount the previous sessions and content. They were also asked what aspects they liked and disliked and how they would apply what they had covered in day-to-day life.

RESULTS

The nature and frequency of bullying

Overall, in the PP intervention school there was a significant reduction in reports of bullying, with 70.6 per cent of pupils saying they had not been bullied in the past two weeks pre-test and 79.2 per cent post-intervention ($\chi^2(1) = 4.33$, $p \leq 0.01$) (see Table 7.1), with reports of name calling having the most significant reduction ($\chi^2(1) = 4.9$, $p \leq 0.01$). Interestingly, while no significant differences were found between boys and girls pre intervention in terms of reports of physical bullying (hitting and kicking), significantly fewer females reported being hit or kicked post-intervention ($\chi^2(1) = 4.19$, $p \leq 0.05$). In the control school, no significant increase or decrease in bullying was reported across the nine-week period. The most common types of reported bullying were namecalling, hitting and kicking and rumour-spreading. Significant differences were found between genders pre-test. Girls reported significantly fewer experiences of hitting and kicking, theft and threats compared with boys ($\chi^2(1) = 4.38$, $p \leq 0.05$; $\chi^2(1) = 7.07$, $p \leq 0.05$; and $\chi^2(1) = 6.11$, $p < 0.01$, respectively). Post-test, girls reported significantly less hitting and kicking, name calling and theft of personal possessions than boys ($\chi^2(1) = 4.89$, $p \leq 0.05$; $\chi^2(1) = 3.99$, $p \leq 0.05$ and $\chi^2(1) = 4.81$, $p \leq 0.05$, respectively).

General well-being

Pupils completed the KINDL-R questionnaire, in which higher scores represent perceptions of a better quality of life when compared with lower scores. Mean scores were analysed using a One-Way ANOVA. Pupils from the PP intervention school reported feeling significantly better about their physical health at post-test ($F(1, 447) = 7.56$, $p \leq 0.01$) and they also reported significantly better feelings about their family ($F(1, 437) = 4.27$, $p \leq 0.05$) and feelings in general ($F(1, 445) = 5.26$, $p \leq 0.05$). Notably, feelings about school did not improve, nor did feelings about themselves and friends. The aggregate scores across the six sub-scales generated a mean general well-being score. Pupils in the PP intervention school reported feeling significantly better overall ($F(1, 448) = 6.53$,

■ **Table 7.1** Nature and prevalence of bullying

Item	Test	Experimental			Control	
		Yes (%)	χ^2		Yes (%)	χ^2
I haven't been bullied in the	Pre	70.6			68.5	
past two weeks	Post	79.2	4.33*		68.3	0.00
I've been called names about	1	7.5			5.6	
my ethnicity or colour	2	5.4	0.78		6.8	0.23
I've been hit or kicked	1	8.7			11.7	
	2	6.9	0.48		10.6	0.11
I've been called other names	1	22.5			22.2	
	2	14.4	4.90*		18	0.89
Rumours have been spread	1	8.3			9.9	
about me	2	6.9	0.30		8.1	0.32
No one speaks to me	1	2			4.3	
	2	1.5	0.16		1.2	2.82
I have been frightened when a	1	2.4			4.9	
particular person looks or stares	2	2	0.08		3.1	0.70
at me						
I've had my belongings taken	1	4.7			5.6	
	2	4.5	0.02		4.3	0.25
I've been threatened with	1	2.8			6.8	
violence	2	2	0.30		4.3	0.92
My homework has been taken	1	0			1.2	
or destroyed	2	0.5	1.26		0.6	0.33
I've seen graffiti about me	1	2			1.9	
	2	2	0.00		1.2	0.20
I've been pressured into smoking	1	1.6			2.5	
	2	0	3.22		1.9	0.14
I've been pressured into `	1	2			0	
drinking alcohol	2	0.5	1.89		1.2	2.03
I've been pressured into	1	1.2			0.6	
taking drugs	2	0	2.41		0	1.00
I've been bullied in other ways	1	4			8	
	2	3	0.32		5.6	0.75

* = $p \leq 0.05$

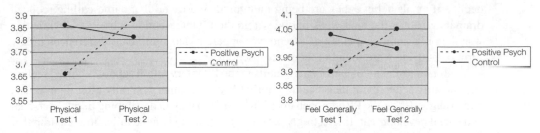

Figure 7.1 Physical.

Figure 7.2 Feeling in general.

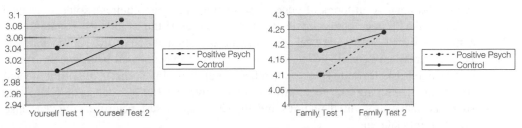

Figure 7.3 Feelings about yourself.

Figure 7.4 Feelings about family.

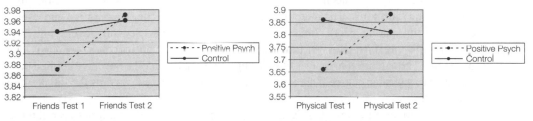

Figure 7.5 Feelings about friends.

Figure 7.6 Feelings about school.

$p \leq 0.01$). Within the control sample, no significant differences were found pre-and post-test across the six sub-scales and the total wellbeing mean score (see Figures 7.1–7.6).

Mental health

Pre- and post-test scores were compared using a One-Way ANOVA. No significant differences were found in either of the two schools.

DISCUSSION

The PP approach aimed to reduce the levels of bullying by building pupils' interpersonal qualities using activities delivered in PSHE lessons. Overall, reports of bullying by type did decline by approximately one third after nine weeks, which is encouraging, although, as Naylor and Cowie (1999) point out, interventions can sometimes hypersensitise pupils to the issues of bullying, which can result in an increase in reports, or even a potential decline if pupils believe they are being monitored. We found that name-calling reduced dramatically over the nine-week period within the PP intervention school, and while this was the only significant change, a trend was apparent. No significant differences in any form of bullying were found in the control school.

In terms of general well-being, pupils in the PP intervention school reported feeling significantly better about their health, family life and feelings generally after nine weeks, which suggests that the PP approach does have a role to play in developing pupils' personal and social development. Interestingly, as researchers we may have fallen into the trap that Seligman and his colleagues warn against: namely attempting to introduce an intervention in isolation, ignoring the 'whole school' – the well-being of teachers, other pupils and of course parents. Notwithstanding this flaw, it is clear that students in the PP intervention school did improve in terms of general well-being, and this requires explanation. One aspect of the PP intervention involved pupils listing three things they were grateful for, at the end of each day for one week. This was an adaptation of Seligman's (2005) gratitude visit. This may have contributed in some small measure to better well-being scores at post-test, as pupils had learnt to spend time reflecting upon positive aspects of family life and friendship, thus taking their focus away from negative experiences such as bullying. This supports Seligman's initial findings and suggests that these types of exercise are also effective for children.

Developing their own interpersonal qualities was a key focus in this intervention, and may have been particularly rewarding for those pupils (bullies and victims alike) who experienced low self-esteem, and in re-structuring pupils' views towards amiability, altruism and team spirit. The intention here was to develop better cooperation and a sense of amiability among peers. Indeed, much of the work focused on developing these qualities in a specific contextual framework (i.e. how such qualities can be used to reduce bullying). The reduction in reports of bullying suggests that pupils may have applied these qualities to a greater degree than before or perhaps in a different way, as the intervention exampled.

We did not find any significant change in pupils' mental health between the pre- and post-test in the PP intervention school. Clearly, the PP intervention did not have an immediate or direct impact on mental health, and it may have been overly ambitious of us to expect to see discernable improvement in such a short period of time. While the six BSI dimension scores varied considerably in the control school at pre- and post-test, with no discernable pattern, in the PP intervention school the scores remained stable, which can be interpreted in positive terms. However, it seems likely with such a short intervention, that measures of mental health are unlikely to prove useful indicators of change.

There were limitations in conducting this study, largely related to organisational issues in the schools concerned. Initially, it was envisaged that the whole of KS3 and KS4 in each school would participate. Owing to factors such as revision for examinations, examination timetabling and work experience, this was not possible. Only one year in both schools was available during the time of participation (Year 7), so we were unable to work with the 'whole school', and thus the pupils in the study undertook this programme in isolation. The schools participated at different times of the year: the PP intervention study school began the intervention in March 2004, and the control school undertook the pre-test questionnaire in January 2005.

CONCLUSION

Results indicated that, among those pupils who experienced the PP intervention pro-gramme, levels of bullying reduced, and they scored marginally better in terms of general well-being but not mental health. The short duration of this study is likely to have militated against effectively evaluating the potential benefits of PP in terms of pupils' mental health. Overall, it seems likely that PP's contribution to school-based anti-bullying interventions will be in terms of supporting long-term rather than short-term initiatives, and could perhaps represent an important component of a wider 'whole-school' anti-bullying intervention.

REFERENCES

Carr, A. (2004) *Positive psychology: the science of human happiness and human strengths*, New York: Brunner-Routledge.

Costa, P. and McCrae, P. (1992) *Revised NEO personality inventory (NEO-PI-R and NEO five-factor inventory (NEO-FFI)) professional manual*, Odessa, FL: Psychological Assessment Resources.

Demaray, M.K. and Malecki, C.K. (2003) 'Perceptions of the frequency and importance of social support by students classified as victims, bullies, and bully/victims in an urban middle school', *School Psychology Review*, Vol. 32: 471–489.

Department for Education and Skills (2005) *Every child matters: change for children*, London: DfES.

Derogatis, L.R. (1975) *Brief symptom inventory*, Minneapolis: NCS Pearsons.

Due, P., Holstein, B.E., Lynch, J., Diderichsen, F., Gabhain, S.N., Scheiddt, P. and Currie, C. (2005) 'Bullying and symptoms among school aged children: international comparative cross sectional study in 28 countries (Electronic version), *The European Journal of Public Health*, Vol. 15, No. 2: 128–132.

Eisenberg, N., Fabes, R.A., Murphy, B., Karbon, M. and Smith, M. (1996) 'The relations of children's dispositional empathy-related responding to their emotionality, regulation, and social functioning', *Developmental Psychology*, Vol. 32: 195–209.

Eslea, M. and Mukhtar, K. (2000) 'Bullying and racism among Asian school children in Britain', *Educational Research*, Vol. 42, No. 2: 207–217.

Feinberg, T. (2003) 'Bullying preventions and intervention', *Principal Leadership (middle school edn)*, Vol. 4: 10–14.

Fullan, M. (2001) *Leading in a culture of change*, San Francisco: Jossey-Bass.

Galloway, D. (1994) 'Bullying: the importance of a whole school approach', *Therapeutic Care and Education*, Vol. 3: 315–329.

Haynie, D.L., Nansel, T., Eitel, P., Crump, A.D., Saylor, K., Yu, K. and Simons-Morton, B. (2001) 'Bullies, victims, and bully/victims: distinct groups of at-risk youth', *Journal of Early Adolescence*, Vol. 21, No. 1: 29–49.

Keyes, J. (1998) 'Social wellbeing', *Psychology Quarterly*, Vol. 61: 121–140.

Nabuzoka, D. and Smith, P.K. (1993) 'Sociometric status and social behaviour of children with and without learning difficulties', *Journal of Child Psychology & Psychiatry*, Vol. 34, No. 8: 1435–1448.

Naylor, P. and Cowie, H. (1999) 'The effectiveness of peer support systems in challenging school bullying: the perspectives and experiences of teachers and pupils', *Journal of Adolescence*, Vol. 22: 467–479.

Office for Standards in Education (2003) *Bullying: effective action in secondary schools*, London: Ofsted (HMI 465).

Oliver, C. and Candappa, M. (2003) *Tackling bullying: listening to the views of children and young people*, Thomas Coram Research Unit, Research Report no. RR400: University of London.

Olweus, D. (1991) 'Bully/victim problems among school children: basic facts and effects of a school-based intervention program', in Rubin, K. and Pepler, D. (eds) *The development and treatmen of childhood aggression*, Hillsdale, NJ: Lawrence Erlbaum: 411–488.

Olweus, D. (1993) Bullying at school: what we know and what we can do, Oxford: Blackwell.

Olweus, D. (1999) 'Norway', in Smith, P.K., Morita, Y., Junger-Tas, J., Olweus, D., Catalano, R. and Slee, P. (eds) *The nature of school bullying: a cross national perspective,* London: Routledge: 28–48.

Olweus, D. (2004) 'The Olweus bullying prevention programme: design and implementation issues and a new national initiative in Norway', in Smith, P.K., Pepler, D. and Rigby, K. (eds) *Bullying in schools: how successful can interventions be?* Cambridge: Cambridge University Press: 13–36.

Peterson, C. and Park, N. (2003) 'Positive psychology as the even-handed positive psychology views it', *Psychological Inquiry*, Vol. 14: 141–146.

Peterson, C., Park, N. and Seligman, M.E.P. (2005) 'Orientations to happiness and life satisfaction: the full life versus the empty life', *Journal of Happiness Studies*, Vol. 6: 25–41.

Rappaport, J. (2000) *Evaluation of programs and measures to reduce problem behaviour and develop social competence*, Oslo, Norway: Kirkeundervisnings.

Ravens-Sieberer, U. and Bullinger, M. (1998) 'News from the KINDL-questionnaire – a new version for adolescents', *Quality of Life Research*, Vol. 7: 653.

Rivers, I. and Duncan, N. (2002) 'Understanding homophobic bullying in schools: building a safe educational environment for all pupils', *Youth and Policy*, Vol. 75: 30–41.

Salmivalli, C., Kaukiainen, A., Kaistaniemi, L. and Lagerspetz, K.M.J. (1999) 'Self-evaluated self-esteem, peer-evaluated self-esteem, and defensive egotism as predictors of adolescents' participation in bullying situations', *PSPB*, Vol. 25, No. 10: 1268–1278.

Seligman, M. (1998) *Learned optimism: how to change your mind and your life* (2nd edition), New York: Pocket books.

Seligman, M. (2003) *Authentic happiness: understanding the new positive psychology to realise your potential for lasting fulfilment*, London: Nicholas Brealey.

Seligman, M.E.P. (2004) Positive psychology network paper, www.psych.upenn.edu/seligman/ppgrant.htm; accessed 1 December 2004.

Seligman, M.E.P., Steen, T.A., Park, N. and Peterson, C. (2005) 'Positive psychology progress: empirical validation of interventions', *American Psychologist*, Vol. 60, No. 5: 410–421.

Smith, P.K., Pepler, D. and Rigby, K. (2004) 'Working to prevent bullying: key issues', in Smith, P.K., Pepler, D. and Rigby, K. (eds) *Bullying in schools: how successful can interventions be?* Cambridge: Cambridge University Press: 1–12.

Snyder, C.R. and Lopez, S. (2002) *Handbook of positive psychology*, New York: Oxford University Press.

Tattum, D.P. (1993) 'What is bullying?', in Tattum, D. (ed.) *Understanding and managing bullying*, London: Heinemann.

Vandiver, T. (2001) 'Children's social competence, academic competence, and aggressiveness as related to ability to make judgments of fairness', *Psychological Reports,* Vol. 89, No. 1: 111–121.

Weinhold, B.K. (2000) 'Bullying and school violence: the tip of the iceberg', *The Teacher Educator,* Vol. 35: 28–33.

Yule, W. (ed.) (1999) *Post-traumatic stress disorders: concepts and therapy*, Chichester: Wiley.

MEETING INDIVIDUAL DIFFERENCES

INTRODUCTION

Each pupil in your class is different. A cohort of same-age pupils is likely to contain individuals at different stages of maturity, arising from differences in physical or cognitive development and bringing with them varied cultural experiences; these features of development interact. Differences in achievement, motivation and behaviour may be more marked in a mixed ability class, although substantial differences remain in streamed or setted classes. Cultural, religious and economic backgrounds of your pupils may strongly affect their response to schooling, and, whereas some pupils respond to academic challenge, others see little point in such demands. Yet other pupils are gifted and need special attention, as do pupils with learning or behavioural difficulties. The differences between pupils show a remarkable range of variation and, when faced with twenty to thirty pupils for whom you have planned a particular topic with particular learning outcomes, you may find that every pupil could take something different from your teaching.

READINGS IN THIS SECTION ARE:

Reading 8
The effects of social class and ethnicity on gender differences in GCSE attainment: a secondary analysis of the Youth Cohort Study of England and Wales 1997–2001
Paul Connolly

Reading 8 links with Unit 4.4, 'Responding to diversity'. The author has analysed data from the Youth Cohort Study (YCS), a longitudinal study of successive cohorts of pupils leaving school at 16, and analysed their performance then and at 19 years old in terms of social class, gender and ethnicity. Three cohorts of pupils were studied, with sample sizes approaching 15,000, 14,000 and 17,000. The study shows that social class and ethnicity have a far greater influence on GCSE performance than does gender. Further, that there is no evidence of systematic variation in the size of gender differences in educational attainment that exist across social class and ethnicity. The reading emphasises that categorising and comparing performance simply in terms gender, ethnicity or class are no longer useful, but that pupils need to be helped according to their individual circumstances.

Reading 9
Educational psychology and the effectiveness of inclusive education/mainstreaming
Geoff Lindsay

The second reading in this section addresses the recent development in England of the notion of inclusion (Lindsay, 2007). Many educationalists and psychologists have argued for pupils with special educational needs (SEN) to be taught in the mainstream classes rather than in special schools or be segregated in some way. This reading has focused primarily on research evidence of the effectiveness of inclusive education. However, it is also argued that there is a separate conceptual framework that must be considered, which concerns values and rights. Inclusive education has been driven by a belief that this is the correct approach, to include rather than segregate and exclude. The evidence from this review does not provide a clear endorsement for the positive effects of inclusion. There is a lack of evidence from appropriate studies, and, where evidence does exist, the balance was only marginally positive. It is argued that the policy has been driven by a concern for pupils' rights. The important task now is to research more thoroughly the mediators and moderators that support the optimal education for pupils with SEN and disabilities and, as a consequence, develop an evidence-based approach to these pupils' education.

Reading 10
Setting or mixed ability? Teachers' views of the organisation of pupils for learning
Chris M.M. Smith and Margaret J. Sutherland

The third reading in this section (Smith and Sutherland, 2003) addresses two important issues. The first issue is concerned with the way pupils are grouped in schools for subject teaching, and, the second, the awareness of teachers of research findings and their influence, or lack of it, on teachers' views of the best way to group pupils for teaching. Teachers believed that setting increased the motivation of pupils, but recognised that this may only be true of top sets. Another belief was that examination results are improved by setting, an opinion at odds with the evidence. Another dimension to the research was the opinion of pupils. Very little notice appeared to be taken by teachers of pupils' views; there is evidence to suggest that, in part, they were at odds with teachers views.

Reading 11
Moral education in practice
Colin Wringe

The final reading in this section (Wringe, 2006) is an extract from a book on moral education, and the reading cited here, 'Moral education in practice', discusses ways to approach moral education, their advantages and disadvantages, addressed through both a practical and theoretical standpoint. The author asks whether it is appropriate for schools to concern themselves with moral education at all, especially in communities where the cultural, and often religious, rights of communities are a matter of principle and concern. The reading touches on many familiar situations in school, teacher–pupil relationships, of subject approaches to moral education and discusses the role of cognitive development and motivation on moral development.

A recurring point in the reading is the need for morality to be caught rather than taught; a matter of engagement rather than instruction; and that, for effective development, discussion is essential. Moral education is seen as developing in a community context. As well as looking at the value of developing a sound basis for moral judgement, the author discusses the issues of sanctions where behaviours are at odds with the prevailing rules and values. A theme running through the reading is whether moral education requires its own curriculum slot or should be part of every subject and teacher's role.

FURTHER READING

Boaler, J. (1997) *Experiencing school mathematics: teaching style, sex and setting*, Buckingham: Open University Press.

This is a comparative study of pupils in two comprehensive schools, documenting their differences in knowledge and understanding of mathematics and their motivation and attitude towards the subject. One school taught in a traditional way, through rule-learning then application, whereas the other linked mathematics to the everyday life of pupils, using open-ended project work as one teaching strategy. One conclusion from the study was that pupils in mixed-ability classes did as well as pupils taught in ability sets. Another finding was that some pupils in top sets, being taught in the traditional way, were more likely to experience stress because of the need to keep up. Some girls were disadvantaged by a traditional approach to teaching mathematics.

The above further reading links with Unit 4.1 of the 5th edition of *Learning to teach in the secondary school*.

Hallam, S. and Ireson, J. (2005) 'Secondary school teachers' pedagogic practices when teaching mixed and structured ability classes', *Research Papers in Education*, Vol. 20, No. 1: 3–24.

This research uses questionnaires to compare secondary school teachers' pedagogical practices in mixed and ability-grouped classes. The sample included mainly teachers of mathematics, science and English. The findings showed that the curriculum was differentiated more in ability-grouped classes by content, depth, the activities undertaken and the resources used. Grouping less able pupils led to more opportunities for rehearsal and repetition, more structured work, more practical work, fewer opportunities for discussion, less access to the curriculum, less homework with less detailed feedback; lessons were easier and slower.

The above further reading links with Units 4.1 and 4.3 of the 5th edition of *Learning to teach in the secondary school*.

British Medical Association (BMA) (2003) *Adolescent health*, BMA Board of Science and Education; available at www.BMA.org.uk.

This report focuses on the problems facing adolescents and examines the evidence surrounding adolescent health, behaviour and interventions. It reviews four important areas in adolescent health: nutrition, exercise and obesity; smoking, drinking and drug use; mental health; and sexual health. It discusses the prevalence of the problems involved; examines which adolescents are affected; describes the interventions used to address the issues; and evaluates the effectiveness of these strategies. This report provides an overview of adolescent health issues and the policy environment.

The above further reading links with Unit 4.2 of the 5th edition of *Learning to teach in the secondary school*.

Adey, P. (2000) 'Science teaching and the development of intelligence' in Monk, M. and Osborne, J. *Good practice in science education*, Buckingham: The Open University Press: Chapter 10: 158–173.

The chapter challenges all teachers, not only science teachers, to help pupils learn how to think. The author suggests that science teaching can raise pupils' intelligence, with similar gains in other subjects. The claim is based on a plastic model of intelligence (see Adey *et al.*, 2007), supported by extensive evidence from studies of cognitive development (e.g. Adey and Shayer, 1994) and advances in neuroscience (see Goswami, 2004). The time spent helping pupils to 'learn how to learn' pays off in improved academic achievement.

The papers referred to above are

Adey, P., Csapo, B., Demetriou, A., Hautamäki, J. and Shayer, M. (2007) 'Can we be intelligent about intelligence? Why education needs the concept of plastic general ability', *Educational Research Review*, Vol. 2, No. 2: 75–97.

Adey, P. and Shayer, M. (1994) *Really raising standards: cognitive intervention and academic achievement*, London: Routledge.

The above further reading links with Unit 4.3 of the 5th edition of *Learning to teach in the secondary school*.

5   Department for Children, Schools and Families (DCSF) (2003) *Aiming high: raising the achievement of minority ethnic pupils: Summary*, London: DCSF.

The report surveys and brings together research evidence related to the academic performance of different ethnic groups of pupils in England and identifies factors contributing to their performance. The authors paint a complex picture. While acknowledging that lower performance of pupils is often linked to socio-economic disadvantage, other contributing factors are identified, including national and local policies and practice. The report identifies five features contributing to the success of pupils in schools.

The above further reading links with Unit 4.4 of the 5th edition of *Learning to teach in the secondary school*.

6   Rivers, I. (2000) 'Social Exclusion, absenteeism and sexual minority youth', *Support for Learning*, Vol. 15, No. 1: 13–18.

The author compares two groups of bisexual, gay and lesbian adults who have reported having been subjected to abuse at school because of their sexual orientation. The subjects report on the effect on school attendance and its consequences for achievement and on the promotion of suicidal feelings and the possibility of self-harm. The author moves on to discuss ways to promote anti-harassment measures in school and the creation of a safe environment.

The above further reading links with Unit 4.4 of the 5th edition of *Learning to teach in the secondary school*.

7   Younger, M. and Warrington, M. (2005) *Raising boys' achievement*, London: DfES.

A report of a four-year research study addressing the underachievement of some boys relative to girls' achievement. While acknowledging the evidence, it points out that all pupils' performance has improved in recent years, that many boys do well, and that the gender gap, while real, is not increasing. Strategies for improving pupil performance must not hinder that of girls. Preconditions for intervention strategies are identified, including whole-school approaches, individual approaches and a focus by staff on shifting teaching and learning towards the needs of the individual learner.

The above further reading links with Unit 4.4 of the 5th edition of *Learning to teach in the secondary school*.

8   Fletcher-Campbell, F. (2005) 'Moderate learning difficulties', in Lewis, A. and Norwich, B. (eds) *Special teaching for special children? Pedagogies for inclusion*, Maidenhead: Open University Press: Chapter 14: 180–191.

The book addresses the question 'what is special' about teaching pupils with special or exceptional learning needs?' Some special needs groups, e.g. dyslexics, have argued for the need for particular specialist approaches. In contrast, others argue that 'good teaching is good teaching for all', and that all pupils benefit from similar approaches. Both positions fail to scrutinise this issue rigorously and coherently, and it is this aspect that distinguishes this book. The selected chapter gives you a flavour of the debate.

The above further reading links with Unit 4.6 of the 5th edition of *Learning to teach in the secondary school.*

THE EFFECTS OF SOCIAL CLASS AND ETHNICITY ON GENDER DIFFERENCES IN GCSE ATTAINMENT

A secondary analysis of the Youth Cohort Study of England and Wales 1997–2001

Paul Connolly

A NOTE FROM THE EDITORS

This reading uses data from the national large-scale longitudinal Youth Cohort Study in England and Wales in order to explore the impact of social class, gender and ethnicity on pupil achievement in GCSE.

This reading links with Unit 4.4 of the 5th edition of *Learning to teach in the secondary school*.

QUESTIONS TO CONSIDER

Analyses of the performance of pupils in GCSE examinations and other national tests often focus on the differences in achievement of particular groups of pupils identified, for example, by variables such as gender, social class and ethnicity. Interventions based on such analyses have arisen, such as boosting the performance of boys or addressing the failings of a particular ethnic group. Two questions arise.

1   To what extent are such analyses and interventions helpful, targeting as they do whole cohorts of pupils? Should schools instead focus on the particular learning needs of pupils, as envisaged by the introduction of personalised learning?
2   Are some underachieving pupils held back by factors that are outside the capacity of schools to influence? In these circumstances what actions should be put in place and by whom?

This reading was first published as: Connolly, P. (2006) 'The effects of social class and ethnicity on gender differences in GCSE attainment: a secondary analysis of the Youth Cohort Study of England and Wales 1997–2001', *British Educational Research Journal*, Vol. 32: 3–21.

ABSTRACT

This article is based upon a secondary analysis of three successive cohorts of the Youth Cohort Study of England and Wales and examines the effects of social class and ethnicity on gender differences in General Certificate of Secondary Education (GCSE) attainment for those who left school in 1997, 1999 and 2001 respectively. The article shows that both social class and ethnicity exert a far greater influence on the GCSE performance of boys and girls than gender. Within this it assesses whether there is an interaction effect between gender and social class and also gender and ethnicity in terms of their impact on educational attainment. The article shows that, across all three cohorts, there is no evidence of any systematic variation in the size of the gender differences in educational attainment that exist across either social class or ethnic groups. Simply in terms of the effects of social class, ethnicity and gender on educational attainment, therefore, it is argued that these can actually be understood in terms of a simple 'additive model'. The implications of this for initiatives aimed at addressing gender differences in educational attainment are considered briefly in the conclusion.

INTRODUCTION

Concerns about the misleading and distorting nature of the moral panic that has arisen over the underachievement of boys in education within the UK since the mid 1990s have now been well rehearsed (Epstein *et al.*, 1998a; Francis, 2000; Reed, 1999). Perhaps one of the main criticisms has been focused on the way in which such a panic has tended to rely upon crude comparisons between all boys and all girls, as if they both represent two homogeneous and distinct categories (Epstein *et al.*, 1998a; Jackson, 1998; Mac an Ghaill, 1996; Skelton, 2001). As Lucey and Walkerdine have argued, for example:

all too often simplistic, statistical interpretations which concentrate entirely on gender differences serve to shore up a universal notion of boys' underachievement and present a picture which powerfully obscures and confuses enduring inequalities in attainment.

(Lucey and Walkerdine, 2000: 38)

As Epstein *et al.* (1998b: 11) have also argued, 'the "underachievement" of boys at school is a strongly classed and racialised phenomenon'. Thus, it is not all boys who are underachieving, so it is argued, but working-class boys and boys from particular minority ethnic groups (most notably African Caribbean, Bangladeshi and Pakistani boys). Equally, it is not all girls who are 'overachieving' [*sic*] but, rather, there are certain groups – particularly working-class girls – who are also severely underachieving in education.

There remains a certain lack of clarity, however, regarding the implications of these arguments for how we can actually understand the effects of social class and ethnicity on gender differences in educational attainment. More specifically, there are two competing models that can both be applied to these arguments. The first can be termed the *main effects model* and suggests that gender tends to exert an effect on boys' and girls' levels of achievement, independent of either social class or ethnicity. For this model, it is accepted that there are differences between boys and girls as a whole, and that these are relatively stable across social class and ethnic groups. However, such differences are small and completely overshadowed by the effects of social class and also ethnicity (Demack *et al.*, 2000; Gillborn and Mirza, 2000). Thus, for Bangladeshi working-class boys, for example, their levels of educational attainment may be slightly affected by the fact that they are boys, but the real concerns relate to the adverse effects of social class and ethnicity. In relation to this type of 'additive effects' model, therefore, the concern is that efforts and resources are being targeted at the wrong problem. Interventions to help Bangladeshi working-class boys, for example, need to be targeted at addressing the 'real' problems – issues of racism and socio-economic disadvantage – rather than gender per se.

The second model – which can be termed the *interaction effects model* – goes a stage further than this simple 'additive' approach, to suggest that differences between boys and girls in relation to educational attainment are not actually stable but systematically vary across social class and ethnic groups. In this sense, it is argued that there is likely to be something about the particular combination of gender and class or gender and ethnicity that tends either to reduce, or exacerbate further, gender differences in educational performance. This notion of an interaction effect between social class and gender or between ethnicity and gender is certainly one that may have support from existing qualitative studies of education. In terms of boys and schooling, for example, a number of ethnographic studies have highlighted a diverse range of masculine identities adopted by boys (Connell, 1989; Connolly, 2004; Haywood and Mac an Ghaill, 1996; Mac an Ghaill, 1994; Skelton, 2001). Thus, while expressions of masculinity generally have the tendency to provide some limit on boys' achievement in schools, often through the construction of schoolwork as effeminate and 'uncool', particular constructions of masculinity tend to either exacerbate this further or work against it to a certain extent. In relation to the former, ever since the early studies of Hargreaves (1967), Lacey (1970) and especially Willis (1977), it has been shown that boys from the most marginalised backgrounds are more likely to develop anti-school subcultures that compensate for their relative lack of success in education by gaining status through constructing hyper-forms of masculinity (see also Corrigan, 1979). A similar process has also been found among African Caribbean boys (Mac an Ghaill, 1988;

Gillborn, 1990; Sewell, 1997). Such forms of masculinity therefore tend to exacerbate further the 'underachievement' of these boys.

At the other end of the spectrum is the construction of particular forms of masculinity among middle-class boys based around competitiveness and the displaying of academic ability (Aggleton, 1987; Mac an Ghaill, 1994; Connolly, 2004). For these boys, while being seen to work hard is frowned upon, being able to achieve academically is regarded as a marker of success. In this case, these particular forms of middle-class masculinity tend to dampen down the adverse effects of masculinity more generally. Interestingly, the much smaller number of studies of working-class girls (e.g. Lambart, 1976, 1997) and minority ethnic girls (e.g. Mirza, 1992; Shain, 2003) suggest that social class and ethnicity may not have such clear-cut effects on the responses of girls as they appear to do for boys. All of this certainly suggests that the effects of gender are mediated by social class and ethnicity, such that the nature and extent of gender differences in educational performance could quite possibly vary systematically across differing social groups.

Overall, very little work to date has attempted to clarify which of these two models applies to the issue of gender differences in educational achievement. The comments reported earlier from Epstein *et al.* (1998b: 11), that 'the "underachievement" of boys at school is a strongly classed and racialised phenomenon', can certainly be read using either model. In terms of the main effects model, for example, these comments could be read as implying simply that those boys who are 'underachieving' are doing so because of social class and ethnic factors rather than gender. However, this same statement can also be interpreted from the standpoint of the interaction effects model, in that the emphasis is not so much on 'underachievement' as such but the 'underachievement of boys', which, by default, implies a comparison with girls. In this sense, to say that the 'underachievement of boys' is 'classed and racialised' could be read as implying that the differences between boys and girls vary according to these factors, presumably such that there are little or no gender differences among some social class and/or ethnic groups and much larger and more significant differences among others.

Given the very different readings of gender differences in educational attainment that can arise from these two models, it is surprising that very little published work making use of large-scale, nationally representative data sets exists to date to test either of these. At the time of their review of research in this area, for example, Arnot *et al.* (1998: 69) concluded that, with the exception of Drew and Gray's (1990) study, 'it has not proved possible to identify a more contemporary source of data on young people which simultaneously combines information on social class, ethnicity and gender'. Since then, the only other comparable piece of work published has been that of Demack *et al.* (2000). In drawing upon data from various cohorts of the Youth Cohort Study of England and Wales, Demack *et al.* provide an important analysis of trends in relation to social class, ethnicity and gender between 1988 and 1995. They certainly provide evidence to substantiate some of the arguments associated with the main effects model referred to earlier, that both social class and ethnicity tend to have a much greater effect on differences in educational attainment than gender (see also Gillborn and Mirza, 2000). What is still lacking, however, is any published study aimed explicitly at examining the claims underpinning the second (interaction effects) model. This provides the focus for the current article. Through a secondary analysis of data from three successive cohorts of the Youth Cohort Study of England and Wales, the article will examine what evidence exists for both the main effects and interaction effects models.

METHODOLOGY

The Youth Cohort Study of England and Wales (YCS) is the only publicly available large-scale data set that includes information on the educational achievement of school leavers and their gender and social class and ethnic backgrounds. It is a longitudinal survey of successive cohorts of school leavers that tracks their educational and labour market progress from leaving school at 16 through to the age of 19. A random sample of young people who have reached minimum school leaving age is selected from across England and Wales and is first contacted by means of a postal questionnaire, followed up by telephone interviews, about six to nine months after leaving school. The participants are then contacted again on two further occasions, at twelve-month intervals.

This article is based upon an analysis of data gathered from three successive cohorts of the YCS relating to young people who left school in 1997, 1999 and 2001, respectively. The data gathered during the initial contact with each of these cohorts (Sweep 1) provide the basis for the analysis to follow. A relatively large number of young people returned questionnaires as part of this first sweep for all three cohorts (14,662, 13,698 and 16,707, respectively), reflecting final response rates of 65 per cent, 55 per cent and 56 per cent, respectively. While these are reasonable response rates for surveys of this type, the fact that between 35 and 45 per cent of respondents failed or refused to take part in the studies is likely to introduce an additional element of bias into the findings. In an attempt to correct for non-response bias, the final data sets for each cohort were subsequently weighted in relation to four key variables that are known to be related to non-response: gender, school type, region and GCSE attainment at Year 11. The summary characteristics of the three weighted samples are shown in Table 8.1. However, even with this attempt to correct for non-response bias, a degree of caution should be maintained when interpreting the findings.

As can be seen from Table 8.1, two different measures of social class have been used between these three cohorts, reflecting changes made recently to the YCS in terms of how this variable is coded. The shift from coding social class in terms of socio-economic groups (SEGs) to the use of the more recent National Statistics Socio-Economic Classification (NS-SEC) does make direct comparisons of the effects of social class between cohorts extremely difficult. However, as the intention of this article is more modest and simply focused on examining how gender differences may vary between social class groupings within any particular cohort, then this does not in itself present a problem. It should also be noted that, whichever classificatory scheme has been used over the years, they have all tended to identify the same major divisions (Roberts, 2001), a point that is borne out in relation to the analysis to follow.

In relation to the actual categories listed for both schemes, it has been decided to limit the analysis to follow to the first five categories in each case. The reason for this is that it is not possible to determine the characteristics of those within the remaining 'unclassed' and 'other' categories, and thus it cannot be assumed that they represent homogeneous or coherent groupings. Any findings produced for these categories would therefore be impossible to interpret. The key consequence of limiting the analysis in this way is simply that it is not possible to generalise beyond the five main social class categories used for the respective schemas. The findings reported below are therefore only generalisable to those young people who can be classified into one of the main categories.

As with social class, the YCS data sets only provide one measure of ethnicity that has been used to create the categories listed in Table 8.1. The categories correspond closely

■ **Table 8.1** Characteristics of the weighted samples of the first sweeps of Cohorts 9, 10 and 11 of the Youth Cohort Study of England and Wales[1]

	Cohort 9 (1997[2])		Cohort 10 (1999)		Cohort 11 (2001)	
	n	%	n	%	n	%
Gender						
Male	7,393	50.4	6,939	50.6	8,457	50.6
Female	7,269	49.6	6,760	49.4	8,250	49.4
Ethnicity						
White	12,894	87.9	11,768	85.9	14,621	87.5
Indian	437	3.0	360	2.6	455	2.7
Pakistani	312	2.1	342	2.5	345	2.1
Black	297	2.0	331	2.4	375	2.2
Bangladeshi	122	0.8	134	1.0	117	0.7
Chinese	74	0.5	78	0.6	91	0.5
Other	525	3.6	684	5.0	703	4.2
Social class						
Professional/managerial	3,049	20.8	2,700	20.3		
Other non-manual	2,830	19.3	2,545	18.6		
Skilled manual	4,698	32.0	4,603	33.6		
Semi-skilled manual	1,702	11.6	1,449	10.6		
Unskilled manual	610	4.2	597	4.4		
Unclassed	1,721	11.7	1,677	12.2		
Other	52	0.4	40	0.3		
Higher professional					2,514	15.0
Lower professional					4,156	24.9
Intermediate					3,375	20.2
Lower supervisory					1,802	10.8
Routine					2,233	13.4
Other					2,626	15.7
Total		4,662		13,698		16,707
Response rate	65%		55%		56%	

1 Figures may not sum precisely to the totals for each sample owing to rounding following the application of weights. Percentages may also not sum to 100% owing to rounding.

2 Year in which the young people in each cohort reached school-leaving age and completed their GCSEs.

to the ten-category classification used in the output for the 1991 Census. This was the first census that included a question on ethnicity, and the categories used had undergone significant testing beforehand. As Bulmer (2002) reports, the categories presented few problems and appeared to be clearly understood and commonly used by respondents. This is also reflected in the present three samples, where the non-response rate on this question was very small (under 2 per cent).

One problem with these categories, however, is the size of some of the subsamples. Even with large samples such as these, because they are random samples it is likely that they will result in relatively small subsamples for some of the ethnic categories. If left unaddressed, this would present a problem consequently when attempting to subdivide these groups further to examine the effects of gender and social class. With this in mind, and as can be seen, the three original categories of 'Black African', 'Black Caribbean' and 'Black other' have been conflated into one for the purposes of the present article. While this has been unavoidable, it does create the impression that this newly created group is relatively homogeneous and thus ignores the significant differences that have been shown to exist in terms of educational attainment between Black African and Black Caribbean young people (Gillborn and Gipps, 1996). This should be borne in mind, therefore, when considering the findings for this newly created 'Black' category. In addition, the original data sets included three further categories that were rather ambiguous ('Other', 'Other Asian' and 'Mixed ethnic origin') and unlikely to represent clear and coherent groups of respondents. These have been conflated into the one category 'Other' in Table 8.1. Because of this ambiguity, these categories will be omitted from the main analysis to follow, which will focus, instead, on the larger and more clearly defined ethnic groups.

In terms of GCSE attainment for each respondent, for consistency the measure that will be used will simply be whether an individual has gained five or more GCSE grades A*–C or not. This tends to be the key and most well-known measure of educational performance at this level and continues to provide the basis for comparisons of differences in terms of gender as well as ethnicity and social class. It also tends to be the main measure used in relation to school league tables and the identification of 'successful' and 'failing' [sic] schools. However, it should be noted that there are alternative measures that could have been used. One is simply an extension of the one used, but also incorporates equivalent vocational qualifications attained by respondents. Another is a respondent's GCSE score. This involves allocating a score to each GCSE grade obtained by a respondent (A* = 8, A = 7, B = 6, . . . F = 2, G = 1). Each individual respondent's scores are then summated to provide their own overall GCSE score. Thus a respondent who achieved five B grades would be given an overall score of 30 (i.e. 5×6). Similarly, someone who gained just two E grades and one G grade would achieve an overall score of 7 (i.e. $2 \times 3 + 1 \times 1$). The analysis below (or its equivalent) was run separately using these two additional measures. Interestingly, while minor discrepancies emerged, the key findings remained the same whatever the measure used.

FINDINGS

The main effects model

As regards the main effects model, Table 8.2 provides a breakdown of the proportions of boys and girls gaining five or more GCSE grades A*–C by social class and also ethnicity for the three successive cohorts. Simply in terms of these descriptive data, it can be seen

■ **Table 8.2** Proportions of boys and girls gaining five or more GCSE grades A*–C in England and Wales in 1997, 1999 and 2001[1]

	1997				1999				2001			
	% Total	% Boys	% Girls	Effect Size[2]	% Total	% Boys	% Girls	Effect Size	% Total	% Boys	% Girls	Effect Sizo[2]
Total	46.2	41.9	50.6	.087	48.6	43.8	53.5	.097	50.4	45.6	55.3	.097
Ethnicity												
Chinese	67.1	65.0	69.7	(.050)	74.4	69.6	81.3	(.132)	68.9	67.4	70.5	(.033)
Indian	53.3	51.9	54.8	(.029)	60.3	53.7	66.5	.130	59.2	50.9	67.5	.170
White	47.0	42.7	51.2	.085	49.8	45.1	54.6	.096	50.9	46.1	55.8	.097
Bangladeshi	32.8	23.9	43.6	.209	28.9	15.8	45.8	.328	39.8	33.9	46.4	(.128)
Pakistani	28.8	29.9	27.5	(.026)	28.7	24.5	32.2	(.085)	38.2	34.1	42.7	(.089)
Black	28.7	22.7	35.2	.138	38.4	30.4	45.9	.159	35.7	31.5	39.7	(.085)
Social Class												
Professional/managerial	69.5	65.2	73.9	.094	69.2	64.2	74.6	.113				
Other non-manual	59.8	54.0	66.0	.122	59.7	55.3	64.5	.093				
Skilled manual	40.0	35.6	44.2	.087	45.1	38.7	51.5	.129				
Semi-skilled manual	31.8	26.9	36.6	.104	35.3	31.3	39.2	.083				
Unskilled manual	20.3	17.5	23.2	(.071)	30.3	27.4	32.6	(.056)				
Higher professional									76.8	71.7	82.4	.126
Lower professional									64.0	58.3	69.6	.117
Intermediate									51.2	46.4	55.8	.094
Lower supervisory									34.0	29.3	39.4	.107
Routine									30.7	25.2	36.1	.118

1 Source of data: secondary analysis of data derived from first sweeps of Cohorts 9, 10 and 11 of the Youth Cohort Study of England and Wales.

2 Phi: effect sizes found not to be statistically significant (i.e. $p > .05$) are in parentheses.

that social class and ethnicity appear to exert a greater influence on educational attainment than gender. Just taking the most recent cohort, for example, it can be seen that 45.6 per cent of boys as a whole gained five or more higher-grade passes, compared with 55.3 per cent of girls. In contrast, in relation to social class, 76.8 per cent of those from higher professional backgrounds gained the same, compared with just 30.7 per cent of those from routine occupational backgrounds. Similarly, in terms of ethnicity, 68.9 per cent of Chinese respondents gained five or more GCSE grades A*–C, compared with just 35.7 per cent of Black respondents. It would seem, therefore, that membership of particular social class and ethnic groups has a much greater effect on a respondent's chances of having gained the required five or more GCSE passes than their gender. Moreover, such figures also highlight the dangers of making simplistic comparisons between all boys and all girls. In terms of social class, for example, 71.7 per cent of boys from higher professional backgrounds gained five or more GCSE grades A*–C, compared with just 36.1 per cent of girls from routine occupational backgrounds. Similar comparisons can be made in relation to ethnicity and certainly undermine the popular and universal constructions of 'failing boys' and 'succeeding girls'.

More formally, the relative effects of ethnicity, social class and gender can be measured through the use of a method known as logistic regression.[1] The results of such an analysis performed on all three cohort samples, with whether a respondent has gained five or more GCSE grades A*–C as the dependent variable and with social class, ethnicity and gender all entered as independent categorical variables, are provided in Table 8.3. What

■ **Table 8.3** Relative odds[1] of different categories of pupil gaining five or more GCSE grades A*–C in England and Wales in 1997, 1999 and 2001[2]

	1997	1999	2001
Gender			
Girls	1.499	1.586	1.622
Boys	1.000	1.000	1.000
Ethnicity			
Chinese	7.406	4.090	7.022
Indian	2.903	2.637	3.205
White	1.902	1.397	1.646
Bangladeshi	2.151	(.889)	2.500
Pakistani	1.701	(.750)	1.690
Black	1.000	1.000	1.000
Social class			
Professional/managerial	8.954	5.613	
Other non-manual	5.886	3.679	
Skilled manual	2.540	1.997	
Semi-skilled manual	1.779	1.347	
Unskilled manual	1.000	1.000	
Higher professional			8.064
Lower professional			4.260
Intermediate			2.396
Lower supervisory			1.230
Routine			1.000
% variance explained[3]	10.3%	7.9%	11.9%

1 Calculated by means of a binary logistic regression. Relative odds found not to be statistically significant (i.e. $p > .05$) are in parentheses. See Appendix for full details of regression models.

2 Source of data: secondary analysis of data derived from first sweeps of Cohorts 9, 10 and 11 of the Youth Cohort Study of England and Wales.

3 Cox and Snell, *R square*.

have been included here are simply the relative odds of different categories of pupil gaining five or more GCSE grades A*–C compared with the reference category for that variable (the category with the odds of 1,000). Again, if one takes the most recent cohort (i.e. those leaving school in 2001) as an example, then it can be seen that girls are 1.622 times more likely to gain five or more GCSE grades A*–C than boys. Similarly, in terms of social class, those from routine occupational backgrounds provide the reference category this time. In this case, respondents from higher professional backgrounds are actually just over eight times (8.064) more likely to gain five or more higher-grade GCSE passes than those from routine occupational backgrounds, those from lower professional backgrounds a little over four times more likely (4.260), and so on. Finally, in terms of ethnicity, it can be seen, for example, that Chinese respondents were found to be about seven times (7.022) more likely to gain five or more GCSE passes than Black respondents (the reference category in this case).

The important point to note about these figures is that they represent the effects of one variable (i.e. gender or social class or ethnicity) *once the other two variables are controlled for*. Thus, for example, once we control for gender and social class, White school leavers in 2001 were still over one and a half times as likely (1.646) to gain five or more GCSE grades A*–C than Black school leavers. Overall, by comparing these relative odds, it can be confirmed that social class and ethnicity do have a much greater impact upon the likely odds of a respondent gaining five or more GCSE passes than gender. This, therefore, certainly provides initial support for arguments associated with the main effects model, in that social class and ethnicity do exert independent effects on educational attainment, and both of these tend to overshadow the relatively minor effect exerted by gender. It will be remembered, however, that this model does not take into account interaction effects. In other words, it is assumed that the small gender differences that exist remain relatively constant across social class and ethnic groups. Before this main effects model can be fully accepted, it is therefore important to assess first whether any significant interaction effects exist.

Before moving on to a consideration of the interaction effects model, two additional points are worth noting briefly about the findings in Table 8.3. The first is that the amount of variation in GCSE attainment that these three variables taken together can explain is relatively small. Put another way, the combined effects of gender, ethnicity and social class can only account for about 10 per cent of the variation in GCSE attainment (i.e. between 7.9 per cent and 11.9 per cent, depending upon the cohort). This actually tends to be consistent with the findings of other studies (see Drew and Gray, 1990). This finding does need to be treated with a degree of caution, however. It may well be that this is somewhat of an underestimate, given that the categories used for social class and ethnicity are rather crude and gloss over important variations within each of them. It may well be that, if better and more finely tuned measures of social class and ethnicity could be developed, then they would be likely to account for more of the variation in GCSE attainment. Either way, the proportion of variation in GCSE attainment explained by these three factors does remain relatively low. This in turn suggests that we need to be careful not to be encouraged by the specific focus of this article – limited as it is to a consideration of gender, social class and ethnicity – to assume that these three variables are the most influential factors associated with educational attainment. This will be a point returned to in the concluding section of this article.

The second point to note from the findings in Table 8.3 is the apparent fluctuation in the effects of social class and ethnicity across the three cohorts. As can be seen, social class and ethnicity appear to exert less of an influence on the relative odds of pupils' achieving five or more GCSE higher-grade passes in 1999, compared with 1997 and 2001. There is, however, no simple explanation for this other than random variation in the samples selected for the three cohorts. It is not caused, for example, by the application of respective weightings to the three cohorts. Such a pattern in the data was still evident, even when the analysis was run again without applying such weights. It is also not likely to be a pattern reflecting a broader underlying trend (i.e. the possible decrease in influence of social class and ethnicity on GCSE attainment), as the figures for 2001 have increased again to levels not that dissimilar to those of 1997. In the absence of any further plausible reason, it is therefore likely that the fluctuation in the relative odds across the three cohorts is due simply to random variation in the three samples selected. This in turn reinforces the need to be careful in drawing too many inferences from just one cohort, but rather to focus on patterns evident across a number of cohorts, as done here.

The interaction effects model

A visual inspection of Table 8.2 certainly does not seem to indicate any systematic variation in gender differences across social class categories or ethnic categories for the three respective cohorts. This can be most clearly noted by examining the effect sizes (Phi) for gender within each social class and ethnic category. Phi provides a standardised measure of the size of the effect for gender and can vary between 0 and 1, with values closer to 0 indicating a very small gender effect, and those reaching 1 a very large gender effect. As can be seen, when looking down the effect size columns for the three respective cohorts, there would appear to be little discernible pattern. Given the interaction effects model and the findings of qualitative research in this area to date, one would expect to find the effect size (i.e. the size of the gender differences) to increase as one moved down the social class categories and/or as one examined those ethnic groups with lower overall attainment levels. However, and as can be seen, the variation that does exist seems to be simply random in nature.

The actual existence of any interaction effect can be formally tested using a technique known as log-linear analysis. In this instance, log-linear analysis has been used to estimate what the data should look like if there were no interactions, either between gender and social class, or between gender and ethnicity, in relation to their effects on GCSE attainment for each of the three cohorts. These estimates are then compared with the actual data in each case. The results of such analyses are provided in Table 8.4. For those unfamiliar with log-linear analysis, an explanation of the method and of the findings contained in Table 8.4 is provided at the end of this paper.[2] The key point to note from the results presented in Table 8.4 is that, with just one exception, no statistically significant differences were found between estimates of the data based upon a main effects model and the actual data. In other words, the evidence suggests that the main effects model fits the data sufficiently well and thus confirms formally what was noted from the visual inspection of Table 8.2 discussed earlier, that there is no evidence of any systematic interaction effects between gender and social class or between gender and ethnicity in relation to their impact on educational attainment.

The one exception, as can be noted from Table 8.4, relates to the cohort of young people who left school in 1999, where the main effects model for gender and ethnicity produced an estimate of the data that is significantly different from the actual data ($p = 0.024$). Referring back to Table 8.2, it can be seen that this is most likely to be

■ **Table 8.4** Log-linear analyses examining the interaction effects of gender, ethnicity and social class on whether school leavers in England and Wales gained five or more GCSE grades A*–C In 1997, 1999 and 2001[1]

Year	Hierarchical model[2]	Likelihood ratio chi-square	df	Sig
1997	GE*SC, GE*EX, SC*EX	2.348	4	0.672
	GE*ET, GE*EX, EX*ET	11.850	10	0.295
1999	GE*SC, GE*EX, SC*EX	4.575	4	0.334
	GE*ET, GE*EX, EX*ET	20.641	10	0.024
2001	GE*SC, GE*EX, SC*EX	4.295	4	0.368
	GE*ET, GE*EX, EX*ET	5.500	10	0.855

1 Source of data: secondary analysis of data derived from first sweeps of Cohorts 9, 10 and 11 of the Youth Cohort Study of England and Wales.

2 GE = gender; SC = social class, ET = ethnicity, EX = GCSE attainment.

explained by the relatively higher effect size for Bangladeshi school leavers compared with the other groups ($Phi = 0.328$). Two points are worth noting from this, however. First, and just in relation to this particular cohort, the existence of an interaction effect here does not provide adequate support for the type of interaction effects model proposed earlier. While the size of the gender differences for this particular 'lower-achieving' group does appear to be significantly larger, this is not then replicated for the other groups that are achieving similar levels of educational attainment (i.e. Pakistani and Black school leavers). Moreover, the size of the gender differences does not seem to be any smaller among the higher-achieving groups, such as the Chinese and Indians. Indeed, with the exception of Bangladeshi school leavers, there seems to be no pattern whatsoever.

Second, these figures for Bangladeshi school leavers are not replicated for the other two cohorts. The most likely explanation, therefore, for the larger effect size for gender for this particular group of school leavers is simply the fact that the cohorts were selected randomly. In this sense, and when dealing with relatively small subsamples like this, there are likely to be some fluctuations year on year in terms of the findings from the data, representing the randomly selected nature of the sample itself. It is with this in mind that a degree of caution should be used, more generally, in attempting to identify specific trends in achievement levels for particular ethnic groups across these three years.

CONCLUSIONS

At one level, the findings presented above tend simply to confirm what many within the field of gender and education have been arguing for some time now. While gender does tend to exert an influence on GCSE attainment, such that boys in general tend to achieve less than girls, these differences are relatively small and tend to be overshadowed by the effects of social class and ethnicity. While girls have been about one and a half times more likely to gain five or more GCSE grades A*–C than boys, those from the highest social class backgrounds have been between five and nine times more likely than those from the lowest social class backgrounds. Similarly, those from the top-achieving ethnic group (Chinese) have been between four and seven times more likely to achieve at least five higher-grade GCSE passes than those in the lowest achieving group (Black). Moreover, these overarching effects of social class and ethnicity successfully undermine the simplistic and universal constructions of 'failing boys' versus 'achieving girls'. As has been seen, for example, boys from the highest social class backgrounds have been between two and three times more likely to achieve five or more GCSE grades A*–C than girls from the lowest social class backgrounds.

Where this article has contributed to existing work is in relation to offering a clearer understanding of the precise nature of the relationships between social class, ethnicity and gender, and their impact upon educational attainment. As has been shown, while a number of qualitative studies would seem to suggest that the relative size of the differences between boys and girls is likely to be bigger among those groups (whether defined by social class or ethnicity) that experience the lowest levels of achievement generally, this has not been found to be the case in practice. What the evidence suggests from three consecutive cohorts of the Youth Cohort Study, therefore, is that, while gender differences remain relatively small compared with ethnic and social class differences, they do appear to be relatively stable and constant across all social class and ethnic groups. In other words, the effects of gender appear to be independent of those of social class and ethnicity, thus providing support for the simpler main effects model.

Finally, it is important to note that, simply because the overall effects of gender remain relatively constant across social class and ethnic groups (subject simply to random variation), this does not mean that the actual manifestations and practices of gender (i.e. the ways in which young people construct and reproduce dominant forms of masculinity and femininity) are also constant. Clearly, the wealth of qualitative, ethnographic studies of boys and girls in schools has amply demonstrated that a wide and complex array of differing forms of masculinities and femininities exist. However, and this is the key point, such forms of masculinity and femininity are never just about gender, but are clearly also a reflection of the many differing ways in which gender combines with social class and ethnicity to produce differing and enduring forms of identity.

The key implication arising from this, therefore, is that, simply because it is possible statistically to separate out the effects of gender from social class and also ethnicity, this does not mean that gender differences can actually be addressed practically in isolation from social class and ethnicity. Given the ways in which gender identities are so intertwined with, and mediated by, social class and ethnicity, then there can be no singular programme of intervention that will be appropriate and applicable to all boys or all girls.

With these points in mind, there are three key messages to emerge from the findings of this present article for educational practice. First, the underachievement of boys relative to girls is not just an issue for working-class boys or boys from particular minority ethnic groups. As has been shown, on average boys tend to perform less well than girls, and to a similar extent across all social class and ethnic groups. Second, while it is therefore necessary to address the general problem of boys' underachievement across all these levels, it needs to be accepted that there are no quick-fix or universal solutions. As shown above, different boys (and girls) have very different experiences of education, dependent upon their social class and ethnic backgrounds. In fact, and as seen, for boys and girls gender only plays a relatively minor role in dictating their levels of achievement compared with social class and ethnicity. It is with this in mind that diverse strategies and interventions are required that are based upon the particular needs and experiences of specific groups of boys and girls in particular contexts. Moreover, such strategies need to focus as much (if not more) on factors such as social class and ethnicity as on gender.

Third, and in relation to the last point, it is important that we resist the temptation simply to replace one set of crude generalisations (i.e. concerning all boys or all girls) with another (i.e. concerning all working-class boys or Pakistani girls and so on). The fact that the combined effects of gender, social class and ethnicity were only found to account for about 10 per cent of the variation in GCSE attainment means that we need to be extremely wary of continuing to work with general categories. Whatever specific group we identify, there will remain considerable variation within it (see Connolly, 2006). A danger remains, therefore, in an approach that attempts to construct educational programmes, even for particular groups of pupils such as White working-class boys, in the belief that schools across the country can then simply use these directly with their own pupils. Rather, there is a need for educational interventions that are tailored much more directly to the particular needs and concerns of pupils in specific classes and schools.

APPENDIX: DETAILS OF BINARY LOGISTIC REGRESSION MODELS DERIVED FROM THE THREE COHORTS (SEE TABLE 8.3)

■ **Table 8.5** Binary logistic regression on whether school leavers in England and Wales in 1997 gained five or more GCSE grades A*–C or not[1]

	B	S.E.	Wald	df	Sig.	Exp(B)
Gender[2]						
Girls	0.405	0.038	114.340	1	<.001	1.499
Ethnicity[3]						
Chinese	2.002	0.341	34.436	1	<0.001	7.406
Indian	1.066	0.193	30.389	1	<0.001	2.903
White	0.643	0.159	16.372	1	<0.001	1.902
Bangladeshi	0.766	0.332	5.330	1	0.021	2.151
Pakistani	0.531	0.230	5.338	1	0.021	1.701
Social class[4]						
Professional/managerial	2.192	0.110	306.863	1	<0.001	8.954
Other non-manual	1.773	0.110	261.000	1	<0.001	5.886
Skilled manual	0.932	0.107	76.255	1	<0.001	2.540
Semi-skilled manual	0.576	0.115	24.965	1	<0.001	1.779
Constant	−2.208	0.189	136.885	1	<0.001	0.110

1 Source of data: secondary analysis of data derived from the first sweep of Cohort 9 of the Youth Cohort Study of England and Wales (NCSR (1999)).

2 Reference category: boys.

3 Reference category: Black pupils.

4 Reference category: unskilled manual occupations.

Table 8.6 Binary logistic regression on whether school leavers in England and Wales in 1999 gained five or more GCSE grades A*–C or not[1]

	B	S.E.	Wald	df	Sig.	Exp(B)
Gender[2]						
Girls	0.461	0.039	140.547	1	<0.001	1.586
Ethnicity[3]						
Chinese	1.408	0.305	21.360	1	<0.001	4.090
Indian	0.970	0.184	27.896	1	<0.001	2.637
White	0.335	0.138	5.902	1	0.015	1.397
Bangladeshi	−0.118	0.291	0.164	1	0.685	0.889
Pakistani	−0.287	0.199	2.077	1	<0.150	0.750
Social Class[4]						
Professional/managerial	1.725	0.101	292.435	1	<0.001	5.613
Other non-manual	1.303	0.101	167.551	1	<0.001	3.679
Skilled manual	0.691	0.096	51.497	1	<0.001	1.997
Semi-skilled manual	0.298	0.107	7.685	1	0.006	1.347
Constant	−1.456	0.166	76.611	1	<0.001	0.233

1 Source of data: secondary analysis of data derived from first sweep of Cohort 10 of the Youth Cohort Study of England and Wales.

2 Reference category: boys.

3 Reference category: Black pupils.

4 Reference category: unskilled manual occupations.

Table 8.7 Binary logistic regression on whether school leavers in England and Wales in 2001 gained five or more GCSE grades A*–C or not[1]

	B	S.E.	Wald	df	Sig.	Exp(B)
Gender[2]						
Girls	0.484	0.037	172.148	1	<0.001	1.622
Ethnicity[3]						
Chinese	1.949	0.353	30.439	1	<0.001	7.022
Indian	1.165	0.183	40.297	1	<0.001	3.205
White	0.498	0.142	12.221	1	<0.001	1.646
Bangladeshi	0.916	0.321	8.131	1	0.004	2.500
Pakistani	0.525	0.207	6.398	1	0.011	1.690

■ **Table 8.7** *continued*

	B	S.E.	Wald	df	Sig.	Exp(B)
Social class[4]						
Higher professional	2.087	0.068	931.187	1	<0.001	8.064
Lower professional	1.449	0.058	621.147	1	<0.001	4.260
Intermediate	0.874	0.059	219.008	1	<0.001	2.396
Lower supervisory	0.207	0.070	8.836	1	0.003	1.230
Constant	−1.608	0.149	116.356	1	<0.001	0.200

1 Source of data: secondary analysis of data derived from first sweep of Cohort 9 of the Youth Cohort Study of England and Wales.

2 Reference category: boys.

3 Reference category: Black pupils.

4 Reference category: semi-routine and routine occupations.

NOTES

1 Logistic regression attempts to predict the outcome of a simple binary variable (in this case, whether a pupil has achieved five or more GCSE higher-grade passes or not), using one or more predictor variables (in this case gender, ethnicity and social class). The statistical models that are produced can depend upon the variable selection methods used. The models detailed in Table 8.3 have all been produced using the 'forced entry' method, whereby all three predictor variables were entered into the model in one block, and parameter estimates were calculated accordingly. There are two reasons for using this method. First, the reason for producing these models is to allow comparison of the relative effects of the three predictor variables on GCSE attainment. It is therefore necessary to include all three variables to allow such comparisons to be made. Second, and more substantively, there are significant problems associated with the other selection methods available. These methods, collectively known as 'stepwise methods', set and use statistical criteria for the decision to add or remove predictor variables from the model. The problem with this approach is precisely that it bases decisions as to what variables are important on statistical rather than theoretical criteria. This, in turn, makes the nature of any resultant model especially vulnerable to random variations in the data. Further details on logistic regression and the problems of using stepwise methods for variable selection can be found in Cramer (2003), Field (2005) and Miles and Shevlin (2001).

2 Log-linear analysis is a technique that has been specifically developed for analysing tabular data. Consider, for example, a frequency table consisting of three variables: gender (GE), social class (SC) and GCSE attainment (EX). Gender obviously consists of just two categories (male and female), as does GCSE attainment (whether that person has achieved five or more GCSE higher-grade passes or not), and social class consists of five categories (see Table 8.2 for the five categories). The actual frequency table therefore will consist of 20 cells ($2 \times 2 \times 5$), with the numbers of respondents listed in each cell (i.e. how many respondents, for example, were female, Indian and did not achieve five GCSE higher-grade passes).

    1 The purpose of log-linear analysis is to determine what factors can explain the variation in the data in that table. It could be, for example, that the data in the table

can be explained simply by the independent effects of the three variables, with no interactions between them. Such a model would be depicted as: GE, SC, EX. As there is no interaction between the three variables, then the key conclusion to be drawn from such a model is that neither gender nor social class interacts with GCSE attainment. In other words, GCSE attainment remains constant across gender and social class categories. If such a model fitted our data well, we would conclude from this that there were no gender or social class differences in GCSE attainment.

2   More complex models than this can obviously be developed. For example, an interaction between social class and GCSE attainment could be added, such that the model now becomes: SC*EX, GE. It should be noted that this model is depicted as what is called a 'hierarchical model', and so it is taken that the interaction 'SC*EX' also includes within it the independent effects of 'SC' and 'EX', and so these do not need to be listed separately. For this model, if it fitted our data well, we would conclude that there are social class differences in educational attainment (as there is an interaction between the two), but that there are no gender differences in GCSE attainment (as there is no interaction between gender and GCSE attainment).

3   One could go further to include all two-way interactions and thus produce the following model: GE*SC, GE*EX, SC*EX. As we are interested in GCSE attainment, then our main concern is with what variables interact with GCSE attainment. In this case, the model would be interpreted as suggesting that gender and social class are independently associated with GCSE attainment. This is precisely the model that is included in Table 8.4 for each of the three successive cohorts (1997, 1999 and 2001). In addition, precisely the same analysis can also be conducted but with ethnicity (ET) rather than social class (SC), thus producing the parallel model: GE*ET, GE*EX, ET*EX, which is incidentally the other model listed in Table 8.4.

4   The only model that is more complex than these is the three-way interaction model depicted as: GE*SC*EX, in the case of gender and social class, or: GE*ET*EX, in the case of gender and ethnicity. Again, because this is a hierarchical model, then all lower-level interactions are contained within this (i.e. all possible two-way interactions and all independent effects involving the three variables). In this case, not only are both gender and social class related to GCSE attainment (in relation to the first model), but gender and social class also interact together in relation to their effects on GCSE attainment. This represents the interaction effects model that provides the focus for this article. Thus, in this case, gender differences in GCSE attainment do not remain constant but systematically vary across social class groups (or, equally, social class differences in GCSE attainment vary across gender categories).

5   For any specified model, log-linear analysis can take the existing data and estimate what it should look like for that model. Through a rather complex iterative mathematical procedure, it basically creates another frequency table that estimates what the numbers of respondents should be in each cell for that specified model. These estimates can then be compared with the original frequency table, based upon the actual data, to assess whether that model adequately fits the data or not. Formally, the comparison can be tested using a chi-square test, and the results of such tests are reported in Table 8.4 for each of the six models listed.

6   What the results from these tests tell us is that, with just one exception, there are no statistically significant differences between the models listed and the actual data. In other words, these models tend to describe the data well. As these are all models based upon two-way interactions, then we can conclude from this that the data can be adequately explained by the simple and independent effects of gender and

social class on GCSE attainment (as with model: GE*SC, GE*EX, SC*EX) or the independent effects of gender and ethnicity on GCSE attainment (as with model: GE*ET, GE*EX, ET*EX). In other words, this confirms that there is no significant three-way interaction effect, either between gender and social class on GCSE attainment, or gender and ethnicity on GCSE attainment.

7   For clear and accessible introductions to log-linear analysis, see Cramer (2003), Field (2005) and Miller *et al.* (2002).

REFERENCES

Aggleton, P. (1987) *Rebels without a cause: middle class youth and the transition from school to work*, Lewes: Falmer Press.

Arnot, M., Gray, J., James, M., Ruddock, J. and Duveen, G. (1998) *Recent research on gender and educational performance*, London: Office for Standards in Education. http://qb.soc.surrey.ac.uk/topics/ethnicity/ethnic_census.htm.

Connell, R.W. (1989) 'Cool guys, swots and wimps: the interplay of masculinity and education', *Oxford Review of Education*, Vol. 15: 291–303.

Connolly, P. (2004) *Boys and schooling in the early years*, London: RoutledgeFalmer.

Connolly, P. (2006) 'Summary statistics, educational achievement gaps and the ecological fallacy', *Oxford Review of Education*, Vol. 32, No. 2: 235–252.

Corrigan, P. (1979) *Schooling the Smash Street Kids*, London: Macmillan.

Cramer, D. (2003) *Advanced quantitative data analysis*, Maidenhead: Open University Press.

Demack, S., Drew, D. and Grimsley, M. (2000) 'Minding the gap: ethnic, gender and social class differences in attainment at 16, 1988–95', *Race Ethnicity and Education* Vol. 3: 117–143.

Drew, D. and Gray, J. (1990) 'The fifth year examination achievements of black young people in England and Wales', *Educational Research*, Vol. 32: 107–117.

Epstein, D., Elwood, J., Hey, V. and Maw, J. (1998a) *Failing boys? Issues in gender and achievement*, Buckingham: Open University Press.

Epstein, D., Elwood, J., Hey, V. and Maw, J. (1998b) 'Schoolboy frictions: feminism and "failing" boys', in Epstein, D., Elwood, J., Hey, V. and Maw, J. (eds) *Failing boys? Issues in gender and achievement*, Buckingham: Open University Press

Field, A. (2005) *Discovering statistics using SPSS* (2nd edition), London: Sage.

Francis, B. (2000) *Boys, girls and achievement: addressing the classroom issues*, London: RoutledgeFalmer.

Gillborn, D. (1990) *'Race', ethnicity and education*, London: Unwin Hyman.

Gillborn, D. and Gipps, C. (1996) *Recent research on the achievements of ethnic minority pupils*, London: Office for Standards in Education.

Gillborn, D. and Mirza, H. (2000) *Educational inequality – mapping race, class and gender: a synthesis of research evidence*, London: Office for Standards in Education.

Hargreaves, D.H. (1967) *Social relations in a secondary school*, London: Routledge & Kegan Paul.

Haywood, C. and Mac an Ghaill, M. (1996) 'Schooling masculinities', in Mac an Ghaill, M. (ed.) *Understanding masculinities*, Buckingham: Open University Press.

Jackson, D. (1998) 'Breaking out of the binary trap: boys' underachievement, schooling and gender relations', in Epstein, D., Elwood, J., Hey, V. and Maw, J. (eds) *Failing boys? Issues in gender and achievement*, Buckingham: Open University Press.

Lacey, C. (1970) *Hightown Grammar*, Manchester: Manchester University Press.

Lambart, A. (1976) 'The sisterhood', in Hammersley, M. and Woods, P. (eds) *The process of schooling*, London: Routledge & Kegan Paul.

Lambart, A. (1997) 'Mereside: a grammar school for girls in the 1960s', *Gender and Education*, Vol. 6: 441–456.

Lucey, H. and Walkerdine, V. (2000) 'Boys' underachievement: social class and changing masculinities', in Cox, T. (ed.) *Combating educational disadvantage: meeting the needs of vulnerable children*, London: Falmer Press.

Mac an Ghaill, M. (1988) *Young, gifted and black*, Milton Keynes: Open University Press.

Mac an Ghaill, M. (1994) *The making of men: masculinities, sexualities and schooling*, Buckingham: Open University Press.

Mac an Ghaill, M. (1996) '"What about the boys?" schooling, class and crisis masculinity', *Sociological Review*, Vol. 44: 381–397.

Miles, J. and Shevlin, M. (2001) *Applying regression and correlation*, London: Sage.

Miller, R., Acton, C., Fullerton, D. and Maltby, J. (2002) *SPSS for social scientists*, Basingstoke: Palgrave Macmillan.

Mirza, H.S. (1992) *Young, female and black*, London: Routledge.

National Centre for Social Research (NCSR) (1999) *Youth Cohort Study: Cohort 9 Sweep 1*. Technical Report, London: NCSR.

Reed, L. Raphael (1999) 'Troubling boys and disturbing discourses on masculinity and schooling: a feminist exploration of current debates and interventions concerning boys in school', *Gender and Education*, Vol. 11: 93–110.

Roberts, K. (2001) *Class in modern Britain*, London: Palgrave.

Sewell, T. (1997) *Black masculinities and schooling: how black boys survive modern schooling*, Stoke-on-Trent: Trentham Books.

Shain, F. (2003) *The schooling and identity of Asian girls*, Stoke-on-Trent: Trentham Books.

Skelton, C. (2001) *Schooling the boys: masculinities and primary education*, Buckingham: Open University Press.

Willis, P. (1977) *Learning to labour: how working class kids get working class jobs*, Farnborough: Saxon House.

EDUCATIONAL PSYCHOLOGY AND THE EFFECTIVENESS OF INCLUSIVE EDUCATION/ MAINSTREAMING

Geoff Lindsay

A NOTE FROM THE EDITORS

This reading critically reviews the evidence for the benefits of inclusion of pupils with a wide range of special educational needs and disabilities in mainstream classrooms to the pupils and raises issues that seem to be neglected in the existing research.

This reading links with Unit 4.6 of the 5th edition of *Learning to teach in the secondary school*.

QUESTIONS TO CONSIDER

1   Is a change of name from 'integration' to 'inclusion' relating to the placement of pupils with SEN in mainstream schools and classrooms just a synonymic change, or does it represent a change in attitude of educators towards such pupils?
2   Do the rights of pupils to be educated alongside their peers in mainstream classrooms override the need for the education system to provide appropriate and effective support to meet their special needs, wherever or however it is provided?
3   How is the effectiveness of SEN education measured? What counts as good progress, in contrast to just some progress? What methods are available to study the effects of interventions?

This reading was first published as: Lindsay, G. (2007) 'Educational psychology and the effectiveness of inclusive education/mainstreaming', *British Journal of Educational Psychology*, Vol. 77: 1–24.

ABSTRACT

Background: Inclusive education/mainstreaming is a key policy objective for the education of children and young people with special educational needs (SEN) and disabilities.

Aims: This paper reviews the literature on the effectiveness of inclusive education/ mainstreaming. The focus is on evidence for effects in terms of child outcomes with examination also of evidence on processes that support effectiveness.

Samples: The review covers a range of SEN and children from pre-school to the end of compulsory education.

Method: Following an historical review of evidence on inclusive education/main-streaming, the core of the paper is a detailed examination of all the papers published in eight journals from the field of special education published 2001–2005 (N 1/4 1373): *Journal of Special Education, Exceptional Children, Learning Disabilities Research and Practice, Journal of Learning Disabilities, Remedial and Special Education, British Journal of Special Education, European Journal of Special Needs Education*, and the *International Journal of Inclusive Education*. The derived categories were: comparative studies of outcomes: other outcome studies; non-comparative qualitative studies including non-experimental case studies; teacher practice and development; teacher attitudes; and the use of teaching assistants.

Results: Only 14 papers (1.0%) were identified as comparative outcome studies of children with some form of SEN. Measures used varied but included social as well as educational outcomes. Other papers included qualitative studies of inclusive practice, some of which used a non-comparative case study design while others were based on respondent's judgements, or explored process factors including teacher attitudes and the use of teaching assistants.

Conclusions: Inclusive education/mainstreaming has been promoted on two bases: the rights of children to be included in mainstream education and the proposition that inclusive education is more effective. This review focuses on the latter issue.

The evidence from this review does not provide a clear endorsement for the positive effects of inclusion. There is a lack of evidence from appropriate studies and, where evidence does exist, the balance was only marginally positive. It is argued that the policy has been driven by a concern for children's rights. The important task now is to research more thoroughly the mediators and moderators that support the optimal education for children with SEN and disabilities and, as a consequence, develop an evidence-based approach to these children's education.

BACKGROUND

Inclusive education/mainstreaming is a key policy in a number of countries, including the UK and US. In the UK, the New Labour government addressed the issue through its Green Paper (Department for Education and Employment, 1997) within months of taking office. Policy developments have taken place, with inclusion at their centre, in England and Wales and within the separate legislative framework for Scotland (Department for Education and Skills (DfES) 2001a, 2001b; Special Education Needs and Disability Act

2001; Standards in Scotland's Schools Act 2000) and in the US (The Education for All Handicapped Pupils Act (PL-94–142) and Individuals with Disabilities Education Act (PL 99–457)). A major driver has been concern that children's rights are compromised by special education, segregated from typically developing peers and the mainstream curriculum and educational practices. This position concerning rights and the values that underlie them is important but primarily sets out what proponents believe should be the case. A separate issue concerns the relative effectiveness of different educational approaches. This rests on empirical evidence rather than values and ideologies, although it is acknowledged that these issues interact. It is not argued that educational psychology is 'value free', but rather that it is important to separate discussion of rights and values from that of effectiveness.

Given the very clear international policy imperative, it is reasonable to ask: to what extent is the development of inclusive education evidence-based? Educational psychology can contribute to the conceptualization of the nature, appropriateness and effectiveness of education for children with disabilities and special educational needs (SEN). The present paper focuses on the latter and the role of educational psychology in providing evidence regarding educational practice, with particular reference to inclusive education/mainstreaming.

It is important to recognize that research evidence is only one factor in policy formulation. Politics is also about values and ideology, and indeed about expediency and the art of the possible. Values provide a second pillar, along with research evidence, that might reasonably be considered to support policies concerning the education of children and young people with disabilities and SEN. Hence, both evidence for differential effectiveness of processes and outcomes, and compliance with the values and aspirations of society are factors in policy development, including the determination of children's rights (Lindsay, 2003).

Evidence from many writers in favour of inclusion, however, suggests their interest is only in terms of the rights position and that research evidence is considered, at best, not central to such considerations or even irrelevant (Booth, 1996; Rustemier, 2002). Research evidence to the contrary, perhaps showing negative effects of inclusion, may be rejected, not as a scientific argument, but because such evidence cannot be used as the basis for what ought to be. Poor outcomes may be found but, it is argued, these should drive us to greater efforts to discover how to implement a policy seen as inherently correct. For a trenchant criticism of ideologically driven positions see Kavale and Mostert (2003). The focus of this paper is not policy analysis, rather an examination of the evidence for the effectiveness of inclusive education. However, the tensions between rights- and evidence-based policies will be considered.

METHODOLOGICAL ISSUES

The evaluation of the effectiveness of inclusion presents the researcher with substantial challenges. It is comparable in scale and potential impact with the very large educational interventions noted by Pressley *et al.* (2006), which comprise thousands of smaller interventions many of which are prerequisite to later interventions. This is a rational approach to major educational interventions. However, this magnitude of scale is associated with diversity of approach, and so examination of studies of the effectiveness of inclusive education requires consideration of a number of methodological issues, including terminology, the nature of interventions and research methods.

Terminology

The variation in terminology across time and countries poses a challenge for exploring comparability of studies, whereas, from a medical perspective, the ICD-10 and DSM-IV classificatory systems provide standardized diagnostic criteria, which reduce variation. In this paper, UK terminology will be generally used. The generic term SEN has been widely used in the UK, for nearly thirty years, to cover all children who have developmental difficulties that affect: their learning; their behavioural, emotional and social development; their communication; and their ability to care for themselves and gain independence. It was intended to replace disability categories (DfES, 1978), but these have continued to be used, even if they have changed. The eleven categories of the 1945 Regulations have been reduced to four categories in the SEN Code of Practice (DfES, 2001a), although a larger set of twelve categories (plus Other) is also used by the DfES in collecting data for the Pupil Level Annual School Census (PLASC). There is inconsistency over time (e.g. 'educational subnormality' was not used after the 1970s, to a large extent replaced by 'moderate learning difficulties'); between constituent counties in the UK (e.g. England: behavioural, emotional and social difficulties (BESD); Scotland: social, emotional and behavioural difficulties (SEBD)); between education and health services (e.g. learning difficulties or learning disabilities); between practitioners (e.g. specific language impairment or specific speech and language difficulties: Dockrell *et al.*, 2006); and between the UK and the US and other countries (e.g. the US term specific learning disabilities is comparable with the UK term specific learning difficulties). While some of these difficulties may be minor, others reflect different sensitivities, e.g. the term 'subnormal', or conceptual frameworks. For example, the earlier extensive use of measures of cognitive ability (e.g. IQ) has reduced in the UK, as exemplified by the SEN Code of Practice criteria for identifying learning and cognition needs, although they continue to be used by local authorities in the SEN identification procedures (Norwich and Kelly, 2005).

The terms 'inclusion' or 'inclusive education' have largely replaced 'integration' and are intended to represent a different concept; 'integration' may be seen as a child adapting to a host setting (typically a school), while 'inclusion' may refer to the host adapting in order to meet the needs of actual (and potential) pupils. However, this distinction is not always clear in practice. Some argue that the change in terminology reflects a shift from a needs-based to a rights-based agenda, or that integration may be seen as politically neutral and a form of service delivery, while inclusion has a strong ideological element (Pirrie *et al.*, 2006). The term 'mainstreaming' has continued to be used by others, especially in the US, although inclusion is becoming more common internationally. Each of these terms is used to refer to a range of practices.

Interventions

There are difficulties in defining interventions with respect to location. Much of the debate on inclusion concerns the difference(s) between mainstream compared with special schools, or mainstream classes versus special classes. Mainstream schools are not homogeneous; they vary greatly in their social mix, levels of achievement and behavioural ethos (Office of Her Majesty's Chief Inspector, 2005).Within both the US and the UK, for example, there has been a broadening of types of individual mainstream school (e.g. US: charter schools; UK: academies and specialist schools), with different policies on admissions even within a broad concept of comprehensive schooling. Grouping of schools building upon earlier networks and clusters to form partnerships and federations has also occurred. These arrangements may be 'soft', largely by agreements that are relatively informal, through to 'hard' federations, which may have different forms of governance and management, such as a single governing body and/or an executive head teacher for more than one school (Lindsay *et al.*, in press). With a focus on SEN, schools might, individually or as a group, develop specialist, enhanced provision for pupils with SEN. These have varying names, including units, integrated resources and designated special provision, and, more importantly, may operate in different ways, for example staffing numbers and expertise, nature of pupils and severity of SEN. The difficulty in defining a 'mainstream' school is therefore significant (Pirrie *et al.*, 2006).

Research methods and analysis

The last variable to be considered here concerns the nature of the evaluative research. There has been substantial and often trenchant criticism of educational research in the UK (Hillage *et al.*, 1998; Tooley and Darby, 1998). These critiques addressed both policy relevance and the quality of studies. Although the latter in particular was itself subject to critical commentary from the research community, the point here is that both were funded by government agencies (the DfES and Ofsted, respectively) because of concerns about the nature and usefulness of educational research. The debate has also been strong in the US, with promotion of the need for better research (National Research Council, 2002) and promotion of experimental research and the use of randomized control trials (RCTs) (Gersten *et al.*, 2005). In addition to debate about education research in general, there has been particular discussion of research in special education (Graham, 2005).

These concerns reflect a number of debates, but the focus here is on appropriate methods to enable evaluation of the effectiveness of interventions. RCTs are often proposed as a 'gold standard', as random allocation, experimental manipulation and valid comparisons of treatments provide the best evidence of causal relationships between intervention and outcome (National Research Council, 2002; What Works Clearinghouse, 2006). However, attaining true randomization and true control (comparison) group design is often highly problematic. In a study of reading and maths interventions, Seethaler and Fuchs (2005) found only 34 of 806 relevant articles in five journals (4.22 per cent) used random allocation, indicating a 'drop in the bucket' in terms of evidence based on this method. Their study reinforces an early analysis by Gersten *et al.* (2004), which found a significant reduction in the proportion of experimental research in the US funded for the two-year period of 1997–1998 compared with 1987–1988.

Hence, although promoted as a method of choice, RCTs are relatively rare in educational research. They are most suitable for providing evidence on outcomes not processes. Examination of processes is also necessary, particularly when these are complex or not well understood. A number of researchers have also argued the benefits of other methodologies (National Research Council, 2002; Odom *et al.*, 2005): rigorous correlation studies (Thompson *et al.*, 2005), well-constructed, single-subject designs (Horner *et al.*, 2005) and sound qualitative studies (Brantlinger *et al.*, 2005). The National Reading Panel's (2000) decision not to include qualitative or single-case studies in their review of effective methods of teaching reading, nor to argue for the benefits of studying an educational intervention using a variety of methodologies, has been criticized (Pressley *et al.*, 2006). The development of quality standards has been promoted as a more relevant approach rather than adherence to one particular method, especially one that is very difficult to implement successfully in educational research (Gersten *et al.*, 2000; Gersten *et al.*, 2005). Longitudinal studies using triangulated data sources can also provide important information relevant to inclusive education. Dockrell *et al.* (2007), in a study of children with specific language and communication needs, aged between 8 and 17 years, report changes in educational provision (mainstream and special) experienced by a substantial proportion of the young people, as well as a lack of evidence for the superiority of either inclusive or special provision. The present paper adopts a broad approach to evaluation and, hence, to the types of study considered.

EVALUATING THE EFFECTIVENESS OF INCLUSIVE EDUCATION

Examining to what degree, or even whether, an intervention described as inclusive education or mainstreaming may be considered effective is complicated by variations with respect to participants (the range of SEN types, severity, persistence and comorbidity), intervention definition (contextual factors, nature of the intervention) and the type of evaluative method (e.g. RCTs, correlational research, meta-analyses and single-study design). A formidable set of issues has been revealed for researchers, yet these must be addressed if research is to lead to effective practice. Therefore, the rest of this paper will explore research, which may shed light on the main questions concerning the effectiveness of inclusive education. The review will be presented in two parts. The main section will comprise a review of the papers in specified journals, 2000–2005, together with other studies mainly produced during this period. This review will therefore consider current evidence about efficacy. Prior to this, a brief review will be presented of the historical evidence.

An historical perspective

A key paper in the history of the move to inclusive education was that by Dunn (1968). Indeed, a recent survey reported that this was the most highly cited paper in the field of learning difficulties (McLeskey, 2004). It is interesting to note, therefore, that Dunn's paper is largely an opinion piece, radical and inspiring, with an analysis of the then-current system in the US, together with a blueprint for change, much of which would be recognized now; his section of efficacy studies comprises just three paragraphs. Also worthy of note is Dunn's purpose. He sets out clearly that his concern is mainly 'A better education than special class placement is needed for socioculturally deprived children with mild learning problems who have been labelled mentally retarded' (p. 5). It is this element of special education that he argued 'in its present form is obsolete and unjustifiable' (p. 6). Note also his statement:

> We are not arguing that we do away with our special education programmes for the moderately and severely retarded, for other types of more handicapped children or for the multiply handicapped.
>
> (Dunn, 1968: 6)

■ **Table 9.1** An analysis of three meta-analytic studies of the effects of inclusive placements (from Baker et al., 1994)

	Carlberg and Kavale	Wang and Baker	Baker
Year published	1980	1985–6	1994
Time period	Pre-1980	1975–1984	1983–1992
Academic effect size	0.15	0.44	0.08
Social effect size	0.11	0.11	0.28

Around this time, a number of studies were undertaken to investigate the efficacy of different placements and for different groups, the majority conducted in the US. These studies identified the methodological problems discussed above, leading to questions about the individual studies' validity, including the equivalence of children in comparative studies and attrition. For example, Blackman (1967: 8), quoted in Christoplos and Renz (1969), argues that a study by Goldstein et al. (1965) 'blends into the long line of negative findings that have characterized this area of research for the past 30 years' by failing to indicate the superiority of special classes. However, although using a random allocation design, it suffered substantial attrition, losing three quarters of the original sample.

Several reviews of inclusive education were undertaken in the 1980s (e.g. Madden and Slavin, 1983) and 1990s (e.g. Baker et al., 1994; Hegarty, 1993; Sebba and Sachdev, 1997). These adopted different methodologies, including overviews, reviews and meta-analyses, but failed to provide clear evidence for the benefit of inclusive education. Baker et al. reviewed several meta-analyses and found positive but generally small effect sizes, the highest for academic achievement, but primarily in only one of the three analyses (Table 9.1).

A further review of eight model programmes by Manset and Semmel (1997) found evidence of varying degrees of effectiveness and argued that 'inclusive programming effects are relatively unimpressive for most students with disabilities especially in view of the extraordinary resources available to many of these model programmes' (p. 117). Interaction effects between level of child difficulties and placement were reported by a number of studies using RCT or at least quasi-experimental designs. For example, Mills et al. (1998) found no overall differences in placement effects for groups of pre-schoolchildren with disabilities, but higher-performing children benefited more from integrated special education class placement, whereas lower-performing children benefited more from mainstream or segregated placements (see also Cole et al., 1991).

By the end of the twentieth century, therefore, the evidence for the effectiveness of inclusive education/mainstreaming might best be described as equivocal, although, equally, there was little evidence for the superiority of special education. Rather, there was a degree of support for effectiveness but this was tempered by a number of caveats. Some concerned the methodology of the studies, while others may be interpreted not as critiques but realistic appraisals of the complexity of the topic. That is, it might not be realistic to ask if inclusive education was effective, but it would be better to focus on which models were more effective for which children, including the relative importance of different moderators (Lindsay, 1989).

Post-2000

Following Seethaler and Fuchs (2005), this section focuses on a target group of journals. This differs, therefore, from systematic reviews that explore the whole field using keywords to identify appropriate publications, such as studies in the UK through the Evidence for Policy and Practice Information and Coordinating (EPPI) Centre (e.g. Kalambouka *et al.*, 2005). For the present study, eight journals from the field of special education were selected. The *Journal of Special Education* (125 papers), *Exceptional Children* (135), *Learning Disabilities Research and Practice* (150), *Journal of Learning Disabilities* (282) and *Remedial and Special Education* (225) are major US journals, overwhelmingly publishing studies undertaken in the US. The *British Journal of Special Education* (169) has been the major UK journal for SEN, and the *European Journal of Special Needs Education* (145) is the major European journal: the former largely publishes UK studies, whereas the latter reports studies mainly from across Europe. Finally, the *International Journal of Inclusive Education* (142) has a wider brief and includes papers from many countries across the world.

Each issue, from 2000 to the end of 2005 was examined, six full years, and papers were selected that had relevance to the effectiveness of inclusive education. No restriction was placed on methodology, and, hence, both quantitative and qualitative designs were potentially acceptable. Each abstract was read, and its relevance was evaluated. This process also allowed the generation of a range of categories concerning effectiveness. This differed from Seethaler and Fuchs's more focused paper, which selected only those studies examining reading and maths interventions, with group designs and random assignment to treatment conditions. The derived categories were: opinion; comparative studies of outcomes; other outcome studies; non-comparative qualitative studies, including non-experimental case studies; teacher practice and development; teacher attitude; and the use of teaching assistants. In addition, a category of research methodology was identified.

Following the reading of the abstracts, papers were selected for detailed reading that appeared to address the effectiveness of inclusive education. As the selection criteria were deliberately set to be broad, this resulted in papers varying from those with a clear focus on effectiveness research questions through to others that addressed effectiveness in passing. The definition of 'effectiveness' was not tightly drawn, so allowing studies that reported on various child outcomes. Also, studies were selected on the basis of their investigating effectiveness, not whether inclusion was found to be effective.

A total of 1,373 papers were considered. Despite the broad categorization of 'effectiveness', only fourteen papers (1.0 per cent) were identified that reported comparative outcome studies of children with some form of SEN. Other papers presented qualitative studies of inclusive practice, some using non-comparative case study methods, but others reporting descriptions of practice, which may include respondents' judgements. In this section, the fourteen comparative outcome studies will be reported, followed by discussion of non-comparative, qualitative studies. In the following section, process studies will be reported, including research on teacher practice, teacher attitudes and the use of teaching assistants, as these studies provide information about effectiveness, even if they were not effectiveness studies per se. Finally, other recent research will be reviewed, focusing on school effectiveness and inclusion.

Studies of outcomes

COMPARATIVE STUDIES OF OUTCOMES

Fourteen papers were identified as comparative studies of outcomes, of which two were reviews. There was substantial variation on several dimensions. None used a RCT method. Only nine compared the performance of children with SEN in different settings, and, in the other five (including two reviews), outcomes for children with SEN were compared with those for typically developing (TD) children, where both were attending mainstream schools (Table 9.2). The nature of children's SEN varied greatly, as did age of sample, with studies ranging from children in preschool/kindergarten to 17 year olds. Most studies (nine) included measures of social, emotional or behavioural development, together with academic development (including academic engagement), and the other five

■ **Table 9.2** Studies of the effect of inclusion

Study	Age range	Comparison	Focus	Effect
Comparison by setting				
1 Rafferty *et al.* (2003)	Preschool	Mainstream vs. special class	Language, cognitive, social	(+)(+)(ı)
2 Buysse *et al.* (2002)	Preschool	Mainstream vs. special class	Social	(+)
3 Allodi (2000)	9–13	Mainstream vs. units	Self-concept	=
4 Karsten *et al.* (2001)	Up to 13	Mainstream vs. special school	Academic, social	= =
5 Wiener and Tardiff (2004)	9–13	In class support vs. resource room vs. inclusion class vs. special class	Social	+
6 Rea *et al.* (2002)	12	Mainstream vs. pull out	Academic, behaviour, attendance	(+) = +
7 Myklebust (2002)	14–16	Mainstream vs. special class	Academic, drop out	+ –
8 Markussen (2004)	16	Mainstream vs. special class vs. TD peers	Academic	+
9 Elbaum (2002)	Kindergarten–17	Resource room vs. special class vs. special school SEN vs. TD	Self-concept	=
10 Zeleke (2004)	6–17	SEN vs. TD	Self-concept: academic, social, general	– = =
11 Monchy *et al.* (2004)	9–12	SEN vs. TD	Social	–
12 Wallace *et al.* (2002)	High school	SEN vs. TD	Academic, behaviour	= =
13 Cawley *et al.* (2002)	11–12	SEN vs. TD	Academic, behaviour	= =
14 Cambra and Silvestre (2003)	10–11	SEN vs. TD	Self-concept	–

Note: ı: positive inclusion effect; (+): positive inclusion effect but with caveat(s); =: no difference between conditions; –: negative inclusion effect.

addressed social factors only, including self-concept. The studies are discussed by age of participants.

An interaction effect was reported by Rafferty *et al.* (2003), who researched a US preschool setting, where between 53 and 75 per cent of the children in the inclusion classes had disabilities, and all children in segregated classes had disabilities. The former contained twelve to eighteen children, one special education teacher and one early childhood teacher; the latter contained six children, one special education teacher and one aide. The children in the inclusive classes had higher levels of functioning at pre-test, but, using a covariance model, the study found an interaction between settings and degree of disability. Type of setting had no differential impact on children with low levels of disability in terms of either language ability or social competence, but children with severe disabilities in inclusive settings had greater gains than those in segregated classes. The very high proportion of children with disabilities raises questions about whether these classes can be considered inclusive.

An interaction effect was also found by Buysse *et al.* (2002) in a US study of 333 preschool children (120 with disabilities and 213 TD) attending one of two forms of inclusive early childhood programme; specialized settings had a majority of children with disabilities, whereas, in child-care settings, the opposite was the case. Disability covered a wide range of problems, including deafness, autistic spectrum disorder and mental retardation. Children in the child-care settings had more playmates and were more likely to have a TD friend than those in specialized settings, but this could be due to the differences in availability of TD children in each setting.

Other studies have produced mixed or equivocal results. A Dutch study comparing over 400 matched pairs of at-risk children in special and regular (mainstream) education (age up to 13 years) found no differences by setting on either academic or psychosocial development (Karsten *et al.*, 2001). A Swedish study of 183 pupils (9–13 years) found no difference in self-concept between those receiving support from special educators in mainstream schools (Allodi, 2000), although there was some evidence of those supported in mainstream having lower levels of self-concept for academic competence compared with those in small groups in special units.

Wiener and Tardiff (2004) report a Canadian study of 117 children (grades 4–8) with learning disabilities (LDs) educated in one of four different service delivery models: In-class or Resource Room Support for those judged to need a lower intensity of service; Inclusion or Self-Contained Special Education classrooms for those needing a higher intensity of support. On a range of social factors addressing friendship, loneliness, self-perceptions and social skills, the comparisons of each pair of models tended to favour the more inclusive approach, although the overall levels of social and emotional functioning were lower than children without LDs, and the large number of comparisons increased the risk of Type I errors in the number of statistically significant differences found.

A study comparing 8th-grade students in middle schools in the US, one inclusive, the other operating a pull-out special education system, with matched groups of students with LDs, found that the inclusive education group achieved significantly higher levels on a range of academic measures and equivalent scores on others (Rea *et al.*, 2002). These children also had better attendance and equivalent levels of suspension. The features of this relatively successful model included a 'teaming model', whereby teachers planned work together and classes rotated during the day.

A positive finding for inclusion was also reported from a Norwegian study of 592 students with general learning problems over the three years of upper secondary schooling

(Myklebust, 2002). The study compared students who were taught exclusively in small groups outside the classroom, receiving adapted teaching during their first year of upper secondary, with those who were taught in ordinary classes. After three years, the latter group had made better progress: 40 per cent, compared with 10 per cent, were academically 'on schedule'. The drop-out rate showed the opposite effect, however. This study therefore suggests a complex situation, whereby the special class support in the first year helped to reduce the risk of drop-out, but was less effective than general class placement at that time for academic progress. Markussen (2004) compared 777 students with SENs, 285 attending special classes with reduced numbers of students, and 492 attending ordinary classes, with a comparison group of 463 non-SEN students. The SEN students in special classes achieved a lower level of success compared with those in ordinary classes, after other factors had been controlled. However, there were no differences among the SEN group attending ordinary classes in achieving formal competence, irrespective of whether they received help in class or in small groups outside the classroom.

A meta-analysis of self-concept of students with learning disabilities, derived from an analysis of thirty-six research reports allowing sixty-five different placement comparisons (Elbaum, 2002), provides more substantial evidence. This found no overall relationship between self-concept and setting (regular classroom for all instruction, part-time resource, self-contained for all academic instruction and special school) for four out of five comparisons, suggesting that students fared no better or worse in terms of self-concept in regular or separate classrooms. A review by Zeleke (2004) of forty-one studies examining self-concept of children with learning difficulties compared with normally achieving children in mainstream also found strong evidence of the former having significantly lower scores on academic self-concept, while evidence of social self-concept overall indicated they fared no worse.

The studies, such as Zeleke's, that have examined outcomes for children with SENs compared with TD children, rather than by setting, provide different evidence regarding inclusion. A Dutch study of twenty-five 9–12 year olds with behaviour problems in full-time regular education produced negative findings regarding inclusion, as these children were socially included less than their peers without SEN (Monchy et al., 2004). Furthermore, the teachers were judged to have too positive a view of these children's social integration and to have underestimated the frequency of their being bullied and of bullying others. However, two other studies provide more positive results. Wallace et al. (2002), in a study of 118 inclusive classrooms in four US high schools selected from 114 success-ful schools, showed that students with and without disabilities had equivalent high levels of academic engagement and low levels of inappropriate behaviour. Cawley et al. (2002) report a successful science programme in an inner-city US school with very high levels of poverty. Students with LDs and severe emotional disturbance were integrated into science lessons taught jointly by the regular and science teachers who had been on a 100-hour training programme. No behavioural problems were found, and the success rate of the special educational students was equivalent to that of the general education students.

Cambra and Silvestre (2003) studied the self-concept and social preference of Spanish students with a range of SENs and comparison TD children in a mainstream school with Special Experimental School status (35 per cent had SENs of various kinds). The typically developing group had significantly more positive social and academic self-concepts and were also more likely to be selected and less likely to be rejected. Hence, mainstreaming in this study was not associated with equivalent socio-emotional development for the SEN group.

Qualitative methodology has been used to investigate the progression of children but some do not provide sufficient data to allow a judgment on the findings. For example, Peters (2002), in case studies of two US schools, claims a variety of gains for students with significant SENs, but no data are presented to support this conclusion. Other studies typically focus on processes rather than child outcomes, often using very small samples. For example, Hall and McGregor (2000) show that three children with disabilities were involved in a variety of peer relationships during Kindergarten and Grade 1, but this level of involvement reduced by upper elementary grades (10–13 years), e.g. reciprocal nominations as playmate for two of the three boys reduced from eleven at Kindergarten/Grade 1 to only one positive reciprocal nomination at upper elementary level. They were also less involved in shared activities, although these children continued to play with, and be accepted by, peers in the playground. Hall and McGregor speculate that, by the end of elementary schooling, these boys may have been in classrooms but not perceived as part of a class. Hanson *et al.* (2001) found that only about 10 per cent of the twenty-five children originally in inclusive preschool settings remained in inclusive settings five years later. They identified five factors influencing this change: professional influences, families' abilities to access information, influence of advocates, match between family and school needs and expectations, and the influence of child and family characteristics. This qualitative study, based on annual interviews and observations, reveals the tensions between a desire for inclusive education and the problems of meeting children's needs with the available resources. Other case studies have focused more on the processes operating within schools rather than on the children, suggesting possible areas for development, but, in the absence of child-level data, these findings are speculative (e.g. Carrington and Elkins, 2002).

Where outcomes have been examined, mixed results have been found. Pijl and Hamstra (2005), in a Norwegian study, report that seven of twenty-four pupils (29 per cent) in a fully inclusive model of education had social-emotional development judged as 'worrying' by independent assessors, although the teachers and parents were more positive. Pavri and Monda-Amaya (2000, 2001) in two studies of twenty and thirty children, respectively, report that, although children with LDs felt part of a social network, many felt loneliness at school. In an interview study of fourteen young people (12–18 years) with Down's syndrome, attending either their local mainstream secondary school or a resourced mainstream school, Cuckle and Wilson (2002) found that the young people were positive about friendships and having role models among mainstream peers, but friendships were mainly limited to school. More truly reciprocal friendships were noted with peers who also had SEN, including others with Down's syndrome. Cuckle and Wilson suggest this reflects the closer match of interests, emotional maturity and communication skills. A study of twenty-four young people (mean age 22 years), who had transferred from a special school for pupils with moderate learning difficulties to mainstream, presents an even gloomier picture (Hornby and Kidd, 2001). Only three of the twenty-four were working full time and one part time, and none was married.

Studies of process

TEACHER PRACTICE

At the heart of all education is the practice of teachers; consequently, the role of teachers in developing inclusion is central to its effectiveness. A number of studies have explored teacher practice; these have typically been small-scale. Flem *et al.* (2004) studied the practice of one teacher recommended as achieving effective inclusive practice in Norway over four months, working with a class of twenty-three 7th-grade students, including three with SEN. The study identified elements of practice considered to lead to effectiveness. These included general educational practice applied to the pupil with SEN (e.g. effective scaffolding; developing and modelling positive interactions and ambience; contingency management; and effective instructional methods, including feedback). Also identified as important were collaboration with other teachers and the school administration.

Other studies have supported these factors. Additional special teachers to work with Kindergarten teachers (Takala and Aunio, 2005) and collaborative teams to work with 4th-grade students with severe disabilities or considered at-risk in general educational classrooms (Hunt *et al.*, 2003) have been found useful. The importance and effectiveness of individualized Unified Plans of Support (UPSs) were indicated by observed changes in the students' behaviour, with levels of engagement increasing substantially, as did an increase in initiating interactions with teachers and other children, together with team members' opinions of improved performance. The UPS stressed team action, and Hunt *et al.* speculate that a key element in its success was that team members had time to reflect together.

The development of a positive ethos, with a values-based commitment to inclusion, has also been shown to have an important role (Fisher *et al.*, 2002; Kugelmass, 2001). However, teachers may not share these views, even if there is a national policy for inclusion. A sense of lacking competence (Dockrell and Lindsay, 2001), lack of resources or additional training and support for teachers to develop their own skills, and an unrealistic or lack of awareness of the prevalence of developmental problems (Dockrell, Shield, and Rigby, 2003) may undermine teachers' development of inclusive education (Freire and César, 2003; Skårbrevik, 2005).

TEACHER ATTITUDES

Teacher attitudes, as well as their behaviours, have been proposed as a key factor in successful inclusive education. Reviews have identified a number of important factors affecting teacher attitudes to inclusion (Avramidis and Norwich, 2002; Scruggs and Mastropieri, 1996). Although a general shift to a more positive attitude to inclusion has been identified, there is no evidence of acceptance of a policy of total inclusion.

The nature of children's disability or SEN appears critical, with teachers generally having more favourable attitudes to including children with physical and sensory impairment than those with learning difficulties or BESD (e.g. Clough and Lindsay, 1991). There is a lack of consistent evidence concerning teachers' age and gender and age of pupils taught, but teachers' beliefs and training are important (Avramidis and Norwich, 2002). There is mixed evidence concerning experience of contact with children with SEN (e.g. Center and Ward, 1987; Praisner, 2003). Resources, both physical, including ICT and teaching materials, and human, including teaching assistants, are important, as is support from the head teacher (Marshall *et al.*, 2002). Furthermore, restructuring of the physical environment and organizational changes may also be necessary for successful inclusion (Avramidis *et al.*, 2002).

Hence, teachers may have positive attitudes in principle, but they temper these by a number of practical considerations (Croll and Moses, 2000; Frederickson *et al.*, 2004). This is particularly the case with respect to meeting curricular demands rather than addressing social inclusion (Flem and Keller, 2000), and attitudes may vary with curriculum subject (Ellins and Porter, 2005).

TEACHING ASSISTANTS

Teaching assistants in the UK have had many roles over the years, from general duties around the classroom, to specific work with individual pupils with SENs. Increasingly, a more general SEN role to support inclusion, working in collaboration with the teacher, is being promoted. However, the UK context has been made more complex by the tradition of these non-SEN roles being undertaken by other personnel working as assistants and the recent workload agreement aimed at reducing teachers' responsibilities for non-teaching tasks. There have also been many different terms used, a common one for those with the SEN role having been 'learning support assistants'. In the US, the term 'paraprofessional' is the most common. In this paper, teaching assistant (TA) will be the preferred term. The key issues to consider are the nature of TA practice, the training they receive to carry it out, and how this helps to support the inclusion of children with SENs.

The employment of TAs to support children with SENs increased substantially during the 1990s (Farrell *et al.*, 1999). However, their role has been unclear, often left to schools to determine. Teachers have typically been positive about the support available from TAs (Moran and Abbott, 2002; Ofsted, 2002), but often have not been able to articulate clearly the academic benefits they believe the pupils have attained (Blatchford *et al.*, 2004). French (2001) found little evidence of scheduled planning meetings between paraprofessionals and teachers.

The main practice provided by TAs has been direct support of pupils with SEN (Amaiz and Castejón, 2001; Blatchford *et al.*, 2004; Giangreco *et al.*, 2001; Groom and Rose, 2005), but see Emanuelsson (2001) for some variations. However, the specific nature of such support has varied to include direct teaching of academic skills, life skills or vocational skills; supporting pupils with challenging behaviour to prevent or ameliorate possible disruption and optimize both conduct and learning; facilitating interactions with other pupils; and providing personal care or supporting self-help skills in children, e.g. toileting and feeding.

There have been concerns regarding the potential overlap with teaching and confusion over what TAs actually do and what professionals think they should be doing (Giangreco *et al.*, 2001). One concern is the distinction of role between the TA and teacher: should the TA support, supplement, extend or replace the teacher? Given the implications for conditions of service, this issue has raised concerns beyond the pedagogic into the political arena. However, the use of TAs to support inclusion is now well established, but lack of training has been highlighted as a major concern for successful undertaking of a pedagogic role (Blatchford *et al.*, 2004; Farrell *et al.*, 1999; Riggs and Mueller, 2001). This has been addressed within the UK by a number of training initiatives (www. teachernet.gov.uk/wholeschool/teachingassistants/training/; accessed 3 March 2006). In the US, Giangreco *et al.* (2003) report a large-scale innovative programme for planning TA support, which was rated highly by participants.

Giangreco *et al.* (2001) argue that the literature has been 'top-heavy with non-databased articles on roles and training of paraprofessionals calling for role clarification as well as more and better training' (p. 57). In the UK, there is indirect evidence to support impact on children, beyond the opinions of the teachers with whom TAs work. Ofsted (2002) report that the evidence from their inspections of schools shows the quality of teaching in lessons with TAs is better than in lessons without them, but point out that schools rarely evaluate the impact of TAs on pupils' learning and attainment. Blatchford *et al.* (2004), in a large-scale study, report that TAs had an indirect effect on teaching by increasing pupil engagement and helping teachers focus on teaching; with a TA present, there was a more active form of interaction and more individualized teacher attention. Evidence for social benefits comes from an evaluation of a training programme aimed to teach four TAs how to facilitate interactions between pupils with severe disabilities and their peers. Although small scale, a comparison of baseline and post-intervention observational data indicates the training was successful in not only doubling TA facilitative behaviour but also student interaction, which increased twenty-five-fold and was maintained (Causton-Theoharris and Malmgren, 2005).

The use of TAs is now very well established. Teachers and TAs are developing collaborative teamwork, and training is now more widespread. Nevertheless, concern remains. The evidence of positive impact remains limited, both in absolute terms and also with respect to specific training programmes, for which further evidence of replicability is required. Broer *et al.* (2005) have raised important questions about the negative as well as positive aspects of TA support from a study of pupil perspectives that identified the TA being seen as having four roles: mother, friend, protector and primary teacher. Hence, the nature of TAs' work and the role taken and perceived by the child, and the relationship between role and child outcomes require more research.

SCHOOL EFFECTIVENESS AND INCLUSION

Although the focus of this paper so far has been on the impact of inclusion on pupils with SENs, it is also reasonable to examine the impact on pupils without SEN. Indeed, England's Special Educational Needs and Disability Act 2001 states that a child with SENs must be educated in a mainstream school, unless this is incompatible with the parents' wishes or the provision of efficient education of other children. Two research strands may be identified: the direct impact on non-SEN children and the impact on overall school standards and effectiveness.

In a systematic review of twenty-six studies, Kalambouka *et al.* (2005) identified 23 per cent positive findings, 15 per cent negative, 53 per cent neutral and 10 per cent mixed findings, with respect to impact of inclusion on non-SEN pupils. Most studies concerned the inclusion of pupils with difficulties in learning or cognition, and there was evidence of more negative findings where inclusion concerned pupils with emotional and behavioural difficulties; however, no study reported negative impact when the included children had physical, sensory or communication difficulties. Studies such as those reviewed by Kalambuka *et al.* are relatively small scale but have the advantage of data drawn from individual pupil profiles derived from instruments designed to focus on specific domains. Large-scale studies of school-level impact typically use less sensitive measures. For example, the recent availability of PLASC data in England has allowed large-scale, national studies, but using less specific criteria. PLASC allows analysis of SEN by two major criteria: whether a child has a statement of SEN or is at the next lower level (School Action Plus), and the primary need identified (e.g. moderate learning difficulties).

Lunt and Norwich (1999) found a substantial negative correlation between attainment at 16 years (GCSE, average points score for the school) and level of inclusion in a sample of 3,151 secondary schools. Not more than 3 per cent of the top 20 per cent GCSE performers were schools within the top 20 per cent in terms of proportion of SEN pupils. However, this study did not take account of social disadvantage, a factor that has been found to be associated with higher levels of identified SEN (Lindsay *et al.*, 2006; Skiba *et al.*, 2005). A national study using PLASC data by Dyson *et al.* (2004) found a very small, negative relationship between pupil attainment (GCSE and GNVQ average points score) and level of inclusivity (the proportion of pupils at School Action Plus and with a Statement). However, there was evidence of socio-economic disadvantage being a confounding factor: more inclusive schools were more likely to have higher proportions of pupils suffering socio-economic disadvantage, as indicated by eligibility for free school meals.

Neither of these large-scale analyses addressed inclusion in terms of more refined measures of inclusion, such as classroom processes, resources and curricula, although the same criticism could be made of many small-scale studies. Furthermore, Dyson *et al.* (2004) report that analyses of sixteen case studies in their study indicated that categorization of schools on their measures of inclusivity and performance was 'somewhat unstable over time' (p. 57). Also Lindsay *et al.* (2006) report that socio-economic disadvantage is differentially related to different categories of SEN, with a substantial relationship with BESD but not sensory impairment.

DISCUSSION

Inclusion has been a major policy initiative, designed to improve the educational opportunities of children with special educational needs and disabilities. Support for inclusion is based on two foundations: that children have a right to inclusion within mainstream schools, and that inclusive education is more effective. The present review has focused on the latter question (see Lindsay (2003) for a discussion of the former). Nevertheless, both are important. Effectiveness must be judged relative to the criteria used, which are partly derived from values, as well as technical considerations.

Overall, the weight of evidence reviewed in this paper cannot be said to provide a clear endorsement for the positive effects of inclusion (see also Zigmond, 2003). Just 1 per cent of over 1,300 studies, published 2000–2005, that were reviewed addressed effectiveness, and the results from these studies were only marginally positive overall, although comparability between outcomes for SEN and TD children could be interpreted as positive rather than non-difference. Furthermore, the studies covered a range of ages and methods of inclusion; used a variety of methods; and produced evidence on a number of different outcome variables. Taken as a whole, and with the pre-2000 evidence, which presents a similar picture, there is a lack of a firm research base for inclusive education to support either whether this is a preferable approach in terms of outcomes, or how inclusion should be implemented. The review has highlighted the importance of interaction effects and, hence, the need to examine moderators and mediators affecting outcomes. This amounts to a clear indication of the power of policies argued to be supporting children's rights (to be included) rather than of evidence of optimal practice. The research base is more helpful in identifying processes that facilitate inclusion. The differential benefit of training TAs is a case in point. However, there is a lack of rigorous studies that demonstrate positive child outcomes rather than improved teaching processes.

Can inclusive education be evaluated?

Some educationists question the value of research in this field, as inclusion is considered appropriate de facto, and, hence, what is needed is a commitment to ensure it is implemented. Negative findings may be viewed as indicating limitations in present practice that must be addressed, rather than as presenting a challenge to the basic position in support of inclusion (e.g. Booth, 1996). This stance sits uneasily with other researchers who are committed to evidence-based policy and practice. Also, a difficulty with this position is that the relative standing and priority of rights are not universally agreed; often there may be competing rights (Mithaug, 1998). Others do use the research literature but argue that the evidence more strongly supports inclusion, whereas the position on the basis of the present review is that it is barely more than equivocal (see also Norwich and Kelly, 2005).

Those who are committed to research also have significant difficulties in examining the effectiveness of inclusion. First, problems in the definition of variables are endemic. How is 'inclusion' to be operationally defined? Dyson *et al*. (2004) used the proportion of pupils designated as having SENs as a measure of inclusivity. This is highly problematic, as they recognized. The categorization of a child as having SENs and the specification of the severity of the SEN (as judged by the pupil having a Statement or being at the lower level of School Action Plus in the English system) are both contentious. Each is related to objective measures but is also influenced by school policies, including attempts to secure resources. Categories representing lesser severity are even less reliable (Lindsay *et al*., 2006). Attribution to certain categories of SEN (e.g. moderate learning difficulties) and the definition of locational variables are also problematic. Mainstream schools vary greatly (e.g. in terms of socio-economic disadvantage, overall levels of attainment and ethnic profiles), and locational distinctions within 'mainstream' may be complex. It cannot be assumed that terms such as resource base, unit, integrated resource and designated special provision refer to comparable provision, or even that there is commonality within each category. Variation also exists, despite the National Curriculum in England, in curriculum content, pedagogy, grouping, and use of ICT and teaching assistants. Such variations increase further when systems in different countries are considered.

A second difficulty concerns the changing nature of schooling. Many special schools have developed link/outreach programmes, where pupils attend both mainstream and special schools. The use of relatively segregated special unit provision in schools has changed to a more diffuse system of class/resource base plus support within mainstream classrooms. Furthermore, the mainstream school system itself is changing, for example with the development of Charter schools in the US and federations of schools in England. These changes present methodological challenges in terms of comparative research in this field, as 'inclusion' can no longer be conceptualized as the opposite of 'segregation'. Rather, 'inclusion into what?' becomes a key research question, and hence adds complexity to comparative studies. For example, federations of schools in England have developed a range of collaborative partnerships with varying purposes, forms of leadership and governance, and degree of focus on SEN (Lindsay *et al*., in press). Some have paired a successful school with one in difficulties; others have developed a broader-based sharing of expertise; one school, which opened only at Easter 2006, combines a primary, secondary and the only special school in the local authority into one school building, under an executive director for all three schools.

A third theme concerns the use of TAs, which has developed substantially, with indications of potential benefit (Blatchford *et al*., 2004; Ofsted, 2002). Although their introduction in the past may have been seen as a cheap approach to inclusion, the size of this professional force now presents a major opportunity for development. There is evidence for the effectiveness of training (Causton-Theoharris and Malmgren, 2005); what is now needed is evidence of effectiveness of different support regimes for children with different types of SEN. In particular, it is important to compare not only outcomes related to trained vs. untrained TAs, but also to compare TAs against regular and specialist trained teachers, both with regard to child outcomes and cost-benefits.

A fourth theme concerns the effectiveness of pedagogy and needs to be focused on the nature of different SENs. Brookes (2002), Graham (2006) and Pressley *et al.* (2006) have reviewed successful pedagogy for literacy intervention, while Seethaler and Fuchs (2005) have examined both reading and maths. Key principles that optimize achievement, of both TD children and those with literacy difficulties, have been identified. Other studies have identified comparable principles for other domains, including BESD (Evans *et al.*, 2004). Both Davis and Florian (2004) and Lewis and Norwich (2005) have taken a broader perspective in an attempt to identify whether there is a separate special education pedagogy, reviewing evidence across the range of categories of SEN. The general findings from their reviews are that there are principles that can be applied to optimize learning, but that these must be both conceptualized and operationalized in relation to the individual child's learning and developmental needs and to the setting in which the teaching and learning are to take place.

Finally, it is necessary to consider the use of teams of practitioners. Teams have a chequered history. The child guidance team model was heavily criticized in the early 1970s (Tizard, 1973), but other forms of teams have developed. In England, the development of Children's Trusts and the Every Child Matters agenda requires the development of children's services with clear integration of functions to avoid vulnerable children falling through gaps in services. Teams may be focused at school level to support inclusion. However, this is currently an under-researched area, and both the earlier studies and recent evaluations provide mixed findings (e.g. Heath *et al.*, 2004).

A WAY FORWARD

This paper has focused primarily on research evidence of the effectiveness of inclusive education. However, it was also argued that there is a separate conceptual framework that must be considered. This concerns values and rights. Inclusive education has been driven by a belief that this is the correct approach, to include rather than segregate and exclude. Policies of various governments have pursued this line (e.g. Department of Education and Skills, 2001b). However, there are signs of change. The UK House of Commons Committee on Education and Skills (2006) urged the government to clarify its position on inclusion, which, it argued, was confusing, with policy statements indicating an expectation of fewer special schools, whereas the Minister's witness statement to the Committee stated that the Government would be 'content' if, as a result of local authority decisions, the current 'roughly static portion of special schools continues' (p. 5). The Committee was strident in its criticism:

> The government's clear ideological stance to promote inclusion is leading to parental backlash based on fear, frustration and confusion. This duplicitous approach by the government undermines people's confidence in its ability to deliver in the genuine interests of those children with SEN.
>
> (UK House of Commons Committee on Education and Skills, 2006: 125)

However much educational psychologists may wish that evidence should drive policy, the reality is that research evidence is only one of several influences taken into account by politicians. Nevertheless, it is important that, as researchers and practitioners, we continue to produce research evidence to influence policy.

Given that the government policy in many countries is often confused, but generally supportive of inclusion, but the evidence for the effectiveness of inclusive education is, at best, marginally in support of inclusive education, the task now is twofold. First, there is a need for further conceptualization of the options of inclusive education. It is necessary to consider inclusive education as a multifaceted practice, built upon foundations grounded in a belief that children with developmental difficulties and SENs require appropriate education that optimizes their life chances as individuals to become full members of society. The proposition that this should largely, if not entirely, be facilitated by education in mainstream schools should be recognized as a values-based, not empirically based, position. There are indications of practices that appear to support inclusion, but there is a need for a more analytical consideration of combined (interactional) effects of relevant mediator and moderator factors concerning pupil diversity; curricular and assessment specifications; and the education system, which, being in a state of increasing change and diversity may support more effective education, partly by providing more flexibility in the system (Odom *et al.*, 2004; Wedell, 2005).

The agenda proposed here, therefore, accepts the basic premise that children's needs should be addressed within an inclusive education system in the broadest sense, but views this as more than simply a question of mainstream vs. special school or that inclusion can only mean full-time education in a mainstream class. The research evidence on effectiveness cannot be used to justify either position. This approach also requires its own research agenda that develops beyond simple comparative studies to a series of complementary research strands. These would include large-scale analyses of data sets, together with detailed analyses of the implementation of inclusion in different settings. In particular, there is a need to focus on mediator and moderator influences on processes and outcomes rather than location (Zigmond, 2003). Studies designed on this basis could also be usefully shaped by drawing upon psychological theories to a greater extent than is apparent from past research. This approach would be grounded in an ecological systems approach, with studies drawing appropriately on both quantitative and qualitative methods. Furthermore, there could be greater use of longitudinal studies to explore the impact of educational systems on the children over time. This approach is research-based and, hence, actively rejects both the view that research is unnecessary as inclusion is a right, and a simple model of 'full inclusion for all' (see also Kavale and Mostert, 2003).

There is an opportunity to implement and evaluate a variegated system of inclusive education appropriate to this century's complex societies and patterns of schooling, where inclusion in its widest sense is impartial, addressing religion, ethnicity, social class and other social dimensions as well as SEN and disability. Parents will be important contributors on behalf of their children, as will children themselves, to shape up both the implementation of inclusion and its evaluation. The task is to examine, carefully and analytically, how inclusive education can be effective in meeting the different needs of individual children with disabilities and special educational needs.

REFERENCES

Allodi, M.W. (2000) 'Self-concept in children receiving special support at school', *European Journal of Special Needs Education*, Vol. 15: 69–78.

Amaiz, P. and Castejón, J.-L. (2001) 'Towards a change in the role of the support teacher in the Spanish education system', *European Journal of Special Needs Education*, Vol. 16: 99–110.

Avramidis, E., Bayliss, P. and Burden, R. (2002) 'Inclusion in action: an in-depth case study of an effective inclusive secondary school in the south-west of England', *International Journal of Inclusive Education*, Vol. 6: 143–163.

Avramidis, E. and Norwich, B. (2002) 'Teachers' attitudes towards integration/inclusion: a review of the literature', *European Journal of Special Needs Education*, Vol. 17: 129–147.

Baker, E.T.,Wang, M.C. and Walberg, H.J. (1994) 'The effects of inclusion on learning', *Educational Leadership*, Vol. 52: 33–35.

Blatchford, P., Russell, A., Bassett, P., Brown, P. and Martin, C. (2004) *The role and effects of teaching assistants in English primary schools (Years 4 to 6) 2000–2003: results from the Class Size and Pupil Adult Ratios (CSPAR) KS2 project* (Research Report RR605), Nottingham, UK: Department for Education and skills.

Booth, T. (1996) 'Changing views about research on integration: the inclusion of students with special needs or participation for all?', in Sigston, A., Curran, P., Labram, A. and Wolfendale, S. (eds) *Psychology in practice with young people, families and schools*, London: David Fulton: 181–194.

Brantlinger, E., Jiminez, R., Klinger, J., Pugach, M. and Richardson, V. (2005) 'Qualitative studies in education', *Exceptional Children*, Vol. 71: 195–207.

Broer, S.M., Doyle, M.B. and Giangreco, M.F. (2005) 'Perspectives of students with intellectual disabilities about their experiences with paraprofessional support', *Exceptional children*, Vol. 71: 415–430.

Brookes, G. (2002) *What works with children with literacy difficulties? The effectiveness of intervention schemes* (Research Report 380), Nottingham, UK: Department for Education and Skills.

Buysse, V., Goldman, B.D. and Skinner, M.L. (2002) 'Setting effects on friendship formation among young children with and without disabilities', *Exceptional Children*, Vol. 68: 503–517.

Cambra, C. and Silvestre, N. (2003) 'Students with special educational needs in the inclusive classroom: social integration and self-concept', *European Journal of Special Needs Education*, Vol. 18: 197–208.

Carrington, S. and Elkins, J. (2002) 'Comparison of a traditional and an inclusive secondary school culture', *International Journal of Inclusive Education*, Vol. 6: 1–16.

Causton-Theoharris, J.N. and Malmgren, K.W. (2005) 'Increasing peer interactions for students with severe disabilities via paraprofessional training', *Exceptional children*, Vol. 71: 431–444.

Cawley, J., Hayden, S., Cade, E. and Baker-Kroczynski, S. (2002) 'Including students with disabilities into the general education science classroom', *Exceptional Children*, Vol. 68: 423–435.

Center, Y. and Ward, J. (1987) 'Teachers' attitudes towards the integration of disabled children into regular schools', *Exceptional Children*, Vol. 34: 41–56.

Christoplos, F. and Renz, P. (1969) 'A critical examination of special education programs', *Journal of Special Education*, Vol. 3: 371–379.

Clough, P. and Lindsay, G. (1991) *Integration and the support service*, Slough, UK: NFER.

Cole, K., Mills, P., Dale, P. and Jenkins, J. (1991) 'Effects of preschool integration for children with disabilities', *Exceptional Children*, Vol. 58, No. 1: 36–45.

Croll, P. and Moses, D. (2000) 'Ideologies and utopias: education professionals' views of inclusion', *European Journal of Special Needs Education*, Vol. 15: 1–12.

Cuckle, P. and Wilson, J. (2002) 'Social relationships and friends among young people with Down's syndrome in secondary schools', *British Journal of Special Education*, Vol. 29: 66–71.

Davis, P. and Florian, L. (2004) *Teaching strategies and approaches for pupils with special educational needs: a scoping study* (Research Report 516), Norwich, UK: Her Majesty's Stationery Office.

Department for Education and Employment (1997) *Excellence for all children: meeting special educational needs*, London: HMSO.

Department for Education and Science (1978) *Special educational needs* (The Warnock Report), London: HMSO.

Department for Education and Skills (2001a) *Special educational needs code of practice*, London: HMSO.

Department for Education and Skills (2001b) *Inclusive schooling: children with special educational needs*, Nottingham, UK: HMSO.

Dockrell, J. and Lindsay, G. (2001) 'Children with specific speech and language difficulties: the teachers' perspectives', *Oxford Review of Education*, Vol. 27, No. 3: 369–394.

Dockrell, J.E., Lindsay, G., Letchford, C. and Mackie, C. (2006) 'Educational provision for children with specific speech and language difficulties: perspectives of speech and language therapy managers', *International Journal of Language and Communication Disorders*, Vol. 41: 423–440.

Dockrell, J.E., Lindsay, G., Palikara, O. and Cullen, M.A. (2007) *Raising the achievements of young people with specific language and communication needs and other special educational needs through school to work and college* (Research Report), Nottingham, UK: Department for Education and Skills.

Dockrell, J.E., Shield, B.M. and Rigby, K. (2003) 'Acoustic guidelines and teacher strategies for optimising learning conditions in classrooms for children with hearing problems', in Fabry, D. and DeConde Johnson, C. (eds) *ACCESS: Achieving Clear Communication Employing Sound Solutions,* Chicago: Phonak: 217–229.

Dunn, L.M. (1968) 'Special education for the mildly retarded – is much of it justifiable?', *Exceptional Children*, Vol. 35: 5–22.

Dyson, A., Farrell, P., Polat, F., Hutcheson, G. and Gallannaugh, F. (2004) *Inclusion and pupil achievement* (Research Report RR578), Nottingham, UK: Department for Education and Skills.

Elbaum, B. (2002) 'The self-concept of students with learning disabilities: a meta-analysis of comparisons across different placements', *Learning Disabilities Research and Practice*, Vol. 17: 216–226.

Ellins, J. and Porter, J. (2005) 'Departmental difficulties in attitudes to special educational needs in the secondary school', *British Journal of Special Education*, Vol. 32: 188–195.

Emanuelsson, I. (2001) 'Reactive versus proactive support coordinator roles: an international comparison', *European Journal of Special Needs Education*, Vol. 16: 133–142.

Evans, J., Harden, A. and Thomas, J. (2004) 'What are effective strategies to support pupils with emotional and behavioural difficulties (EBD) in mainstream primary schools? Findings from a systematic review of research', *Journal of Research in Special Educational Needs*, Vol. 4: 2–16.

Farrell, P., Balshaw, M. and Polat, F. (1999) *The management, role and training of learning support assistants* (Research Report RR161), Nottingham, UK: Department for Education and Skills.

Fisher, D., Roach, V. and Frey, N. (2002) 'Examining the general programmatic benefits of inclusive schools', *International Journal of Inclusive Education*, Vol. 6: 63–78.

Flem, A. and Keller, C. (2000) 'Inclusion in Norway: a study of ideology in practice', *European Journal of Special Needs Education*, Vol. 15: 188–205.

Flem, A., Moen, T. and Gudmunsdottir, S. (2004) 'Towards inclusive schools: a study of inclusive education in practice', *European Journal of Special Needs Education*, Vol. 19: 85–98.

Frederickson, N., Dunsmuir, S., Lang, J. and Monsen, J. (2004) 'Mainstream-special school inclusion partnerships: pupil, parent and teacher perspectives', *International Journal of Inclusive Education*, Vol. 8: 37–57.

French, N.K. (2001) 'Supervising paraprofessionals: a survey of teacher practices', *Journal of Special Education*, Vol. 35: 41–53.

Frieire, S. and César, M. (2003) 'Inclusive ideals for inclusive practices: how far is a dream from reality? Five comparative case studies', *European Journal of Special Needs Education*, Vol. 18: 341–354.

Gersten, R., Baker, S. and Lloyd, J.W. (2000) 'Designing high quality research in special education', *Journal of Special Education*, Vol. 34: 2–18.

Gersten, R., Baker, S.K., Smith-Johnson, J., Flojo, J.R. and Hagan-Burke, S. (2004) 'A tale of two decades: trends in support for federally funded experimental research in special education', *Exceptional Children*, Vol. 70: 323–332.

Gersten, R., Fuchs, L.S., Compton, D., Coyne, M., Greenwood, C. and Innocenti, M.S. (2005) 'Quality indicators for group experimental and quasi-experimental research in special education', *Exceptional Children*, Vol. 71: 149–164.

Giangreco, M.F., Edelman, S.W. and Broer, S.M. (2001) 'Respect, appreciation, and acknowledgement of paraprofessionals who support students with disabilities', *Exceptional Children*, Vol. 67: 485–498.

Giangreco, M.F., Edelman, S.W. and Broer, S.M. (2003) 'Schoolwide planning to improve paraeducator supports', *Exceptional Children*, Vol. 70: 63–79.

Giangreco, M.F., Edelman, S.W., Broer, S.M. and Doyle, M.B. (2001) 'Paraprofessional support of students with disabilities: literature from the past decade', *Exceptional Children*, Vol. 68: 45–63.

Goldstein, H., Moss, J.W. and Jordan, L.J. (1965) *The efficacy of special class training on the development of mentally retarded children* (Cognitive Research Report 619), Washington, DC: Department of Health, Education, and Welfare (HEW), Office Education.

Graham, S. (2005) 'Preview', *Exceptional Children*, Vol. 71: 135.

Graham, S. (2006) 'Writing', in Alexander, P. and Winne, P. (eds) *Handbook of educational psychology*, Mahwah, NJ: Erlbaum.

Groom, B. and Rose, R. (2005) 'Supporting the inclusion of pupils with social, emotional and behavioural difficulties in the primary school: the role of teaching assistants', *Journal of Research in Special Education*, Vol. 5: 20–30.

Hall, L.J. and McGregor, J.A. (2000) 'A follow-up study of the peer relationships of children with disabilities in an inclusive school', *Journal of Special Education*, Vol. 34: 114–126.

Hanson, M.J., Horn, E., Sandall, S., Beckman, P., Morgan, M., Marquart, J. *et al.* (2001) 'After preschool inclusion: children's educational pathways over the early school years', *Exceptional Children*, Vol. 68: 65–83.

Heath, N.L., Petrakos, H., Finn, C.A., Karagiannakis, A., McClean-Heywood, D. and Rousseau, C. (2004) 'Inclusion on the final frontier: a model for including children with emotional and behaviour disorders (E/BD) in Canada', *International Journal of Inclusive Education*, Vol. 8: 241–259.

Hegarty, S. (1993) 'Reviewing the literature on integration', *European Journal of Special Needs Education*, Vol. 8: 194–200.

Hillage, J., Pearson, R., Anderson, A. and Tamkin, P. (1998) *Excellence in research on schools* (Research Report RR74), London: Department for Education and Employment.

Horner, R.H., Carr, E.G., Halle, J., McGee, G., Odom, S. and Wolery, M. (2005) 'The use of single-subject research to identify evidence-based practice in special education', *Exceptional Children*, Vol. 71: 165–179.

Hornby, G. and Kidd, P. (2001) 'Transfer from special to mainstream – ten years on', *British Journal of Special Education*, Vol. 28: 10–17.

House of Commons Education and Skills Committee (2006) *Special educational needs: third report of session 2005–6*, Vol. 1, London: The Stationery Office.

Hunt, P., Soto, G., Maire, J. and Doering, K. (2003) 'Collaborative teaming to support students at risk and students with severe disabilities in general education classrooms', *Exceptional Children*, Vol. 69: 315–332.

Kalambouka, A., Farrell, P., Dyson, A. and Kaplan, I. (2005) *The impact of population inclusivity on student outcomes*, London: University of London, Institute of Education, Social Science Research Unit, EPPI-Centre.

Karsten, S., Peetsma, T., Roeleveld, J. and Vergeer, M. (2001) 'The Dutch policy of integration put to the test: differences in academic and psychosocial development of pupils in special and mainstream schools', *European Journal of Special Needs Education*, Vol. 16: 193–205.

Kavale, K.A. and Mostert, M.P. (2003) 'River of ideology, islands of evidence', *Exceptionality*, Vol. 11: 191–208.

Kugelmass, J.W. (2001) 'Collaboration and compromise in creating and sustaining an inclusive school', *International Journal of Inclusive Education*, Vol. 5: 47–65.

Lewis, A. and Norwich, B. (2005) *Special teaching for special children? Pedagogies for inclusion*, Maidenhead, UK: Open University Press.

Lindsay, G. (1989) 'Evaluating integration', *Educational Psychology in Practice*, Vol. 5: 7–16.

Lindsay, G. (2003) 'Inclusive education: a critical perspective', *British Journal of Special Education*, Vol. 30: 3–12.

Lindsay, G., Muijs, D., Harris, A., Chapman, C., Arweck, E. and Goodall, J. (2007) *Evaluation of the federations programme* (Research Report), Nottingham, UK: Department for Education and Skills.

Lindsay, G., Pather, S. and Strand, S. (2006) *Special educational needs and ethnicity* (Research Report 757), Nottingham, UK: Department for Education and Skills.

Lunt, I. and Norwich, B. (1999) *Can effective schools be inclusive schools?* London: University of London, Institute of Education.

Madden, N.A., and Slavin, R.E. (1983) 'Mainstreaming students with mild handicaps: academic and social outcomes', *Review of Educational Research*, Vol. 53: 519–569.

Manset, G. and Semmel, M.I. (1997) 'Are inclusive programmes for students with mild disabilities effective? A comparative review of model programmes', *Journal of Special Education*, Vol. 31: 155–180.

Markussen, E. (2004) 'Special education: does it help? A study of special education in Norwegian upper secondary schools', *European Journal of Special Needs Education*, Vol. 19: 33–48.

Marshall, J., Ralph, S. and Palmer, S. (2002) 'I wasn't trained to work with them: mainstream teachers' attitudes to children with speech and language difficulties', *International Journal of Inclusive Education*, Vol. 6: 199–215.

McLeskey, J. (2004) 'Classic articles in special education', *Remedial and Special Education*, Vol. 25: 79–87.

Mills, P.E., Cole, K.N., Jenkins, J.R. and Dale, P.S. (1998) 'Effects of differing levels of inclusion on preschoolers with disabilities', *Exceptional Children*, Vol. 65: 79–90.

Mithaug, D.E. (1998) 'The alternative to ideological inclusion', in Vitello, S.J. and Mithaug, D.E. (eds) *Inclusive schooling: national and international perspectives*, Mahwah, NJ: Erlbaum.

Monchy, M., de Pijl, S.J. and Jan-Zandberg, T.S. (2004) 'Discrepancies in judging social inclusion and bullying of pupils with behaviour problems', *European Journal of Special Needs Education*, Vol. 19: 317–330.

Moran, A. and Abbott, L. (2002) 'Developing inclusive schools: the pivotal role of teaching assistants in promoting inclusion in special and mainstream schools in Northern Ireland', *European Journal of Special Needs Education*, Vol. 17: 161–173.

Myklebust, J.O. (2002) 'Inclusion or exclusion? Transitions among special needs students in upper secondary education in Norway', *European Journal of Special Needs Education*, Vol. 17: 251–263.

National Reading Panel (2000) *Teaching children to read: an evidence-based assessment of scientific research literature on reading and its implications for reading instruction*, Washington, DC: National Institute of Child Health and Human Development.

National Research Council (2002) 'Scientific research in education', in Shavelson, R.J. and Tourne, L. (eds) *Committee on scientific principles for educational research*, Washington, DC: National Academy Press.

Norwich, B. and Kelly, N. (2005) *Moderate learning difficulties and the future of inclusion*, London: RoutledgeFalmer.

Odom, S.L.K., Viztum, J.,Wolery, R., Lieber, J., Sandall, S., Hanson, M.J., Beckman, P., Schwartz, I. and Horn, E. (2004) 'Preschool inclusion in the United States: a review of research from an ecological systems perspective', *Journal of Research in Special Educational Needs*, Vol. 4: 17–49.

Odom, S., Brantlinger, E., Gersten, R., Horner, R.H., Thompson, B. and Harris, K.R. (2005) 'Research in special education: scientific methods and evidence-based practice', *Exceptional Children*, Vol. 71: 137–148.

Office of Her Majesty's Chief Inspector (2005) *The annual report of Her Majesty's Chief Inspector of Schools 2004/05*, London: Ofsted.

Office for Standards in Education (2002) *Teaching assistants in primary schools: an evaluation of the quality and impact of their work*, London: Ofsted.

Pavri, S. and Monda-Amaya, L. (2000) 'Loneliness and students with learning disabilities in inclusive classrooms: self-perceptions, coping strategies and preferred interventions', *Learning Disabilities Research and Practice*, Vol. 15: 22–33.

Pavri, S. and Monda-Amaya, L. (2001) 'Social support in inclusive schools: student and teacher perspectives', *Exceptional Children*, Vol. 67: 391–411.

Peters, S. (2002) 'Inclusive education in accelerated and professional development schools: a casebased study of two school reform efforts in the USA', *International Journal of Inclusive Education*, Vol. 6: 287–308.

Pijl, S.J. and Hamstra, D. (2005) 'Assessing pupil development and education in an inclusive setting', *International Journal of Inclusive Education*, Vol. 9: 181–192.

Pirrie, A., Head, G. and Brna, P. (2006) *Mainstreaming pupils with special educational needs*, Edinburgh: Scottish Executive Education Department.

Praisner, C.L. (2003) 'Attitudes of elementary school principals toward the inclusion of students with disabilities', *Exceptional Children*, Vol. 69: 135–145.

Pressley, M., Graham, S. and Harris, K.R. (2006) 'The state of educational research', *British Journal of Educational Psychology*, Vol. 76: 1–20.

Rafferty, Y., Piscitelli, V. and Boettcher, C. (2003) 'The impact of inclusion on language development and social competence among preschoolers with disabilities', *Exceptional Children*, Vol. 69: 467–479.

Rea, P.J., McLaughlan, V.L. and Walther-Thomas, C. (2002) 'Outcomes for students with learning disabilities in inclusive and pullout programmes', *Exceptional Children*, Vol. 68: 203–223.

Riggs, C.C. and Mueller, P.H. (2001) 'Employment and utilization of paraeducators in inclusive settings', *Journal of Special Education*, Vol. 35: 54–62.

Rustemier, S. (2002) *Social and educational justice: the human rights framework for inclusion*, Bristol, UK: Centre for Studies on Inclusive Education.

Scruggs, T.E. and Mastropieri, M.A. (1996) 'Teacher perspectives of mainstreaming-inclusion, 1958–1995: a research synthesis', *Exceptional Children*, Vol. 63: 59–74.

Sebba, J. and Sachdev, D. (1997) *What works in inclusive education?*, Ilford, UK: Barnado's.

Seethaler, P.M. and Fuchs, L.S. (2005) 'A drop in the bucket: randomized contact trials testing reading and math interventions', *Learning Disabilities Research and Practice*, Vol. 20: 98–102.

Skårbrevik, K.J. (2005) 'The quality of special education for students with special needs in ordinary classes', *European Journal of Special Needs Education*, Vol. 20: 387–401.

Skiba, R.J., Simmons, A.B., Poloni-Staudinger, L., Feggins-Azziz, L.R. and Chung, C. (2005) 'Unproven links: can poverty explain disproportionality in special education?', *Journal of Special Education*, Vol. 39: 130–144.

Takala, M. and Aunio, P. (2005) 'Exploring a new inclusive model in Finnish early childhood special education: a 3-year follow-up study', *International Journal of Inclusive Education*, Vol. 9: 39–54.

Thompson, B., Diamond, K.E., McWilliam, R., Snyder, P. and Snyder, S.W. (2005) 'Evaluating the quality of evidence from correlational research for evidence-based practice', *Exceptional Children*, Vol. 71: 181–194.

Tizard, J. (1973) 'Maladjusted children and the child guidance service', *London Educational Review*, Vol. 2: 22–37.

Tooley, J. and Darby, D. (1998) *Educational research: a critique*, London: Ofsted.

Wallace, T., Anderson, A.R., Bartholomay, T. and Hupp, S. (2002) 'An ecobehavioral examination of high school classrooms that include students with disabilities', *Exceptional Children*, Vol. 68: 345–359.

Wedell, K. (2005) 'Dilemmas in the quest for inclusion', *British Journal of Special Education*, Vol. 32: 3–11.

What Works Clearinghouse (2006) *Standards* (US Department of Education), www.whatworks. ed.gov/reviewprocess/standards.html; accessed 14 February 2006.

Wiener, J. and Tardiff, C.Y. (2004) 'Social and emotional functioning of children with learning disabilities: does special education placement make a difference?', *Learning Disabilities Research and Practice*, Vol. 19: 20–32.

Zeleke, S. (2004) 'Self-concepts of students with learning disabilities and their normally achieving peers: a review', *European Journal of Special Needs Education*, Vol. 19: 145–170.

Zigmond, N. (2003) 'Where should students with disabilities receive special education services? Is one place better than another?', *Journal of Special Education*, Vol. 37: 193–199.

SETTING OR MIXED ABILITY?

Teachers' views of the organisation of pupils for learning

Chris M.M. Smith and
Margaret J. Sutherland

A NOTE FROM THE EDITORS

This reading reviews the attitudes of teachers about the different ways of grouping pupils.

This reading links with Unit 4.1 of the 5th edition of *Learning to teach in the secondary school*.

QUESTIONS TO CONSIDER

1   Evidence over recent decades suggests that setting pupils for teaching purposes does not have significant advantages for pupil achievement. Why do many teachers and parents believe that setting or streaming is preferred to mixed ability teaching despite this evidence? Should evidence not related to achievement be used in identifying teaching groups?

2   To what extent should the views of pupils about the experience of being placed in particular teaching groups be considered in identifying a policy for grouping?

3   Is identifying the best way to group pupils another example of trying to 'square the circle'. Just as there is evidence that many girls do better in single sex classrooms and some boys do better in a mixed gender class, so too low-achieving pupils do better in a mixed ability classroom, but high achievers do well in a streamed situation. Are there ways forward?

This reading was first published as: Smith, C.M.M. and Sutherland, M.J. (2003) 'Setting or mixed ability? Teachers' views of the organisation of pupils for learning', *Journal of Research in Special Educational Needs*, Vol. 3: 141–146.

ABSTRACT

This paper examines how staff in schools formulate decisions about pupil organisation. A small sample of primary and secondary schools from across Scotland was involved in the study. In 1996 Her Majesty's Inspectors published a report entitled *Achievement for All* (SOEID, 1996) which, it was envisaged, would form the basis of school evaluations into the effectiveness of classroom organisation. This report, and in particular the six principles on which it suggested effective organisational arrangements should rest, formed the organising framework for the study.

The study had three main aims:

1   to ascertain the extent to which the principles outlined in the HMI report had been used by school staff when making decisions about which form of organisation to use
2   to comment on the perceptions of teaching staff of how well the arrangements in place were working
3   to ascertain how the impact on teaching and learning was being evaluated.

INTRODUCTION

Achievement for all (SOEID, 1996) identified a number of key principles governing the organisation of pupils by class, or within class, in Scottish schools and concluded that:

> The application of these principles does not give rise to one, universally best method of organising pupils into classes. If used effectively, both mixed ability and setting may be appropriate forms of organisation ... It is important that the forms of organisation employed in schools are subject to rigorous analysis and evaluation to ensure that they meet the key principles ... Decisions about class organisation must be based on an objective appraisal of what is likely to be the effect for pupils and upon realistic expectations of teachers.
>
> (SOEID, 1996: para. 5.4)

This conclusion is in keeping with available reviews of research on the topic. In the year following the publication of *Achievement for all,* The Scottish Council for Research in Education (SCRE) published a review of research related to setting and streaming in schools (Harlen and Malcolm, 1997). This review concluded that there is: 'no consistent and reliable evidence of positive effects of setting and streaming in any subjects or for students of particular ability levels' (p. 40). This confirmed the conclusions of an earlier review by Slavin (1990) that found no effects of ability grouping on pupils' achievements for any level of ability. More recently, research by Ireson *et al.* (2002) confirmed that 'neither setting nor mixed ability provide significant advantages in terms of raising achievement' (p. 1).

However, tensions in *Achievement for all* are evident, in particular between the advice being offered, that is, 'The main consideration in organising pupils into classes should be to create the best conditions for effective learning and teaching ...' (SOEID, 1996: para. 2.1) and the main recommendations:

> In primary schools attainment groups should be the principal means of organising pupils in English language and mathematics.
>
> (SOEID, 1996: para. 5.12)

> In secondary schools, much greater use should be made of attainment groups in all subjects. Broadband setting should be introduced in English and mathematics from S1 [age 11–12] and, where feasible, in a number of other subjects by S2 [age 12–13], particularly in science and modern languages.
>
> (SOEID, 1996: para. 5.13)

Despite an absence of research evidence to favour setting as the most effective organisational arrangements, many schools have changed their organisational procedures in line with the recommendations outlined in the HMI document (*Times Educational Supplement Scotland*, 2002) and as advocated by the Right Honourable Jack McConnell MSP, First Minister of the Scottish Parliament (McConnell, 2002), in a speech to Scottish head teachers.

There is, therefore, a contradiction evident with policy makers in that setting continues to be advocated, although it is also recognised that there is no significant research evidence to favour this form of organisation. Schools are caught between these two conflicting messages:

> As neither setting nor mixed ability organisation appears to offer great advantages in terms of raising standards, decisions about the best way to group pupils should be based on other considerations. It is time for a reassessment of the organisation of pupils to achieve a better alignment between grouping, pedagogy and learning outcomes. Social outcomes should also be considered.
>
> (Ireson *et al.*, 2002: 12)

METHODOLOGY

A total of eleven schools were included in the investigation (four primary and seven secondary). All schools had been identified by HMI as exemplifying good practice in recent inspections.

One department in each of the secondary schools was included in the research. This involved four subject areas: English, mathematics, science and modern languages. Four secondary schools organised pupils by broad-band setting, two used mixed ability teaching, and one used within-class setting. Thus five departments organised pupils by setting (either within class or across classes). In each secondary school, one member of the management structure (with responsibility for pupil organisation), the principal teacher of the subject and two classroom teachers from within the same department were interviewed.

All four primary schools in the research used broad-band setting in mathematics and English language. These primary schools also organised the pupils by mixed ability for class work in the other curricular areas. Thus, all the teachers interviewed in the primary schools had current experience of both methods of organisation. In each primary school, one member of the senior management team and two teachers involved in the set arrangements were interviewed.

All staff were interviewed using a semi-structured interview schedule. In total, thirty-three members of staff were interviewed.

The interview schedule included four key sections pertinent to this paper:

1   knowledge and use of Scottish Office Education and Industry Department (SOEID) principles;
2   rationale for the organisational procedures currently in place;
3   perspectives on how well the current arrangements were meeting the six principles outlined in the SOEID report, *Achievement for All*;
4   evaluation of the current arrangements.

The interview schedules – detailing the areas and topics to be covered – were issued to schools in advance of the visit in order to give individuals time to consider their responses. Prior to each visit, researchers obtained relevant policies and documentation from each school to provide background information.

KNOWLEDGE AND USE OF THE SOEID PRINCIPLES

Achievement for all (SOEID, 1996) provided key principles around which schools might reflect and base decisions. In order to ensure effective learning and teaching, it suggested the organisation of pupils by class or within class should:

■   create conditions that motivate all pupils to make sustained progress in learning within a common curriculum framework;
■   be flexible in responding to pupils' academic, personal and social development;
■   make it clear that the achievements and progress of each pupil are valued;
■   promote teaching that builds on the prior learning and attainments of pupils;
■   free teachers to spend most of their time on direct teaching and enable pupils to work effectively on challenging tasks; and be feasible and appropriate in terms of expectations of teachers and pupils.

(SOEID, 1996: para. 2.2)

It became clear, however, that the schools in this study were not utilising the advice contained in the *Achievement for all* document when deciding on the organisational arrangements that would be adopted. While the staff of three schools were familiar with the existence of the document, only two of the school personnel interviewed had actually read it. No school used it or any other framework to evaluate the effectiveness of the organisational arrangements in place or to help in the decision-making process when a change in organisational procedures was being contemplated.

RATIONALE FOR THE ORGANISATIONAL PROCEDURES CURRENTLY IN PLACE

All schools believed firmly in their choice and could offer a rationale for the organisational arrangements adopted. For those schools using set arrangements, their reasons included the following:

■   it is easier for teachers to deal with a smaller range of ability;
■   it was a way of separating out pupils with behaviour problems so that at least some could have a chance to learn;

- ■ it would improve results;
- ■ more able pupils could be challenged more easily;
- ■ mixed ability encourages teaching to the middle and therefore is inappropriate for a good number of pupils in the class.

For those schools using mixed ability arrangements, their reasons included the following:

- ■ it did not stigmatise pupils;
- ■ it reduced the possibilities of bullying;
- ■ pupils helped one another and contributed to a more positive class ethos;
- ■ setting was a divisive and elitist approach.

STAFF PERSPECTIVES OF THE IMPACT ON TEACHING AND LEARNING OF THE ARRANGEMENTS RELATED TO THE SIX PRINCIPLES IN *ACHIEVEMENT FOR ALL*

Create conditions that motivate all pupils to make sustained progress in learning within a common curriculum framework

The class ethos was acknowledged to be of vital importance to learning. In this respect, schools reported that, when the pupils were placed in sets, the work was *more purposeful* and *focused*.

Staff in primary schools felt they worked more collaboratively when pupils were set. This was viewed as a positive development and motivating for the staff involved: 'I'm much more involved with my colleagues than I was in my last school; you can't work this system unless you do work as a team.'

Motivating particular groups of pupils was acknowledged to be difficult in both mixed ability and set arrangements. It was perceived that it was easier to motivate pupils who work more slowly than others through mixed ability arrangements; however, the motivation of 'more able pupils' was more difficult within mixed ability classes. A particular problem of motivation was identified with set arrangements at the S2 stage: 'in S2 the motivation aspect is more difficult to maintain'.

Be flexible in responding to pupils' academic, personal and social development

Flexibility was perceived to be harder to achieve in set arrangements. There was a tendency to keep top sets full and lower sets deliberately small. However, this led to problems if a pupil did well enough to be 'moved up' and there was no room in the higher set. There could be an awkward transition period when a pupil moved from one set to another, but the difficulty seemed to be exacerbated if a pupil moved 'up' a set: 'if a pupil moves up a set there can be a problem of matching the work during the transition period'. The reality in schools utilising set arrangements was that there was very little movement between sets once they had been established.

In contrast, the range of ability within mixed ability classes was seen to allow pupils to work at their own pace and progress without such organisational barriers.

Make it clear that the achievements and progress of each pupil are valued

All schools mentioned record keeping as the main way of tracking progress:

■ profiling is done through work on the curriculum;
■ a checklist is provided for the purpose of checking that essential elements have been covered;
■ staff keep and maintain records that include all assessments which are made.

Only one school interpreted this point in terms of the messages that pupils receive about their achievement and progress, although one school did mention that 'the ethos is one of cooperation amongst pupils and support for one another rather than competition between them'. There are implications for how pupils perceive that their progress and achievements are valued if the focus for staff is on the more formal procedures of recording and monitoring progress.

It was interesting to note that staff did not refer directly to tests as a means of letting pupils know about their achievement and progress. This was in contrast to the findings in a survey of pupils where testing was identified as a key way in which they received feedback about their achievement and progress (Smith and Sutherland, 2002).

Promote teaching that builds on the prior learning and attainments of pupils

Staff spoke in depth about the information transfer arrangements in place within their school and across sectors. The notion of building on prior learning was generally acknowledged to be an essential feature of effective learning and teaching. However, it became apparent that some issues exist in relation to this principle. Several comments indicated that some teachers equate building on prior learning with pupils having the same teacher over an elongated period of time.

> If you know the children well it can have positive and negative effects. Knowledge of a child is certainly very important, but it may be that they and you need a change.

> When you have the same class in S1 and S2 you really know the pupils and so you can work the class to suit their needs.

Some reservations were expressed by primary teachers who felt that the information collected and transferred to the local secondary schools was not being used.

> Secondary schools must acknowledge the learning that has taken place in primary schools.

In one secondary school it was stated that the pupils were retested on entry to the secondary schools, as the results from the associated primary schools were inconsistent and unreliable.

Free teachers to spend most of their time on direct teaching and enable pupils to work effectively on challenging tasks

While direct teaching, as defined by *Achievement for all*, includes one-to-one tuition, small group lessons and whole-class teaching, schools had interpreted this as equating almost exclusively to whole-class teaching. In set arrangements, it was perceived that more direct teaching (in the form of whole-class teaching) could and would occur. Thus, in those schools that used set arrangements, the dominant pedagogy was whole-class teaching for all levels of sets.

In contrast, in those schools operating mixed ability arrangements, direct teaching was less dependent on whole-class sessions. The term had been interpreted to encompass small group teaching and individual tuition, as well as the possibility of whole-class sessions. Two ways of maximising direct teaching opportunities were mentioned: the encouragement and facilitation of independent learning by pupils, and the use of other adults in the room (for example, learning support staff). Teachers operating with mixed ability classes were acutely aware of the range of abilities within their classes and identified the use of all forms of direct teaching as a means of catering for this diversity.

Be feasible and appropriate in terms of expectations of teachers and pupils

Setting was perceived to reduce pressure on a teacher in terms of preparation and class management: 'Setting is easier to plan and prepare for.' On the other hand, with mixed ability arrangements, it was felt that 'a lot more is expected of teachers and it takes a great deal more effort than other methods of organisation.' This perception was borne out in the findings from the survey of pupils (Smith and Sutherland, 2002), where pupils overwhelmingly perceived setting as being easier to manage for the teacher.

STAFF EVALUATION OF THE CURRENT ARRANGEMENTS

No formal evaluation procedures (that focused on the organisational arrangements for pupils) were carried out in any school. However, given that reasons could be offered for the adoption of particular organisational arrangements (see above), and that both advantages and disadvantages of adopting set arrangements could be identified (see below), there was evidence that teachers had been involved in a good deal of reflection on the issues.

In total, six schools had experience of mixed ability from which to draw. For the two secondary departments using mixed ability arrangements, the decision to continue with organising pupils on a mixed ability basis involved a conviction that the arrangements in place were working well and that there would be no advantage in changing them. Both departments referred to favourable HMI reports and good exam results as evidence that the arrangements were working. The four primary schools involved in the study also had experience of mixed ability organisation for general class work, and their perceptions of this work are included here. Staff interviewed from the six schools operating mixed ability organisation perceived the advantages of mixed ability to be that:

■   there was less likelihood of pupil stigmatisation;
■   it was easier to maintain the motivation of those pupils working at a slower rate;

- there was greater flexibility for pupils to progress at their own rates;
- pupils benefited from peer support.

Disadvantages were also identified:

- it required a good deal – sometimes inordinate amounts – of organisation and preparation for staff;
- it could be difficult to provide appropriate challenges for the most able pupils;
- it meant that whole-class lessons were difficult to undertake because of the range of abilities in the class.

Nine schools in total were involved in organising their pupils by setting: five secondary departments and all four primary schools. Staff perceived the advantages of setting to be that:

- it encouraged teamwork and collaboration with colleagues in primary schools;
- it permitted a different ethos to be created. In particular it focused attention, and work became more purposeful;
- the preparation and 'set management' were easier for the teacher;
- more whole-class teaching could take place.

Disadvantages were also identified:

- motivating pupils in the slower sets was difficult;
- the sets were often fairly rigid and inflexible;
- moving pupils from one set to another, particularly those moving 'up a set', was problematic in two ways. First, if the top set was full, then these was no space for a pupil who may be better placed in that top set. Second, the curriculum was perceived to be so different between sets that a smooth transition between one set and another was difficult to achieve;
- staffing issues arose. In set arrangements three, and in some cases four, members of staff were required to cover two classes. If, as in the case of primary schools, this involved senior management team members, then the impact of other duties could mean set arrangements being abandoned.

Of concern to the researchers was the fact that pupils' perceptions had not influenced these reflections by staff. In fact, pupil perceptions had not formally been sought by any of the schools involved. There was evidence in two schools that pupils had been invited informally to offer their opinions on the organisational arrangement in place. When pupils were interviewed as part of a larger study into perceptions of organisational arrangements in schools (Smith and Sutherland, 2002), it was found that, in some schools, pupils held opposing views to teachers as to the effectiveness of the pupil organisation in place. In one school, for example, the staff were clear that no stigmatisation occurred as a result of set arrangements, while the pupils interviewed reported several instances of verbal bullying taking place.

DISCUSSION

The mixed messages from policy, inspections and research put schools in a difficult position. It was clear, from the rationale that could be offered and the identification of advantages and disadvantages of each organisational arrangement in place, that staff had formed opinions about the effectiveness of the arrangements. Some of the same principles as were outlined in *Achievement for all* (SOEID, 1996), in particular motivation, flexibility and feasibility for staff, were considered to be indicators of the effectiveness of the arrangements. However, other principles in *Achievement for all,* in particular valuing progress and achievement, building on prior learning and the appropriateness of the arrangements for the pupils, had not been considered by staff as being particularly related to the organisational arrangements in place.

The staff in the study reported that it was harder to motivate pupils in the lower sets; however, there was no recognition of the dangers for other groups in set arrangements. It has been established, for example, that girls can be demotivated by fast pace and pressure to succeed (Boaler, 1997a–c). There was some evidence that a similar ethos was being cultivated in top sets in this study. The schools involved had reported that the ethos had become more purposeful and focused, and this was viewed as a positive outcome of the set arrangements. However, Ireson *et al.* (2002) found that pupils in top sets suffer because the fast pace and heightened focus on coverage of the curriculum mean that they cannot do things in depth. A recent response to the national debate on education by the Scottish Executive Education Department (SEED, 2003) acknowledged that an overcrowded curriculum dominated by a testing and exam culture had been to the detriment of creativity and a narrow focus on key academic areas.

The findings of the research raise the question of why set classes appear more purposeful and focused than mixed ability classes. The introduction of setting would appear to coincide with increased pressure and pace – at least for the top sets. It may relate partly to the fact that primary schools reported greater involvement in teamwork with colleagues when setting was in place. This involvement may mean that staff members themselves are more focused and purposeful, and that this is carried over into the ethos of the set classes. Further investigation as to why this might be the case and why focus and purpose are less likely to be associated with mixed ability classes is required.

It was generally recognised by schools in the study that a lack of flexibility posed some problems within set arrangements. There were particular problems acknowledged in set arrangements in respect of pupils moving from one set to another due to the differing pace at which the sets worked. This was compounded by the tendency to keep numbers in the top sets high, thus limiting the possibilities for movement. As with the current study, Ireson *et al.* (2002) found that, 'there is limited movement between groups, so that even if pupils improve they may not be allowed to be moved to higher sets' (p. 11). An assumption that a set comprised a much more homogenous group of learners led to the increased use of certain pedagogical methods, such as whole-class teaching. However, this has been found to be flawed thinking, as Ireson *et al.* (2002: 11) suggest: 'even when fine setting is used set sizes of 25–30 inevitably contain pupils with a range of attainments.' Further, Hallam *et al.* (cited by Ireson *et al.*, 2002) suggest that teachers working with set arrangements use a limited pedagogy, even though they may be capable of, and had previously utilised, a wider range.

The wide spread of attainment in sets would be less problematic if appropriate teaching methods were used, with a variety of activities and differentiated work within the classroom. Evidence suggests that this is unlikely, as even teachers who use these methods with mixed ability classes fail to employ them when teaching sets.
(Hallam *et al.*, cited by Ireson *et al.*, 2002: 11)

One of the principles of *Achievement for all* was that achievements and progress should be valued. However, the focus by those schools using set arrangements was on monitoring and recording progress rather than on valuing of achievement and progress. This was evident in the section of the study that looked at pupils' perceptions of the arrangements in place (Smith and Sutherland, 2002). In this concurrent study, pupils reported dissatisfaction with the use of formal test results as a dominant factor in selection into sets. They particularly felt that this did not accurately reflect their achievements and progress. Staff acknowledged that teaching should build on prior learning but equated the effectiveness of this with teaching the same classes from one year to another. This was specifically related to the secondary sector, where staff see pupils for only a limited number of periods per week. Pressure on teachers to cover the curriculum and to achieve targets may impact on their ability to forge meaningful relationships with pupils in their class. This may be especially difficult when class sizes are at their maximum (in Scotland that is thirty in primary classes P1–3 for 4–6 year-olds, thirty-three in primary classes P4–6 for 7–10 year-olds, and thirty in non-practical classes in secondary S1 and S2).

It would appear that an issue still exists with the transition period from primary to secondary education, with primary schools still reporting that information passed on is not being used. It would appear that there is a lack of confidence in the information being transferred from one sector to another. The recent response to the national debate by the Scottish Executive (SEED, 2003) has suggested that teachers should be able to teach in both sectors, and that this may increase continuity at the transition phase.

The question of whether the adoption of particular organisational arrangements impacts on pedagogy remains to be addressed fully. As with Hallam *et al.* (cited by Ireson *et al.*, 2002), this study found that teachers involved in set arrangements held a narrower definition of direct teaching than those involved in mixed ability arrangements. An assumption of homogeneity led to the belief that all pupils could work at the same pace and in the same way. This, once again, contradicted what more than one pupil reported in the concurrent study: 'although it's ability it's still mixed!' (Smith and Sutherland, 2002). There was a clear perception from staff interviewed for this study that setting was easier for the teacher to manage. Thus, while sets may be *feasible* (SOEID, 1996) in terms of teacher workload, it would appear that they may not, necessarily, be more *appropriate* (SOEID, 1996) in terms of pupil learning.

CONCLUSIONS

Given that the document *Achievement for all* (SOEID, 1996) was not used by schools in this study, it raises the question of the place and use of such reports in and by schools. In addition, all of these schools had received recent favourable reports from HMI who, presumably, did use the principles from the document in their evaluations. It may be that, from the teachers' point of view, some principles relate more closely to the organisational arrangements in place than others, and that both forms of organisation can meet all six principles satisfactorily for the purposes of HMI inspections. Particular forms of organisation, however, would appear to be able to meet some of the six principles more easily than others.

In set arrangements, it would appear that motivation might be an issue for some pupils, and there is a lack of flexibility in the allocation of pupils to sets and in movement between sets. Sets were, however, perceived to be easier for the teachers to organise and manage and, although research evidence may dispute the perception, more motivating for the more able pupils. In mixed ability arrangements, the motivation of the most able pupils can prove difficult, and it is perceived as much harder for teachers to cater adequately for everyone in the class. However, mixed ability is perceived to offer greater flexibility.

Some of the perceptions of staff seem to be at odds with the research evidence currently available. It was felt by schools which utilised setting arrangements that motivation of those in the top sets was easier to achieve. There is some research evidence to suggest that the fast pace and competition that emerge in these top sets can prove to be an issue for the motivation of girls in particular. It also emerged from the rationale of those schools adopting setting that there was a belief that this would improve results. The research available would suggest that this is not the case. The issue that emerges is not whether schools and staff are reflecting on the issues – they clearly are; it perhaps relates more to the utilisation of research findings in their decision-making and their procedures for formal evaluation of the arrangements.

Finally, it would seem that inclusion of pupils' opinions and insights into the impact of organisational arrangements on their learning would be an invaluable source of information in any evaluation procedure. Indeed, recent legislation (The Standards in Scotland's Schools etc. 2000 Act) requires schools to involve pupils in the decision-making processes that affect their learning. The omission of this crucial group in the consideration of such important issues remains to be addressed.

REFERENCES

Boaler, J. (1997a) 'Setting, social class and survival of the quickest', *British Educational Research Journal*, Vol. 23, No. 5: 575–595.

Boaler, J. (1997b) 'When even the winners are losers: evaluating the experiences of "top set" students', *Journal of Curriculum Studies*, Vol. 29, No. 2: 165–182.

Boaler, J. (1997c) *Experiencing school mathematics: teaching styles, sex and setting*, Buckingham: Open University Press.

Harlen, W. and Malcolm, H. (1997) *Setting and streaming: a research review*, Edinburgh: SCRE.

Ireson, J., Hallam, S. and Hurley, C. (2002) 'Ability grouping in the secondary school: effects on GCSE attainment in English, mathematics and science'. Paper presented at the *British Educational Research Association Annual Conference*, 10–14 September, Exeter University, Exeter.

McConnell, J. (2002) 'The future of education'. Speech given by the First Minister of the Scottish Parliament to an audience of head teachers, 5 November, Glasgow.

SEED (2003) *Educating for excellence, choice and opportunity: the executive's response to the national debate*, Edinburgh: HMSO.

SOEID (1996) *Achievement for all*, Edinburgh: HMSO.

Slavin, R.E. (1990) 'Student achievement effects of ability grouping in secondary schools: a best evidence synthesis', *Review of Educational Research*, Vol. 60: 471–499.

Smith, Chris M.M. and Sutherland, M.J. (2002) 'Setting or mixed ability? Pupils' views of the organizational arrangement in their school'. Paper presented at the *Annual Conference of the Scottish Educational Research Association* (SERA), Dundee.

Times Educational Supplement Scotland (TESS) (2002) 'Setting versus mixed ability', *Scotland Plus*, 22 November: 2–3.

MORAL EDUCATION IN PRACTICE

Colin Wringe

Having considered in some detail both the scope and content of moral education and what it is to be morally educated, we might be tempted to say that the manner in which moral education is to be achieved is a matter for empirical rather than philosophical enquiry, or simply one of personal or professional experience. Different children, different groups of children, children in different personal and social circumstances, we might feel, need to be dealt with differently, and only individual experience and individual insight can enable educators, be they parents, teachers or youth workers, to sum up individual learners and the situation in which they find themselves. Neither philosophical deduction nor, indeed, empirical generalisation can identify the child for whom moral considerations are not yet an issue, or the one committed to a notion of good conduct that is uncritical and one-sided. A similar point may be made about groups of pupils or other learners. In some school classes, there may be a strong sense of doing what is sensible in the interests of all, of justice and fair play, but not much sign of caring for those who lose out in life, while the members of other groups may respond with care and concern for each others' joys and sorrows but not have much awareness or commitment to the rights, interests and reasonable expectations of those outside the group. Does one attempt to build outwards from the strengths of the pupils one has, or begin by tackling what one sees as weaknesses and shortcomings? This will depend on the educator's judicious assessment, not only of the learners concerned, but of his or her own strengths and weaknesses and what McLaughlin and Halstead (1999) term pedagogic phronesis.

Formal empirical enquiries into the effectiveness of moral education need to be framed with some care. Those that attempt to correlate inputs or structural conditions with behavioural outcomes may mislead or simply be beside the point, given the centrality of reasons for conduct rather than observable conduct itself in the evaluation of moral development. On the other hand, a difficulty with more individualised, interpretive enquiries is that young people are bound to see researchers as adults whose approval they may seek or against whom they may wish to protect their private thoughts. If skilfully constructed and sensitively carried out, however, such enquiries may be helpful in bringing to the attention of educators the range of moral attitudes among both learners and moral educators themselves. Though the professional experience of teachers and other groups involved in various ways in the task of moral education and the accumulating wisdom of parents and other carers may lead to the development of strategies for coping on a day-to-day basis with the task of moral education, there nevertheless remain a number of general points to be made about the practice of moral education in the light of our understanding of this task.

Some writers (Kymlicka, 1999; Pritchard, 1996) have felt it appropriate to touch upon the issue of whether it is appropriate for maintained schools to concern themselves with moral education at all. This question seems to have been principally of interest to writers in the United States, where the cultural and especially the religious rights of communities have been a matter of particular concern. The issue is whether a programme of moral education carried out in publicly maintained schools amounts to a programme of indoctrination, infringing the rights of parents to bring up their children according to their own moral and religious traditions. As we have suggested, this concern may be partly met by distinguishing clearly between the behavioural requirements of morality and those of religion and recognising the validity of both for those who believe. It is nevertheless easy to understand the anxieties of those who wish their children to grow up to behave according to religious requirements, that their offspring may be led astray by the less restrictive requirements of rational secular morality. In the process of moral education, schools at least need to recognise, and even explicitly acknowledge, that what may be perfectly acceptable in purely moral terms is, nevertheless, a sin in some religions and therefore to many pupils in the school and to their parents.

This concern of some parents cannot, however, be a reason for totally excluding moral education from schools, and the writers who raise this issue mainly appear to do so in order to dismiss it. Pritchard notes that some 80 per cent of American parents are in favour of schools undertaking some form of moral education, though he admits that the portmanteau term moral education may cover a multitude of meanings. In Britain, there has been little public or parental protest against the affirmation, in the 1988 Education Act, of the longstanding tradition that moral education is an integral part of the function of schools. To this extent, we must suppose that these parents assume that the work schools undertake in this area is continuous with the moral upbringing they would wish to provide at home.

Both Kymlicka (1999) and Crittenden (1999) draw attention to the overlapping requirements of what we may describe as reasonable morality and those of most commonly practised religions. They also point out that most school pupils, of whatever community background, will later interact with the wider community and need to behave in a way that will not only be morally acceptable but also enable them to achieve a measure of social acceptance in that community. They will also need to understand, and to some extent accommodate, the values and moral assumptions of conscientious and well-intentioned members of the wider society, which may be in some regards less restrictive than their own. Children are not the property of either their parents or their community and have the right to develop those virtues and other qualities of character that will lead to their being approved of in the wider community of their peers. They are also entitled to what Feinberg (1980) terms 'an open future', in the sense of being in a position to make their own rational assessment of the life they are to lead, even though they may ultimately be drawn to that embraced by their parents and others in their community. Development of the capacity for considered choice is not indoctrination but the antidote to indoctrination, which neither parents nor communities are entitled to practise at the expense of the younger generation. Schools also have a duty to society at large as well as to parents. This is not to concede that rationality and rational morality are just another ideology that it suits mainstream society to inculcate into its citizens. A younger generation committed to the application of rational judgement may be highly critical of mainstream society and the values it currently embraces. Such, indeed, will be part of the aim of any well-conceived programme of moral education in a society whose moral perfection is as yet incomplete!

Schools cannot, in principle, opt out of the task of moral education. All institutions must embody both rules and values if they are not to descend into chaos, and those who spend a formative part of their lives in those institutions, unless they are irremediably alienated, are bound to absorb some of those values, be they good or bad. It is just possible to conceive of a school attempting to inculcate certain bodies of knowledge and skill in a sterile and morally antiseptic way, keeping order where necessary by coercion and fear, but such an institution would scarcely be morally neutral. The message conveyed by such a school, where teachers withheld any intimation, let alone promotion, of their own views regarding kindness, the avoidance of violence and cruelty, honesty, cooperation and mutual respect, would be the morally devastating one that such considerations were of no account to those we are expected to emulate in our adult lives.

As with many valid educational methodologies, there is a strong presumption of congruence between ends and means of moral education: the link between teaching and learning to be good is not contingent. Aristotle's dictum that we become virtuous by performing virtuous acts is, however, all too easily misinterpreted as advocating a training or habituation model of moral education. In such a view, one learns courage by facing threatening situations, fortitude by being made to endure hardship, truthfulness by being made to acknowledge untrue statements and tidiness by putting away one's things before going to bed. Though this may produce morally acceptable and reliable members of the adult community and satisfy many advocates of more effective moral education in schools, it is scarcely likely to lead to more moral responsibility, moral autonomy, moral courage or moral wisdom or, necessarily, more flourishing lives for the individuals concerned. Debating whether simply instilling the habits of good behaviour truly constitutes moral education, or whether this is merely socialisation or training, may seem to be to engage in the game of definitions for its own sake, for teachers, parents and others charged with the task of bringing up the young must sometimes engage in all three. It is, however, helpful to identify moral education as something peculiarly appropriate to moral beings or those on the way to becoming so. To develop as a moral being, we have suggested, is to become someone who not only chooses to do what is right but chooses to do so because it is right. Baby's moral education only begins when he or she can be persuaded to stop trying to poke Kitty's eye out with a spoon because it is unkind to Kitty, or to stop pulling Daddy's hair because it hurts Daddy. To drink up his (her) milk 'like a good boy (girl)' indicates moral progress, while doing so in response to the threat of some minor sanction does not.

It is sometimes supposed there is an issue about whether there should be specific periods or specific activities set aside for the purpose of moral education in schools, or whether we should, in some way, use other subjects as a medium for moral education. More vaguely still, it may be suggested that we should simply expect values to be absorbed from the whole school environment. Quite clearly, these are not exclusive alternatives, and there is a strong case for making the best possible use of all these approaches. There is no reason why we should neglect any opportunity to educate morally, intellectually or in any other way. Schools certainly need to embody the values they wish to transmit, and no doubt the most important of these will be publicly celebrated in school mottos, prospectuses, mission statements, public addresses on speech days and the like. These are all helpful in making values explicit, though a sense of style and judgement is necessary if they are not to seem smug, complacent or so blatantly at variance with actual practice in the school as to engender cynicism rather than commitment. The goals of moral education are, no doubt, best achieved when young people grow up in a moral community, where what is done is done because, for one reason or another, it is right. Communities exist in which a range of different reasons for doing things may predominate: pride, vanity, family or local prestige, hostility to certain outsiders, ease and pleasure, commercial profit or whatever. In themselves, these motives may not necessarily be inconsistent with acting morally or even, other things being equal, with acting for moral reasons. In a community where the predominant driving motive is financial profit, individuals may be fiercely righteous, even in their commercial dealings. So also may educational institutions strongly committed to the pursuit of knowledge and the development of human skills and capacities. Danger only arises when those learning to be moral or otherwise perceive, as adolescents are quick to perceive, that moral reasons play a secondary role to reasons of a less worthy kind and may, in fact, sometimes be given in pursuit of less worthy goals. The conclusion all too readily drawn in such circumstances is that moral reasons are always used in this way.

Reasons for action may, however, be genuinely mixed. This is a common literary theme, particularly in the genres of comedy and satire. Such literary treatments may perform the morally educative function of setting us on our guard against self-deception or the deception of others, but it is wrong to assume that publicly given reasons are always insincere. The uncritical assumption that they must always be so is one of the more morally corrosive habits of mind and speech that, without stifling healthy scepticism where it is merited, moral educators may need to pick up on and correct. Some sincere nineteenth-century philanthropists may have felt it expedient to argue before their shareholders that it was in their companies' commercial interests to treat their workers more humanely, while idealistic politicians may defend their contributions to overseas development by maintaining, for the sake of their more hard nosed supporters, that they are in the long-term national interest.

The importance, from the point of view of moral education, of acting rightly because it is right makes it clear that any programme of moral education that neglects the cognitive and the question of specifically moral motivation, does so at the risk of not being a programme of moral education at all but one of socialisation into conformity. The young person therefore needs to grow up in a community that not only behaves morally but one in which moral reasons are articulated, however cursorily and infrequently this may be done. This poses something of a problem. In the everyday life of adults, those who justify their actions too often tend to be unpopular, if not actually suspect. They may seem to be either setting themselves up as paragons or trying to coerce us into cooperating in their projects. It is important, however, that those parents, teachers and others whose role is an educative one should not be too inhibited by such thoughts. They are, after all, supposed to be guiding, and even where necessary controlling, the actions of the young. Besides, if reasons are given, this needs to be done not so much by way of justification – that way hypocrisy is learned – but simply as explanation. In such a situation, a young person might learn to do what requires courage, endurance or some personal inconvenience because older people they like, admire or identify with seem to do it naturally because there are reasons for doing it. 'This will make a lot of difference to old Tom and it won't really take us long', 'Others depend on our doing it and would do the same for us', 'It's only fair to Mrs. Jones', 'We care about people, our town, the environment, don't we?', 'Doing it will be an achievement', 'This is something to take a pride in doing'. From this, it necessarily follows that if the older generation is to be successful in morally educating the young it must begin by reforming itself. We cannot expect young people to learn kindness and caring where the weak are bullied and abused, tolerance and respect where role models are destructive and censorious, truthfulness where school mission statements, while avoiding literal falsehood, are couched in terms calculated to impress rather than enlighten and guide, or justice where privileged and underprivileged alike are bound to perceive that neither material advantages nor life chances are distributed fairly.

Schools are likely to be more powerful as agents of moral education if they are experienced by their pupils as communities of which they themselves are members, rather than as somewhere you have to go each morning and stay there until 3.30, or somewhere you go with the instrumental aim of eventually obtaining certain educational qualifications. If teachers are to be morally significant figures in the lives of pupils, they need to be experienced as part of the 'we', older and, of course, more influential members of that community, rather than purely as figures of authority or objects of hostility, alien figures who dispense the instruction one goes there to get, who are there to keep order or actively persecute one or one's friends as the case may be. How successful a school is in turning itself into a community rather than an institution will depend on many things: interpersonal relations between staff and between staff and pupils, the accessibility of the school and its facilities, so that pupils come to see it as 'theirs', the richness of out-of-school activities and the number and success of whole-school social events in which pupils, parents and staff take part.

Insofar as teachers are significant figures in the lives of pupils, their own conduct is likely, for good or for ill, to be influential. This is not an argument for the old-fashioned view that teachers should be persons of irreproachable private lives. More important is the way teachers interact with their pupils and the way they are seen by pupils to do their job. Children are not the shrewd judges of character they are sometimes said to be. Arrogant bullies are often thought to be 'strict but fair' by those who are lucky enough not to be victimised by them, and those who are conscientious and kindly may be thought of as weak unless they sometimes go out of their way to use the word 'must' and mean it. They are nevertheless capable of deciding which of their teachers are conscientious, care enough about them to prepare proper lessons, do not waste their time and show sufficient respect to hand back work promptly and decently marked. They also know which are lazy, ill-organised, self-opinionated or wretchedly mean-minded.

The importance of growing up in a community in which values are explicitly articulated obliges us to touch once again upon the complex relationship between religion and moral education. While distinguishing between morality and religion as a source of values and noting that the requirements of the two may not exactly coincide, we also acknowledged that many religious traditions embody codes of value and conduct that demand our approval, not to say in many cases our extreme admiration. Religious observance, sermons, the words of hymns, prayers and blessings offer some of the few occasions in modern life where virtues may be articulated and celebrated without awkwardness or embarrassment, while the public offering of explicit guidance remains part of the approved role of ministers of religion and a privilege we no longer accord to other authority figures, such as employers, politicians, royalty or other members of the traditional upper classes.

It would be unconscionable, not to say offensive to sincere believers, for the secular world to be seen to use religion for its own educational purposes, like the free-thinking squire who thought that regular church attendance was a useful means of keeping the peasantry in their places. Nevertheless, the manner in which religions embody and explicitly celebrate independently justifiable moral values provides one reason for retaining the study of religion and the opportunity for nonsectarian religious observance in schools. Needless to say, this needs to be of a strictly non-evangelising character, and, with due sensitivity towards religiously committed pupils and communities, critical distinctions need to be drawn between those many values that are independently justifiable and those that, along with other articles of belief, are simply part of a particular religion. It remains, of course, possible that, however critically the study of religions and religious observance is undertaken in an educational context, it may result in some pupils finding meaning in one or other of the great religions whose values and beliefs are considered. Such a pupil may eventually come to embrace that religion in its entirety, including those articles of faith and those injunctions and prohibitions that seem to the non-believer not to stand up to critical scrutiny. This possibility may seem troubling to some. Others may think that educators in a democratic society, in which autonomy and the individual choice of a meaningful life are valued, should not view such a possibility with too much anxiety.

We have suggested that the morally educated person both knows what it is to be moral and is committed to the ideal of moral conduct in the sense not merely of behaving according to a set of socially approved rules, but of striving to do what is right, even when to do so seems to conflict with some of those rules. We saw that to see the point of moral conduct was in itself in a sense to approve of it and be committed to it. It might be thought that one difference between moral education and other aspects of the educational curriculum resides in the fact that, while other subjects are largely technical, being primarily concerned with knowledge and skills, moral education is more importantly a matter of motivation and behaviour. It is important, it is sometimes said, that children not only should know what is the right thing to do but should both be committed to doing it and actually do it in practice. There are many who see no problem in determining what ought to be done and regard the whole task of moral education as one of ensuring conformity to what are seen as established and simple moral norms. If there is a distinction to be drawn between moral and other aspects of education, it is one of degree rather than of essentials. Much has already been said about the importance of the cognitive aspect of moral education, but it is equally a mistake to dismiss the motivational and performative aspects of other educational areas. We should think little of the aesthetic education of someone who, though knowledgeable about the various arts, showed no interest in them or was unconcerned about his or her own personal appearance, surroundings or possessions, or of the historical education of someone who did not care about the past or his or her society's heritage and traditions.

We should not minimise the crucial importance of motivation in the process of moral education, or the dilemmas it poses. Direct instruction is not always well regarded these days and, by itself, is inadequate as an educational strategy. It is, nevertheless the most basic and obvious way both of transmitting information and belief and of influencing behaviour. 'Such and such is the case.' 'These are the reasons for believing that such and such is the case.' 'Please do so and so.' 'You really ought to do so and so.' Without making too many sweeping assumptions about human nature or relying too heavily on Milgram's (1974) findings, it can be said that, both as children and as adults, we are often inclined to go along with the wishes of others and are glad to receive their approval. Praise and blame are powerful motivators, and at various stages in their lives children are pleased to be thought of as 'big', 'clever', 'nice' or 'good' boys and girls and are pleased to be included in the community of those who are approved and admired. Teachers' guiding and controlling discourse offers numerous opportunities for explicit reference to values, both in acknowledging kind, thoughtful, considerate or responsible actions on the part of children and in the issuing of rebukes, which must inevitably happen from time to time in every classroom. 'Stop that. No-one talks in my lessons. Do it again and you'll regret it. Is that understood?' and 'Don't do that, please, Michael. Susan wants to get on with her work. If you do it again you'll be behind at break, which would be a pity when you were so helpful to Peter when he spilt his paint.' Both ways of phrasing the rebuke may achieve, or fail to achieve, the desired result, and it should not be assumed that the second will necessarily be less effective. But the moral message conveyed by each is somewhat different.

There are obvious caveats to be observed with regard to the use of praise and blame in moral education. Teachers, parents and others should not be coy about saying what they consider good or bad or in expressing approval or disapproval, but it is important that young people should eventually be weaned off dependence on the approval of others. In many cases this will occur all too readily in adolescence, when young people seek independence and come to see the older generation as naïve and out of touch. At this point, though it remains important to continue to guide, the terms of approval need to be more carefully chosen and more subtly expressed. Where undue dependence on approval appears to persist, it may be necessary to nudge some young people in the direction of criticism. 'Yes, I know so and so is keen for you to do such and such, but do you think he is right?'

Beyond the immediate family and school, the case has been made (Advisory Group on Citizenship, 1998) for quasi-formal community involvement on the part of young people as part of a programme of citizenship education, and social service units have long been part of the extracurricular offering of many schools. Not a great deal has been said about the actual educational rationale for such activities. The services such units provide are no doubt welcome to their recipients and to the community generally when members of the school visit people in hospital, help old folk tidy their gardens or give their time in cleaning up the local environment. The so-called Crick Report merely speaks in a somewhat circular fashion of 'pupils learning about and becoming involved in the life and concerns of their communities, including learning through community involvement and service to the community' (Advisory Group on Citizenship, 1998: 40).

Insofar as these are to be educative experiences, as opposed to merely useful ways of occupying young people's time, it is because of their group nature. These are essentially social activities, and young people are involved together in doing something that both they and others recognise as worthwhile and to that extent satisfying. Younger members of the group become committed through following the example of those who are older, and school pupils come into contact with obviously worthy and admirable adult members of the community, prepared to give their own time and effort for no apparent material gain to themselves. The notion of disinterested activity in pursuit of a worthwhile end, of doing something because it is a good thing to do, becomes a real and meaningful possibility in a way that no amount of purely verbal exhortation can achieve.

This is no mere example of virtue being acquired through the performance of virtuous actions. If virtue is acquired in such circumstances, it is being caught rather than taught, through the performance of worthwhile actions in the company and emulation of others. The activity is validated by the approval and participation of others like oneself, those one aspires to resemble, those by whose approval one sets some store. If it is important, from the point of view of moral education, that young people should learn not only to act well but to do so because it is the right thing to do, appropriate reasons for community involvement or voluntary activity need, however tacitly, to be both recognised and acknowledged in the group. School heads who sell these activities as a good thing to be able to include in one's curriculum vitae or university applications risk jeopardising their morally educative value if it is done in too hardnosed a way. We referred earlier to the possible compatibility of generous and self-interested motives. The ability to harness the two together without either agonising too grievously or falling too complacently into self-deception may also be an important part of moral education. If certain activities are useful for inclusion in one's curriculum vitae or university applications, it is because they are in themselves worthy, and no harm is done if this point is made explicit to pupils.

Expressions of moral approval and disapproval may not always be sufficient to influence the behaviour of children and young people in the desired direction, and this must necessarily lead us to a discussion of the issue of sanctions and punishment in an educational context and the part they have to play in moral education. During several stages of their development, children clearly wish not only to please but also to be approved of. Praise, reinforcement of the child's self-image as a good boy or girl and the gentlest of chiding or expressions of disappointment are motivation enough. At others, these seem totally ineffective. During the tantrum stage of toddlerhood, physical containment may seem the only option. One can scarcely speak of punishment here, and the voice of reason only seems to fan the flames of fury. The firmness of containment at this stage is sometimes seen as contributing to moral development by establishing firm boundaries, but an alternative interpretation is to regard moral education as simply having been put on hold until the stage is past. Something similar may be said with regard to the period of adolescence, when certain 13–14-year-old classes are described by experienced teachers as needing a firm hand and may seem unresponsive to anything but stern authority and the certainty of immediate sanctions.

What is important here is that parents, educators and those involved in the process of correction and reform should not, at any of these stages including the earliest, feel guilty about the use of sanctions or constraint. There is, of course, an obligation to ensure that these are used at a level of severity that is the minimum at which they are unmistakeably effective. Anything less may only harden resistance and prolong the undesirable behaviour. The intention must be to bring about an improvement in the learner's behaviour, insofar as this is possible, rather than simply to prevent the educator or his or her institution from losing face. It goes without saying that, if moral education and reform are our concern, reasonable steps need to be taken to help the individual to see why his or her actions are unacceptable, rather than simply ensure conformity under threat of more severe sanctions in future. Sometimes, however, through no fault of our own, we may be unsuccessful in this endeavour. There are no doubt mature offenders upon whom, for whatever reason, moral considerations have no purchase and who may see moral reasoning as no more than a rhetorical device, which only the gullible take seriously. There are also those who are calculating and ruthless but succeed in never actually falling foul of the law. These are in no sense on the path to becoming moral beings capable of responding to moral constraint, or even appreciating the meaning of right and wrong. We cannot win all battles, though we should, perhaps, not give up trying too readily. The point at which we may reasonably do so is itself a moral issue, but both the adult world and civilised society are perfectly justified in taking reasonable steps to protect themselves and their own tolerable lives against those who may find themselves temporarily or permanently outside them.

The view that traditionally reward and punishment have been the instruments of moral education is scarcely even half the truth, for little is said of the use of pleasure as opposed to pain in the history of moral education. The ferocious punishments meted out to Roman slaves or the eighteenth-century poor may or may not have achieved social control but will have effected little moral education in the community at large. Happily, the infliction of physical pain as a means of correcting the conduct of children seems to be on the way out in civilised countries. Behavioural psychologists have seemed to demonstrate that the use of positive reinforcement is more effective than punishment in the shaping of behaviour, as it is logically bound to be where moral initiative rather than mere conformity is required. It is, however, a solecism to equate either reward or punishment with mere positive or negative reinforcement in the behavioural sense. Such deliberate behaviour shaping in respect of potentially rational beings is scarcely conscionable and can no more be regarded as part of moral education than 'sleep learning' (if such a process were possible) could be regarded as part of education in other fields. Even punishment used as a threat to deter is a long way from the Skinnerian notion of negative reinforcement, for it assumes that the recipient of the threat consciously generalises the nature of the forbidden act and makes a deliberate judgement whether or not to do it. To be educationally effective, rather than simply inculcating submission to the will of the stronger, the threat of punishment has to be coupled with an understanding and acceptance of the wrongness of what is forbidden. From an educational perspective, the point of punishment is not so much the infliction of displeasure upon the offender as the unambiguous expression of disapproval by a respected authority and the ignominy of having had such a mark of censure inflicted upon one. This necessarily assumes that the punishing authority is respected by the offender and others in his or her social group, and that the offender has reason to want to be approved of by the punisher. The offender must come to see him- or herself as someone who has fallen short of a standard to which he or she aspires and who has been brought back into line, not as a heroic martyr resisting an arbitrary and vindictive oppressor with the support and approval of his or her peers.

The appropriate severity of sanctions also raises a number of dilemmas. In the world of adult criminals who are assumed to choose to do wrong, the severity of punishments may need to be significant so that the risk of being caught at least outweighs the benefit of the crime to the offender. The punishment of crimes against individuals also needs to inflict a sanction proportionate to the harm suffered by the victim, so that justice seems to favour the victim rather than the criminal. Somewhat different considerations apply in an educational context, if we consider that most childish or adolescent misdemeanours are the result of thoughtlessness or impulse rather than the deliberate calculation of advantage. The point of the punishment is to bring home the seriousness both of what has been done and the disapproval of the educator. It does matter, and is not just a hilarious bit of fun, if a teacher's lessons are constantly disrupted. It does matter if people fool around with dangerous power tools in the metalwork room or damage expensive equipment by using it without proper supervision or failing to follow proper procedures. It does matter and should be a cause of shame if younger or more vulnerable children are bullied or treated unkindly. Adults may sometimes point these things out over and over again without avail, until some form of significant sanction is employed to make the point that their rebukes are something more than empty words.

Sometimes, more serious misdemeanours may happen in schools: deliberate and malicious damage, systematic theft, severe acts of violence leading to injury, the use and distribution of drugs. Dealing with such events only remains within the educator's competence for as long as there remains some possibility that the perpetrator's future conduct may be improved by the use of sanctions and other resources available to the school. Where serious material harm results from a pupil's actions, it may, in any case, be necessary to involve authorities outside the school. Similar comments obviously apply when a pupil's behaviour, though less serious in its consequences, is in other ways problematic and does not seem to respond to the normal resources and procedures available to the educator. The role of educators differs from that of both policemen and psychologists, though they may sometimes be called upon to cooperate with and seek the cooperation of both.

We referred earlier to the ways in which other school subjects and activities may contribute to moral education. Various philosophers of education (Arnold, 1989, 1997; Butcher and Schneider, 1988; Carr, 1979; Drewe, 2001; Meakin, 1981; Wright, 1987) have written about the potential contribution of physical education and sport to this goal, and this, along with promoting health and fitness, has traditionally been given as a reason for their inclusion in the curriculum. Suggested moral benefits have included the development of 'character' by learning to show determination in rigorous training to improve performance; facing the physical hardship and risk of knocks and bruises in some sports; notions of fair play within an agreed set of rules; a readiness to exert oneself or sacrifice one's own opportunities to shine for the sake of the team; the opportunity to show generosity towards opponents in appreciating and applauding their achievements in both victory and defeat; and the ability to combine intense competition within the game with decent social relations off the field.

These possibilities are not to be denied, though it is all too easy to be naïve in our attempts to find educational justification for including physical education and sport in the curriculum. Competitive games are not always played in a morally edifying spirit. Happily, some professional sports have recently seen the importance of cleaning up their act, and some star performers have shown responsibility in recognising their influence as role models for the young. Even at school and youth levels, however, the desire to win at all costs, or for one's team to win if one is a coach, may sometimes exert a more powerful influence upon attitudes and behaviour than the ideals of sportsmanship, fair play and respect for opponents. Achievement in sport may lead to arrogance, machismo or locker-room bullying. Generosity and appreciation are not always shown towards the efforts and achievements of the physically ungifted, and the importance of excelling, which is inherent in the nature of so many sports, necessarily brings with it the dangers of exclusiveness and elitism. As with many opportunities for moral education and moral development, teachers need to do more than simply institute a promising activity and expect the educational results to occur of their own accord. If moral development is part of the justification of physical education and sport in the curriculum, it must be explicitly recognised as an aim of the subject, for the achievement of which teachers must see themselves as responsible, along with, but in many ways educationally more important than, success in promoting achievement and excellent performance in the sports themselves.

The extent to which some other school subjects should serve as vehicles of moral education has not been entirely uncontroversial. Some purists may feel that the inherent standards of their subject are compromised or diluted if they are used for this or any other wider educational purpose, and this may even be seen as indoctrinatory. Of course, there have been the unfortunate examples of Lysenko and his politically motivated attempts to prove that acquired characteristics may be inherited, and Nazi pseudo-scientific theories of racial characteristics, not to mention the nineteenth-century use of history teaching in many countries to inspire patriotism or, more recently, to demonstrate the superiority of democratic government. We must necessarily be on our guard, for to corrupt the rigour of academic disciplines is an insidious form of dishonesty and scarcely an appropriate mode of moral education. The making of valid moral judgements implies a prior effort to gain an accurate view of the situation being judged, and this in itself is an important moral lesson. Moral judgements must not only be based on sound reasoning and valid moral premises. A point less frequently made is that their other premises, their factual ones, must be sound also, and intellectual rigour may be essential to ensuring that this is so. Intellectual rigour is a fastidious moral virtue and sophisticated form of honesty, and, if morality is to count as anything more than opinion or ideology, its conclusions must be susceptible of rigorous support. This is not to suppose that rigorous argument in morality follows the same rules as rigorous argument in science or mathematics. One of the grosser errors that those with no education in moral reasoning often commit is to demand that it should do so or abandon its claim to intellectual respectability. But the underlying demand for honesty in reasoning is common to both. One cannot cheat on the laws of arithmetic or change them by stamping one's foot or throwing a tantrum. This is an important moral lesson, and many fallacious moral arguments trade on a refusal to take proper account of numbers. All disciplines have their characteristic areas of rigour and their characteristic temptations. One does not massage one's results in the physical and social sciences, quote literary texts with misleading disregard for context, or apply value-loaded descriptors to the personalities and events of history to suit one's ideological prejudices.

The facts of science may have moral implications. To draw attention to these may not itself be science, but it is certainly a proper part of scientific education, for it is to give such facts part of their due significance in human life. When vice in literary works is punished and virtue rewarded, this is morally satisfying, but it would be crass to treat such works as if they were simply improving tales. Quite frequently it is the reverse that happens, but the moral point of view is rarely absent from such works. We are usually left in no doubt as to which characters we should detest and despise and which we should identify with. We would rather be the virtuous hero and heroine who are doomed than their odious persecutor who triumphs over them. The amiable rogue may have moral qualities that, in human terms, seem more important than the mere respectability of his or her oppressors or victims. It is one of the characteristics of many literary works to bring out the subtlety required in our judgement of character, actions and situations, in a manner that entirely accords with the goals of moral education. To bring out these subtleties does not subvert the proper aims of literary studies: to fail to do so is to neglect an important aspect of them.

Similar comments apply in the case of history. Unlike literature, neither its personalities nor its events have been created with a moral perspective in mind, and one of the tasks of academic historians may be to rid our perception of them of any such aura. This, however, is not to deny that there have existed genuinely estimable men and women, as well as villains, traitors and tyrants, noble achievements and acts of mercy, as well as treacheries, cruelties and mindless acts of slaughter. These quite properly evoke admiration or contempt. Insofar as this is true, History teaching may, without abandoning its essential integrity, evoke idealism and admiration for achievement, as well as humility in face of its transience. Whatever the claims of moral objectivity upon the academic historian, it can scarcely be the aim of school history teaching to entirely extinguish such responses in order that such personalities and events should entirely leave them cold.

It is, finally, difficult to think of good reasons why some quite specific portion of curricular time should not be set aside for purposes of moral education. I do not take seriously or propose to address the objection that the curriculum is already so over-crowded as to make this impossible. The kind of person someone grows up to be is ultimately more important than the various skills and items of academic knowledge he or she may also possess. If this is true at an individual level, it is also true socially. It is difficult to doubt that a society of morally aware and morally sensitive individuals is likely to make possible a greater degree of human flourishing than one whose members are merely well informed and highly skilled. Nor is it obvious that such a society would be less prosperous economically, nor, certainly, that such prosperity would be less justly distributed. Moral education, as we have argued, necessarily includes important aspects of citizenship and sex education, and someone's personal and social development is also part of their moral character. Given that our moral judgements must take due account of facts about the world, moral education will also need to make reference to current events and information mainly dealt with by other subject areas. Overridingly, however, an understanding of and commitment to what are valid reasons for action are essential to morally aware citizens in their private and their social and public conduct and in their response to the conduct of others. Various teaching and learning strategies will naturally be used during the time dedicated to moral education, and the level of lesson objectives will necessarily be appropriate to the age, capacities and existing knowledge of the learners concerned. Moral education is too serious a matter to be left to the whims and fancies of individual teachers to be added on as an appendage to other subjects or dealt with at odd moments in form periods after registration. It is an area in which acknowledged bodies of content and argument exist and in which it is perfectly possible to put together a programme of balanced coverage capable of being delivered in an expert and professional way, by appropriately qualified teachers.

For a number of reasons, discussion is likely to figure prominently among the teaching strategies employed by those involved in the regular teaching of moral education. Though such discussions may bear some resemblance to 1970s experimental work, they are likely to be conducted in a rather different spirit and on the basis of rather different assumptions, given now commonly accepted reservations. We are nowadays less confident of Piaget's and Kohlberg's stage-related picture of moral development, taking place spontaneously in response to stimulus materials and more or less unguided discussion. We are now less ready to accept that grasp of higher-order rational concepts such as justice represents the pinnacle of such development. The reaching of sound moral conclusions no longer seems to us purely a matter of pitting one higher-order principle against another. Though as doubtful as ever of the absolute validity of certain traditional moral injunctions and prohibitions, we no longer think that individuals should reach their own moral conclusions and live according to them, irrespective of the feelings and moral assumptions of others. Going along with the accepted customs and practices of society, provided they are not the cause of suffering or injustice, no longer seems the act of moral cowardice and enslavement it once did. To be critical is no longer to challenge everything put to us by a member of the older generation, and we no longer assume that individuals are bound to reach sound conclusions in morality, or indeed anything else, except by building on the achievements of others. In particular, we no longer suppose that the goals of moral education are achieved simply by reaching sound intellectual conclusions.

Nevertheless, discussion remains, as it has always been, a key feature of progressive teaching and learning, particularly in the fields of moral, literary or aesthetic judgement where there are no chains of irrefutable argument nor bodies of authoritative record nor tangible evidence to be transmitted. There is no reason for teachers to disguise their own point of view or attempt to play the neutral chairman. Besides being arrogant and supercilious, this deprives learners of one, hopefully valuable, perspective. The teacher has, after all, lived longer and probably seen more than most pupils and has presumably given some thought to the issues being discussed. Those hoping to succeed in their role as moral educators will necessarily seek to lead their pupils to what seem to be morally reputable conclusions rather than attempting to inculcate such conclusions by force of authority. They will also appreciate that recourse to coercion, moral browbeating, factual misrepresentation and other devices of indoctrination, even if apparently successful in achieving persuasion, are in fact contrary to the aims of moral education. Successful moral education is less about instruction than engagement. Discussion is an essentially social activity, in which not only shared views but also group commitments are generated.

Insofar as moral education is, in part, cognitive and conceptual, these aspects need to be developed, and sometimes this may require direct teacher intervention and explanation, but without interaction there is no feedback. The teacher does not know what is understood, far less what is believed, except by the crude and relatively inaccurate methods of teacher-controlled question and answer or more formal modes of assessment. In moral as in other kinds of education, critical understanding cannot be achieved if the learner does not have the chance both to try out and rehearse his or her understanding of what has been learned and be coached in the modes of criticism appropriate to the kinds of discussion taking place. Some of the *Schools Council Humanities Curriculum Project's* recommendations with regard to the conduct of discussion remain as valid as they have ever been in civilised educational circles. Everyone needs to be encouraged to participate, and reason rather than rhetoric or abuse has to prevail. The suggestion that consensus needs to be avoided seems less valid. The tone needs to be that of seeking a common understanding rather than of an adversarial war of all against all, for it is the point of morality that we can reach commonly acceptable agreements as to what ought to be done or how life ought to be lived, while recognising that there remain questions between us upon which judgement may be reserved (Gert 1998).

In addition to developing the conceptual apparatus of moral reflection and commitment to supporting the implementation of morally acceptable conclusions, discussion may have a further important role to play in moral education. Ours is, or aspires to be, a society of equals, both politically and in domestic life. The nature of modern work increasingly requires consultation with colleagues rather than the independent performance of our allotted role, and the consultation of subordinates increasingly comes to be seen as good management practice. Consultation in the workplace no doubt most frequently concerns such practical questions as the best way to complete a certain task, but, especially in the public services and caring professions, discussion may also touch upon the rightness or otherwise of what is being done or the moral acceptability of the demands being made of individuals. This is all part of the valued moral climate of our society, one of our valued traditions, albeit perhaps a fairly recently established one, which it is part of the task of moral education to support and preserve. The skills of moral debate, identifying relevant issues, the avoidance of browbeating, recognition of the rights and point of view of others, the reasonable weighing of conflicting considerations, all need to be learned, and this may possibly be best achieved under the tutelage of a skilled and committed teacher.

Notwithstanding the importance of discussion in the pedagogy of moral education, there will be, as in other subjects, certain aspects that are best introduced by means of direct teacher input or presentation. With older and relatively able groups, this may perfectly well include the explanation of various kinds of moral justification and the differences between them, as well as presentation of factual information about current situations and events that have moral implications. These are genuinely of interest to many children as they grow up, and passionately so to many adolescents. They are also issues on which one-sided, extreme and ill-informed views may be embraced, simply for want of reasoned discussion and criticism. Straightforward didactic moral instruction and, indeed, preaching have traditionally been part of this process, and, despite the obvious shortcomings of teaching as telling as an educational process when employed alone, it is an absurd prejudice that we can learn nothing of value by simply being told it, and the direct presentation of a point of view at least has this to be said morally in its favour, that it is explicit and up for scrutiny in a way that ideas delivered by other approaches may not be. Needless to say, any such presentation would normally be followed by discussion and opportunities for debate in a way quite foreign to more authoritarian styles of moral instruction in the past. To be of genuine value to either society or the younger generation, the programme of moral education needs to ensure that pupils have, at a suitable level, some notion of our society's principal moral perspectives: the general good, rights and social contract, respect for persons, the celebration of certain virtues and values, and caring. At the same time, it needs to address such general issues as mindless relativism and cynicism, as well as equally mindless and inflexible absolutism; the relationship between morality and religion; and the way in which, in many cases requiring moral judgement, the appeal to principles, though helpful, may not resolve the issue without careful scrutiny of the particular situation.

It will, hopefully, not appear from the above remarks that what is being suggested bears any resemblance to any authoritarian and inculcatory approaches to moral education suggested by some writers. Morality is, indeed, a serious and sometimes demanding guide to conduct, but it is not to be trivialised by being reduced to a set of narrow formulae to be dictated to the supposedly ignorant and uncomprehending, or used by members of one generation to protect their comfortable lives and world view from disturbance by the adventurous and occasionally wayward explorations of the next. Moral reflection opens up a universe of possibilities for understanding the way we are and the way things might be. The overriding goal of moral education must be to make this universe accessible to the young as they eventually surpass us in the continuing quest to discover the good life for human beings and the manner in which human life may best be lived.

REFERENCES

Advisory Group on Citizenship (1998) *Education for citizenship and the teaching of democracy in schools*, London: Department for Education and Employment/Qualifications and Curriculum Authority.

Arnold, P. (1989) 'Competitive sport, winning and education', *Journal of Moral Education*, Vol. 18: 15–25.

Arnold, P. (1997) *Sport, ethics and education*, London: Cassell.

Butcher, R. and Schneider, A. (1988) 'Fair play as respect for the game', *Journal of Philosophy of Sport*, Vol. 25: 1–22.

Carr, D. (1979) 'Aims of physical education', *Physical Education Review*, Vol. 2: 91–100.

Crittenden, B. (1999) 'Moral education in a pluralist democracy', in J.M. Halstead and T.H. McLaughlin (eds) *Education in morality*, London: Routledge.

Drewe, S. (2001) *Socrates, sport and students: a philosophical enquiry into physical education and sport*, Lanham, MD: University Press of America.

Feinberg, J. (1980) 'The child's right to an open future', in W. Aiken and H. Lafollette (eds) *Whose child?*, Totowa, NJ: Littlefield Adams.

Gert, B. (1998) *Morality*, New York/Oxford: Oxford University Press.

Kymlicka, W. (1999) 'Education for citizenship', in J.M. Halstead and T.H. McLaughlin (eds) *Education in morality*, London: Routledge.

McLaughlin, T.H. and Halstead, J.M. (1999) 'Education in character and virtue', in J.M. Halstead and T.H. McLaughlin (eds) *Education in character and virtue*, London: Routledge.

Meakin, D. (1981) 'Physical education: an agency of moral education?', *Journal of Philosophy of Education*, Vol. 15: 241–253.

Milgram, S. (1974) *Obedience to authority: an experimental view*, London: Tavistock.

Pritchard, M. (1996) *Reasonable children*, Lawrence, KS: University Press of Kansas.

Wright, L. (1987) 'Physical education and moral development', *Journal of Philosophy of Education*, Vol. 21: 93–101.

HELPING PUPILS LEARN

INTRODUCTION

This section focuses on helping pupils to learn. It therefore focuses on theories of teaching and learning, including teaching methods which promote learning and teaching styles. There are three readings in this section. The first focuses on influences on the outcomes of learning, and the second two focus on relatively recent foci within education: personalised learning and neuroscience.

READINGS IN THIS SECTION ARE:

Reading 12
Personal understanding and target understanding: mapping influences on the outcomes of learning
Noel Entwistle and Colin Smith

Few theories of learning have been developed specifically for education. Additionally, although the individual activities of the learner and the design of the learning context are both important in education, most theories have explained learning in terms of either the individual learner or the context. Entwistle and Smith (2002) review qualitative research on learning carried out in classrooms to identify some of the major influences on the quality of learning outcomes. They use this to develop a conceptual framework to explain differences in levels and forms of understanding. This framework emphasises the activities of both teachers and pupils and the influences on learning outcomes of both the individual and the social context. The differing ways in which curriculum designers, teachers and pupils define knowledge and conceptualise the teaching–learning process are highlighted in the distinction between 'target' and 'personal' understanding in the framework. How these conceptualisations influence the level of understanding reached by pupils is also highlighted. The likely effects of the tasks and conditions being provided for pupils, and ways to strengthen the emphasis on conceptual understanding, are highlighted by the framework.

Reading 13
Personalised learning: ambiguities in theory and practice
R.J. Campbell, W. Robinson, J. Neelands, R. Hewston and L. Mazzoli

The government in England (initially the Department for Education and Skills (DfES) and now the Department for Children, Schools and Families (DCSF)) has introduced a personalised learning initiative. This focuses on tailoring learning to pupils' individual needs, interests and aptitudes, with the aim of ensuring that all pupils achieve the highest standards possible for their abilities, regardless of their personal background and circumstances, and are autonomous in their learning to enable them to cope in the rapidly changing world of work. Reading 13, by Campbell *et al.* (2007), traces the origins of the concept of personalisation, as it has developed in public services in general, and then how it applies to the personalised learning initiative in school education. The lack of conceptual clarity of the term and ambiguities in theorising personalisation of learning are identified as issues which have not been adequately addressed and which, it is argued, contribute to the initial conceptualisation of 'deep' personalisation being lost in the process of development, dissemination and implementation and being transformed into 'shallow' personalisation. This paper presents an interesting and critical review of the agenda, drawing on a range of research. It flags up some of the problems of translating policy into practice and is based on some useful academic sources that are worth following up in their own right.

Reading 14
Neuroscience and education
Usha Goswami

The relevance of the relatively new discipline of neuroscience (encompassing neurology, psychology and biology) to education and its potential impact on pedagogy are increasingly recognized by scientists, educationalists and policy makers. The development of neuroscience over the last hundred years is considered by Goswami (2004). She then considers how this increased understanding of brain development and function might be used to explore educational questions. Although a number of neural 'markers' have been identified by cognitive neuroscience that can be used to assess development and are useful for investigating educational questions, Goswami argues that bridges need to be built between neuroscience and basic research in education in order for the potential for neuroscience to make contributions to educational research to be realized.

FURTHER READING

Auster, E. and Wylie, K. (2006) 'Creating active learning in the classroom: a systematic approach', *Journal of Management Education*, Vol. 30, No. 2: 333–354.

Although this article relates to adult learners on business courses, it provides a clear outline of key features of active learning, which you can apply to a secondary school context.

The above further reading links with Unit 5.2 of the 5th edition of *Learning to teach in the secondary school*.

Black, P., McCormick, R., James, M. and Pedder, D. (2006) 'Learning how to learn and assessment for learning: a theoretical inquiry' *Research Papers in Education*, Vol. 21, No. 2: 119–132.

This article provides an introduction to the Teaching and Learning Research Programme (TLRP) Learning How to Learn Project. It also provides the context for the other articles in the issue. The article describes the origins of the research, the overall development and research design, as well as the ways in which different forms of quantitative and qualitative data analysis are being integrated to interrogate a 'logic model', both at whole-sample level and in case studies.

The above further reading links with Units 5.1, 5.2 and 6.1 of the 5th edition of *Learning to teach in the secondary school*.

Teaching and Learning Research Programme and Economic and Social Research Council (TLRP and ESRC) (2007) *Principles into practice: a teaching guide to research evidence on teaching and learning*, London: Institute of Education, University of London, available online.

The TLRP has six distinct aims. They relate to performing and promoting excellent educational research and ensuring that it is used to enhance learning. The aims relate to: learning, outcomes, lifecourse, enrichment, expertise and improvement.

There is a considerable amount of information on the programme available at: www.tlrp.org/ index.html. Several special editions of journals stem from research conducted on this programme. These can be accessed through: www.tlrp.org/pub/journals.html.

The above further reading links with Chapter 5 of the 5th edition of *Learning to teach in the secondary school*.

Topping, K.J. and Trickey, S. (2007) 'Collaborative philosophical inquiry for school children; cognitive effects at 10–12 years', *British Journal of Educational Psychology*, Vol. 77, No. 2: 271–288.

There is little evidence of maintained gains from thinking skills interventions in education. This study reports the cognitive effects of collaborative philosophical inquiry, two years after the participants had transferred to secondary (high) school, without experiencing further philosophical inquiry in the interim. The ninety-six pupils in the experimental group, who engaged in collaborative inquiry for 1 hour per week over 16 months, were interviewed using the Cognitive Abilities Test. The significant pre–post cognitive ability gains in the experimental group in primary school were maintained towards the end of their second year of secondary school. Higher achieving pupils were somewhat advantaged in sustaining these gains. The control group showed an insignificant but persistent deterioration in scores from pre- to post-test to follow-up. The study provides evidence of maintained cognitive gains from collaborative philosophical inquiry, transferred across contexts.

The above further reading links with Units 5.1 and 5.6 of the 5th edition of *Learning to teach in the secondary school*.

Burton, D.M. (2007) 'Psychopedagogy and personalised learning', *Journal of Education for Teaching*, Vol. 33, No. 1: 5–17.

This article explores the extent to which moulding pedagogy from a superficial reading of psychological ideas is educationally viable and suggests that pedagogical research is becoming increasingly self-referential. The paper examines the widespread acceptance of ideas such as metacognition, multiple forms of intelligence, learning styles, learning preferences, thinking skills, brain functioning, emotional intelligence and neuro-linguistic programming and their apparent validation within government documentation in England.

The above further reading links with Unit 5.5 of the 5th edition of *Learning to teach in the secondary school*.

Bransford, J.B., Brown, A.L. and Cocking, R. (2000) 'Learning and transfer' in Bransford, J.B., Brown, A.L. and Cocking, R. (eds) *How people learn: brain, mind, experience and school: expanded edition*, Washington: National Academy Press: Chapter 3: 39–66.

This book provides an overview of research on learners and learning and on teachers and teaching. It is organised around three foci: research on human learning, including new developments from neuroscience; learning research that has implications for the design of formal instructional environments, such as schools and colleges; and research that explores the possibility of helping all individuals achieve their fullest potential.

The chapter entitled 'Learning and transfer' (pp. 51–79) focuses on understanding 'the kinds of learning experiences that lead to transfer, defined as the ability to extend what has been learned in one context to new contexts (e.g. Byrnes, 1996: 74)'. The chapter explores:

> key characteristics of learning and transfer that have important implications for education: initial learning is necessary for transfer, and a considerable amount is known about the kinds of learning experiences that support transfer; knowledge that is overtly contextualised can reduce transfer, abstract representations of knowledge can help promote transfer; transfer is best viewed as an active, dynamic process rather than a passive end-product of a particular set of learning experiences; all new learning involves transfer based on previous learning, and this fact has important implications for the design of instruction that helps students learn.
>
> (Bransford *et al.*, 2000: 53)

The above further reading links with Units 4.3, 5.1 and 5.6 of the 5th edition of *Learning to teach in the secondary school*.

PERSONAL UNDERSTANDING AND TARGET UNDERSTANDING

Mapping influences on the outcomes of learning

Noel Entwistle and Colin Smith

A NOTE FROM THE EDITORS

This reading reviews qualitative research in learning to identify some of the major influences on the quality of learning outcomes, and then uses this to develop a conceptual framework, which emphasises the activities of both teachers and pupils and the influences on learning outcomes of both the individual and the social context.

This reading links with Unit 5.5 of the 5th edition of *Learning to teach in the secondary school*.

QUESTIONS TO CONSIDER

1   Models of learning have changed over the years; what are various models that have been used over time, why have they changed, and why has this change occurred? What does the changing conceptualisation of learning mean for teaching and learning?

2   What does knowledge of the concept of deep and surface learning mean for teachers and learners in classrooms today? Is deep learning achieved and, if not, what are some of the possible reasons why?

3   The ways teachers interact with pupils depend on professional knowledge but also on their beliefs about teaching and learning. Why are beliefs so important in influencing the way teachers teach, and what impact is this likely to have on pupils?

4   How does knowledge of the major influences on the outcomes of learning identified in the theory of learning articulated in this paper influence your views of the way you teach?

This reading was first published as: Entwistle, N. and Smith, C. (2002) 'Personal understanding and target understanding: mapping influences on the outcomes of learning', *British Journal of Educational Psychology*, Vol. 72: 321–342.

ABSTRACT

Background: Among the many theories of learning, few have been developed specifically for education. Most have explained learning in terms of *either* the individual activities of the learner *or* the design of the learning context; yet both are important in education. Each theory applies strictly only to the context for which it was developed, and yet quite general implications for education are often suggested.

Aims: 1. To review qualitative research on learning carried out within the classroom and to identify some of the major influences on the quality of learning outcomes. 2. To develop a conceptual framework based on this research which seeks to explain differences in levels and forms of understanding.

Method: Model building based on reviews of research on learning in schools and universities.

Analysis: A conceptual framework was developed from the review of the literature which emphasises the activities of both teachers and students and the influences on learning outcomes of both the individual and the social context. The framework introduces a distinction between 'target' and 'personal' understanding to draw attention to the differing ways in which curriculum designers, teachers and students define knowledge and conceptualise the teaching–learning process. It also suggests how these conceptualisations influence the level of understanding reached by students. The framework is intended to encourage teachers and curriculum designers to think about the likely effects of the tasks and conditions they are providing for students, and to consider ways of strengthening the emphasis on conceptual understanding. By drawing on research findings from both schools and universities, a way of thinking about teaching and learning is indicated which can, to some extent, be generalised across educational contexts.

INTRODUCTION

Educational and psychological researchers have made repeated attempts at providing satisfactory conceptual frameworks to describe classroom learning and improve the quality of teaching. Over the years, models of learning have changed radically, with a steady progression from functionalism and behaviourism, through cognitive theories, to competing forms of constructivism (Phillips, 2000), situated cognition (Brown *et al.*, 1989) and cognitive apprenticeship (Lave and Wenger, 1991). The early theories were philosophical and introspective, but thereafter ideas depended on empirical data, collected in differing ways within varying contexts. The aim of all these theories has been to produce ideas with wide generality, and many have been used to suggest ways of improving the effectiveness of learning within education. They do, however, all too often appear to contradict each other, and may also seem unrealistic. The teacher is faced with an array of principles, all of which claim to improve learning, yet few of which have their origins specifically within classroom contexts.

Psychological theories of learning

Although there has been a growing recognition of the importance of ecological validity in psychology, there is still a tendency to draw implications for education from widely disparate settings. The differing theories are a product, not just of the conditions and contexts within which the data were collected, but also of the prevailing philosophical *Zeitgeist*. Each theory is, to some extent, a product of its time, being affected by the social and political circumstances within which it originates (Bredo, 2000). Wolf *et al.* (1991) identified similar changes in educational thinking, contrasting an earlier epistemology of 'intelligence' with the more recent one of 'mind'. The former emphasised norm-referencing, numerical scales and rank-ordering of students, while the latter focused on criterion referencing, qualitative differences and the assumption that all individuals are able to construct knowledge for themselves.

As early as the 1950s, Kelly (1955) suggested that each theory had a limited 'focus of convenience', and this seems especially true of attempts to explain classroom behaviour and thinking. In particular, education has been described with an emphasis on either the social setting within which it takes place or the changes occurring in the learner. As Bredo (2000) points out, most psychological theories have tended to be rather one-sided, favouring explanations based either on the environment or on the individual:

> Behaviourism . . . meant a focus on the effects of the structure of the environment, such as its reinforcement contingencies. It was an attempt to describe 'learning' in purely environmental terms without having to know about the structure of the organism . . . Cognitivists took the opposite tack, emphasising the effects of the structure of the organism . . . Thus, the structuring or organising of behaviour was seen as due to the organism rather than to the environment . . . In this conception, 'learning' is a change in the rules or procedures used to manipulate symbolic expressions. But what is omitted are the circumstances that lead to conceiving of the problem in a certain way in the first place.
>
> (Bredo, 2000: 40)

Bredo finds the arguments from situated cognition no more convincing, with the individual dimension lacking and the social context over-emphasised. Criticisms of constructivism have concentrated on its almost exclusive focus on the construction of meaning, while omitting issues such as individual cognitive and motivational differences. (This is, though, not equally true of all constructivist theories – see, for example, von Glasersfeld, 1988.) While accepting the value of the instructional methods associated with constructivism, Fox (2001) points out these limitations and argues that the role of the teacher has also been largely ignored:

Learners do need to interact, to have dialogues, to solve problems and to make sense of new ideas; but they also often find it difficult to see why they should make the effort, fail to pay attention, misconstrue new concepts, forget what they learned ten minutes ago and fail to apply fragile new knowledge effectively to new contexts. They can be helped by the expertise of teachers and they need instruction, demonstration and practice, as well as challenging problems and investigations, to make progress.

(Fox, 2001: 33–34)

The attempt to provide a theoretical framework to describe learning in general, of all kinds and across quite different contexts, is likely to prove as elusive as the 'theory of everything' sought by physicists. Different perspectives on the nature of mind and intellectual development can only be partial stories (Cobb, 1994). As a result, we have to select theories that fulfil a specific purpose. Bredo (2000) argues that we need pragmatic educational theories for describing the types of learning found in classrooms, and suggests that the much earlier functional perspective adopted by William James and John Dewey was, in fact, much more suited for dealing with learning in context:

Functional psychology was a sophisticated attempt to avoid [the] split between organism and environment, mind and body, theory and practice . . . It viewed adaptation as a dynamic, collaborative affair between organism and environment . . . Adopting it [now] requires something more like a naturalistic or anthropological approach to research . . . [which] may not convey the traditional sense of 'scientific' certainty, but perhaps this is simply a loss of false pretensions.

(Bredo, 2000: 41–42)

Contrasting learning processes

In developing a conceptual framework to guide thinking within education, it is crucial to identify the kinds of learning that we wish to support. One of the apparent reasons for the current popularity of constructivist theories is that they present learning in terms of the development of individual understanding, rather than as the reproduction of a body of information or the acquisition of a repertoire of appropriate behaviour. The distinction between 'learning by heart' and achieving understanding has run through discussions about the quality of education over successive centuries (see, for example, Watts (1810) and Dewey (1938)), but there has been continuing agreement that rote learning is a limited, and limiting, process. Ausubel distinguished *meaningful learning* from *rote learning*, and also *discovery learning* from *reception learning* (Ausubel *et al.*, 1978). While discovery learning was viewed as desirable, it was seen as very time consuming. To provide sufficient coverage, Ausubel argued that schoolwork must necessarily involve a substantial amount of meaningful reception learning, and even some rote learning. Nevertheless, he criticised the extent to which schools, at that time, relied on passive rote learning, rather than encouraging the active, meaningful learning which would create firmly established ideas which could more readily be utilised across a variety of tasks and contexts.

Although there have been many changes in education since Ausubel's work, there are continuing concerns about the limited extent to which understanding is emphasised in schools, expressed for example by Project Zero researchers at Harvard (e.g., Wiske, 1998), and by Newton (2000) at Newcastle, who commented:

In spite of good reasons to value understanding, it is not a central concern in every classroom: . . . there has been a tendency to favour a reproduction of information . . . For instance, in primary science lessons, 'why' questions can be fairly rare events . . . At the same time, there is evidence that children may not always see the point of the exercise . . . Further, an anxiety about learning in a subject can lead to a reliance on memorisation when it is not appropriate . . . Examination success (is seen) as the primary goal: understanding is less fortunate. Some examinations may place little emphasis on understanding. When they do, understanding may be one path to success but a mix of understandings and memorisation may achieve the same goal, perhaps more readily.

(Newton, 2000: 10–11)

While constructivism may be seen as the most obvious candidate for a theoretical framework aimed at ensuring that understanding becomes a more conscious aim of teachers, it is actually too diffuse a set of ideas to provide a coherent, integrative framework (Phillips, 2000). Some forms of constructivism emphasise the activities of the learner, while others are more concerned with the setting. In social constructivism, there seems to be an important gap in the logic, noted by Katz (2000). He asks how the subjective understanding constructed by the 'knower' is supposed to be linked to accepted knowledge, to allow what counts as 'good work' to be recognised. We need a theory which is directly focused on education and yet broad enough to encompass both individual and contextual perspectives in addressing the activities of both students and teacher. It also has to provide the link between individual knowledge and the accepted norms and standards of educational achievement.

Educational theories of learning

Bereiter (1990) distinguished between explanatory and instructional theories of learning. He pointed out that the former lacked convincing connections with educational practice, while the latter often failed to provide adequate explanations of how teaching affected learning outcomes. Perkins (in press) has argued that teachers need 'action theories', which carry with them practical guidance on teaching procedures, such as the curriculum guidelines he and his colleagues developed within Project Zero. They built on constructivist ideas to offer a *Teaching for Understanding* (TfU) framework (Wiske, 1998). The underlying theory suggests that understanding can best be supported and developed by ensuring that students undertake closely linked *understanding performances*, all of which have been carefully chosen to make understanding an essential requirement (Perkins, 1998). These understanding performances not only demonstrate understanding, they also develop it by requiring higher-level thinking:

Performances of understanding require students to show their understanding in an observable way. They make students' thinking visible. It is not enough for students to reshape, expand, extrapolate from, and apply their knowledge in the privacy of their own thoughts . . . Such an understanding would be untried, possibly fragile, and virtually impossible to assess.

(Blythe *et al.*, 1998: 63)

The TfU framework, as a whole, provides a coherent sequence of curriculum design and implementation procedures. The starting point involves identifying *overarching goals* for the course, which are subsequently used as *throughlines* for students, reminding them how topics and themes cohere. From the goals, generative topics are established which are 'issues, themes, concepts, ideas, and so on that provide enough depth, significance, connections, and variety of perspective to support students' development of powerful understandings' (Blythe *et al.*, 1998: 18.). Then, *understanding aims* are produced which suggest tasks designed specifically to encourage *understanding performances*. Finally, the framework insists that assessment should be *ongoing* or formative, providing students with feedback about their work and also allowing both teacher and students to assess progress towards understanding.

Could this, then, be a theory of learning which is both practical and sufficiently broad to meet the criteria we have set up? It is impressively practical, but does not explicitly address student thinking; nor does it seem to offer a sufficiently active role to the teacher, once the curriculum has been set up. The TfUframework implies that all that is required to help students reach understanding is the repeated experiences of understanding performances. The role of the teacher is seen as essentially that of 'coach', but most students probably need direct teaching as well. Learners may need help in seeing that understanding is part of the exercise, and in grasping what understanding really involves in a discipline (Newton, 2000; Newton and Newton, 1999). Ideas from TfU will nevertheless form a good platform for exploring what else may be needed in developing a classroom-based theory of learning that has direct implications for teaching.

Our approach involves looking at the various influences on students' learning in schools and universities from the perspectives of the participants in teaching–learning processes. From a review of relevant literature, a conceptual framework has been developed to describe influences on the outcomes of learning. It represents a pragmatic theory of learning within educational contexts, designed to take account of the activities of both teachers and students – of the individual and the social context. Its descriptions of a recognisable classroom reality are intended to encourage teachers and curriculum designers to think about the likely effects of the tasks and conditions they are providing for students, and to consider ways of strengthening the emphasis on conceptual understanding.

Our starting point will be research on student learning at university which has demonstrated the links that exist between approaches to studying and perceptions of the teaching–learning environment, but these relationships prove to apply equally at school level. Contrasting approaches lead to qualitatively different levels of understanding, which are next to be considered. These two sections concentrate on the student's perspective, while the following one looks at how teachers conceptualise teaching and learning. The distinction between 'target' and 'personal' understanding is then used to develop a conceptual model of the interaction between teachers and learners in the classroom, to indicate important influences on the quality of the learning outcomes.

RESEARCH ON STUDENT LEARNING

We begin, then, with the research on student learning at university level which has shown how teaching–learning environments (broadly defined to include teaching, assessment, learning materials and so on) influence learning outcomes. The findings come from the research tradition originated in the 1970s by Marton and his colleagues in Gothenburg (Marton and Booth, 1997; Marton *et al.*, 1997). Using naturalistic experiments, these researchers drew attention to qualitative differences in the ways in which students went about the task of reading an academic article (Marton and Saljo, 1976, 1997). The main distinction was between *deep* and *surface* approaches to learning. The approach depended on the students' intentions and motives and on their perceptions of the task demands. The decision to seek meaning (deep) or to reproduce the information provided (surface) was seen as a consequence of how students had interpreted the task and the setting (context), and how they viewed the content.

The surface approach involves routine use of rote memorisation, while the deep approach draws predominantly on making connections with previous knowledge and carrying out logical reasoning. The link between memorisation and the surface approach has, however, proved to be an oversimplification, as research on Chinese learners has demonstrated (Kember, 1996; Watkins and Biggs, 1996). Memorisation can also be used, for example, to master unfamiliar terminology by initial rote learning, as a first step towards developing understanding, or when committing an understanding to memory. Where memorisation involves meaningful learning, it has been described as *deep memorising* (Tang, 1991) or *memorising with understanding* (Marton *et al.*, 1997; Meyer, 2000). This is not just a characteristic of Chinese learners; British university students have also been found to use this approach, at least in revising for final examinations (Entwistle and Entwistle, 2001). Practising teachers have also made this distinction. In recent development work, teachers indicated that the rote learning of, for example, the activity series of metals could contribute to understanding when the list was used to make predictions about how metals behave, rather than merely to recite it back (Smith, 2001, 2002a). The main characteristic of a surface approach is thus not memorisation per se, but the routine and unreflective use of rote memorisation and procedural ways of learning, stemming from the intention simply to reproduce the material presented by the teacher.

In one of the Gothenburg studies, Fransson (1977) set out experimentally to induce different approaches to learning by varying the context so as to produce anxiety or a relaxed condition as students read an article. He also contrasted a group expected to have an immediate interest in the content with one where the potential interest was less obvious. The initial analysis showed no difference in approaches to learning between the various experimental conditions. However, Fransson also asked the students to rate how they *felt* about the situation. He found that students who reported actually being anxious were more likely to adopt a surface approach, while those who saw the content as interesting adopted a deep approach to the reading. These experiments alerted subsequent researchers to the potentially strong influence of students' perceptions of the learning context on their ways of studying.

A large-scale survey of British university students subsequently used both interviews and inventories to show that the deep and surface categories could be used to describe equivalent differences in everyday studying, including reading articles, writing essays and preparing for examinations (Entwistle and Ramsden, 1983). However, an additional category was needed to describe variations in studying, as opposed to learning, and this was described as a *strategic approach*. Only by adding this category was it possible to explain how students adjusted their ways of studying to take account of formal assessment. The study showed that each approach to learning and studying was associated with characteristic forms of motivation: deep with intrinsic motivation and interest in the subject matter; surface with extrinsic motivation and fear of failure; and strategic with achievement motivation. Looking at students' perceptions of the teaching–learning environment, it was also found that a deep approach appeared to be influenced by 'good teaching' and 'freedom in learning', while heavy workloads and fact-based assessment procedures induced a surface approach.

When students are asked about their experiences of lectures, either in interviews (Hodgson, 1997; Ramsden, 1997) or through evaluation questionnaires (Marsh, 1987), a clear picture emerges of what constitutes 'good lectures' from the students' perspective. They are described in terms of seven main categories – level, pace, structure, clarity, explanation, enthusiasm and empathy. And of these, it is the last three that are the most likely to evoke and support a deep approach to learning.

These categories represent some of the general indicators of good teaching from the students' perspective, but there are still important individual variations. Meyer (1991) described these in terms of *study orchestration* – the co-variation of students' descriptions of their ways of studying and of their study environment. He demonstrated that perceptions of teaching as supporting deep or surface approaches mapped onto the same area within three-dimensional axes as the equivalent approaches to studying (Meyer and Muller, 1990). The composite of approaches to learning and perceptions of the teaching–learning environment represented the orchestrations shown by the students. And when students were asked directly about their *preferences* for 'deep' or 'surface' methods of teaching, they tended to choose methods that would support their reported approaches to studying (Entwistle and Tait, 1990).

Figure 12.1 presents a conceptual model describing the teaching–learning process in higher education. It begins the process of mapping influences on learning by drawing attention to the interactions that exist between teaching and learning in higher education. The central ellipse indicates the differing learning strategies and outcomes that the model is seeking to explain. The top half of the diagram suggests the main influences on approaches to learning (on the left) and approaches to studying (on the right). The lower half describes aspects of the teaching–learning environment which have also been shown to affect the learning strategies and outcomes. On the left are the defining features of good teaching as reported by the students and illustrated by the example of lecturing. Influences depending more strongly on departmental or institutional policies are shown on the right. The central box indicates the selection and organisation of content in preparing teaching material, which has become of major concern in more recent research, as we shall see.

Across the middle of the diagram, attention is drawn to *perceptions* – of meaning and relevance (linked to experiences of teaching) and of task requirements (associated with departmental policy). The position of this band across Figure 12.1 is intended to emphasise that perceptions depend as much on the students' own characteristics as on the actual teaching–learning environment. Thus, students with differing abilities and motives may perceive the same context in quite different ways.

One of the first publications from the Gothenburg research group argued that there was a logical and inevitable relationship between a deep approach and thorough understanding (Marton and Säljö, 1976). If students intend to reproduce information (surface approach), they cannot be expected to develop higher levels of understanding. Subsequent empirical findings have confirmed this contention and established a causal chain from intention to perceptions of context and approaches to studying, and from those to contrasting learning outcomes. And a similar pattern of relationships between approaches to studying and perceptions of the teaching–learning environment has also been found at school level (see, for example, Entwistle *et al.*, 1989). To make these relationships clearer, however, we need to be able to describe the expected qualitative differences in learning outcomes.

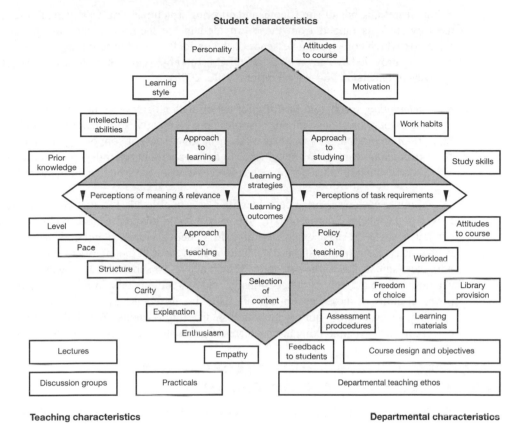

■ **Figure 12.1** Conceptual model of the teaching–learning process in higher education.

RESEARCH ON QUALITATIVE DIFFERENCES IN THE OUTCOMES OF LEARNING

Qualitative differences in levels of understanding were extensively explored by Peel and his students in relation to the onset of Piagetian formal operations in secondary school (Peel, 1971). They looked at the answers students gave to questions which demanded conceptual understanding and distinguished essentially three different levels – *mentioning*, *describing* and *explaining*. Further development along similar lines came from Biggs and Collis (1982) in their SOLO taxonomy (structure of observed learning outcomes) based on the ways in which secondary students used information to answer questions. Their five levels were described as *pre-structural* (naïve or tautological responses), *uni-structural* (focusing on one relevant piece of information), *multi-structural* (several pieces but unrelated), *relational* (using the information provided and showing relationships within it) and *extended abstract* (going beyond information given and considering alternative explanations).

More recently, a series of studies has looked at the understanding developed and experienced by undergraduates as they prepared for their final examinations (Entwistle and Entwistle, 1997, 2001). Contrasting forms of understanding were described in terms of both increasing breadth and depth, and differing structures. The organising frameworks used by students ranged from those provided in the lectures to individually created structures which conveyed the essence of the topic. Relating these findings to the earlier categories provided by Peel, and to the SOLO taxonomy, suggests the following hierarchy in levels of understanding (based on Entwistle, 2000):

- *mentioning* incoherent bits of information without any obvious structure;
- *describing* brief descriptions of topics derived mainly from material provided;
- *relating* outline, personal explanations lacking detail or supporting argument;
- *explaining* using relevant evidence to develop structured, independent arguments;
- *conceiving* individual conceptions of topics developed through continuing reflection.

Similar categories have been identified at school level. Tan and Novak (undated) looked at the levels of understanding in physics classrooms in the USA, while Burns and her colleagues (1991) have explored similar differences in New Zealand students' responses to chemistry. Both studies showed qualitative differences in the quality of understanding, with clear similarities to the categories shown above. At school level, however, the final category was found only very occasionally, and in a rudimentary form. Nevertheless, the potential utility of these descriptions of qualitative differences, as well as influences on learning, seem to apply quite widely across differing contexts. We shall find a similar correspondence when looking at how teachers conceptualise teaching and learning.

TEACHERS' BELIEFS ABOUT TEACHING AND THE CREATION OF OBJECTS OF STUDY

The knowledge, beliefs and attitudes of schoolteachers were explored in a major review by Calderhead (1996). That analysis indicated that the ways in which teachers interact with their students depend on their own knowledge and beliefs about teaching and learning. Studies often identify three main forms of knowledge related to teaching – about subject matter, teaching and managing learning, and relationships with the learner (Wittrock, 1986). Shulman (1987) argued that a combination of content knowledge and pedagogical knowledge – *pedagogical content knowledge* – plays a crucial role.

Teaching staff in universities have also been found to differ in both their knowledge and their beliefs about teaching, which affect the way they teach (Prosser and Trigwell, 1999). Interviews with lecturers have suggested a series of categories describing conceptions of teaching which, to some extent, reflect the distinctions between formal and informal teaching found in schools. At the least sophisticated level, the conception focuses solely on the transmission of knowledge, while the higher ones increasingly include the development of self-awareness and an understanding of how learning takes place. As Dall'Alba (1991) commented:

> The categories . . . are ordered from less to more complete understandings of teaching. At the lowest level, teaching is seen in terms of the teacher alone and, more particularly, in terms of what the teacher does. From there, the focus shifts to incorporate the content and, at higher levels, students' understanding of the content becomes prominent. Finally, the most complete conception focussed on the relationship between teacher, student and content.
>
> (Quoted in Prosser and Trigwell, 1999: 143)

Similar variations in conceptions have been found consistently across a range of teaching contexts (Watkins and Mortimore, 1999) and are generally associated with equivalent approaches to teaching and assessment.

This pattern of relationships is summarised in Figure 12.2 (adapted from Entwistle, 2000; Entwistle and Walker, 2002; Entwistle *et al.*, 2000). The top half of the diagram suggests how differing conceptions affect the choice of both teaching methods and assessment procedures and, hence, learning outcomes. Those choices then influence the approaches to studying adopted by students, and, hence, the levels of understanding they reach. The emergence of the more sophisticated conceptions suggests an expanding awareness of the nature of teaching and learning (Entwistle and Walker, 2002), which incorporates the differing forms of knowledge and emotional reponses previously identified in research into school teaching (Calderhead, 1996). Within the classroom, such expanded awareness allows the teacher to employ a varied repertoire of teaching methods, and also to show a greater 'strategic alertness' (Entwistle and Walker, 2002), recognising and capitalising on the 'teachable moments' which occur from time to time (Woods and Jeffrey, 1996).

Marton and Booth (1997) have commented on the importance of an interaction between teachers and students which takes the idea of 'good teaching' even further. For them, it also requires a mutual awareness of the teaching–learning process:

> [Pedagogy depends on] meetings of awarenesses, which we see as achieved through the experiences that teachers and learners undertake jointly . . . Teachers mould experiences for their students with the aim of bringing about learning, and the

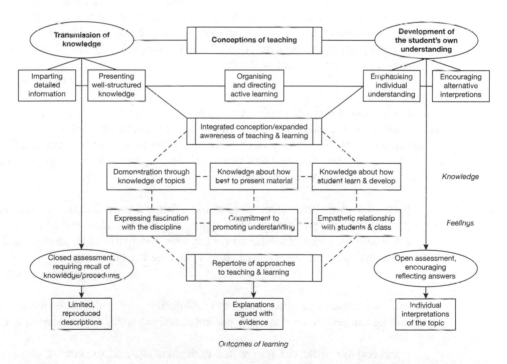

Figure 12.2 Suggested relationships between conceptions of teaching and outcomes of learning.

essential feature is that *the teacher takes the part of the learner* . . . The teacher focuses on the learner's experience of the object of learning. Here we have [what we call] 'thought contact', [with] the teacher moulding an object of study [for the students].

(Marton and Booth, 1997: 179)

This idea of 'moulding an object of study' implies that individual teachers may interpret and teach the same topic in importantly different ways. At one level that may seem to be a truism, but when explored more fully it throws light on some of the difficulties students have in seeing the teacher's meaning. Recent work has been examining in detail how different teachers construct an object of study for their students within a specific subject area. Patrick (1998), for example, distinguished three groups of history teachers in secondary schools who were teaching in quite different ways. One group appeared to have a 'transmission' model of teaching, emphasising the content, mode of delivery and teaching technique. The subject matter, and how their students saw it, were both unproblematic for these teachers. A second group of teachers saw historical knowledge as an entity which, while requiring interpretation, could still be offered to students as material to be learned, first, by the acquisition of knowledge and, then, by discussing and interpreting that knowledge. But the understanding expected as a result of this process was still that of the teacher, and the students were expected to reach an equivalent form of understanding. The final group of teachers tried to share their ways of thinking about the subject and emphasised the contested nature of historical knowledge:

> Considering how the study of history was constructed in these classes enables us to see the significance of the teacher's role. Teachers are not neutral. They were not [showing] merely different ways of manipulating 'pedagogical content knowledge' . . .; nor [was it] merely a question of individual style . . . [It] involved adopting or refusing a position of political critique.
>
> (Patrick, undated: 16)

Patrick found equivalent differences among physics teachers, not in terms of the recognition of problematic knowledge, but rather of the relative emphasis on procedural or conceptual aspects of the subject, or on the nature of scientific experiment and thinking. But again it was clear that teachers using the same syllabus were setting before their students very different objects of study:

> It is plain from the students' responses that we need to take a nuanced and discriminating view of the teacher's impact. Students, like teachers, bring to the classroom their expectations and conceptions of what is to be studied, and these views interact with the object of study which the teacher constructs.
>
> (Patrick, undated: 17)

In another classroom observation study, Molander (1997) also found marked differences among teachers in the ways they presented and explained topics. He found that:

> [teachers] use different frames for understanding and explaining biology: and even if . . . teachers are governed by the same curricula and teach the same topics . . . there would nevertheless be appreciable differences in their instruction . . .

What successful students have is an understanding of the subject matter that corresponds to their teacher's understanding, together with the ability to express it.

(Molander, 1997: 193, 214)

From this review, it is now clear that teachers do not uniformly put a high priority on the need for students to develop understanding for themselves. And even when they do, the form of understanding encouraged can vary markedly, depending on how the object of study is shaped for the students. Patrick found that the predominant response of students to the teaching they had experienced paralleled the approach adopted by their teachers. In dealing with historical sources, for example, some classes concentrated on summarising salient details, while others focused on the arguments presented, or interpreted the material from their own perspective, with each approach also affecting the students' attitudes to the study of history itself. This discussion of the interplay between teachers' and students' understandings can now be taken a stage further.

TARGET UNDERSTANDING AND PERSONAL UNDERSTANDING

From an extensive review of the literature on understanding, Smith (1998) drew attention to the distinction between *target understanding* and *personal understanding*. 'Target understanding' derives in part from the formal requirements of the syllabus but is interpreted from the teacher's own perspective. 'Personal understanding' reflects how the student comes to see the topic presented by the teacher, influenced by the teacher's view, but also by the student's prior educational and personal history.

In science education, a similar distinction between target and personal understanding has also been drawn by Newton (2000), who comments:

All understandings are more or less idiosyncratic. This is in part due to differences in prior knowledge which learners bring to a situation. Nevertheless, in some subjects there are patterns and relationships that are generally accepted by a professional community, sometimes referred to as authorised or public understandings ... Reasonably, these understandings are targets that teachers want students to construct ... The emphasis is on the construction of a representation which reflects the structure of the target. However, there are occasions when target structures are relatively few. Understanding can amount to making connections of a personal and unique significance ... You must make what personal understanding of it you will.

(Newton, 2000: 24–25)

Smith's earlier exploration of the use of the terms 'target' and 'personal' in relation to understanding had, however, taken their meanings further than in Newton's comment above.

Target understanding

Smith (1998) discussed target understanding in terms of a selection of topics and ideas from a universe of knowledge within each subject area. He used Scottish Higher Biology (for age 17+) as an illustration of the ways in which an official syllabus is devised and communicated to teachers, describing its creation by a working party of teachers, together with officials from the Scottish Examination Board and the Scottish Office. University lecturers also contributed to the process by suggesting content and commenting upon draft versions. This working party had to decide what a student should know about biology by the end of school education. In constructing the syllabus, not only had topics to be described, but specifications for the level of understanding had also to be set. These targets were built out of the syllabus constructors' conceptualisations of the subject, negotiated then into agreed, formalised statements, after comments from schools. This process was explained in an interview by one of the officials involved:

> Because of the vast nature of the subject, there were many areas which had claims for inclusion, but we didn't want to make it all embracing . . . After a lot of debate, there was agreement on the major topics which should be included . . . We then had topic authors who produced, I don't know how many drafts . . . In the light of discussion [with university experts], the draft copies were modified, . . . amended and refined.

The syllabus which emerged from this process was intended to tread a careful line between tight prescription to guide question setters, and opportunities for teachers and students to 'go beyond the words' of the syllabus. The final descriptions are necessarily reduced to brief statements about what is required. For example:

> Candidates should have a clear understanding of photosynthesis, cell structure, cell respiration, diffusion.

Teachers are, however, also provided with notes on the syllabus, which indicate the limits to the understanding being required and suggest areas where students may find difficulty. For example:

> Organelles are introduced only where a knowledge of their structure is essential in order to understand their function . . . Teachers may find it helpful to separate the teaching of photosynthesis and respiration; candidates often confuse the biochemical pathways involved in the two processes.

In such an examination system, teachers adjust their teaching to the syllabus notes, the types of question set and the pattern of marks their students are obtaining. In this way, the syllabus becomes interpreted, and the 'target understanding' more precisely fixed. However, the target experienced by the students is filtered still further through the individual teacher's understanding of the subject and expectations about attainable levels of understanding. This perceived target is an 'object of study', built up from teachers' comments and explanations over many occasions. This process of transmission inevitably leaves the target somewhat hazy in the students' minds, affecting their ability to achieve the understandings expected by the teacher or examiner.

Personal understanding

In the earlier discussion of different levels of understanding, the focus was on the extent to which the students' understandings were structured in ways which were acceptable to their teachers. In science education, in particular, there is an extensive literature which charts the differences which exist between scientific thinking and the misconceptions or alternative frameworks which are often used by students (see, for example, Driver and Erickson, 1983). While the origin of misconceptions is often the types of explanation provided by parents or peers, another source of variation lies in how the tasks set by teachers are perceived by their students. For example, Bereiter and Scardamalia (1989) point out that students often fail to recognise that they are expected to learn something for themselves, seeing their job as simply satisfying the teacher:

> Studying is work of course, but that is not the point. The work that characterizes classroom life may have originally been conceived with learning goals in mind, and it may even achieve some learning objectives, but from the standpoint of the students, *doing schoolwork is what school is about*. It is their job, not attaining learning goals.
>
> (Bereiter and Scardamalia, 1989: 377; emphasis added)

Even doing schoolwork to the satisfaction of the teacher depends on being able to make sense of the tasks set. An intriguing study by Saljo (1991) illustrated how an authentic task may produce unanticipated difficulty. Students in primary school were asked to solve a problem by using a table of postage charges. They first tried to apply routines from conventional numerical problems, and then to think logically and independently about what would be 'fair': neither of these approaches was successful. The problem could be solved only when they fully appreciated the function of the postage table in everyday life.

Such misunderstandings are commonplace and have led Halldén (1988, 1999) to distinguish between the *task* set by the teacher, and the *problem* perceived or 'contextualised' by the student. As Scheja (2001) comments in relation to a more recent study:

> For the learner, it comes down to putting a reasonable construction on the information provided by the teacher, and . . . to allocate [the task] to a context in which it makes sense . . . Importantly, the learner's contextualisation involves, not only understandings about the conceptual requirements of a given task, but also . . . perceptions about the social (communicative) setting in which this task has been presented.
>
> (Scheja, 2001: 7)

From his review of the literature, Smith (1998) extended his use of the term 'personal understanding' to include not just the contextualisation of the task but also other effects of the wide range of contexts that students experience. Young people's behaviour and thinking in school are, as we know, substantially influenced by their experiences at home, by 'significant others' and by their peer group. Students bring to any situation in the classroom, not just varying levels and mixes of abilities, prior knowledge and understanding, and approaches to studying, but also differing sets of motives, expectations and beliefs about educational learning and its relevance. All of these affect their intentions and their readiness to engage with the tasks set by the teachers, and also their understanding of what is required in the classroom. What is accepted within the home as an adequate explanation to a scientific question, for example, may be nothing like the answer a teacher expects.

'Personal understanding' thus becomes the product of all these experiences and may involve overlapping, potentially contradictory or fuzzy conceptions. Even when the feeling of understanding is strong, it may remain idiosyncratic or incorrect in comparison to target understanding. This sense of 'personal understanding' can be captured in the phrase, 'It is *my* understanding that . . .'.

> This is a meaning of understanding which implies something particular to an individual. It is that individual's interpretation of context or a particular aspect of that context. In this sense, a person always has an understanding of the context . . . This may also be the sense of the term which is implied when writers talk about the growth of social . . . or language understanding. At any rate, understanding in these cases is clearly not one of either fully understanding or of not understanding. It is open to variations in depth or level, and to variations in interpretations of what is the case or what is being meant.
>
> (Smith, 1998: 73)

All these influences thus affect the ways in which students interpret and approach the tasks set by teachers, who are themselves having to decide how best to present the required curriculum. A chain of individual constructions of rather different meanings can then be envisaged. It leads from the formal syllabus to the students' perceptions of the work they have to do, and accounts, at least in part, for the different ways in which the tasks are carried out, and the wide variations in forms and levels of understanding reached.

MAPPING INFLUENCES ON THE OUTCOMES OF LEARNING

This discussion of recent educational research on learning and teaching was designed to produce a more general conceptual model of teaching and learning. Derived in part from the earlier model, Figure 12.3 summarises, in diagrammatic form, some of the influences which lead to qualitatively different learning levels and forms of understanding. Besides being more generally applicable than the previous one, this model introduces recent ideas on the differing perceptions and conceptions held by both students and teachers. Yet it remains a partial representation of the complexities of classroom learning. It does not include all the influences on learning; nor indeed should it. The whole purpose of such a map is to simplify complexity and remove unnecessary detail, so as to make the landscape more readily recognisable. This particular diagram serves simply as a mnemonic device to keep in mind, or in 'simultaneous awareness' (Bowden and Marton, 1998), a substantial set of influences on learning.

Of course, the particular set of concepts chosen is open to challenge, and each of the boxes can be seen as a portal to related ideas and concepts which include, but go well beyond, those discussed earlier. These ideas include substantive suggestions about teaching practice, which are currently being explored. The model also cannot convey the idea of the development which underlies it, although arrows are used to suggest that the understandings of both students and teacher will develop over time. Moreover, the dotted line on the left indicates that our concepts are affected by departmental and institutional ethos, as well as the much broader cultural influences, all of which lie beyond the scope of this article.

As in the earlier model, Figure 12.3 places the characteristics of students and teachers above and below the central part of the diagram, where the learning outcomes are positioned. The concept boxes imply explanations of differences in the levels of under-standing reached. In this model, the distinction between target and personal understanding

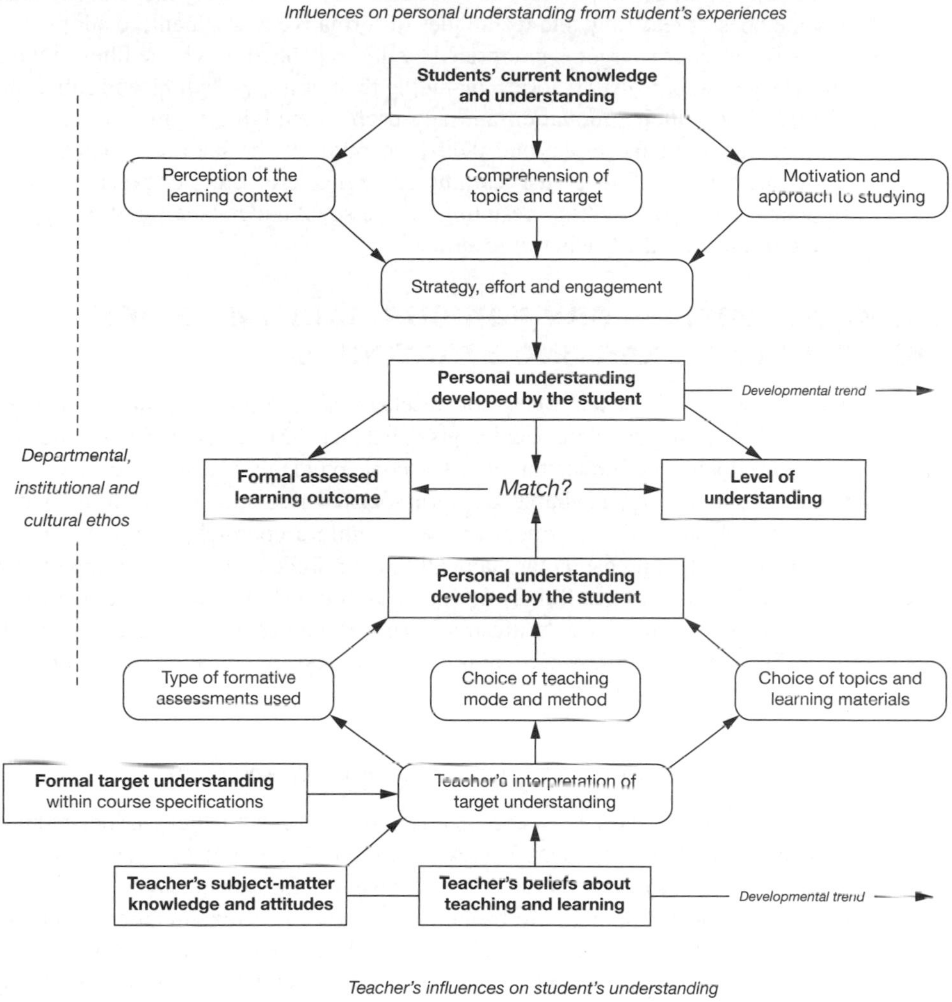

Influences on personal understanding from student's experiences

Teacher's influences on student's understanding

■ **Figure 12.3** Conceptual model of influences on students' levels of understanding.

has been introduced to organise the interrelationships being suggested, with the idea of contrasting perceptions playing an essential supporting role. Here, though, the outcome of learning is judged in terms of the extent of the match between the target understanding being expected by the teacher or examiner, and the level of understanding actually reached by an individual student.

Target understanding is shown as originating in decisions taken by the curriculum designers about course specifications or examination syllabuses; these produce the formal target. Interpreting that target, teachers are influenced by their own knowledge and attitudes about the subject, and by their beliefs about teaching and learning. The interpreted target or object of study is then presented to the class, both by direct teaching and through the implicit messages conveyed by teachers' attitudes and emphases. Teachers choose topics and decide the importance to place on each of them; they then decide which modes and methods of teaching, and techniques of formative assessment, to adopt.

The teacher's target is interpreted by the students through the filter of their existing knowledge and personal histories, including their attitudes, beliefs and self-concepts. All of these affect their motivation and approach to studying within the classroom, their comprehension of the target and their perception of the learning context. These three components then influence the learning strategies, effort and engagement that students show in carrying out the task, resulting in a personal understanding of the topic, which is then evaluated by the teacher or examiner.

USING THE FRAMEWORK FOR CURRICULUM DESIGN AND TEACHING–LEARNING STRATEGIES

The framework is intended to help both teachers and researchers to think more clearly about how understanding develops. It attempts to balance the roles played by teacher and student in the development of understanding. The conceptual model also brings into sharper relief the effects of the formal syllabus and its associated assessment procedures. Thus, teacher, student, syllabus and assessment are seen within a complex, interacting process, with components affecting each other, and all of them influencing the learning outcomes.

Implications of the framework are currently being developed along several lines. These are briefly introduced to illustrate its potential 'pedagogical fertility', in other words its ability to provoke innovative thinking and produce practical improvements in teaching and learning (Entwistle, 1994).

Formal target understanding within secondary schools

The model emphasises how examination syllabuses and their associated assessment procedures form an initial target. Pressure for public accountability, and for reliability of measurement, may lead to an overemphasis on factual accuracy and pre-packaged descriptive understandings. Our framework has led to a re-examination of our earlier look at biology in Scottish secondary schools. There is clear evidence in syllabuses at both Standard Grade (14–16) and Higher (17+) of the emphasis on predominantly factual knowledge. Where understanding *is* specified, no more than the 'descriptive' level seems to be expected. Moreover, even in the most recent versions of the Higher syllabus, there is little attempt to present the subject as a coherent whole – a limitation noted by one of the curriculum designers interviewed previously (Smith, 1998):

I: You might have expected some linking themes – adaptation, perhaps?

R: Absolutely right. I wanted that . . . I wanted to show how these concepts permeate the whole thing – like adaptation . . . to give them one or two models and to justify big changes in the examination paper. I was furious when I didn't get a chance . . . We sold the teachers short over this lack of cohesion in the subject. It's all in wee dollops, packages of information with no ways in which teachers could look at it from a synthetic aspect . . . What we really need is some way in which we can synthesise the aspects of biology. The skilful teacher has to sit back and look at where the integrating themes are, and that can be difficult because of the way it is put together and the time they have.

The descriptions of what is required for each grade level (A, B, C, etc.) within the Higher examination does suggest that integration of the content will be expected for the highest grade. One section in the examination does involve integration across course units, as well as a greater emphasis on explanations rather than descriptions (Higher Still Development Unit, 1998). However, the actual questions indicate that only limited integration is being required, as they do not involve the broader themes needed to produce a coherent understanding of the subject. At present, few syllabuses explicitly include the equivalent of the 'through-lines' offered within the TfU framework to focus students' attention on the coherence of the course, nor do they model higher forms of understanding. It is possible to draw on and extend the TfU framework to suggest ways of implementing a curriculum that would provide a more explicit requirement for understanding (Smith, 2002b).

Formal syllabuses, and the type of examination questions set, substantially affect how teachers present their target understandings to students. Teachers, though, are still free to encourage students to reach the highest level of understanding of which they are capable. They are also, given time, able to build up a sense of coherence in the subject in the way suggested in the previous quotation. The problem remains, however, that neither students nor staff may see the point of going beyond what the formal target understanding appears to demand. The syllabus can thus form a serious limitation on the quality of understanding being sought, although it also offers the most immediate opportunity for improvement. It would be relatively easy for examination boards to ensure that grade-related criteria set a more demanding target of integrative understanding to achieve a top grade.

The development of secondary teachers' thinking about understanding

The framework, and the discussion which preceded it, drew attention to teachers' beliefs about learning and teaching, and to the ways in which they interpret and present a target understanding to form an object of study. By emphasising the role of the teacher in interpreting the target and then deciding on appropriate teaching and learning strategies, the framework can be used to initiate discussions among staff. One of the authors (Colin Smith) has been using the model to provoke the development within his own school of a purpose-built framework that reflects the teachers' own ideas about encouraging students' understanding. The intention has been to create a shared form of action theory or 'living theory' (Whitehead, 1989) which directly encourages reflection on the improvement of practice. Such a shared set of ideas and principles then encompasses teachers' beliefs about learning and teaching, and the interpretation of target understanding (Smith, 2001).

A group of teachers is currently applying these ideas to their attempts to support, in everyday practice, understanding of topics within the curriculum (Smith, 2001). A shared living theory of this type gains strength from the teachers' involvement in its design and can have a direct impact on development planning by obliging management to provide school structures which support its implementation. As the development process is taken further, students will also be involved in the discussions. By being introduced to the outlines of the theory, they should then be better able to share the 'mutual awareness' which Marton and Booth (1997) see as crucial to good teaching and learning. Specifically, they can become active partners in the attempt to improve the match between realistic, but demanding, targets, and the forms and levels of personal understanding achieved.

Exploration of the relationship between intuitive theories and academic discourse

Personal understanding is essentially a developmental concept. Our framework indicates, in broad outline, how people's life experiences affect the development of their understanding within educational contexts. And it offers an educational learning theory that complements psychological theories of cognitive development, by keeping both individual and context in mind simultaneously. This combination may offer an important breakthrough in exploring the relationships between intuitive theories and scientifically accurate conceptions.

Smith and Williams (2002) are currently using the distinction between target and personal understanding to explore the relationship between young people's intuitive understanding of genetics and the public understanding of science. In some cultures, science education avoids challenging everyday experience and intuitive or local explanations while emphasising that science is also a source for certain practical knowledge. In contrast, Western education seeks to replace everyday notions with generalised scientific knowledge (Popli, 1999), thus losing the linguistic and conceptual connection with everyday experience. It might prove more effective to reconsider the forms of target understanding that would appropriately build on or challenge 'intuitive genetics', so that the scientific meaning serves to extend people's understanding of it in their everyday lives.

CONCLUSION

These three examples indicate the potential value of the framework developed out of recent educational research. It provides a pragmatic theory of learning within education that summarises some of the major influences on the outcomes of learning. The model brings together the syllabus, as the initial target, the teacher's interpretation of that target, and the differences in experience and approach of the students. All of these influences affect the form and level of personal understanding reached by the student. While this cannot offer anything approaching complete coverage of the intricacy and complexity of the relationships met within the classroom, it does offer a way of thinking which teachers can readily adapt to their own circumstances and ideas about education. And it derives from educational research that has clear ecological validity.

Delineating the boundaries of any model of education is difficult. There are always reasons for extending them further, to include more and more of the contexts which influence learning (Bronfennbrenner, 1979). Pragmatism suggests, however, that a more limited focus of convenience is chosen. If we are to be able to offer a way of thinking about teaching which is research-based, and yet professionally sound, we need an ecologically valid theory which uses, as far as possible, accessible terms and describes everyday classroom situations and contexts. We have argued that our framework offers just such a set of ideas and principles, ones that cover important aspects of teaching–learning processes identified from research while remaining recognisable to teachers. Our model also retains everyday classroom contrasts, such as teacher and learner, individual understanding and shared understanding, prescribed curriculum and what is actually taught. It thus offers at least one way of conceptualising the teaching–learning process which may be of direct value for teachers.

REFERENCES

Ausubel, D.P., Novak, J.S. and Hanesian, H. (1978) *Educational psychology: a cognitive view*, New York: Holt, Rinehart &Winston.

Bereiter, C. (1990) 'Aspects of an educational learning theory', *Review of Educational Research*, Vol. 60: 603–624.

Bereiter, C. and Scardamalia, M. (1989) 'Intentional learning as a goal of instruction', in Resnick, L.B. (ed.) *Knowing, learning and instruction: essays in honour of Robert Glaser*, Hillsdale, NJ: Erlbaum: 361–392.

Biggs, J.B. and Collis, K.F. (1982) *Evaluating the quality of learning: the SOLO taxonomy*. New York: Academic Press.

Blythe, T. *et al.* (1998) *The 'Teaching for Understanding' guide*. San Francisco: Jossey-Bass.

Bowden, J. and Marton, F. (1998) *The university of learning*, London: Kogan Page.

Bredo, E. (2000) 'The social construction of learning', in Phye, G.D. (ed.) *Handbook of academic learning: construction of knowledge*, New York: Academic Press: 3–46.

Bronfennbrenner, H. (1979) *The ecology of human development: experiments by nature and design*, Cambridge, MA: Harvard University Press.

Brown, J.S., Collins, A. and Duguid, P. (1989) 'Situated cognition and the culture of learning', *Educational Researcher*, Vol. 18, No. 1: 32–42.

Burns, J., Clift, J. and Duncan, J. (1991) 'Understanding of understanding: implications for learning and teaching', *British Journal of Educational Psychology*, Vol. 61: 276–289.

Calderhead, J. (1996) 'Teachers: beliefs and knowledge', in Berliner, D. and Calfree, R. (eds) *Handbook of educational psychology*, New York: Macmillan: 709–725.

Cobb, P. (1994) 'Where is the mind? Constructivist and sociocultural perspectives on mathematical development', *Educational Researcher*, Vol. 23: 13–20.

Dall'Alba, G. (1991) 'Foreshadowing conceptions of teaching', *Research and Development in Higher Education*, Vol. 13: 293–297.

Dewey, J. (1938) *Experience and education*, New York: Collier Macmillan.

Driver, R. and Erickson, G. (1983) 'Theories in action: some theoretical and empirical issues in the study of students' conceptual frameworks in science', *Studies in Science Education*, Vol. 10: 37–60.

Entwistle, N.J. (1994) 'Generative concepts and pedagogical fertility: communicating research findings on student learning', *EARLI News*, June: 9–15.

Entwistle, N.J. (2000) 'Approaches to studying and levels of understanding: the influences of teaching and assessment', in Smart, J.C. (ed.) *Higher education: handbook of theory and research*, Vol. XV, New York: Agathon Press: 156–218.

Entwistle, N.J. and Entwistle, A.C. (1997) 'Revision and the experience of understanding', in Marton, F., Hounsell, D.J. and Entwistle, N.J. (eds) *The experience of learning* (2nd edition), Edinburgh: Scottish Academic Press: 145–158.

Entwistle, N.J. and Entwistle, D.M. (2001) *The interplay between memorising and understanding in preparing for examinations*. Paper presented at the *9th Conference of the European Association for Research into Learning and Instruction*, August, Fribourg, Switzerland.

Entwistle, N.J. and Ramsden, P. (1983) *Understanding student learning*, London: Croom Helm.

Entwistle, N.J. and Walker, P. (2002) 'Strategic alertness and expanded awareness in sophisticated conceptions of teaching', in Hativa, N. and Goodyear, P. (eds) *Teacher thinking, beliefs and knowledge in higher education*, Dordrecht: Kluwer: 15–40.

Entwistle, N.J., Kozéki, B. and Tait, H. (1989) 'Pupils' perceptions of school and teachers. II – Relationships with motivation and approaches to learning', *British Journal of Educational Psychology*, Vol. 59: 340–350.

Entwistle, N.J., Skinner, D.J., Entwistle, D.M., and Orr, S.M. (2000) 'Conceptions and beliefs about "good teaching": an integration of contrasting research areas', *Higher Education Research and Development*, Vol. 19: 5–26.

Entwistle, N.J. and Tait, H. (1990) 'Approaches to learning, evaluations of teaching, and preferences for contrasting academic environments', *Higher Education*, Vol. 19: 169–194.

Fox, R. (2001) 'Constructivism examined', *Oxford Review of Education*, Vol. 27: 23–35.

Fransson, A. (1977) 'On qualitative differences in learning: IV – Effects of motivation and test anxiety on process and outcome', *British Journal of Educational Psychology*, Vol. 47: 244–257.

Halldén, O. (1988) 'Alternative frameworks and the concept of task: cognitive constraints in pupils' interpretations of teachers' assignments', *Scandinavian Journal of Educational Research*, Vol. 32: 123–140.

Halldén, O. (1999) 'Conceptual change and contextualisation', in Schnotz, W., Vosniadou, S. and Carretaro, M. (eds) *New perspectives on conceptual change,* Mahwah, NJ: Lawrence Erlbaum: 53–66.

Higher Still Development Unit (1998) *Biology Workshop Papers, Section 6*, Edinburgh.

Hodgson, V. (1997) 'Lectures and the experience of relevance', in Marton, F., Hounsell, D.J. and Entwistle, N.J. (eds) *The experience of learning* (2nd edition), Edinburgh: Scottish Academic Press: 159–171.

Katz, S. (2000) 'Competency, epistemology and pedagogy: curriculum's holy trinity', *Curriculum Journal*, Vol. 11: 133–144.

Kelly, G.A. (1955) *The psychology of personal constructs*, New York: Norton.

Kember, D. (1996) 'The intention to both memorise and understand: another approach to learning', *Higher Education,* Vol. 31: 341–354.

Lave, J. and Wenger, E. (1991) *Situated learning: legitimate peripheral participation*, Cambridge: Cambridge University Press.

Marsh, H. (1987) 'Students' evaluations of university teaching: research findings, methodological issues, directions for future research', *International Journal of Educational Research*, Vol. 11, No. 3: whole issue.

Marton, F. and Booth, S. (1997) *Learning and awareness*, Mahwah, NJ: Lawrence Erlbaum.

Marton, F. and Säljö, R. (1976) 'On qualitative differences in learning: I – Outcome and process', *British Journal of Educational Psychology*, Vol. 46: 4–11.

Marton, F. and Säljö, R. (1997) 'Approaches to learning', in Marton, F., Hounsell, D.J. and Entwistle, N. J. (eds) *The experience of learning* (2nd edition), Edinburgh: Scottish Academic Press: 39–58.

Marton, F., Hounsell, D.J. and Entwistle, N.J. (eds) (1997) *The experience of learning* (2nd edition), Edinburgh: Scottish Academic Press.

Marton, F., Watkins, D. and Tang, C. (1997) 'Discontinuities and continuities in the experience of learning: an interview study of high-school students in Hong Kong', *Learning and Instruction*, Vol. 7: 21–48.

Meyer, J.H.F. (1991) 'Study orchestration: the manifestation, interpretation and consequences of contextualised approaches to learning', *Higher Education*, Vol. 22: 297–316.

Meyer, J.H.F. (2000) 'Variation in contrasting forms of "memorising" and associated observables', *British Journal of Educational Psychology*, Vol. 70: 163–176.

Meyer, J.H.F. and Muller, M.W. (1990) 'Evaluating the quality of student learning. I – An unfolding analysis of the association between perceptions of learning context and approaches to studying at an individual level', *Studies in Higher Education*, Vol. 15: 131–154.

Molander, B.-O. (1997) *Joint discourses or disjointed courses*, Stockholm: HLS Forlag, Stockholm Institute of Education Press.

Newton, D.P. (2000) *Teaching for understanding*, London: RoutledgeFalmer.

Newton, D.P. and Newton, L.D. (1999) 'Knowing what counts as understanding in different disciplines', *Educational Studies*, Vol. 25: 35–54.

Patrick, K. (1998) 'Teaching and learning: the construction of an object of study'. Unpublished Ph.D. thesis, University of Melbourne.

Patrick, K. (undated) 'Doing history'. Unpublished paper, University of Melbourne

Peel, E.A. (1971) *The nature of adolescent judgement*, London: Staples Press.

Perkins, D.N. (1998) 'What is understanding?', in Wiske, M.S. (ed.) *Teaching for understanding. Linking research with practice*, San Francisco: Jossey-Bass: 39–57.

Perkins, D.N. (in press) 'Knowledge into action' in *Knowledge directions*.

Phillips, D.C. (ed.) (2000) *Constructivism in education*, Chicago, IL: National Society for the Study of Education.

Popli, R. (1999) 'Scientific literacy for all citizens: different concepts and contents', *Public Understanding of Science*, Vol. 8: 123–137.

Prosser, M. and Trigwell, K. (1999) *Understanding learning and teaching: the experience in higher education*, Buckingham: SRHE/Open University Press.

Ramsden, P. (1992) *Learning to teach in higher education*, London: Kogan Page.

Ramsden, P. (1997) 'The context of learning in academic departments', in Marton, F., Hounsell, D.J. and Entwistle, N.J. (eds) *The experience of learning* (2nd edition), Edinburgh: Scottish Academic Press: 198–216.

Säljö, R. (1991) 'Learning and mediation: fitting reality into a table', *Learning and Instruction*, Vol. 1: 262–272.

Scheja, M. (2001). 'Contextualising studies in higher education: an empirical study of first-year students' experiences of studying in tertiary engineering education'. Paper presented at the *9th Conference of the European Association for Research on Learning and Instruction*, August, Fribourg, Switzerland.

Shulman, L.S. (1987) 'Knowledge and teaching: foundations of the new reform', *Harvard Educational Review*, Vol. 57: 114–135.

Smith, C.A. (1998) 'Personal understanding and target understanding: their relationships through individual variations and curricular influences'. Unpublished Ph.D. thesis, University of Edinburgh.

Smith, C.A. (2001) 'Linking research with practice: living theories and learning and teaching policies'. Paper presented at the Scottish Educational Research Association Conference, September, Perth.

Smith, C.A. (2002a) 'School learning and teaching policies as shared living theories: an example'. Manuscript submitted for publication.

Smith, C.A. (2002b). 'Modelling understanding using the syllabus: biology education as an example'. Manuscript submitted for publication.

Smith, C.A., and Williams, J. (2002) 'Models in promoting public understanding of science: understanding genetics as an example from biology'. Manuscript in preparation

Tan, S.K. and Novak, J.D. (undated) 'Student meanings of understanding in the physics classroom'. Unpublished manuscript, University of Sains Malaysia, Penang, Malaysia.

Tang, C. (1991) 'Effects of different assessment methods on tertiary students' approaches to studying'. Unpublished Ph.D. Dissertation, University of Hong Kong.

Von Glasersfeld, E. (1988) 'Learning as a constructivist activity', in Stelle, L. (ed.) *Proceedings of the International Conference of Mathematical Education, Hungary*, Mahwah, NJ: Lawrence Erlbaum.

Watkins, C. and Mortimore, P. (1999) 'Pedagogy: what do we know?', in Mortimore, P. (ed.) *Understanding pedagogy and its impact on learning*, London: Paul Chapman: 1–19.

Watkins, D.A. and Biggs, J.B. (eds) (1996) *The Chinese learner: cultural, psychological and contextual influences*, Hong Kong: Comparative Education Research Centre and Australian Council for Educational Research.

Watts, I. (1810) *The improvement of the mind*, London: Gale & Curtis.

Whitehead, J. (1989) 'Creating a living educational theory from questions of the kind, "How do I improve my practice?"', *Cambridge Journal of Education*, Vol. 19: 41–52.

Wiske, M.S. (1998) 'What is teaching for understanding?', in Wiske, M.S. (ed.) *Teaching for understanding. Linking research with practice*, San Francisco: Jossey-Bass: 61–85.

Wittrock, M. (ed.) (1986) *Handbook of research on teaching* (3rd edition), New York: Macmillan.

Wolf, D., Bixby, J., Glenn III, J. and Gardner, H. (1991) 'To use their minds well: new forms of student assessment', *Review of Research in Education*, Vol. 17: 31–74.

Woods, P. and Jeffrey, B. (1996) *Teachable moments*, Buckingham: Open University Press.

PERSONALISED LEARNING

Ambiguities in theory and practice

R.J. Campbell, W. Robinson, J. Neelands, R. Hewston and L. Mazzoli

---

A NOTE FROM THE EDITORS

This conceptual reading presents a critical review of the personalisation agenda, drawing on a range of research and drawing attention to some of the problems of translating policy into practice.

This reading links with Chapter 5 of the 5th edition of *Learning to teach in the secondary school*.

QUESTIONS TO CONSIDER

1   The concept of personalisation of learning is contested; how was personalisation conceived by Demos (Leadbetter, 2003) for public services in general? What did this conception mean for education?
2   What is deep personalisation, and how does it differ from shallow personalisation?
3   Personalisation has been dismissed by some as no more than differentiation, which is an integral part of effective teaching. Why are these views held?
4   What, if any, research has been conducted on the impact of the framework developed by DfES (2004) on schools and teachers' practice in classrooms? What research needs to be conducted?

This reading was first published as: Campbell, R.J., Robinson, W., Neelands, J., Hewston R. and Mazzoli L. (2007) 'Personalised learning: ambiguities in theory and practice', *British Journal of Educational Studies*, Vol. 55, 135–154.

ABSTRACT

This paper traces the origins of the concept of personalisation in public sector services, and applies it to school education. The original conceptualisation stressed the need for 'deep' rather than shallow, personalisation, if radical transformation of services were to be achieved. It is argued that as the concept has been disseminated and implemented through policy documents, notably the 2005 White Paper, it has lost its original emphasis on deep personalisation. The focus in this article is particularly upon gifted and talented students whose education provides the best case example of how the theory of personalisation might work in practice. Two examples of the lessons in a sixth form college are used to illustrate the character of personalised pedagogy in practice. The implications for theory and practice are discussed.

PERSONALISATION IN THE PUBLIC SERVICES: THEORIES AND AMBIGUITIES

Personalisation is a contestable concept applied to the planning and delivery of public sector services in England. It was introduced into the policy arena following the publication of a paper from a think tank, Demos, by Leadbeater (2003). The concept was at first misunderstood as the individualisation of services, but personalisation is a far more socially-oriented idea. Leadbeater argued that personalisation could operate at five increasingly deeply structured levels. These were:

■ providing more customer friendly services;
■ giving people more say in navigating their way through services;
■ giving users more say over how money is spent;
■ users becoming co-designers and co-producers of services;
■ self-organisation by individuals working with the support and advisory systems provided by professionals.

Leadbeater speculated that personalisation could become as powerful an organising logic for reshaping public sector services in the coming decade as privatisation had been in the 1980s and 1990s.

To illustrate the concept, he contrasted explanations for the 23 per cent decline in deaths from heart disease in England between 1997 and 2002. On the one hand, medical professionals had improved the quality of cardiac services and introduced statins and other technical improvements; on the other, citizens had adopted changes to their lifestyle, giving up smoking, taking exercise, eating more healthy food etc. He argued that, 'Contained in this single story are two very different accounts of how the public good is created.' The first emphasises the role of the state and professionals in providing more effective services:

> The public good goes up the more effective the state becomes in solving society's problems for it. The second account is that the public good – fewer people dying young from heart attacks – comes from millions of people making loosely connected decisions in society to change the way they live, which collectively produces a significant improvement in the public good. In this model, the state does not act upon society; it does not provide a service. Instead, the state creates a platform or environment in which people take decisions about their lives in a different way. This is bottom-up, mass social innovation enabled by the state.
>
> (Leadbeater, 2003: 16)

Leadbeater argues that these two accounts may be constructed as complementary, but they reflect very different assumptions about the role of users and professionals. The former assumes user-dependency, whereas in the latter, users become co-producers of the good in question, having access to information and developing confidence to self-manage their health. The two approaches can contribute to the development of personalised public services, but, he argued, the approach chosen will determine the form such personalisation takes: providing better access and some limited voice about services (shallow personalisation), sustaining improvements in the existing systems; or, a more 'disruptive' innovation, in which users become 'designers and paymasters' of services (deep personalisation).

The deepest level would mean:

self organisation: the public good emerging from within society, in part through the way that public policy shapes millions of individual decisions about how we exercise, eat, smoke, save for our pensions, read to our children, pay our taxes, and so on. Many of our biggest social challenges – reducing obesity and smoking, caring for people with chronic health conditions, promoting learning, creating safer communities – will only be met if we promote a mass social innovation within society: self organising capacity to meet demand, otherwise queues would just lengthen.

(Leadbeater, 2003: 49)

For the argument in this paper, deep personalisation is taken to mean either or both of the last two of Leadbeater's levels, and shallow personalisation the first three, the justification for this distinction being that the last two levels involve action by consumers, whereas the former three require merely that the state acts in a more efficient way to provide services to the consumer.

Under this model of deep personalisation, professionals become advisers and brokers of services, not providing the services themselves so much as helping clients generate pathways through the available range of provision that meets their particular needs. Some public services (for example, emergency and accident treatment in hospitals, defence, police) Leadbeater accepts do not lend themselves easily to the participative concept of personalisation. But deep personalisation would be particularly appropriate in services which are face to face (e.g. social services, non-emergency health), or involve a long-term relationship (e.g. treatment of chronic illness), or depend on direct engagement between professionals and users (e.g. much formal schooling). He cites research showing that self-management by diabetes sufferers was associated with fewer crises and less hospital treatment than those not self-managing.

At this stage, two critical ambiguities emerge in Leadbeater's argument. The first is whether the principal advantage is to the individual (through the development of a more healthy lifestyle, for example) or to the state, through the consequential reduction of state funding for directly provided services, as illustrated in the diabetes example above. The second is whether, under deep personalisation, the assertion that the state ceases to provide direct services goes beyond rhetoric, since, even in this model, the state 'creates the platform' and funds the delivery of most of the professional services that become brokered and co-produced. Unless these activities are seen as merely a transitional stage, they do not obviously reflect the bottom-up mass innovation supposed to characterise deep personalisation.

PERSONALISATION AND EDUCATION

Leadbeater saw the application of personalisation to education as particularly appropriate, drawing upon the concept of a 'script' to envisage how it might work. Children would be enabled to devise a 'greater repertoire of possible scripts for how their education would unfold'. At core there would be a common script – the basic curriculum – but that script could branch out in many different ways, to have many different styles and endings. The foundation would be to encourage children, from an early age and across all backgrounds, to become more involved in making decisions about what they would like to learn and how. The more aware people are of what makes them want to learn, the more effective their learning is likely to be, since, 'personalised learning allows individual interpretations of the goals and value of education' (pp. 68–69).

The aim of personalisation in learning is not marketisation of education so much as the promotion of self-realisation, with children constructed as active and responsible co-authors of their educational script. This would lead to students' setting their own learning targets, adopting continuous self-assessment for learning, and to the development of flexibility in learning beyond the school and outside traditional school hours. Such flexibility to learn out of school would not be an entitlement, but would depend on 'earned autonomy' achieved through students doing well, demonstrating self-motivation and becoming more self-regulating. Schools and teachers would no longer prescribe the content and pace and control of the curriculum, but would form partnerships and networks with other schools and other agencies, so as to broaden the resources and learning opportunities available to students; their role would be to broker students' access to them and to help them make informed choices about pathways through them.

However attractive in theory, this application of the deep personalisation model also rests on substantial ambiguities. As a matter of fact and of law currently, it is not 'schools and teachers' who prescribe the content, pace and control of the curriculum, it is the state, with most estimates showing state prescription, at least up to age 14, of 90 per cent of what is an age-related curriculum. It is difficult to see how this degree of regulation of the curriculum could allow individual interpretations of the goals and values of education. Even if it did, it would shatter the idea that education had a unifying function in society, to initiate the young into the common culture, as Lawton (1975) and others have argued. The second ambiguity is about earned autonomy, which will have to be demonstrated by pupils/students learning the state-controlled, directly delivered and non-negotiable curriculum, which may reward self-motivation, but not self-regulation by pupils/students. Moreover, self-motivation and self-regulation, not to mention educational progress, however desirable intrinsically, are not equally distributed among different classes and cultures in English society, so to ambiguity is added the possibility of continuing, or even increased, educational disadvantage.

The force of the above point is explicitly acknowledged by Leadbeater, who sees the main obstacle to the development of personalisation to be cultural, intellectual and financial capital, with professional-class parents being in a position to exploit the advantages of personalisation for the benefit of their own children. Personalisation, therefore, might increase the already large inequalities in educational provision and achievement, deriving mainly from social and economic status. Leadbeater's answer to this is that public resources would need to be skewed toward the educationally disadvantaged families, with increased and intensive guidance and advocacy from professionals, and compensatory resource allocation, for example in information technology. 'With careful design personalised services need not widen inequalities. On the contrary, they could be most valuable for people most in need' (p. 79).

This proposed solution to the inequality problem will be discussed more fully later in the paper, but at this point it is worth noting that 'not widening inequalities' is not the same as reducing them, and could be read as implying that personalisation does not embody an ambition to *redress* the sources of inequality in educational achievement or even educational provision.

More directly, however, skewing resources in education to redress societal inequalities has had a long and dismal record of ineffectiveness, going back at least as far as the 1970s, with the educational priority areas and community education movements that followed the Plowden Report (1967). Indeed, it could be argued that what has started to reduce inequality in educational achievement is the direct delivery, through interventionist national initiatives such as the literacy and numeracy strategies, of more effective teaching technologies – the educational equivalent of statins. In contrast to the rest of Leadbeater's argument, the treatment of this crucial issue comes over as weak, and possibly naïve, in respect of its assumptions about the ease with which generation of agency in the most disadvantaged groups in society can be realised.

Despite these concerns, the term 'personalisation' appears to have attracted a substantial range of analyses since the Leadbeater paper. The Nuffield Review of 14–19 provision (Hayward *et al.*, 2005), the ESRC Teaching and Learning programme (Pollard and James, 2004), an NCSL special supplement (NCSL, 2004), a government White Paper (DfES, 2005) and a review chaired by Her Majesty's Chief Inspector (HMCI) of schools (Gilbert, 2007) make differentially effective attempts to analyse the term, though none, except Gilbert, refers to Leadbeater's work directly. Possibly for this reason, or possibly because the concept of personalisation has not yet been fully worked out, there is no explicit common definition across these papers. The Nuffield Review, while referring to the ESRC programme, worked (pp. 49–50) with a concept stressing a specified pedagogy – encouraging cooperative learning, mentoring, valuing experiential learning, incorporating learners' personal and social experience, using ICT, providing individual support – and allied this to the development of collaborative partnerships of providers to extend accessible choice for students. In respect of official encouragement for capturing student voice, the Nuffield Review was cautious, articulating a further ambiguity:

> It is not clear for what purpose the 'learner's voice' is thought to be important: whether for understanding how to motivate students (to get them to take an interest in things which teachers or trainers think they should be interested in) or whether for shaping the very aims and purposes of learning.
>
> (Hayward *et al.*, 37)

Nevertheless, the Nuffield Review's treatment came close to Leadbeater's conception of co-producing a public good, but was less explicit about the role of self-organisation represented in Leadbeater's deepest level.

The ESRC analysis (Pollard and James, 2004: 5) drew upon a fivefold framework provided by the DfES (2004). This comprised:

- Assessment for Learning.
- Teaching and Learning strategies that stretch pupils.
- Curriculum entitlement and Choice.
- Student-centred Organisations.
- Partnership beyond the school.

The rationale for including these elements and not others is not made clear, though Assessment for Learning, which involves teachers and students jointly generating what best helps students learn, and developing metacognitive judgements by students about their learning, is palpably part of the personalisation concept. Likewise, partnerships beyond the school will be needed if schools are to act as brokers for wider pathways to learning opportunities that reflect student choice and are responsive to it.

The ESRC analysis, while supporting the principle of personalisation, also illustrated some specific problematic aspects from research programmes already in train. For example, in respect of Assessment for Learning, it argued:

> Personalised learning is not a matter of tailoring curriculum, teaching and assessment to 'fit' the individual but is a question of developing social practices that enable people to become all that they are capable of becoming.
>
> (Pollard and James, 2004: 6)

It is clear that this reconceptualisation directly challenges the model in the White Paper, as will be argued below. However, it accords very closely with the pedagogy we found in classrooms, two illustrations of which are provided below.

In respect of consulting students in order to empower student voice, the issues of equity and authenticity were raised: 'Does the consultation consist of questions that teachers think are important or questions that pupils think are important?' (Pollard and James, 2004: 11).

This questioning of the purpose of generating student voice resonates with the Nuffield Review's concern on the issue.

The ESRC analysis raised three more ambiguities, which it saw as arising in part from the rapid development of the concept, and in part from the 'lack of clarity' about the concept, according to the DfES itself. The first is whether lack of clarity could be con-structed as an advantage, since the ESRC analysis cites a paper from the DfES in 2004, to the effect that, 'Personalised Learning is an aspiration or a philosophy providing space within which others can operate'. The second issue was identified as the relationship between the component parts of the fivefold framework:

> Its logical and empirical base can be challenged. How are its components chosen and what do they involve? Committed educationalists within the DfES have been working on the factors which they hope will, if implemented appropriately, enhance learning outcomes and provide equity and excellence. But these conclusions are still a theory – a set of propositions.
>
> (Pollard and James, 2004: 23)

Third, there was the issue of the reception of the idea by the profession. 'The new concept of personalised learning is likely to generate scepticism in some circles. Does it represent genuine new thinking about how teaching and learning can most effectively take place?' Noting the contrast between the learner-centred character of personalisation and the previous and current state-centred approaches to curriculum and assessment, the ESRC analysis doubts whether a 'simple switch' between the two modes can be achieved.

As with the Nuffield Review, the ESRC analysis has strong, though implicit, assumptions that are close to the Leadbeater concept, perhaps most strongly in respect of its emphasis on student voice, and the role that assessment for learning plays in helping learners understand how they learn most effectively, though there is little detailed treatment about the concept of co-production of knowledge, which is restricted to a brief comment on constructivism. It may be that taking the DfES fivefold framework, whatever its advantages for tying in the argument to current education policy developments, deflected the ESRC team's attention from the more generalised Leadbeater model, which is not restricted to education, and certainly not to the statutory period of schooling, since his examples include aspects of adult learning.

The special supplement from the NCSL offers a mix of small reports of practice in particular schools, and outlines of the idea of personalised learning. There is continuity with the DfES fivefold model analysed by the ESRC team, with particularly strong emphasis on the role of Assessment for Learning and brokering learning through partnerships. This is probably because the supplement was produced in partnership with the DfES Innovation Unit and has a contribution from its director.

The most analytical contribution comes from Professor David Hopkins, head of the DfES Standards and Effectiveness Unit at the time:

> It's building schooling around the needs and aptitudes of individual pupils, shaping teaching around the way different youngsters learn. It's also about making sure that the talent of each pupil is supported and encouraged, and about personalising the school experience to enable pupils to focus on their learning . . . personalised learning has to be a system-wide achievement so that it impacts on every student in every school.
>
> (NCSL, 2004: 7)

Hopkins goes on to stress the importance of pedagogic change and assessment for learning and, unlike the Nuffield and ESRC analyses, asserts that a whole-school ethos and approach must be implemented. He sees these elements as implicated in delivering the government's commitment to 'excellence and equity' in education.

The supplement concludes with twenty-three bullet points for school leaders to help them put the theory of personalisation into practice. Most focus on improving organisational understanding and efficiency (e.g. 'Exploit the opportunities of workforce reform to involve more adults in preparing for and assisting in learning'). Our assessment is that only three of the twenty-three are directly concerned with students actively generating their own understandings and knowledge as co-constructors with teachers. The supplement therefore can be interpreted as operating at the shallower end of personalisation, at least in its ideas about how personalisation can be put into practice. This may be a risk associated with any attempt to articulate theory into practice.

The 2005 White Paper (DfES, 2005) gives particular attention to personalised learning, devoting a whole chapter to the topic. Unlike Nuffield and the ESRC, however, there is very little to connect the text to the Leadbeater theorising. Indeed, the chapter is distinguished by its refusal to attempt to define conceptually what it understands by the term. There is descriptive rhetoric but no conceptualisation. For example:

> Personalisation is the key to tackling the persistent achievement gaps between different social and ethnic groups. It means a tailored education for every child and young person, that gives them strength in the basics, stretches their aspirations, and builds their life chances.
>
> (DfES, 2005: para 4.1)

Personalisation is not new. Our best schools provide a tailored education which combines: extra small group or one to one tuition for those who need it not as a substitute for excellent whole class teaching, but as an integrated part of the child's learning opportunities for all children to get extra support and tuition in subjects they are interested in, as well as access to a range of opportunities beyond the school day, including weekend and holiday courses and online learning, exciting whole class teaching, which gets the best from every child, setting or grouping children of similar ability and attainment, a rich flexible and accessible curriculum and, for older pupils, one that allows them to mix academic and vocational learning, innovative use of ICT, both in the classroom and linking the classroom with the home.

(DfES, 2005: para 4.2)

Most important of all, it means excellent, tailored whole class teaching with all the resources available, from extra support staff to improved ICT being used to ensure that every pupil gets the education they need.

(DfES, 2005: para 4.6)

Central to personalised learning is schools' use of data to provide structured feedback to pupils and parents on their progress.

(DfES, 2005: para 4.50)

Of course, the target audience for a White Paper might be thought to be somewhat different from those of the Nuffield Review and the ESRC, but nevertheless the lack of clarity in conceptualising personalised learning, and the absence of any sense of ambiguity or tentativeness in the White Paper treatment, contrasts with the two academic reviews.

Four other points need making about the assumptions in the White Paper. First, in its perspective, if anyone is going to be involved in co-producing knowledge it is the teachers and the parents, not the learners themselves. Second, there is almost no reference to student voice, and choice appears to be limited to 'allowing' older students to mix academic and vocational learning. Third, there is a strong role asserted for personalisation in tackling the persistent achievement gaps between different social and ethnic groups, but the White Paper interprets this primarily in the limited sense of improving attainment in English and mathematics. It does not present the problem as having political, cultural and economic dimensions, as the Leadbeater analysis does. Perhaps most importantly, the White Paper separates out treatment of personalisation from other linked policy initiatives, such as increasing parental choice of school, thereby avoiding facing up to the contradictions inhering in educational policy making overall. As Harris and Ranson (2005) argue, 'customising' education for the individual student sits uneasily with the marketisation of education through parental choice. They might have added that it sits even more uneasily with a national curriculum and testing programme, dominated by age-relatedness.

Thus, despite the known interest in the DfES in the Leadbeater model, the White Paper runs the risk of transmitting an image of personalisation in only the shallow sense of making the existing services provided in schools and other educational settings more streamlined, more accessible and more efficient. There is very little sense of deep personalisation, in the form of students and teachers as co-producers of educational knowledge, at least in relation to formal schooling.

The review chaired by HMCI Gilbert (Gilbert, 2007) was more informed by the Leadbeater analysis, which it referred to explicitly. Her review looked forward to the nature of teaching and learning in 2020 and drew heavily on the language of personalisation. It characterised personalisation as transformational in schooling, and gave strong emphasis to some aspects in the other documents cited above, such as Assessment for Learning. Like the NCSL paper, it emphasised a whole-school approach, arguing that personalisation should be reflected in all school policies and plans. It treated the arguments for strengthening pupil voice significantly more substantively than the White Paper, and proposed that each pupil should have a learning guide to help in exercising personalised choice, conceptualising students as 'partners' in learning. In this way, it hinted at a deeper sense of personalisation than in other semi-official documents. However, the review, in an apparent attempt to be as comprehensive as possible, proposed a model of learning so broad-ranging as to be able to be interpreted as almost anything and everything in the school system. For example, it included monitoring developments in the National Curriculum, designing buildings and facilities for personalisation, altering secondary, but not primary, school pastoral arrangements, innovative use of ICT, reducing attainment gaps between different social and ethnic groups, parental participation, models of school leadership, workforce reform and a model for teacher development focused on in-school practice. Thus the radical, 'disruptive' character of Leadbeater's model, involving changed power relations over knowledge production, gets lost, possibly because the process of innovation by committee tends to include all the special interests of committee members.

PERSONALISATION IN THE EDUCATION OF GIFTED AND TALENTED STUDENTS: PEDAGOGY AS THE CO-PRODUCTION OF KNOWLEDGE

Where deep personalisation of education can be envisaged most easily is with older and more able students (and also in the adult education/lifelong learning sector). We could hypothesise that deep personalisation as a model would be most realisable in the universities and in schools/colleges providing education in the 16–19 age range, where student voice and student choice have high salience, given the range of providers in the education marketplace and the relatively high levels of ability and maturity in the students as consumers. It could be particularly applicable to those school students identified as gifted and talented, and it is worth examining how it might work for such students. If it cannot be realised for these students, it is difficult to see how it could be for younger, less mature or less able students. In this article, the focus is upon pedagogy, perhaps the most difficult component of personalised learning to envisage since, for obvious logistical reasons, 'tailoring' teaching cannot mean individualised instruction, generally, other than in one-to-one tutorials. You can have a bespoke suit, even today, but bespoke learning in classes of twenty or more students is difficult to realise, even were it thought desirable.

The teaching and learning sessions described below are from a leading edge sixth-form college (for 1700 16–19 year-olds) in a university city. The college is over-subscribed and attracts high-attaining students, including a proportion of students identified as gifted and talented. The teaching in all subjects was assessed as outstanding by inspectors in the most recent report on the college by the Office for Standards in Education. The descriptions are from field notes made during direct observation of the sessions. The interpretations of the purpose and practice of the pedagogy were discussed with the teachers concerned directly after the sessions, and they were in broad agreement with them.

The English surgery

The first session, taken by Martina, was a lunchtime 'surgery', which could be attended by students preparing for an advanced extension award in English. Twelve students, three boys and nine girls, were in the session, though, it being lunchtime, they were joined by two others some ten minutes after the start, and one girl left half way through. The session ran from 12.50–13.50, preceded by ten minutes of settling in, waiting for students to arrive and individual conversations.

12.50: Martina distributes a previous examination paper, drawing attention to a specific task item relating to a definition of formalism in literature offered in an excerpt from a literary critic. She writes the definition on the whiteboard and identifies three aspects to analyse the definition that she wants the students to use as a framework – Approach, Insights and BUTS (reservations).

12.55: Martina sets paired/triad tasks and then visits each small group, challenging individuals about their initial judgements, and they test out their responses on her. In five minutes she has worked with six individuals; in seven minutes she has worked with all of the students in the pairs/triads. The pace is fast and business-like, but unhurried; the teacher personality is quiet and unshowy.

13.03: She calls together the whole group to share ideas. Students readily offer ideas, she accepts what they say and turns it back to other students to comment on, then adds her ideas to it. The discourse is characterised by a gradual and collective accumulation of ideas, incorporating a readiness to challenge and be challenged. For example, one student argues that, 'formalism as defined, implies that literature is special or superior. But why, what's the justification? Why are other kinds of writing, say journalism or non-literary texts, inferior? And it would exclude non-standard language.' This generates high-level articulation of the problems associated with intrinsic and extrinsic judgements, and how authorial intention is to be understood. The exchange then explores the effect the social and historical context of a literary work has upon its interpretation, with one student instancing the way Shakespeare's vocabulary often meant something different in his time from now. 'What's more,' argued another student, 'formalism implies a kind of stasis – that we have established all the criteria for literary excellence, that our criteria are not changing.' Throughout this section of the session the students challenge each other's ideas, the teacher challenges them, and they challenge the teacher, and through this iterative process ideas are shared and constructively built upon. All students are unselfconsciously on task.

13.15: Martina sets a new task for pairs/triads. 'Can you come up with an example that would disprove his point? But we need specific examples.' The groups work together on this task, with Martina intervening to trigger clearer articulation of the examples, and the argument that the examples disprove the critic's point. All students are on task.

13.27: There is whole-class sharing of these ideas, again characterised by high-order questioning by the students of each other and by students contributing to the ideas of their peers. Again all students engage with the task.

13.35: Martina draws this session to a close by setting an extension task as an assignment to be completed in preparation for the next surgery, a week later. 'Here is a new piece of text, which you need to read independently first of all. The task is: How does this new text take today's argument on? Give three examples from your reading. This will be the focal point for our discussion next time.'

13.40–13.50: The session ends with guidance on completing the examination entry form.

The history lesson

The second teaching session was a modern history lesson, taken by Peter, the head of the history department. There were twenty-two 17-year-old students, roughly equal numbers of boys and girls, in a fairly conventional, though cramped, arrangement of a U-shaped line of students, against two sides and the back wall of the room, with areas of the U shape filled in with other students, so that all were facing the teacher and most could see and talk to each other without turning round. The lesson lasted from 11.35 to 12.40 and focused on an analysis of the Nazi State. The description below does not reflect the highly charismatic, often extremely entertaining, classroom persona of the teacher.

11.35: Peter explains the materials the students will be needing and the topic. He sets in outline the homework for next week, reminding them that they will be preparing for an examination-conditions test. He reminds them also that they have his email address and they can raise any issues or problems with him. He responds directly to two email queries he had had since the last lesson. Then he sets the first task. 'You've got three labels – they're in the materials, in the text. Polycratic, Feudal, Chaos. You have to produce the examples to support the case that the Nazi state was Polycratic or Feudal or Chaotic.'

11.40: Peter sets the task for pairs or triads, with different groups required to analyse the argument for justifying different labels. He tests individual understandings before they work in their groups. 'OK what have you got to say about Feudal?' One student problematises the label: 'Does it work at two levels – does it work for the state? Does it work for the people? You might get different answers for each of those levels.' Peter elaborates on the answer for the rest of the class, raising the possibility that the answers they arrive at may be too complex for a single label, but the purpose of the task was to press that questioning of the task itself – 'Test the label to destruction!' 'The same with Polycratic – What's it mean and can it be applied to help us understand the nature of the Nazi state.' One student explains what she understands by the label – different competing power groups – but has reservations about its appropriateness. 'I'm not sure that the state was Polycratic, because all the power groups were dependent on Hitler's support. So it's probably Autocratic we need, not Polycratic.' Peter says, 'So you've got reservations, very good, you'll need to test them out in your group. Now Feudal – let me remind you of your Year 7 work at your secondary school – Barons. You'll all know what Feudalism is, won't you?' Then he sets them to work in pairs. All students are on task.

12.00: Peter brings the class together to 'test out' the judgements the students have made, taking first the pairs who have worked on Feudal, then Chaos, then Polycratic. Student responses are tentatively expressed, but the reasons for their judgement are clearly articulated. For example, one student said, 'I don't know if I'm right but I'll try. Under feudalism the barons were the top group under the monarch, but I'm not sure that applies to Nazi Germany. The power distribution amongst the various groups wasn't as straightforward.' 'Yes,' says Peter, 'but does the concept of feudalism help explain the power distribution. You're only half way there, I think. What about Chaos?' 'I think Chaos is useful to explain the growth of anti-Semitism,' argues one student. Peter queries this: 'Is that Chaos in the sense we have used earlier, and in the text?' 'Well it would cause chaos! And it applies as well as the other two to explaining anti-Semitism,' answers the student. The pace of these and later interactive sections of the lesson is very fast, requiring students and teacher to think on their feet. In a period of ten minutes, Peter has involved nine individual students, representing all but one of the pairs.

12.10: Peter refers to the lecture given yesterday by a visiting Professor of Modern History, developing his theory of the 'dual state'. 'Can we work that into our explanations?'

12.15: Peter poses the question to the whole class: 'OK you've heard ideas on all three labels. Which works best and why?' One student proposes: 'I wouldn't settle for any one idea, I'd want to use all three because they offer different, like, perspectives on the same state.' Peter pushes the student to elaborate on her approach and then re-formulates it for the class as a whole.

12.20: Peter sets the individual students the task of writing down in note form the case for one, or some, or all the labels as explanations for the Nazi state. They all work on this task in silence until one student queries whether the 'Nazi state' is what they should be thinking about. Peter suggests that what he means is that it was such a unique state that they should be attempting to analyse the 'Hitler state', which might be a simpler way to analyse the system. He is challenged by a student who points out the reasons for using the Nazi state as developed in the text. She also argues that the discussion so far has ignored the role of the churches to which the text refers. 'Alright, hold all those points in play and I'll need a little time to think through this, while you complete the task. But I'll retain the right to disagree with the book, and for that matter with you,' Peter responds. The students settle back to the writing task, in silence.

12.30: Class still working in silence. Peter brings them together, reminding them of the nature of the lesson, that is, to analyse the Nazi state. 'We need two students to promote the case for a label as useful, and the rest of the class to listen and evaluate it – that is weigh up the strength of the case being made.' This is done for Chaos, with some students arguing that that label is the most useful, and others taking a more multi-layered model, drawing together arguments from the text, from their paired work, from the whole class discourse and from their note taking.

12.40: Lesson ends, and students leave still talking about the arguments.

INTERPRETATION

These sessions illustrated the pedagogy involved if teachers have as their primary aim the co-construction of classroom knowledge in understandings, skills and contestation of ideas; the teachers saw their role as helping students produce their ideas and improve them by building upon their initial ideas and subjecting them to the scrutiny of their peers and the teachers themselves. This collective learning in the classroom was extended by individual activity outside it, which would then be the basis for further collective learning in the next session.

The teachers identified four principal conditions for this kind of pedagogy. First, they themselves needed very high levels of subject expertise, since they were not engaged in individualising learning – letting individual students generate their own ideas, as might happen under some interpretations of 'progressivism' or 'student-centred' learning. Co-constructing knowledge can work only if the teacher has such a high level of subject expertise to bring to bear upon the students' ideas that s/he can respond authoritatively to their ideas and help take them further. Second, the teachers could assume, because of the college's ethos and value system, high levels of on-task behaviour and student self-motivation. Participation in, and commitment to, learning were givens in the college culture and illustrate the way whole-school values influenced pedagogy. Third, the value assumption that knowledge is tentative, contestable and revisable permeated the classroom pedagogy. This was not 'instruction', nor was it the 'whole-class interactive teaching' promoted under the national literacy and numeracy initiatives, since the knowledge, skills, understandings and values being collectively generated were constructed tentatively; the objectives for the sessions were not cognitive outcomes specified in advance, so much as pedagogical processes to be adhered to.

Finally, relationships were informal but courteous, but underlying the informality was a very clear structure to the sessions, with the pace, direction and transition from one activity to another primarily controlled by the teacher.

Three other points arose from these sessions. First, they did not rely on high levels of information technology, the dominant mode of learning being spoken discourse – language for learning, so to speak. Information technology played a strong role in personalising the out-of-class learning since the teachers and students used email to communicate about learning tasks set outside the class. Second, this pedagogy was being used in what was in effect a preparation for conventional, unseen external examinations, which is often used as a justification for a much more transmission mode of teaching.

Finally, it is sometimes implied that a particularly charismatic persona is needed to achieve good pace and challenge in classroom interaction. This was true in one case, where teacher charisma drove the classroom learning with liveliness and witty exchanges, but not in the other, where a quiet, authoritative and respected, but unshowy, teacher personality was outstandingly effective in creating and driving the learning. Power to teach (Robinson, 2004) does not always, or necessarily, require a drama queen in the classroom.

A final comment on these teaching sessions is fundamental to our understanding the pedagogy. The surface features (identifying the purposes, setting tasks in pairs, sharing views with the whole class, setting out-of-class tasks) are significant, but much less important than the underlying values and aims of the teacher – in this case to engage with students in the co-production of classroom learning. In other subjects or in other sessions in these subjects, the surface features might not be there; the key to understanding the pedagogy is to understand what the teachers were trying to achieve.

DISCUSSION

There are three principal points to raise about personalised pedagogy as illustrated above. First, personalisation is a collective activity, not an individualised one, but the collective frame leads to the individual developing her/his learning. The teacher, the student group and the individual student produce together the meanings and understandings that the individual achieves. In the terms of the ESRC analysis quoted earlier, it is social, not individualised, practice. It is also collective in another sense: the values and attitudes that teachers and students bring to learning are derived from, and embedded in, a collective organisational ethos.

Second, this pedagogy is not new. It is elsewhere called the transacted curriculum or constructivist learning. The characteristic of constructivist learning, which is derived from Vygotskian social theory, is that the teacher 'scaffolds' the learning of the student; provides the structured support to enable the learners to construct knowledge for themselves. It has been one of the standard approaches taught in teacher training courses, but has frequently been derided as too theoretical. It is interesting to see its survival, and possibly its celebration and legitimisation, under the personalisation agenda.

Third, the sessions illustrated are in the fields of history and English literature, where a heavy emphasis is placed on developing knowledge as judgements and justification rather than knowledge as objective truth. The extent to which this pedagogy is generalisable across different subjects is open to question and needs further research.

There are, finally, three problematic issues in considering how far this model of personalised learning is generalisable. They relate to age, ability and social background. It was argued earlier that the best case to illustrate personalised learning should be derived from investigating how it might work with the most able and mature students, and that, following Leadbeater's concern, social background might play a part, in the sense that high levels of cultural capital might be necessary, because personalisation favoured those groups whose values and orientation were aligned with middle-class socialisation. The students in the illustrations above were older, very able and largely from professional-class families.

We have to be speculative at this stage, but it is argued (e.g. Wells and Chang-Wells, 1992) that constructivist learning is effective with much younger students, and that it is particularly appropriate for learning in primary schools and preschool settings. So the age/maturity argument may not be valid. On the issue of ability, the pitch and cognitive demand are particularly relevant for very able students, but the question is whether the aim of co-producing knowledge in the classroom is appropriate for all ability levels. Following Bloom (1968), what seems a prerequisite for this kind of co-productive learning is high performance in evaluating, synthesising and other forms of higher-order thinking, so we could hypothesise that it might be difficult to implement this pedagogy in classes where such thinking is not habitual.

The social class issue is less clear cut. It has long been argued (Bernstein, 1971, 1973) that pedagogy, especially pedagogy dependent on spoken language, is skewed towards advantaging children from middle-class family socialisation, though this has been contested by cultural relativists (e.g. Labov, 1970). It will be particularly important to research this issue further, since some studies in the USA suggest that a different pedagogy for low socio-economic students, which emphasises rote learning and direct instruction, is needed in contrast to that which is effective with higher socio-economic students (see Campbell *et al.*, 2004 for a review of the field). However, Mortimore (1999) has argued that structure and direction in pedagogy need not imply a narrower curriculum.

Nevertheless, addressing the relationship between poverty and learning is not merely a matter of pedagogy; at the very least, a working hypothesis is that those most at risk from the implementation of deep personalisation in learning are students from those social groups least well equipped, in terms of their families' cultural, social and financial capital, to develop self-regulation in learning and access to, choice over, and voice in, learning opportunities beyond the formal schooling. Nothing in Leadbeater, the White Paper or the NCSL document seriously examines how to resolve this problem, which is admittedly not created by the concept of deep personalisation, but may well be exacerbated by it. One approach being developed in England is the GOAL project at the National Academy for Gifted and Talented Youth at Warwick University. This is an intervention programme offering a combination of funding and mentoring to provide access to wider schooling opportunities for disadvantaged gifted students. It resonates with the shallow aspects of the personalisation concept (making the system more efficient, more customer-friendly, more navigable), but its effectiveness at delivering deep personalisation is yet to be tested.

These macro-level concerns, however, are speculative and should be the focus of further research. What seems much more securely embedded in these teaching and learning sessions is the way in which, reflecting the view of Hopkins referred to earlier, the whole-school values and whole-school ethos feed into the classroom behaviour of students and teachers. In this particular college, these values had been collectively developed, including development through the student council, the teachers and the governing body. They concerned values about learning behaviour, respecting differences in views, taking account of student voice, and the importance of self-motivation for learning. This set of values was the underpinning infrastructure of the personalised pedagogy, and without their influence on the attitudes and behaviour of teachers and students in classrooms it is probable that the pedagogy would collapse.

Finally, we have demonstrated earlier the ambiguities in theorising personalisation in education. This lack of conceptual clarity, most obvious in the White Paper, is unfortunate, since the danger that personalisation will be implemented only in its shallower form in schooling is very real. It is easier to implement reforms that merely increase system efficiency, but much more difficult to implement the 'disruptive' innovation in role relationships between teacher and learner envisaged by deep personalisation in Leadbeater's terms. In the end, what Leadbeater is arguing for is a radical change in the control of educational knowledge production, and bringing about such change will be hampered where the basic concept is fuzzily transmitted by the Department for Education and Skills, a government department not renowned over the last twenty years for its enthusiasm for relinquishing its control over curriculum, pedagogy and assessment.

REFERENCES

Bernstein, B. (1971) *Class, codes and control, Volume 1. Theoretical studies towards a sociology of language*, London: Routledge & Kegan Paul.

Bernstein, B. (1973) *Class codes and control, Volume 3. Towards a theory of educational transmissions*, London: Routledge & Kegan Paul.

Bloom, B.S. (1968) *Learning for mastery*, Washington, DC: ERIC.

Campbell, J., Kyriakides, L., Muijs, D. and Robinson, W. (2004) *Assessing teacher effectiveness*, London and New York: RoutledgeFalmer.

DfES (2004) *A national conversation about personalised learning*, available online at www.standards.dfes.gov.uk/personalisedlearning.

DfES (2005) *White Paper: Higher standards, better schools for all*, London: Department for Education and Skills.

Gilbert, C. (2007) *2020 vision*, a report to the Secretary of State on behalf of the Teaching and Learning in 2020 Review Group, London: OFSTED.

Harris, A. and Ranson, S. (2005) 'The contradictions of educational policy: disadvantage and achievement', *British Educational Research Journal*, Vol. 31, No. 5: 571–587.

Hayward, G., Hodgson, A., Johnson, J., Oancea, A., Pring, R., Spours, K., Wilde, S. and Wright, S. (2005) *Annual Report of the Nuffield Review of 14–19 education and training*, Oxford: University of Oxford Department of Educational Studies.

Labov, W. (1970) 'The logic of non-standard English', in Williams, F. (ed.) *Language and poverty*, Chicago: Markham: 153–189.

Lawton, D. (1975) *Class, culture and the curriculum*, London: Routledge & Kegan Paul.

Leadbeater, C. (2003) *Personalisation through participation*, London: Demos.

Mortimore, P. (ed.) (1999) *Understanding pedagogy and its impact on learning*, London: Paul Chapman.

NCSL (National College for School Leadership) (2004) *Personalised learning*, Special LDR Supplement, Nottingham: NCSL.

Plowden Report (1967) *Children and their primary schools*, London: The Stationery Office.

Pollard, A. and James, M. (eds) (2004) *Personalised learning, a commentary by the teaching and learning research programme*, London: Economic and Social Research Council.

Robinson, W. (2004) *Power to teach*, London and New York: RoutledgeFalmer.

Wells, G. and Chang-Wells, Gen Ling (1992) *Constructing knowledge together: classrooms as centers of inquiry and literacy*, Portsmouth, NH: Heinemann.

NEUROSCIENCE AND EDUCATION

Usha Goswami

A NOTE FROM THE EDITORS

This reading considers the development of the field of neuroscience and then how this increased understanding might be used to explore educational questions.

This reading links with Unit 5.6 of the 5th edition of *Learning to teach in the secondary school*.

QUESTIONS TO CONSIDER

1   Why could an understanding of the processes by which the brain learns and remembers be useful to teachers? What level of understanding of cognitive neuroscience will be helpful to teachers?

2   Links between neuroscience and education are only just beginning to be developed; there are some studies in cognitive development which could lead to specifically educational questions. What are some of the questions that need to be asked to enable neuroscience to make a valuable contribution to more effective teaching and learning?

3   Neuroscience is a new discipline applied to education. In time, it is likely to sit alongside other foundational disciplines applied to education. How can this potentially help you as a teacher?

This reading was first published as: Goswami, U. (2004) 'Neuroscience and education', *British Journal of Educational Psychology*, Vol. 74. 1–14.

ABSTRACT

Neuroscience is a relatively new discipline encompassing neurology, psychology and biology. It has made great strides in the last 100 years, during which many aspects of the physiology, biochemistry, pharmacology and structure of the vertebrate brain have been understood. Understanding of some of the basic perceptual, cognitive, attentional, emotional and mnemonic functions is also making progress, particularly since the advent of the cognitive neurosciences, which focus specifically on understanding higher level processes of cognition via imaging technology. Neuroimaging has enabled scientists to study the human brain at work *in vivo*, deepening our understanding of the very complex processes underpinning speech and language, thinking and reasoning, reading and mathematics. It seems timely, therefore, to consider how we might implement our increased understanding of brain development and brain function to explore educational questions.

INTRODUCTION

The study of learning unites education and neuroscience. Neuroscience, as broadly defined, investigates the processes by which the brain learns and remembers, from the molecular and cellular levels right through to brain systems (e.g. the system of neural areas and pathways underpinning our ability to speak and comprehend language). This focus on learning and memory can be at a variety of levels. Understanding cell signalling and synaptic mechanisms (one brain cell connects to another via a synapse) is important for understanding learning, but so is examination of the functions of specific brain structures such as the hippocampus by natural lesion studies or by invasive methods. Brain cells (or neurons) transmit information via electrical signals, which pass from cell to cell via the synapses, triggering the release of neurotransmitters (chemical messengers). There are around 100 billion neurons in the brain, each with massive connections to other neurons. Understanding the ways in which neurotransmitters work is a major goal of neuroscience. Patterns of neural activity are thought to correspond to particular mental states or mental representations. Learning broadly comprises changes in connectivity, either via changes in potentiation at the synapse or via the strengthening or pruning of connections. Successful teaching thus directly affects brain function, by changing connectivity.

Clearly, educators do not study learning at the level of the cell. Successful learning is also dependent on the curriculum and the teacher, the context provided by the classroom and the family, and the context of the school and the wider community. All of these factors of course interact with the characteristics of individual brains. For example, children with high levels of the MAOA gene (monoamine oxidise A) who experience maltreatment and adverse family environments seem to be protected from developing antisocial behaviours (Caspi *et al.*, 2002), possibly via moderating effects on their neural response to stress. Diet also affects the brain. A child whose diet is poor will not be able to respond to excellent teaching in the same way as a child whose brain is well nourished. It is already possible to study the effects of various medications on cognitive function. Methylphenidate (Ritalin), a medication frequently prescribed for children with ADHD (Attention Deficit Hyperactivity Disorder), has been shown to improve stimulus recognition in medicated children (in terms of attention to auditory and visual stimuli as revealed by neuroimaging; see Seifert *et al.*, 2003). Neuroimaging techniques also offer the potential to study the effects of different diets, food additives and potential toxins on educational performance.

TEACHING

It is notable, however, that neuroscience does not as yet study teaching. Successful teaching is the natural counterpart of successful learning, and is described as a 'natural cognition' by Strauss (2003). Forms of teaching are found throughout the animal kingdom, usually related to ways of getting food. However, the performance of *intentional acts* to increase the knowledge of others (teaching with a 'theory of mind') does seem to be unique to humans, and is perhaps essential to what it means to be a human being (Strauss *et al.*, 2002). The identification and analysis of successful pedagogy are central to research in education, but are currently a foreign field to cognitive neuroscience. There are occasional studies of the neural changes accompanying certain types of highly focused educational programme (such as remedial programmes for teaching literacy to dyslexic children; see below), but wider questions involving the invisible mental processes and inferences made by successful teachers have not begun to be asked. Strauss suggests that questions such as whether there are specialized neural circuits for different aspects of teaching may soon be tractable to neuroimaging methods, and this is a thought-provoking idea. Teaching is a very specialized kind of social interaction, and some of its aspects (reading the minds of others, inferring their motivational and emotional states) are after all already investigated in cognitive neuroscience.

Used creatively, therefore, cognitive neuroscience methods have the potential to deliver important information relevant to the design and delivery of educational curricula as well as the quality of teaching itself. Cognitive neuroscience may also offer methods for the early identification of special needs, and enable assessment of the delivery of education for special needs. At the same time, however, it is worth noting that 'neuromyths' abound. Some popular beliefs about what brain science can actually deliver to education are quite unrealistic. Although current brain science technologies offer exciting opportunities to educationists, they complement rather than replace traditional methods of educational enquiry.

A QUICK PRIMER ON BRAIN DEVELOPMENT

Many critical aspects of brain development are complete prior to birth (see Johnson (1997) for an overview). The development of the neural tube begins during the first weeks of gestation, and 'proliferative zones' within the tube give birth to the cells that compose the brain. These cells migrate to the different regions where they will be employed in the mature brain prior to birth. By 7 months gestation, almost all of the neurons that will comprise the mature brain have been formed. Brain development following birth consists almost exclusively of the growth of axons, synapses and dendrites (fibre connections): this process is called synaptogenesis. For visual and auditory cortex, there is dramatic early synaptogenesis, with maximum density of around 150 per cent of adult levels between 4 and 12 months, followed by pruning. Synaptic density in the visual cortex returns to adult levels between 2 and 4 years. For other areas, such as prefrontal cortex (thought to underpin planning and reasoning), density increases more slowly and peaks after the first year. Reduction to adult levels of density is not seen until some time between 10 and 20 years. Brain metabolism (glucose uptake, an approximate index of synaptic functioning) is also above adult levels in the early years, with a peak of about 150 per cent somewhere around 4–5 years.

By the age of around 10 years, brain metabolism reduces to adult levels for most cortical regions. The general pattern of brain development is clear. There are bursts of synaptogenesis, peaks of density and then synapse rearrangement and stabilization with myelinization, occurring at different times and rates for different brain regions (i.e. different sensitive periods for the development of different types of knowledge). Brain volume quadruples between birth and adulthood, because of the proliferation of connections, not because of the production of new neurons. Nevertheless, the brain is highly plastic, and significant new connections frequently form in adulthood in response to new learning or to environmental insults (such as a stroke). Similarly, sensitive periods are not all-or-none. If visual input is lacking during early development, for example, the critical period is extended (Fagiolini and Hensch, 2000). Nevertheless, visual functions that develop late (e.g. depth perception) suffer more from early deprivation than functions that are relatively mature at birth (such as colour perception; Maurer *et al.*, 1989). Thus, more complex abilities may have a lower likelihood of recovery than elementary skills. One reason may be that axons have already stabilized on target cells for which they are not normally able to compete, thereby causing irreversible reorganization.

It is important to realize that there are large individual differences between brains. Even in genetically identical twins, there is striking variation in the size of different brain structures and in the number of neurons that different brains use to carry out identical functions. This individual variation is coupled with significant localization of function. A basic map of major brain subdivisions is shown in Figure 14.1. Although adult brains all show this basic structure, it is thought that, early in development, a number of possible developmental paths and end states are possible. The fact that development converges on the same basic brain structure across cultures and gene pools is probably to do with the constraints on development present in the environment. Most children are exposed to very similar constraints, despite slightly different rearing environments.

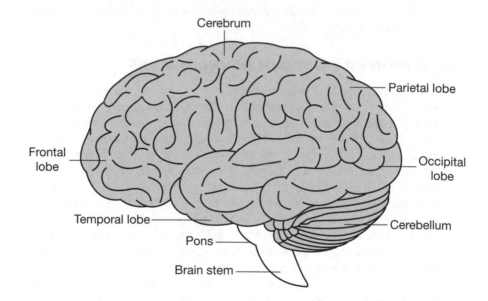

■ **Figure 14.1** The major subdivisions of the cerebral cortex. The different lobes are specialized for different tasks. The frontal lobe is used for planning and reasoning and controls our ability to use speech and how we react to situations emotionally. The temporal lobe is mainly concerned with memory, audition, language and object recognition. The parietal lobe controls our sense of touch and is used for spatial processing and perception. The occipital lobe is specialized for vision. Structures such as the hippocampus and the amygdala are internal to the brain, situated beneath the cerebral cortex in the midbrain.

Large differences in environment, such as being reared in darkness or without contact with other humans, are thankfully absent or rare. When large environmental differences occur, they have notable effects on cognitive function. For example, neuroimaging studies show that blind adults are faster at processing auditory information than sighted controls, and that congenitally deaf adults are faster at processing visual information in the peripheral field than hearing controls (e.g. Neville and Bavelier, 2000; Neville et al., 1983; Röder et al., 1999).

Nevertheless, neurons themselves are interchangeable in the immature system, and so dramatic differences in environment can lead to different developmental outcomes. For example, the area underpinning spoken language in hearing people (used for auditory analysis) is recruited for sign language in deaf people (visual/spatial analysis) (Neville et al., 1998). Visual brain areas are recruited for Braille reading (tactile analysis) in blind people (see Röder and Neville, 2003). It has even been reported that a blind adult who suffered a stroke specific to the visual areas of her brain consequently lost her proficient Braille-reading ability, despite the fact that her somatosensory perception abilities were unaffected (Jackson, 2000). It has also been suggested that all modalities are initially mutually linked, as, during early infancy, auditory stimulation also evokes large responses in visual areas of the brain, and somatosensory responses are enhanced by white noise (e.g. Neville, 1995). If this is the case, a kind of 'synaesthesia' could enable infants to extract schemas that are independent of particular modalities, schemas such as number, intensity and time (see Röder and Neville, 2003). If this mutual linkage extends into early childhood, it may explain why younger children respond so well to teaching via multi-sensory methods.

NEUROIMAGING TOOLS FOR DEVELOPMENTAL COGNITIVE NEUROSCIENCE

Neuroimaging studies are based on the assumption that any cognitive task makes specific demands on the brain which will be met by changes in neural activity. These changes in activity affect local blood flow, which can be measured either directly (PET) or indirectly (fMRI). Dynamic interactions among mental processes can be measured by ERPs.

PET (positron emission tomography) relies on the injection of radioactive tracers and is not suitable for use with children. Brain areas with higher levels of blood flow have larger amounts of the tracer, allowing pictures of the distribution of radiation to be created and thereby enabling the localization of different neural functions. fMRI (functional magnetic resonance imaging) also enables the localization of brain activity. This technique requires inserting the participant into a large magnet (like a big tube) and works by measuring the magnetic resonance signal generated by the protons of water molecules in neural cells. When blood flow to particular brain areas increases, the distribution of water in the brain tissue also changes. This enables measurement of a BOLD (blood oxygenation level dependent) response, which measures changes in the oxygenation state of haemoglobin associated with neural activity. The change in BOLD response is the outcome measure in most fMRI studies. It is very noisy inside the magnet, and participants are given headphones to shield their ears and a panic button (the magnet is claustrophobic). Because of these factors, it has been challenging to adapt fMRI for use with children (who also move a lot, impeding scanning accuracy). However, with the advent of specially adapted coils and less claustrophobic head scanners, such studies are growing in number.

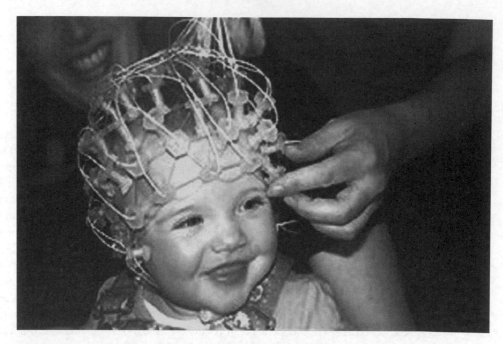

■ **Figure 14.2** A child wearing a specially adapted headcap for measuring ERPs (evoked response potentials). I am grateful to Professor Mark Johnson, Director of the Cognitive and Brain Development Centre, Birkbeck College, London, for this image.

A different and widely used neuroimaging technique that can be applied to children is that of the event related potential (ERP). ERPs enable the timing rather than localization of neural events to be studied. Sensitive electrodes are placed on the skin of the scalp, and then recordings of brain activity are taken. Recording of the spontaneous natural rhythms of the brain is called EEG (electroencephalography). ERP refers to systematic deflections in electrical activity that may occur to precede, accompany or follow experimenter-determined events. ERP rhythms are thus time-locked to specific events designed to study cognitive function. The usual technique is for the child to watch a video while wearing a headcap (like a swimming cap) that holds the electrodes (see Figure 14.2). For visual ERP studies, the video is delivering the stimuli; for auditory ERP studies, the linguistic stimuli form a background noise, and the child sits engrossed in a silent cartoon. The most usual outcome measures are (i) the latency of the potentials, (ii) the amplitude (magnitude) of the various positive and negative changes in neural response, and (iii) the distribution of the activity. The different potentials (characterized in countless ERP studies) are called N100, P200, N400 and so on, denoting negative peak at 100 ms, positive peak at 200 ms and so on. The amplitude and duration of single ERP components such as the P200 increase until age 3 to 4 years (in parallel with synaptic density), and then decrease until puberty. ERP latencies decrease within the first years of life (in parallel with myelinization) and reach adult levels in late childhood. ERP studies have provided extensive evidence on the time course of neural processing and are sensitive to millisecond differences. The sequence of observed potentials and their amplitude and duration are used to understand the underlying cognitive processes.

SELECTED STUDIES FROM COGNITIVE NEUROSCIENCE WITH INTERESTING IMPLICATIONS FOR EDUCATION

How valuable is cognitive neuroscience to educational psychologists? Current opinions vary (Bruer, 1997; Byrnes and Fox, 1998; Geake and Cooper, 2003; Geary, 1998, Mayer, 1998; Schunk, 1998; Stanovich, 1998), but in general the consensus is moving away from early views that neuroscience is irrelevant because it only confirms what we already knew. The eventual answer will probably be that it is very valuable indeed. The tools of cognitive neuroscience offer various possibilities to education, including the early diagnosis of special educational needs, the monitoring and comparison of the effects of different kinds of educational input on learning, and an increased understanding of individual differences in learning and the best ways to suit input to learner. I will now describe briefly some recent neuroscience studies in certain areas of cognitive development and give a flavour of how their methods could contribute to more specifically educational questions.

Language

Despite sharing 98.5 per cent of our genome with chimpanzees, we humans can talk, and chimps cannot. Interestingly, genes expressed in the developing brain may hold part of the answer. For example, a gene called FOXP2 differs in mouse and man by three amino acid differences, two of which occurred after separation from the common human–chimp ancestor about 200,000 years ago (Marcus and Fisher, 2003). This gene is implicated in a severe developmental disorder of speech and language that affects the control of face and mouth movements, impeding speech. Neurally, accurate vocal imitation appears to be critical for the development of speech (Fitch, 2000). Hence, when linguistic input is degraded or absent for various reasons (e.g. being hearing impaired, being orally impaired), speech and language are affected. Studies of normal adults show that grammatical processing relies more on frontal regions of the left hemisphere, whereas semantic processing and vocabulary learning activate posterior lateral regions of both hemispheres. For reasons that are not yet well understood, the brain systems important for syntactic and grammatical processing are more vulnerable to altered language input than the brain systems responsible for semantic and lexical functions. ERP studies show that, when English is acquired late due to auditory deprivation or late immigration to an English-speaking country, syntactic abilities do not develop at the same rate or to the same extent (Neville *et al.*, 1997). Late learners do not rely on left hemisphere systems for grammatical processing, but use both hemispheres (Weber-Fox and Neville, 1996). ERP studies also show that congenitally blind people show bilateral representation of language functions (Roder *et al.*, 2000). Blind people also process speech more efficiently (Hollins, 1989); for example, they speed up cassette tapes, finding them too slow, and still comprehend the speech, even though the recording quality suffers.

Reading

Neuroimaging studies of both children and adults suggest that the major systems for reading alphabetic scripts are lateralized to the left hemisphere. These studies typically measure brain responses to single-word reading using fMRI or ERPs. Reviews of such studies conclude that alphabetic/orthographic processing seems mainly associated with occipital, temporal and parietal areas (e.g. Pugh *et al.*, 2001). The occipital–temporal areas are most active when processing visual features, letter shapes and orthography. The inferior occipital–temporal area shows electrophysiological dissociations between words and non-words at around 180 ms, suggesting that these representations are not purely visual but are linguistically structured. Activation in temporo-occipital areas increases with reading skill (e.g. Shaywitz *et al.*, 2002) and is decreased in children with developmental dyslexia.

Phonological awareness (the ability to recognize and manipulate component sounds in words) predicts reading acquisition across languages, and phonological processing appears to be focused on the temporo-parietal junction. This may be the main site supporting letter-to-sound recoding and is also implicated in spelling disorders. Dyslexic children, who typically have phonological deficits, show reduced activation in the temporo-parietal junction during tasks such as deciding whether different letters rhyme (e.g. P, T = yes; P, K = no). Targeted reading remediation increases activation in this area (e.g. Simos *et al.*, 2002). Finally, recordings of event-related magnetic fields (MEG) in dyslexic children suggest that there is atypical organization of the right hemisphere (Heim *et al.*, 2003). This is consistent with suggestions that compensation strategies adopted by the dyslexic brain require greater right hemisphere involvement in reading.

Although to date neuroimaging studies have largely confirmed what was already known about reading and its development from behavioural studies, neuroscience techniques also offer a way of distinguishing between different cognitive theories (e.g. whether dyslexia has a visual basis or a linguistic basis in children). Neuroimaging techniques also offer a potential means for distinguishing between deviance and delay when studying developmental disorders. For example, our preliminary studies of basic auditory processing in dyslexic children using ERPs suggest that the phonological system of the dyslexic child is immature rather than deviant (Thomson, *et al.*, in preparation). Dyslexic children show remarkable similarity in N1 response to younger reading level controls, while showing much larger N1 amplitudes than age-matched controls. Finally, PET studies have shown that the functional organization of the brain differs in literate and illiterate adults (Castro-Caldas *et al.*, 1998). Portuguese women in their sixties who had never learned to read because of lack of access to education were compared with literate Portuguese women from the same villages in word and nonword repetition tasks. It was found that totally different brain areas were activated during nonword repetition for the illiterate versus literate participants. Learning to read and write in childhood thus changes the functional organization of the adult brain.

Mathematics

For mathematics, cognitive neuroscience is beginning to go beyond existing cognitive models. It has been argued that there is more than one neural system for the representation of numbers. A phylogenetically old 'number sense' system, found in animals and infants as well as older participants, seems to underpin knowledge about numbers and their relations (Dehaene *et al.*, 1998). This system, located bilaterally in the intraparietal areas, is activated when participants perform tasks such as number comparison, whether the comparisons involve Arabic numerals, sets of dots or number words. Because mode of presentation does not affect the location of the parietal ERP components, this system is thought to organize knowledge about number quantities. Developmental ERP studies have shown that young children use exactly the same parietal areas to perform number comparison tasks (Temple and Posner, 1998). A different type of numerical knowledge is thought to be stored verbally, in the language system (Dehaene *et al.*, 1999). This neural system also stores knowledge about poetry and overlearned verbal sequences, such as the months of the year. Mathematically, it underpins counting and rote-acquired knowledge such as the multiplication tables. This linguistic system seems to store 'number facts' rather than compute calculations. Many simple arithmetical problems (e.g. $3 + 4$, 3×4) are so overlearned that they may be stored as declarative knowledge. More complex calculation seems to involve visuospatial regions (Zago *et al.*, 2001), possibly attesting to the importance of visual mental imagery in multi-digit operations (an internalized and sophisticated form of a number line; see Pesenti *et al.*, 2000). Finally, a distinct parietal–premotor area is activated during finger counting and also calculation.

This last observation may suggest that the neural areas activated during finger counting (a developmental strategy for the acquisition of calculation skills) eventually come to partially underpin numerical manipulation skills in adults. If this were the case, then perhaps finger counting has important consequences for the developing brain and should be encouraged in school. In any event, neuroimaging techniques offer ways of exploring such questions. They can also be used to discover the basis of dyscalculia in children. For example, dyslexic children often seem to have associated mathematical difficulties. If dyslexia has a phonological basis, then it seems likely that the mathematical system affected in these children should be the verbal system underpinning counting and calculation. Dyslexic children with mathematical difficulties may show neural anomalies in the activation of this system, but not in the activation of the parietal and premotor number systems. Children with dyscalculia who do not have reading difficulties may show different patterns of impairment. Knowledge of the neural basis of their difficulties could then inform individual remedial curricula.

Direct effects of experience

Although it is frequently assumed that specific experiences have an effect on children, neuroimaging offers ways of investigating this assumption directly. The obvious prediction is that specific experiences will have specific effects, increasing neural representations in areas directly relevant to the skills involved. One area of specific experience that is frequent in childhood is musical experience. fMRI studies have shown that skilled pianists (adults) have enlarged cortical representations in auditory cortex, specific to piano tones. Enlargement was correlated with the age at which musicians began to practise, but did not differ between musicians with absolute versus relative pitch (Pantev *et al.*, 1998). Similarly, MEG studies show that skilled violinists have enlarged neural representations for their left fingers, those most important for playing the violin (Elbert *et al.*, 1996). Clearly, different sensory systems are affected by musical expertise, depending on the nature of the musical instrument concerned. ERP studies have also shown use-dependent functional reorganization in readers of Braille. Skilled Braille readers are more sensitive to tactile information than controls, and this extends across all fingers, not just the index finger (Röder *et al.*, 1996). The neural representations of muscles engaged in Braille reading are also enlarged. Finally, it is interesting to note that London taxi drivers who possess 'The Knowledge' show enlarged hippocampus formations (Maguire *et al.*, 2000). The hippocampus is a small brain area thought to be involved in spatial representation and navigation. In London taxi drivers, the posterior hippocampi were significantly larger than those of controls who did not drive taxis. Furthermore, hippocampal volume was correlated with the amount of time spent as a taxi driver. Again, localized plasticity is found in the adult brain in response to specific environmental inputs.

Plasticity in children, of course, is likely to be even greater. Our growing under-standing of plasticity offers a way of studying the impact of specialized remedial pro-grammes on brain function. For example, on the basis of the cerebellar theory of dyslexia, remedial programmes are available that are designed to improve motor function. It is claimed that these programmes will also improve reading. Whether this is in fact the case can be measured directly via neuroimaging. If the effects of such remedial programmes are specific, then neuroimaging should reveal changes in motor representations but not in phonological and orthographic processing. If the effects generalize to literacy (for example, via improved automaticity), then changes in occipital, temporal and parietal areas should also be observed.

Sleep and cognition

The idea that sleep might serve a cognitive function dates from at least the time of Freud, with his analysis of dreams. Recent neuroimaging studies suggest indeed that Rapid Eye Movement (REM) sleep is not only associated with self-reports of dreaming but is important for learning and memory. Maquet and colleagues (Maquet *et al.*, 2000) used PET to study regional brain activity during REM sleep, following training on a serial reaction time task. During task learning, volunteer students were trained to press one of six marked keys on a computer in response to associated visual signals on the computer screen. Training lasted for 4 hours, from 4.00 p.m. until 8.00 p.m. The participants were then scanned during sleep. Controls were either scanned when awake while receiving the training, or were scanned when asleep following no training. It was found that the brain areas most active in the trained awake group when performing the task were also most active during REM sleep in the trained participants. They were not active during sleep in the untrained participants. Hence, certain regions of the brain (in occipital and premotor cortex) were actually *reactivated* during sleep. It seems that REM sleep either allows the consolidation of memories or the forgetting of unnecessary material (or both together). When tested again on the computer task on the following day, significant improvement in performance was found to have occurred. Although the cellular mechanisms underlying this are not understood, it seems likely that memory consolidation relies on augmented synaptic transmission and eventually on increased synaptic density – the same mechanisms that structure the developing brain. Again, this suggests substantial plasticity even in adulthood, supporting educational emphases on lifelong learning.

Emotion and cognition

It is increasingly recognized that efficient learning does not take place when the learner is experiencing fear or stress. Stress can both help and harm the body. Stress responses can provide the extra strength and attention needed to cope with a sudden emergency, but inappropriate stress has a significant effect on both physiological and cognitive func-tioning. The main emotional system within the brain is the limbic system, a set of structures incorporating the amygdala and hippocampus. The 'emotional brain' (LeDoux, 1996) has strong connections with frontal cortex (the major site for reasoning and problem solving). When a learner is stressed or fearful, connections with frontal cortex become impaired, with a negative impact on learning. Stress and fear also affect social judgements, and responses to reward and risk. One important function of the emotional brain is assessing the value of information being received. When the amygdala is strongly activated, it interrupts action and thought and triggers rapid bodily responses critical for survival. It is suggested by LeDoux that classroom fear or stress might reduce children's ability to pay attention to the learning task because of this automatic interruption mechanism. To date, however, neuroimaging studies of the developmental effects of stress on cognitive function are sparse or non-existent. In the educational arena, studying the role of stress (and emotional affect generally) in classroom learning seems an area ripe for development. Simple ERP measures of attentional processes, such as those used by Seifert *et al.* (2003) to study children with ADHD receiving Ritalin, could easily be adapted for such purposes.

NEUROMYTHS

The engaging term 'neuromyths', coined by the OECD report on understanding the brain (OECD, 2002), suggests the ease and rapidity with which scientific findings can be translated into misinformation regarding what neuroscience can offer education. The three myths given most attention in the OECD report are (1) the lay belief in hemispheric differences ('left brain' versus 'right brain' learning etc.); (2) the notion that the brain is only plastic for certain kinds of information during certain 'critical periods', and that therefore education in these areas must occur during the critical periods; and (3) the idea that the most effective educational interventions need to be timed with periods of synaptogenesis.

Regarding neuromyth 1, the left brain/right brain claims probably have their basis in the fact that there is some hemispheric specialization in terms of the localization of different skills. For example, many aspects of language processing are left-lateralized (although not, as we have seen, in blind people or in those who emigrate in later childhood to a new linguistic community). Some aspects of face recognition, in contrast, are lateralized to the right hemisphere. Nevertheless, there are massive crosshemisphere connections in the normal brain, and both hemispheres work together in every cognitive task so far explored with neuroimaging, including language and face recognition tasks.

Regarding neuromyth 2, optimal periods for certain types of learning clearly exist in development, but they are sensitive periods rather than critical ones. The term 'critical period' implies that the opportunity to learn is lost forever if the biological window is missed. In fact, there seem to be almost no cognitive capacities that can be 'lost' at an early age. As discussed earlier, some aspects of complex processing suffer more than others from deprivation of early environmental input (e.g. depth perception in vision, grammar learning in language), but nevertheless learning is still possible. It is probably better for the final performance levels achieved to educate children in, for example, other languages during the sensitive period for language acquisition. Nevertheless, the existence of a sensitive period does not mean that adults are unable to acquire competent foreign language skills later in life.

Neuromyth 3 concerning synaptogenesis may have arisen from influential work on learning in rats. This research showed that rodent brains form more connections in enriched and stimulating environments (e.g. Greenough *et al.*, 1987). As discussed earlier, any kind of specific environmental stimulation causes the brain to form new connections (recall the enlarged cortical representations of professional musicians and the enlarged hippocampi of London taxi drivers). These demonstrations do not mean that greater synaptic density *predicts* a greater capacity to learn, however.

Other neuromyths can also be identified. One is the idea that a person can either have a 'male brain' or a 'female brain'. The terms 'male brain' and 'female brain' were coined to refer to differences in *cognitive* style rather than biological differences (Baron-Cohen, 2003). Baron-Cohen argued that men were better 'systemizers' (good at understanding mechanical systems) and women were better 'empathisers' (good at communication and understanding others). He did not argue that male and female brains were radically different, but used the terms male and female brain as a psychological shorthand for (overlapping) cognitive profiles.

Another neuromyth is the idea that 'implicit' learning could open new avenues educationally. Much human learning is 'implicit', in the sense that learning takes place in the brain despite lack of attention to/conscious awareness of what is being learned (e.g. Berns *et al.*, 1997; but see Johnstone and Shanks, 2001). Almost all studies of implicit learning use *perceptual* tasks as their behavioural measures (e.g. the participant gets better at responding appropriately to 'random' letter strings in a computer task when the 'random' strings are actually generated according to an underlying 'grammar' or rule system which can be learned). There are no studies showing implicit learning of the *cognitive* skills underpinning educational achievement. These skills most likely require effortful learning and direct teaching.

CONCLUSIONS

Clearly, the potential for neuroscience to make contributions to educational research is great. Nevertheless, bridges need to be built between neuroscience and basic research in education. Bruer (1997) suggested that cognitive psychologists are admirably placed to erect these bridges, although he also cautioned that, while neuroscience has learned a lot about neurons and synapses, it has not learned nearly enough to guide educational practice in any meaningful way. This view is perhaps too pessimistic. Cognitive developmental neuroscience has established a number of neural 'markers' that can be used to assess development, for example of the language system. These markers may be useful for investigating educational questions. Taking ERP signatures of language processing as a case in point, different parameters are robustly associated with semantic processing (e.g. N400), phonetic processing (e.g. mismatch negativity (MMN)) and syntactic processing (e.g. P600). These parameters need to be investigated longitudinally in children. Certain patterns may turn out to be indicative of certain developmental disorders. For example, children at risk for dyslexia may show immature or atypical MMNs to phonetic distinctions (Csepe, 2003). Children with SLI (specific language impairment) may have generally immature auditory systems, systems resembling those of children three or four years younger than them (Bishop and McArthur, in preparation). Characteristic ERPs may also change in response to targeted educational programmes. For example, the MMN to phonetic distinctions may become sharper (as indexed by faster latencies) in response to literacy tuition in phonics (see Csepe, 2003). If this were to be established across languages, education would have a neural tool for comparing the efficiency of different approaches to the teaching of initial reading. For example, one could measure whether the MMN to phonetic distinctions sharpened in response to literacy tuition based on whole language methods. This is only one example of the creative application of currently available neuroscience techniques to important issues in education. Educational and cognitive psychologists need to take the initiative and think 'outside the box' about how current neuroscience techniques can help to answer outstanding educational questions.

REFERENCES

Baron-Cohen, S. (2003) *The essential difference: men, women and the extreme male brain*, London: Penguin/Allen Lane.

Berns, G.S., Cohen, J.D. and Mintun, M.A. (1997) 'Brain regions responsive to novelty in the absence of awareness', *Science*, Vol. 276: 1272–1275.

Bishop, D.V.M. and McArthur, G. (in preparation) *Using event-related potentials to study auditory processing in children with language and literacy impairments*.

Bruer, J.T. (1997) 'Education and the brain: a bridge too far', *Educational Researcher*, Vol. 26, No. 8: 4–16.

Byrnes, J.P. and Fox, N.A. (1998) 'The education relevance of research in cognitive neuroscience', *Educational Psychology Review*, Vol. 10, No. 3: 297–342.

Caspi, A., McClay, J., Moffitt, T.E., Mill, J., Martin, J., Craig, I.W., Taylor, A. and Poulton, R. (2002) 'Role of genotype in the cycle of violence in maltreated children', *Science*, Vol. 297: 851–854.

Castro-Caldas, A., Petersson, K.M., Reis, A., Stone-Elander, S. and Ingvar, M. (1998) 'The illiterate brain. Learning to read and write during childhood influences the functional organization of the adult brain', *Brain*, Vol. 121: 1053–1063.

Csepe, V. (2003) 'Auditory event-related potentials in studying developmental dyslexia', in Csepe, V. (ed.) *Dyslexia: different brain, different behaviour*, New York: Kluwer: 81–112.

Dehaene, S., Dehaene-Lambertz, G. and Cohen, L. (1998) 'Abstract representations of numbers in the animal and human brain', *Trends in Neuroscience*, Vol. 21, No. 8: 355–611.

Dehaene, S., Spelke, E., Pinel, P., Stanescu, R. and Tsirkin, S. (1999) 'Sources of mathematical thinking: behavioural and brain-imaging evidence', *Science*, Vol. 284: 970–974.

Elbert, T., Pantev, C., Wienbruch, C., Rockstroh, B. and Taub, E. (1996) 'Increased cortical representation of the fingers of the left hand in string players', *Science*, Vol. 270: 305–307.

Fagiolini, M. and Hensch, R.K. (2000) 'Inhibitory threshold for critical-period activation in primary visual cortex ', *Nature*, Vol. 404: 183–186.

Fitch,W.T. (2000) 'The evolution of speech: a comparative review', *Trends in Cognitive Sciences*, Vol. 4, No. 7: 258–267.

Geake, J. and Cooper, P. (2003) 'Cognitive neuroscience: implications for education?', *Westminster Studies in Education*, Vol. 26, No. 1: 7–20.

Geary, D.C. (1998) 'What is the function of mind and brain?', *Educational Psychology Review*, Vol. 10, No. 4: 377–387.

Greenough, W.T., Black, J.E. and Wallace, C.S. (1987) 'Experience and brain development', *Child Development*, Vol. 58: 539–559.

Heim, S., Eulitz, C. and Elbert, T. (2003) 'Altered hemispheric asymmetry of auditory P100m in dyslexia', *European Journal of Neuroscience*, Vol. 17: 1715–1722.

Hollins, M. (1989) *Understanding blindness*, Hillsdale, NJ: Lawrence Erlbaum.

Jackson, S. (2000) 'Seeing what you feel', *Trends in Cognitive Sciences*, Vol. 4: 257.

Johnson, M.H. (1997) *Developmental cognitive neuroscience*, Cambridge, MA: Blackwell.

Johnstone, T. and Shanks, D.R. (2001) 'Abstractionist and processing accounts of implicit learning', *Cognitive Psychology*, Vol. 42: 61–112.

LeDoux, J. (1996) *The emotional brain*, New York: Simon Schuster.

Maguire, E.A., Gadian, D.S., Johnsrude, I.S., Good, C.D., Ashburner, J., Frackowiak, R.S. and Frith, C.D. (2000) 'Navigation related structural change in the hippocampi of taxi drivers', *Proceedings of the National Academy of Sciences of the United States of America*, Vol. 97, No. 8: 4398–4403.

Maquet, P., Laureys, S., Peigneux, P., Fuchs, S., Petiau, C., Phillips, C., Aerts, J., Del Fiore, G., Degueldre, C., Meulemans, T., Luxen, A., Franck, G., Van Der Linden, M., Smith, C. and Cleeremans, A. (2000) 'Experience-dependent changes in cerebral activation during human REM sleep', *Nature Neuroscience*, Vol. 3, No. 8: 831–836.

Marcus, G.F. and Fisher, S.E. (2003) 'FOXP2 in focus: what can genes tell us about speech and language?', *Trends in Cognitive Sciences*, Vol. 7, No. 6: 257–262.

Maurer, D., Lewis, T.L. and Brent, H. (1989) 'The effects of deprivation on human visual development: studies in children treated with cataracts', in Morrison, F.J., Lord, C. and Keating, D.P. (eds) *Applied developmental psychology*, San Diego, CA: Academic Press: 139–227.

Mayer, R.E. (1998) 'Does the brain have a place in educational psychology?', *Educational Psychology Review*, Vol. 10, No. 4: 389–396.

Neville, H.J. (1995) 'Developmental specificity in neurocognitive development in humans', in Gazzaniga, M.S. (ed.) *The cognitive neurosciences*, Cambridge, MA: MIT Press: 219–231.

Neville, H.J. and Bavelier, D. (2000) 'Specificity and plasticity in neurocognitive development in humans', in Gazzaniga, M.S. (ed.) *The cognitive neurosciences*, Cambridge, MA: MIT Press: 83–98.

Neville, H.J., Schmidt, A. and Kutas, M. (1983) 'Altered visual-evoked potentials in congenitally deaf adults', *Brain Research*, Vol. 266: 127–132.

Neville, H.J., Coffey, S.A., Lawson, D.S., Fischer, A., Emmorey, K. and Bellugi, U. (1997) 'Neural systems mediating American Sign Language: effects of sensory experience and age of acquisition', *Brain & Language*, Vol. 57: 285–308.

Neville, H.J., Bavelier, D., Corina, D., Rauschecker, J., Karni, A., Lalwani, A., Braun, A., Clark, V., Jezzard, P. and Turner, R. (1998) 'Cerebral organisation for language in deaf and hearing subjects: biological constraints and effects of experience', *Proceedings of the National Academy of Sciences of the United States of America*, Vol. 95, Feb.: 922–929.

OECD (2002) *Understanding the brain: towards a new learning science*, available online at oecd.org.

Pantev, C., Oostenveld, R., Engelien, A., Ross, B., Roberts, L.E. and Hike, M. (1998) 'Increased auditory cortical representation in musicians', *Nature*, Vol. 393: 811–814.

Pesenti, M., Thioux, M., Seron, X. and De Volder, A. (2000) 'Neuroanatomical substrates of Arabic number processing, numerical comparison, and simple addition: a PET study', *Journal of Cognitive Neuroscience*, Vol. 12, No. 3: 461–479.

Pugh, K.R., Mencl, W.E., Jenner, A.R., Katz, L., Frost, S.J., Lee, J.R., Shaywitz, S.E. and Shaywitz, B.A. (2001) 'Neurobiological studies of reading and reading disability', *Journal of Communication Disorders*, Vol. 34: 479–492.

Röder, B. and Neville, H. (2003) 'Developmental functional plasticity', in Grafman, J. and Robertson, I.H. (eds) *Handbook of neuropsychology* (2nd edition, Vol. 9), Oxford: Elsevier Science: 231–270.

Röder, G., Rösler, F. and Neville, H.J. (1999) 'Effects of interstimulus interval on auditory eventrelated potentials in congenitally blind and normally sighted humans', *Neuroscience Letters*, Vol. 264: 53–56.

Röder, G., Rösler, F. and Neville, H.J. (2000) 'Event-related potentials during language processing in congenitally blind and sighted people', *Neuropsychologia*, Vol. 38: 1482–1502.

Röder, G., Rösler, F., Hennighausen, E. and Nacker, F. (1996) 'Event related potentials during auditory and somatosensory discrimination in sighted and blind human subjects', *Cognitive Brain Research*, Vol. 4: 77–93.

Schunk, D.H. (1998) 'An educational psychologist's perspective on cognitive neuroscience', *Educational Psychology Review*, Vol. 10, No. 4: 411–417.

Seifert, J., Scheuerpflug, P., Zillessen, K.E., Fallgater, A. and Warnke, A. (2003) 'Electrophysiological investigation of the effectiveness of methylphenidate in children with and without ADHD', *Journal of Neural Transmission*, Vol. 110, No. 7: 821–829.

Shaywitz, B., Shaywitz, S., Pugh, K., Mencl, W., Fulbright, R., Skudlarski, P., Constable, T., Marchione, K., Fletcher, J., Lyon, G. and Gore, J. (2002) 'Disruption of posterior brain systems for reading in children with developmental dyslexia', *Biological Psychiatry*, Vol. 52, No. 2: 101–110.

Simos, P.G., Fletcher, J.M., Bergman, E., Breier, J.I., Foorman, B.R., Castillo, E.M., Davis, R.N., Fitzgerald, M. and Papanicolaou, A.C. (2002) 'Dyslexia-specific brain activation profile becomes normal following successful remedial training', *Neurology*, Vol. 58: 1203–1213.

Stanovich, K.E. (1998) 'Cognitive neuroscience and educational psychology: what season is it?', *Educational Psychology Review*, Vol. 10, No. 4: 419–426.

Strauss, S. (2003) 'Teaching as a natural cognition and its implications for teacher education', in Pillemer, D. and White, S. (eds) *Developmental psychology and the social changes of our time*, New York: Cambridge University Press.

Strauss, S., Ziv, M. and Stein, A. (2002) 'Teaching as a natural cognition and its relations to preschoolers' developing theory of mind', *Cognitive Development*, Vol. 17: 1473–1787.

Temple, E. and Posner, M.I. (1998) 'Brain mechanisms of quantity are similar in 5-year-old children and adults', *Proceedings of the National Academy of Sciences of the United States of America*, Vol. 95, June: 7836–7841.

Thomson, J., Baldeweg, T. and Goswami, U. (in preparation) *Auditory event-related potential during rise time processing in dyslexic and typically-developing children*.

Weber-Fox, C.M. and Neville, H.J. (1996) 'Maturational constraints on functional specialisation for language processing: ERP and behavioural evidence in bilingual speakers', *Journal of Cognitive Neuroscience*, Vol. 8: 231–256.

Zago, L., Pesenti, M., Mellet, E., Crivello, F., Mazoyer, B. and Tzourio-Mazoyer, N. (2001) 'Neural correlates of simple and complex mental calculation', *NeuroImage*, Vol. 13: 314–327.

ASSESSMENT

INTRODUCTION

In England, since the 1988 Education Reform Act, national testing has taken central stage in monitoring standards in schools. Recently there is growing concern that the amount of assessment has gone beyond acceptable limits, and this section raises also questions about the purposes of assessment.

Assessment is used to provide information about individual pupils' progress, help devise appropriate teaching and learning strategies and give parents helpful information about their child's progress, and to compare pupils in schools and schools across the country. At the same time, the importance of formative assessment in supporting learning and raising achievement has taken the lead in linking assessment with learning rather than just with ranking and certificating pupils. Chapter 6 in *Learning to teach in the secondary school* (Capel, Leask and Turner, 2009) provides an overview of the principles of assessment, of formative and summative assessment, diagnostic testing and ideas of validity and reliability. The difference between norm-referenced testing and criterion-referenced testing is introduced, and the nationally set tests discussed in the light of these principles. Another aspect of that chapter focuses on preparing pupils for public examinations and considers assessment as exemplified by the English National Curriculum Tasks (formerly SATs), GCSE and GCE Advanced Level, raising at the same time issues of teacher accountability. The balance between vocational education and academic education is raised, and contrasts are drawn between the assessment methods used for vocational courses and academic courses. There are three readings in this section.

READINGS IN THIS SECTION ARE:

Reading 15
Testing, Motivation and Learning
Assessment Reform Group, supported by The Nuffield Foundation (based on an extensive review by Wynne Harlen and Ruth Deakin-Crick)

The first study is an example of the work of the Assessment Reform Group (ARG, 2002), which is a body of educationalists interested in, and influential on, the role of assessment in promoting learning in schools, i.e. formative assessment. This reading contains a review of assessment practice and its effects on motivation.

The short reading pulls together research that shows the negative effect of over-testing, particularly on lower-achieving pupils. One consequence of this regime of testing is to increase the gap between high-performing pupils and lower-performing ones. Another feature of the research emphasises that too much testing leads to a concentration on grades rather than learning; that is, testing does not improve learning unless the results of testing are fed back into the teaching and learning cycle. The reading has recommendations for classroom practice and ways forward out of the situations identified and contains many useful references. Readers interested in formative assessment are recommended to access the ARG website: www.assessment-reform-group.org/.

Reading 16

'Troublesome boys' and 'compliant girls': gender identity and perceptions of achievement and underachievement
Susan Jones and Debra Myhill

The second study in this section explores the influence of teachers' beliefs about gender and achievement on the way pupils are supported in their learning; that is, the influence of stereotyping on the way teachers respond to pupil achievement (Jones and Myhill, 2004). The study used four groups of pupils, high-achieving boys and girls and underachieving boys and girls, to explore how teachers' perceptions of gender identity appear to influence achievement levels. Beliefs about gender identity informed the teachers' perceptions in relation to each of the four focus groups, whereby the underachieving boy and the high-achieving girl were seen to conform to gender expectations; the high-achieving boys were seen to challenge gender norms; and the underachieving girl emerges as largely overlooked. The perceived characteristics of the high-achieving girl are presented as describing all girls. There appears to be a tendency to associate boys with underachievement and girls with high achievement. See also Connolly, Reading 8, Section 4.

Reading 17

It's not which school but which set you're in that matters: the influence of ability grouping practices on student progress in mathematics
Dylan Wiliam and Hannah Bartholomew

The final reading in this section focuses on the significance of setting for the GCSE grades in mathematics achieved by pupils in England, comparing those who start from similar achievement levels at Key Stage 3 of the National Curriculum (Wiliam and Bartholomew, 2004). The study took in six schools with favourable Ofsted reports, covering over 950 pupils.

The findings showed that, for pupils with similar KS3 achievements, progress between KS3 and GCSE depended on the set in which the pupils were placed. The study therefore raised issues about how pupils were placed in sets, academic achievement being just one factor in that decision-making process. The study compared the performances of pupils in schools favouring whole-class teaching with those in schools that adopt small-group and individualized teaching. The teaching strategies of teachers of the lower sets are compared with those of teachers responsible for upper sets, and the effects on pupil motivation and learning are described. The case for setting by ability is challenged.

FURTHER READING

Broadfoot, P. and Black, P. (2004) 'The first ten years of "Assessment in Education"', in *Assessment in education: principles, policy and practice*, Vol. 11, No. 1: 7–26.

This paper discusses assessment practice over the last ten years and the changes that have occurred, particularly the shift from assessment for ranking or certification to assessment for learning, and emphasises the increasing importance of assessment in shaping learning and improving teaching.

The above further reading links with Unit 6.1 of the 5th edition of *Learning to teach in the secondary school*.

Black, P. and Wiliam, D. (1998) *Inside the black box: raising standards through classroom assessment*, London: King's College.

The black box is the classroom. The authors describe the black box in terms of inputs (e.g. pupils, teachers, resources, policy) and outputs (improved learning, better test results, teacher satisfaction); they ask 'how can we be sure that new inputs make for better teaching?' and observe that the hardest part of implementing new educational ideas is in the classroom. New assessment practices are discussed and suggestions are provided for how teachers can be helped to adopt these practices.

The above further reading links with Unit 6.1 of the 5th edition of *Learning to teach in the secondary school*.

Black, P. (1998) *Testing: friend or foe? Theory and practice and assessment and testing* (Master classes in Education), London: RoutledgeFalmer.

This book is an introduction to the academic study of assessment, to convey a grasp of the most important concepts of assessment and then to provide some introductory acquaintance with the many conceptual, technical and practical issues that follow. The book is based on the idea that 'clear and compelling principles are not enough to guide the establishment of assessment practices; rather, that assessment practices can only be understood in relation to the historical, cultural and political contexts within which they are worked out and (that) they also entail complex issues both of technique and of principle' (p. 3). There are three main strands throughout the book, namely the general social context, the purposes of assessment and technical issues. These three principles are addressed through chapters on: history; purposes; confidence in assessment, about reliability and validity; what to test, norms, criteria and domains; how to assess, about methods and instruments; teachers' roles in assessment and testing; pupils and assessment; certification and accountability.

The section 'History' (pp. 7–23) contains instructive contrasts of the differences in assessment practice between England and other countries, including USA and European countries.

The above further reading links with Units 6.1 and 6.2 of the 5th edition of *Learning to teach in the secondary school*.

Husbands, C. (2007) 'Using assessment data to support pupil achievement', in Brooks, V., Abbott, I. and Bills, L. (eds) *Preparing to teach in secondary schools*, Maidenhead: Open University Press.

A practical and useful article for all teachers, showing, with examples, the ways in which schools can use assessment data. It is particularly helpful to the student teacher.

TESTING, MOTIVATION AND LEARNING

Assessment Reform Group supported by The Nuffield Foundation (based on an extensive review by Wynne Harlen and Ruth Deakin-Crick)

A NOTE FROM THE EDITORS

This reading contains a review of assessment practice and its effect on motivation, focusing on the concentration on grades rather than learning and the negative effect of over-testing, particularly on lower-achieving pupils.

This reading links with Unit 6.1 of the 5th edition of *Learning to teach in the secondary school*.

QUESTIONS TO CONSIDER

1 Secondary schools gain much of their status from the achievement of their pupils in the GCSE and GCE A Level examinations. Does the influence of these external examinations prevent pupils from learning how to learn, enjoy and gain satisfaction from their learning or to develop learning skills for life?

2 Could GCSE be developed to improve the development of these skills by pupils? Or should public examinations at 16 be scrapped?

This reading was first published as: Harlen, W. and Deakin-Crick, R. (2002) *Testing, motivation and learning*, Cambridge: The Assessment Reform Group.

INTRODUCTION

It is reasonable to expect that testing has an impact on the way pupils learn and on their motivation to learn. The questions we are addressing here are: what is the nature of that impact, and does pupils' learning benefit from it? Pupils need to know how their learning is progressing. Teachers also need to know how their pupils are progressing, to guide both their own teaching and the pupils' further learning. Many others – parents, other teachers, employers – will have an interest in looking back on what has been learned by an individual pupil, often using a grade or mark as an overall summary of that learning. In addition, there has been an increasing tendency for the results from testing and assessment of learning ('summative assessment') to be used, when combined for whole groups of pupils, as indicators of the performance of teachers, schools and the education system.

The issue facing us is not *whether* we should assess to summarise learning, but rather *how* we should do it. How do we use the results obtained from those assessments to promote better learning?

There are different views on this. Some consider that testing raises levels of achievement. According to this view, testing provides incentives to pupils and their teachers to improve their performance. This in turn helps them to gain the rewards or avoid the penalties. Public knowledge of results makes schools realise that they have to show continual improvement. This benefits their pupils: more is expected from them, and more support may be given to them.

Another view is that testing is motivating only for those who anticipate success. Even then, it is argued, it only promotes motivation towards performance goals rather than learning goals. For the less successful pupils, repeated tests lower self-esteem and the effort they put into learning. This has the effect of increasing the gap between high- and low-achieving pupils. It is also claimed that the increase in scores often noted when 'high-stakes' tests are introduced is attributable more to teachers and pupils becoming familiar with test requirements than to real improvements in the quality of pupils' learning. Linked with this is the recognition that the need for 'lifelong learning' places an increased emphasis on motivation. This must come from enjoying learning and knowing how to learn.

What has research to offer in relation to these rival claims about the impact of testing on motivation? In the review of research, we explored several dimensions of the impact of summative assessment and testing on pupil motivation and sought answers to the questions:

■ What is the overall impact on pupil motivation?
■ How does the impact vary with the characteristics of pupils?
■ How does the impact vary with the conditions of assessment/testing?
■ Where impact on pupils has been found, what is the evidence of impact on teachers and teaching?
■ What actions, in what circumstances, are likely to increase the positive and decrease the negative impact on pupil motivation?

In the next section, we summarise the focus and main findings of the review of research, which was funded by the Nuffield Foundation and by the Evidence for Policy and Practice Information and Co-ordination Centre (EPPI-Centre). (See Appendices A and B for details.) We then outline the implications of these findings for policy and practice in relation to: the work of teachers in classrooms; the professional development of teachers; the management of schools; the inspection and evaluation of schools; and national and local assessment policies.

THE FOCUS OF THE REVIEW

The review process sought out evidence from research that links 'summative assessment and testing' to the complex concept of 'motivation to learn'. The former covered any form of judgement of pupils' performance for summative purposes, including formal tests, teacher-made tests and classroom grading. The latter embraced components of motivation such as 'effort', 'self-regulation' and 'self-esteem', as well as acknowledging broad distinctions such as 'intrinsic' and 'extrinsic' motivation. Some of these components are set out and explained in Figure 15.1. As can be seen from the figure, assessment is only one of several factors affecting motivation for learning.

MAIN FINDINGS

A widespread search of published research found 183 studies that were potentially relevant to the review questions. Of these, nineteen were identified as providing sound and valid empirical evidence (the analytical process of selection is explained in Appendices B and C). What emerges is strong evidence of the negative impact of testing on pupils' motivation, though this varied in degree with the pupils' characteristics and with the conditions of their learning. Many aspects of the impact have significant consequences for pupils' future learning and thus are causes for concern. At the same time, the findings indicate ways to increase the positive impact and to decrease the negative impact on pupils' motivation for learning.

None of the studies dealt with all components of motivation to learn, but most of the findings are supported by evidence from more than one study. In the rest of this section, the chief sources of evidence are indicated by numbers in brackets. These refer to the relevant studies listed in Appendix C.

What is the overall impact on pupils' motivation?

An impact on self-esteem was reported in all studies dealing with this aspect of motivation. For example, two studies (4, 5) showed that, after the introduction of the National Curriculum tests in England, low-achieving pupils had lower self-esteem than higher-achieving pupils. Before the tests were introduced, there was no correlation between self-esteem and achievement. Although no cause and effect can be claimed here, an impact can be inferred, since self-esteem is an outcome of educational experience as well as being a factor determining future learning. Put simply, one impact of the tests was the reduction in self-esteem of those pupils who did not achieve well.

Pupils at primary school are also aware that tests give only a narrow view of their learning. When tests pervade the ethos of the classroom, test performance is more highly valued than what is being learned (15, 16). When tests become the main criteria by which pupils are judged, and by which they judge themselves, those whose strengths lie outside the subjects tested have a low opinion of their capabilities (7, 12, 16, 17).

The results of tests that are 'high stakes' for individual pupils, such as the 11+ in Northern Ireland, have been found to have a particularly strong impact on those who receive low grades (11, 12). However, tests that are high stakes for schools rather than for pupils (such as the national tests in England and state-mandated tests in the US) can have just as much impact. Pupils are aware of repeated practice tests and the narrowing of the curriculum (14, 17). Only those confident of success enjoy the tests (12). In taking tests, high achievers are more persistent, use appropriate test-taking strategies and have more positive self-perceptions than low achievers (14). Low achievers become overwhelmed by assessments and de-motivated by constant evidence of their low achievement. The effect is to increase the gap between low- and high-achieving pupils (9, 14, 16).

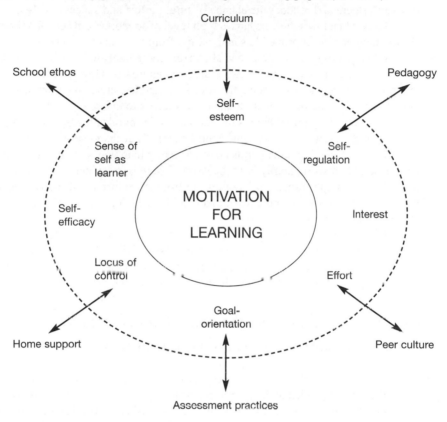

Self-esteem: how one values oneself as a person and as a learner

Self-efficacy: how capable one feels of succeeding in a learning task

Self-regulation: the capacity to evaluate one's own work and to make choices about what to do next

Goal-orientation: whether one's goal is to learn in order to understand or to perform well on a test (which may not reflect secure learning)

Interest: the pleasure from and engagement with learning

Effort: how much one is prepared to try and persevere

Locus of control: how much one feels in control of learning as opposed to it being directed by others

Sense of self as a learner: how confident one feels of being able to learn from the classroom experiences provided.

■ **Figure 15.1** Motivation for learning.

The use of repeated practice tests impresses on pupils the importance of the tests. It encourages them to adopt test-taking strategies designed to avoid effort and responsibility. Repeated practice tests are, therefore, detrimental to higher-order thinking (14).

How does the impact vary with the characteristics of pupils?

Lower-achieving pupils are doubly disadvantaged by tests. Being labelled as failures has an impact on how they feel about their ability to learn. It also lowers further their already low self-esteem and reduces the chance of future effort and success (9, 14).

Only when low achievers have a high level of support (from school or home), which shows them how to improve, do some escape from this vicious circle (18).

Older pupils (that is, age 11 and above) are more likely to have a clear understanding of the meaning of grades than their younger counterparts. However, they are less likely to report teachers' grades as being fair, even though they attach more importance to them (7). Older pupils are more likely to attribute success to effort and ability, while younger ones attribute it to external factors or practice. Older pupils are also more likely to focus on performance outcomes (i.e. scores and levels) rather than learning processes (16).

Lower-achieving older pupils are more likely than younger ones to minimise effort and respond to tests randomly or by guessing. There is no evidence of age differences in test-taking strategies (checking, monitoring time etc.). Instead of motivation increasing with age, older pupils feel more resentment, anxiety, cynicism and mistrust of standardised achievement tests (14).

Girls are reported as expressing more test anxiety than boys (1, 7, 8, 17). Girls are also more likely to think that the source of success or failure lies within themselves rather than being influenced by external circumstances. This has consequences for their self-esteem, especially when they view their potential as fixed (7).

How does the impact vary with the conditions of testing?

The conditions found to affect the impact of testing relate to:

- the degree of self-efficacy (the capacity to undertake a task successfully) of pupils;
- the extent to which their effort is motivated by the prospect of reward or punishment that follows from the test performance (extrinsic motivation). This may have little to do with the learning or the value and satisfaction derived from what is learned (intrinsic motivation);
- the encouragement of self-evaluation and self-regulation and the pressure imposed by adults outside the school.

How assessment of their learning is reported back to the pupil (feedback) affects motivation to learn. It has a central role, since the feeling of self-efficacy is derived from performance in previous tasks of the same kind. If pupils have experienced success in earlier performance, they are more likely to feel able to succeed in a new task (2, 6, 16).

Feedback from the teacher that focuses on how to improve or build on what has been done (described as task-related) is associated with greater interest and effort (3, 16). Feedback that emphasises relative performance, for example marks or grades that are formally or informally compared with those of others, encourages pupils to concentrate on getting better grades rather than on deeper understanding (3).

Teachers' own class testing practices can help to increase pupils' self-efficacy, if teachers explain the purpose and expectations of their tests and provide task-related feedback (2, 6). Further, a school's 'assessment culture' influences pupils' feelings of self-efficacy and effort. Collegiality – meaning constructive discussion of testing and the development of desirable assessment practice in the school – has a positive effect, while an exclusive focus on performance goals has a negative effect (6).

The degree to which learners are able to regulate their own learning also appears to foster pupils' interest and to promote focus on the intrinsic features of their work (15). Pupils who have some control over their work by being given choice and by being encouraged to evaluate their own work are more likely to value the learning itself rather than to focus only on whether or not it is correct (1, 15, 16, 19).

When test scores are a source of pride to parents and the community, pressure is brought to bear on the school for high scores (11, 12). Similarly, parents bring pressure on their children when the result has consequences for attendance at high social status schools. For many pupils, this increases their anxiety, even though they recognise their parents as being supportive (12, 16).

Where impact on pupils has been found, what is the evidence of impact on teachers and teaching?

The evidence suggests that teachers can be very effective in training pupils to pass tests, even when the pupils do not have the understanding or higher-order thinking skills that the tests are intended to measure (9). When test results are used for making decisions that affect the status or future of pupils, teachers or schools ('high-stakes tests'), teachers adopt a teaching style that emphasises transmission of knowledge. This favours those pupils who prefer to learn by mastering information presented sequentially. Those who prefer more active and creative learning experiences are disadvantaged, and their self-esteem is lowered (11, 16). External tests have a constricting effect on the curriculum, resulting in emphasis on the subjects tested at the expense of creativity and personal and social development (9, 14, 17).

High-stakes tests often result in a great deal of time being spent on practice tests, with test performance being highly valued and other pupil achievements undervalued (9, 12, 17). Furthermore, teachers' own assessments become mainly summative in function rather than formative (16).

What actions in what circumstances are likely to increase the positive and decrease the negative impact on pupil motivation?

The research shows that the negative impact of tests can be reduced by ceasing to focus teaching on test content. It can also be reduced by ending the practice of 'training' pupils in how to pass the tests and by preventing the use of class time for repeated practice tests (9, 11, 12, 14, 17). Pupils should not be faced with tests in which they are unlikely to experience success (6, 12, 13, 18).

The review findings also indicate actions that can be taken to decrease the negative and increase the positive impact of summative assessment and tests. In relation to the tests, such actions include:

- involving pupils in decisions about tests (12, 13);
- using assessment to convey a sense of progress in their learning to pupils (6, 18);

■ providing explanations to pupils about the purpose of tests and other assessments of their learning (7, 12, 16);

■ providing feedback that helps further learning (2, 3 6).

In relation to teaching approaches, successful actions include:

■ adopting approaches that encourage self-regulated learning, including collaboration among pupils (6, 15);

■ catering for a range of learning styles (11);

■ cultivating intrinsic interest in the subject (1);

■ putting less emphasis on grades (7);

■ promoting learning goal orientation rather than performance orientation (1, 2, 18, 19);

■ developing pupils' self-assessment skills and their use of criteria relating to learning, rather than test performance (16, 19);

■ making learning goals explicit and helping pupils to direct effort in learning (18).

Actions at the whole school level include:

■ establishing a school climate in which there is constructive discussion about tests and assessment of learning, both among teachers and between teachers and pupils (6);

■ developing a constructive and supportive school ethos to minimise test anxiety (1, 12, 16);

■ ensuring that the demands of the tests are consistent with the expectations of teachers and the capabilities of the pupils (12, 18);

■ broadening the range of information used in assessing the attainment of pupils (9, 14, 17).

IMPLICATIONS FOR THE WORK OF TEACHERS IN CLASSROOMS

The review emphasises what teachers in classrooms can do to avoid the negative impact of tests on motivation for learning. It also indicates the actions that can enhance motivation for learning. To accomplish these goals, teachers should:

do more of this . . .	and do less of this . . .
Provide choice and help pupils to take responsibility for their learning.	Define the curriculum in terms of what is in the tests to the detriment of what is not tested.
Discuss with pupils the purpose of their learning and provide feedback that will help the learning process.	Give frequent drill and practice for test taking.
	Teach how to answer specific test questions.

do more of this . . .	and do less of this . . .
Encourage pupils to judge their work by how much they have learned and by the progress they have made.	Allow pupils to judge their work in terms of scores or grades.
Help pupils to understand the criteria by which their learning is assessed and to assess their own work.	Allow test anxiety to impair some pupils' performance (particularly girls and lower-performing pupils).
Develop pupils' understanding of the goals of their work in terms of what they are learning; provide feedback to pupils in relation to these goals.	Use tests and assessment to tell students where they are in relation to others.
	Give feedback relating to pupils' capabilities, implying a fixed view of each pupil's potential.
Help pupils to understand where they are in relation to learning goals and how to make further progress.	Compare pupils' grades and allow pupils to compare grades, giving status on the basis of test achievement only.
Give feedback that enables pupils to know the next steps and how to succeed in taking them.	Emphasise competition for marks or grades among pupils.
Encourage pupils to value effort and a wide range of attainments.	
Encourage collaboration among pupils and a positive view of each others' attainments.	

IMPLICATIONS FOR PROFESSIONAL DEVELOPMENT

Teachers develop their professional skills in a variety of ways. The process begins in pre-service education and training and continues through formal professional development activities, organised both within and outside schools. Informal learning also takes place through peer observation activities and in the interactions between teachers.

How might we represent the conclusions of this review in these professional development activities? What should be the focus of these activities? In conducting the review, we have identified some of the answers to these questions. It is important that professional development should involve:

■ extending awareness both of the limited validity of tests (and other assessments of learning) and of the ways in which evidence from them can be used to guide learning;
■ recognising how preparation for, involvement in, and responding to, tests and assessment of learning can impact negatively on pupils' motivation;

■   devising strategies to minimise the negative impacts of tests and assessment of learning;

■   understanding the differential impact of tests on pupils including, for example, how the negative impact on low-attaining pupils can be reduced;

■   developing skills in designing tests and using the results from them to maximise their positive impact on the motivation of all pupils. Successful strategies involve the use of peer group learning in systematic revision, in setting questions and in marking papers. In this manner, they can better understand summative assessments and can realise the contribution of such assessments to their learning (Black *et al.,* 2002);

■   discussing and helping the implementation of within-school strategies for emphasising learning goals as distinct from performance goals. Teaching methods that contribute most to the attainment of these goals will also be a feature of such discussions.

IMPLICATIONS FOR THE MANAGEMENT OF SCHOOLS

Assessment and testing of pupils for summative purposes are routine for those who manage schools, whether as head teachers, other senior managers or school governors. They can take several forms, including teacher-made tests, school-devised systems of measuring pupil performance, bought-in tests for specific purposes and high-profile national systems of tests and examinations. Given current external demands for performance measures – both raw test results and value-added scores – there is strong pressure on schools to collect more and more of these kinds of data.

However, the evidence presented here indicates that the experience of testing and assessment of learning can have a negative effect on pupils' motivation to learn. In contrast, a previous review of research, by Black and Wiliam (1998), provides evidence that formative assessment ('assessment for learning') can improve pupils' attainments. Assessment for learning does this by focusing on helping pupils to learn better – without teaching to the test and without increasing test-taking or test practice. Taken together, these two sets of findings strongly suggest that pupils will be better motivated to learn, will learn better and will achieve more, if schools focus on promoting formative assessment practice and use summative assessment only when it is really necessary.

Such a strategy requires school managers to take some risks, though the evidence suggests these risks may be more imagined than real. They need to establish an assessment policy and culture in their schools that promote the value of assessment *for* learning and place assessment *of* learning in perspective. This will involve mediating government policy to staff and parents. Senior managers must not communicate their anxiety for good results to pupils or make them feel burdened by the responsibility for the school performing well. The pupils' priority should be their own learning in all areas of the curriculum, not only those assessed by tests.

The evidence suggests that better school results will follow from better learning and by developing and maintaining pupils' motivation to learn. In addition to promoting formative assessment for learning, school policy also needs to address the issue of when it is appropriate to use summative assessments, and in what form. The ideal situation is to assess pupils only when their teachers judge they have a good chance of success. In this way, the dangers of demotivation, following repeated failure, will be reduced.

Establishing a positive learning culture in schools involves winning the hearts and minds of all: pupils, parents, teachers and the wider school community. This can only be achieved through effective communication, consultation and collegiality. This itself may demand new structures and processes to be developed at whole-school level. Opportunities to work with parents will be especially important.

IMPLICATIONS FOR THE EVALUATION AND INSPECTION OF SCHOOLS

Schools routinely evaluate their own performance and are subject to periodic inspection by external agencies. Indicators derived by combining the results of individual pupils have a significant role in self-evaluation and inspection. However, they can only be indicative of some aspects of a school's performance. The use of such results for these purposes is likely to affect the way in which tests are seen both by teachers and by pupils.

What are the implications of this review for evaluation and inspection? We have identified several conclusions from the findings:

■   performance in tests (and other summative assessments of learning) should be clearly acknowledged as only a partial indication of a school's success in contributing to the learning of its pupils;

■   targets for improvement will necessarily include indices of pupil performance as well as other indices, but they should not be narrowly focused on them;

■   criteria for the inspection of schools should focus at least as much on the quality of learning observed, and on the extent to which assessments contribute to pupils' learning, as on indicators of learning outcomes;

■   inspectors' judgements of assessment policies and practices should include reference to the extent to which the schools have minimised the negative impacts of tests and maximised their contribution to pupils' learning;

■   criteria for school evaluation should refer to all of a school's aims and to all areas of educational activity.

IMPLICATIONS FOR NATIONAL AND LOCAL ASSESSMENT POLICIES

Policies that lead to the introduction of systems for measuring, and reporting on, pupil attainment need to be clearly based on a well-defined set of purposes. This has not always been the case. Some, such as the GCSE in England, Wales and Northern Ireland, have been designed mainly to serve a particular purpose of assessment, i.e. certification. Others, such as National Curriculum assessment, have had ambitions to serve a wide range of purposes.

What does the review evidence suggest that those responsible for designing testing and assessment systems, or using the evidence from them, should do? In reviewing the evidence, we have concluded that designers and users of assessment systems and tests should:

■   be more actively aware of the limited validity of the information about pupil attainment that is being obtained from current high-stakes testing programmes, such as the Key Stage 2 National Curriculum tests;

■   reduce the stakes of such summative assessments by using, at national and local levels, the performance indicators derived from them more selectively and more sensitively. They should take due account of the potential for those indicators to impact negatively on learning, on teaching and on the curriculum;

■ be more aware of the true costs of national systems of testing, in terms of teaching time, practice tests and marking. This in turn should lead policy makers to come to reasoned conclusions about the benefits and costs of each element in those systems;

■ for tracking standards of attainment at national level, consider testing a sample of pupils rather than a full age cohort. This would reduce both the negative impacts of high-stakes tests on pupil motivation and the costs incurred;

■ use test development expertise to create forms of tests and assessments that will make it possible to assess all valued outcomes of education, including, for example, creativity and problemsolving;

■ develop a broader range of indicators to evaluate the performance of schools. Indicators that are derived from summative assessments should therefore be seen as only one element in a more broadly based judgement. This would diminish the likely impact of public judgements of school performance on those pupils whose motivation is most 'at risk'.

APPENDIX A: SOURCES OF INFORMATION

1 The full review report is cited as: Harlen, W. and Deakin Crick, R. (2002) 'A systematic review of the impact of summative assessment and tests on pupils' motivation for learning (EPPI-Centre Review)', in *Research evidence in education library* (Issue 1), London: EPPI-Centre, Social Science Research Unit, Institute of Education.

2 The full review, databases and four user reviews can be found on the EPPI website: http://eppi.ioe.ac.uk.

3 An extended article based on the review with responses from eminent educators in the field of assessment will be published in a special edition of *Assessment in Education*, Vol. 10, No. 2, July 2003.

APPENDIX B: BACKGROUND AND METHODS

This review was prompted by the need to identify the impact of summative assessment and testing, which have burgeoned in many countries in the past decade, on pupils' motivation for learning. While the impact of testing on teachers, teaching and pupils' achievement has been well researched and represented in reviews of research, much less attention had been given to its impact on the affective and cognative (mental activity) outcomes of education. The aim of developing in today's pupils the capacity to continue learning beyond the years of schooling into lifelong learning is widely embraced. If some assessment practices are reducing motivation for learning, the prospect for such pupils' interest in lifelong learning would be a cause for concern. The purpose of the review was therefore to identify and synthesise research evidence about the impact of summative assessment on motivation for learning.

The review was conducted using the procedures for systematic review of research in education being developed by the EPPI-Centre. It involved a wide-ranging search for research studies, written in English, of assessment for summative purposes in schools for pupils between the ages of 4 and 18, which reported on aspects of pupils' motivation for learning. The search for studies involved scanning relevant electronic databases and journals online, following up citations in other reviews, hand-searching journals held in the library, and using personal contacts. This resulted in the listing of 183 studies.

The relevance of each one to the review was judged initially from abstracts, and some were excluded before full texts were read. Successive rounds of applying criteria resulted in the identification of the most relevant studies (of which there were nineteen), which were analysed in depth using the *Guidelines for Extracting Data and Assessing Quality of Primary Studies in Educational Research*, Version 0.94 (EPPICentre, 2001). Judgements were made as to the strength of evidence relevant to the review provided by each study. In the synthesis, greater weight was given to studies providing the strongest evidence.

None of the studies related to all the components of motivation indicated in Figure 15.1, but they could be grouped according to the particular aspects investigated. The three groups, central to motivation for learning and expressed from a learner's perspective, are as follows:

■ *What I feel and think about myself as a learner:* related to self-esteem, self-concept, sense of self as a learner, attitude to assessment, test anxiety, learning disposition.
■ *The energy I have for the task:* related to effort, interest in and attitude to subject, self-regulation.
■ *How I perceive my capacity to undertake the task:* related to locus of control, goal orientation, self-efficacy.

In the report of the review, the synthesis of findings relating to the question 'What is the overall impact on pupil motivation?' is set out under these headings.

The final phase of the review included a presentation of the findings to an expert group at a specially convened consultation conference. This was attended by forty-five experts, representing teachers, local authority or independent advisers on assessment, officials from government or government agencies, teacher educators and academics with research interests in educational assessment and policy. A draft copy of the review report was sent to all participants before the conference, and the methodology and findings were presented in detail during the conference. The outcomes informed the implications in the final report and the summaries in this pamphlet.

APPENDIX C: LIST OF STUDIES USED

1 Benmansour, N. (1999) 'Motivational orientations, self-efficacy, anxiety and strategy use in learning high school mathematics in Morocco', *Mediterranean Journal of Educational Studies*, Vol. 4: 1–15.

2 Brookhart, S. and DeVoge, J. (1999) 'Testing a theory about the role of classroom assessment in pupil motivation and achievement', *Applied Measurement in Education*, Vol. 12: 409–425.

3 Butler, R. (1988) 'Enhancing and undermining intrinsic motivation: the effects of task-involving and ego-involving evaluation on interest and performance', *British Journal of Educational Psychology*, Vol. 8: 1–14.

4 Davies, J. and Brember, I. (1999) 'Reading and mathematics attainments and self-esteem in years 2 and 6: an eight year cross-sectional study', *Educational Studies*, Vol. 25: 145–157.

5 Davies, J. and Brember, I. (1998). 'National curriculum testing and self-esteem in year 2: the first five years: a cross-sectional study', *Educational Psychology*, Vol. 18: 365–375.

6   Duckworth, K., Fielding, G. and Shaughnessy, J. (1986) *The relationship of high school teachers' class testing practices to pupils' feelings of efficacy and efforts to study*, US: Oregon University.

7   Evans, E. and Engelberg, R. (1988) 'Pupils perceptions of school grading', *Journal of Research and Development in Education*, Vol. 21: 44–54.

8   Ferguson, C. and Francis, J. (1979) 'Motivation and mode: an attempt to measure the attitudes of 'O' level GCE candidates to English language', *Educational Studies*, Vol. 5: 231–239.

9   Gordon, S. and Reese, M. (1997) 'High stakes testing: worth the price?', *Journal of School Leadership*, Vol. 7: 345–368.

10 Hughes, B., Sullivan, H. and Beaird, J. (1986) 'Continuing motivation of boys and girls under differing evaluation conditions and achievement levels', *American Educational Research Journal*, Vol. 23: 660–667.

11 Johnston, J. and McClune, W. (2000) 'Selection project sel 5.1: pupil motivation and attitudes – self-esteem, locus of control, learning disposition and the impact of selection on teaching and learning', in *The effects of the selective system of secondary education in Northern Ireland:* Research Papers Volume II, Bangor, Co Down: Department of Education, ISBN 1 897 592 663: 1–37.

12 Leonard, M. and Davey, C. (2001) *Thoughts on the 11 plus*, Belfast: Save the Children Fund.

13 Little, A. (1994) 'Types of assessment and interest in learning: variation in the south of England in the 1980s', *Assessment in Education*, Vol. 1: 201–222.

14 Paris, S., Lawton, T., Turner, J. and Roth, J. (1991) 'A developmental perspective on standardised achievement testing', *Educational Researcher*, Vol. 20: 12–20.

15 Perry, N. (1998) 'Young children's self-regulated learning and contexts that support it', *Journal of Educational Psychology*, Vol. 90: 715–729.

16 Pollard, A., Triggs, P., Broadfoot, P., McNess, E. and Osborn, M. (2000) *What pupils say: changing policy and practice in primary education* (Chapters 7 and 10), London: Continuum.

17 Reay, D. and Wiliam, D. (1999) '"I'll be a nothing": structure, agency and the construction of identity through assessment', *British Educational Research Journal*, Vol. 25: 343–354.

18 Roderick, M. and Engel, M. (2001) 'The grasshopper and the ant: motivational responses of low achieving pupils to high stakes testing', *Educational Evaluation and Policy Analysis*, Vol. 23: 197–228.

19 Schunk, D. (1996) 'Goal and self-evaluative influences during children's cognitive skill learning', *American Educational Research Journal*, Vol. 33: 359–382.

REFERENCES

Black, P., Harrison, C., Lee, C., Marshall, B. and Wiliam, D. (2002) *Working inside the black box: assessment for learning in the classroom,* London: King's College London.

Black, P. and Wiliam, D. (1998) *Inside the black box,* London: King's College London.

'TROUBLESOME BOYS' AND 'COMPLIANT GIRLS'

Gender identity and perceptions of achievement and underachievement

Susan Jones and Debra Myhill

A NOTE FROM THE EDITORS

The research in this reading used focus groups of four groups of pupils, high-achioving boys and girls and underachieving boys and girls, to explore how teachers' perceptions of gender identity appear to influence achievement levels.

This reading links with Units 4.1, 4.4 and 6.1 of the 5th edition of *Learning to teach in the secondary school*.

QUESTIONS TO CONSIDER

In the 1970s, concern was raised about the underachievement of Afro-Caribboan pupils; later that decade, concern shifted to the underachievement and lack of opportunity of girls, particularly in science and mathematics. The relative under-achievement of white working-class boys has also been raised. Recently, the underachievement of boys has dominated many discussions.

1   Does the identification of underachievement in particular groups of pupils inevitably hide the underachievement of pupils outside the target group? How should schools respond to the perceived underachievement of pupils?

2   This reading, by Jones and Myhill, discusses issues of stereotyping of pupils by teachers. Does the identification of particular groups of underachieving pupils lead to such stereotyping or merely reinforce existing stereotyping. How could schools and teachers respond to such evidence?

This reading was first published as: Jones, S. and Myhill, D. (2004) ' "Troublesome boys" and "compliant girls": gender identity and perceptions of achievement and underachievement', *British Journal of Sociology of Education*, Vol. 25: 547–561.

ABSTRACT

Working within a methodological framework that identified four focus groups, high-achieving boys and girls and underachieving boys and girls, this article presents teachers' perceptions of how gender identity is seen to influence achievement levels. Beliefs about gender identity informed the teachers' perceptions in relation to each of the four focus groups, whereby the underachieving boy and the high-achieving girl were seen to conform to gender expectations; the high-achieving boys were seen to challenge gender norms; and the underachieving girl emerges as largely overlooked. The perceived characteristics of the high-achieving girl are presented as describing all girls. There appears to be a tendency to associate boys with underachievement and girls with high achievement.

INTRODUCTION

In the United Kingdom, underachievement has been constructed principally as a gender issue with regard to boys since the early 1990s, although previous discourses of under-achievement have variously focused on the underachievement of girls (Dweck *et al.*, 1978; Leder, 1980; Weinar, 1971) or of children from socially disadvantaged groups (Floud *et al.*, 1957; Halsey *et al.*, 1980). Indeed, some researchers have argued that a far greater predictor of outcome is socio-economic status (Collins *et al.*, 2000; Gillborn and Mirza, 2000). More recently, growing concern for the achievement of pupils from minority ethnic groups has placed children such as those from the Afro-Caribbean community under the spotlight (DfES, 2003). Nonetheless, the thrust of policy initiatives in recent years has been, and continues to be, strongly directed towards the underachievement of boys (Ofsted, 2003a, 2003b).

The link between achievement and gender is one that is frequently used to account for boys' underachievement. Boys' disaffection with schooling is often described as a response to the male culture in which boys find themselves: some boys identify with a set of 'macho' male values that rejects the values of education (Mac an Ghaill, 1994; Martino, 1999). Boys have also been positioned as having weaker language skills, and have been seen as less committed readers and disliking writing activities (Millard, 1997; Gorman *et al.*, 1988). Boys within the classroom have been pictured as cast adrift in an alien environment where the preferred ethos and learning styles, the approved literacy prac-tices, even the testing procedures, all favour female strengths and preferences (Hannan,

1996; Osmont and Davies, 1987; Platten, 1999). The tone of much of the recent debate surrounding the underachievement of boys certainly implies that underachievement is predominantly a concern about males.

However, in the 1970s and 1980s, that same link between gender and achievement was used to explain the underachievement of girls, especially with regard to mathematics and science. It is interesting to compare the social, political and educational contexts and discourses of research as it has been applied to different genders. The discourses surrounding the debate of girls' underachievement were almost exclusively concerned with the effect of gender inequality in the classroom. Girls were pictured as marginalized (Bousted, 1989), the classroom as being dominated by male students (Swann and Graddol, 1988), and girls were said to show low self-esteem and poor self-confidence (Weiner, 1985) and to exclude themselves from traditionally male subjects, such as mathematics and science (Leder, 1980). It was Walkerdine (1989) who pointed out that, while attention was focused on girls' inadequacy with mathematics and science, boys' underachievement in language was being overlooked. She concluded that teachers' beliefs about girls' apparent underperformance in mathematics were based on a misplaced assumption of female failure in mathematics. Her findings, however, did not support this assumption: what they did establish was that 'girls were felt to lack something, even if they were successful', while on the other hand it seemed that 'boys were felt to possess the very thing that girls were taken to lack' (Walkerdine, 1989: 4). Walkerdine argues that beliefs about gender inform teachers' beliefs about learning potential, and so the apparent active, sometimes disruptive, behaviour of boys is perceived as implying an active, inquiring and questioning mind. Boys, she suggests, are being positioned as the 'proper learner'. By contrast, the conforming diligence of girls is perceived as implying rule-bound learning, rather than principled learning. Thus, good behaviour from a girl becomes a problem, while poor behaviour from a boy is interpreted as a quality. In the context of the current debate about boys and underachievement, a very similar set of behaviours has been offered to account for the underachievement of boys and the higher performance of girls. Thus, historically, perceived gender identities have been used to explain both male and female achievement and male and female underachievement.

Although the moving focus of the underachievement debate has shifted from girls to boys, this shift has not been without its critics. In particular, the tendency to see a causative link between masculinity and underachievement has been critiqued for its inability to acknowledge adequately the needs of girls. Osler et al. (2002) consider how the recent focusing of the debate upon boys has rendered many girls, particularly underachieving and low-achieving girls, invisible. Schools perceive boys as a problem, both in terms of behaviour and achievement. Resources, therefore, are aimed disproportionately at boys, while girls view the support that is offered as inappropriate to their needs. Girls, they suggest, only become the focus of concern when teenage pregnancy is an issue. Osler et al. argue that teachers position girls as accepting and upholding the ethos of the school. They suggest, however, that, while girls may not be overtly disruptive, they are more likely to experience anxiety, depression, eating disorders and self-harming. Girls comprise only 17 per cent of the permanent exclusions, but self-exclusion through truanting is widespread among girls. The perception of girls as being largely accepting of the school ethos is challenged by researchers who identify female cohorts who reject conventional educational values. Arnot and Gubb (2001) mention the 'stroppy girl' and the 'intractable girl', while Mac an Ghaill (1994) refers to the 'Posse', who were perceived by teachers as the worst-behaved female student group in the school. Reay (1999) speaks of the 'Spice Girls' who prioritize physical appearance and sexual attraction above success at school. Griffin (1982) comments that existing theories, sociological and psychological, have little to say by way of understanding the experiences of young women.

There is no educated nor any conventional way to describe real female experiences. It is difficult to articulate or theorise women's experience when the words, the ideas and the research traditions are either completely absent, or only present in developing or fragmented forms (Griffin, 1982: 187).

Thus, the positioning of the debate about underachievement as a gender issue in relation to boys, together with the perception that girls do not present problems in the classroom, may be influencing teachers' patterns of expectations for girls and boys in the classroom. This article explores the relationship between teachers' perceptions of gender and achievement.

THE STUDY

Building on the findings of a commissioned study (Project JUDE) investigating the underachievement of boys, the study reported here raises questions about how under-achievement is perceived by teachers, particularly in how it is constructed differentially by gender. The sample in Project JUDE was self-selected, and the research problem owned by the schools, as they had invited the university to explore the issue.

The schools' pyramid involved in the project was made up of six first schools (Years 1–4), three middle schools (Years 5–8) and one high school (Years 9–13). The schools were both rural and urban, including some very small rural first schools. Although the socio-economic profile of the area was predominantly white and middle class, the schools within the sample did reflect different intake profiles. The data in Table 16.1, drawn from Ofsted reports and contextual information provided by the schools, indicate some of this variety, although the data also make clear that the differences between the schools in general are not pronounced. Using free school meals as an indicator, it is evident that none is serving a catchment of significant socio-economic deprivation. The less advantaged catchments reflect the economic deprivation of both urban and rural communities, and it is important to note that some of the rural villages are also affected by a certain amount of social isolation.

The teachers and children who were observed and interviewed formed a purposive sample, designed to capture a balanced cross-section of pupils with variables in age, gender and achievement. In all, thirty-six classes were sampled: six classes each in Years 1, 4, 5, 8, 9 and 10. These year groups represented the oldest and youngest year groups within each phase. Years 4 and 5 and Years 8 and 9 represented the point at which transition between the schools took place, and so, although they were only one year apart, school experience had changed considerably. The class teacher for each class was interviewed; in the high school, all the teachers in the English Department were interviewed, plus a volunteer sample of four teachers from other curriculum areas. In each class, four children were identified by the class teacher as the focus for classroom observation and for inter-view. These four children included a high-achieving boy and girl, and an underachieving boy and girl. There were therefore forty teacher interviews and 144 children (thirty-six in each group) who were interviewed in pairs. There were thirty-six sets of classroom observations.

This article reports principally on data deriving from the teacher interviews, although brief reference is made to some evidence from the classroom observations. The interviews

■ **Table 16.1** The composition of the school sample

School	Roll	Community	Special educational needs (%)	Number of pupils eligible for free school meals	Contextual information
First schools					
F1	149	Rural	27	Well below average	Serves a wide rural catchment with twice the national average of adults with higher-education qualifications
F2	361	Urban	30	A little below average	Area includes a high density of local authority housing
F3	326	Urban	30	Below average	Area of mixed housing
F4	119	Rural	35	Below average	Serves a wide rural catchment
F5	185	Urban	40	Well below average	Area of mixed housing Includes a special unit for children with physical disabilities and learning difficulties
F6	69	Rural	30	Below average	Serves a wide rural catchment
Middle schools					
M1	481	Urban/rural	26	About average	Pupils from widely differing socio-economic backgrounds
M2	415	Rural	35	Below average	Serves several villages Pupils are from widely differing socio-economic backgrounds
M3	577	Urban/rural	20	Well below average	The pupils come from a broad range of socio-geographical and economic backgrounds
High school					
H1	1421	Urban/rural	14	Well below average	The school is working in generally favourable educational and socio-economic circumstances, although it would be wrong to make light of the influences of rural deprivation

were semi-structured, designed to explore teachers' perceptions of gender and of achievement. Since the study had been initiated by the schools, the focus on boys and underachievement would have been known to all involved: however, great care was taken in the design of the interview, and indeed in the design of the study, to look at both girls and boys, and both underachievers and high-achievers, in an attempt to deconstruct the dominant coupling of boys with underachievement. In the opening section of the interviews, teachers were asked to describe the four focus children from their class, to explain why they felt the two underachievers were underachieving and to consider how typical these children were of boys and girls in general. The cluster of prompt questions on gender explored perceptions of parental influences on boys and girls, different learning styles for boys and girls, and curriculum preferences according to gender. The cluster of questions on achievement investigated teachers' views of gender differences in achievement, including whether they believed boys and girls should attain equal outcomes, whether they could account for the differences in achievement of boys and girls, and whether they had found any strategies that successfully raised boys' achievement.

In the pilot phase of the study, it emerged that the term 'underachievement' was proving problematic because, frequently, those selected as underachievers were low achievers, including some pupils with special educational needs. For these teachers, the term underachievement referred to low levels of performance, not to children whose performance was lower than they might have expected. This was despite the focus of the research having arisen from the academic pyramid's analysis of test data that led them to believe that boys were not achieving results matched to their ability. Therefore, following the pilot study, clearer guidelines were given to inform the selection of the underachievers (an underachiever may exhibit only one or several of these criteria): a child who is not achieving in academic tests but who:

■ has oral abilities that are better than their reading or writing;
■ has good general knowledge;
■ grasps ideas and principles quickly;
■ challenges viewpoints or sees things differently from others; or
■ seems unmotivated but capable.

The selection of the four children remained essentially a decision based on the teachers' professional judgement, and some, but not all, made reference to test scores, to inform their decision. At the time of the data collection for this study, use of statistical performance data was not consistent across the schools' pyramid, and there was inconsistent use of other tests, such as Cognitive Ability Tests, which might have informed the decision-making. Thus the initial interview prompts to describe the four children and to explain why they believed they were underachieving permitted further exploration of the designation of particular pupils as underachievers.

Although the research was investigating the issue of boys' underachievement, as already mentioned the research design sought to avoid the coupling of boys with underachievement. The methodological approach taken was to make comparisons between the four groups in order to consider the underachieving boy in relation to other boys and to female underachievers. Thus, from the start, the project engaged with some thorny problems. First, the statistical gap in the performance of boys in relation to girls in national tests and at GCSE only accounts for the existence of the underachieving boy: from this perspective, there are no underachieving girls. Second, the current media and research attention on the underachieving boys, together with the teachers' own perceptions in relation to gender identity, meant that the teachers might well adopt different criteria when selecting boy or girl underachievers. Wrestling with this particular problem was to become a defining issue throughout the study. Much of the research that focuses upon the underachievement of boys does not attempt to identify underachievers; rather, it compares boys with girls more generally. The problem of identifying just who the underachievers are in our classrooms requires further research initiatives, but the findings reported here consider the extent to which teachers' perceptions of underachievement are coloured by their perceptions about gender.

THE FINDINGS

The teachers were asked to express their expectations of finding gender differences in achievement generally, in language ability specifically, and in classroom response and behaviour. When asked directly if they felt boys and girls should achieve the same results, 80 per cent of the teachers said that it was their expectation that boys and girls should get the same results. This commitment to equal achievement, however, was not reflected in teachers' perceptions when prompted to think about classroom attitude and behaviour and ability within different areas of the curriculum. The interviews revealed a more complex picture of teacher perceptions, which were not fully consonant with their espoused belief of equality of outcome by gender. In relation to whether there were gender differences, whether any such differences were learned or innate, and whether there was such a thing as a typical boy or a typical girl, the teachers appeared to be struggling to make sense of conflicting ideas. What teachers believed about gender and achievement, and about equality, did not always appear to be supported by their own experiences in the classroom.

Tables 16.2 and 16.3 illustrate the tendency for teachers to repeat many of the commonly cited gender stereotypes that often go unchallenged as accepted social wisdom. Comments such as 'girls settle down and get on with it' and 'boys don't like writing' were offered without any recognition that they might run counter to an equality of outcome discourse.

These stereotypes not only posit a view of girls as compliant, but posit a counterbalancing view of boys as confidently immature, disruptive and disinclined towards writing. A simple tally of comments made about boys and girls, respectively, revealed fifty-four positive comments made about girls, compared with twenty-two negative comments, and thirty-two positive comments made about boys, compared with fifty-four negative comments. Teachers give voice to a deficit model of male achievement. Boys are principally seen in terms of the things they cannot, will not and do not do. Girls are seen in terms of the things they have achieved and in terms of compliant behaviour. This compliance is spoken of in both positive and negative terms; girls are seen as quieter and more sensible, but as needing more prompting and encouraging.

This polarizing of boys and girls as troublesome boys and compliant girls is reinforced by teachers' comments about behaviour. The most frequent statements were negative comments about boys' behaviour, and the next most common were positive comments about girls' behaviour. Gender difference is observed mostly in terms of behaviour, rather than in terms of achievement, which may well be why, in spite of these comments, 80 per cent of these teachers believed that boys and girls should get the same results. The language relating to girls' behaviour is passive and concerned with compliance; they are 'wanting to please' and 'willing'. Girls are pictured as fitting into the classroom

■ Table 16.2 Teachers' comments about the achievement and behaviour of boys

Positive statements about boys	Negative statements about boys
Achievement	
Boys are good at analytical writing[1]	Boys have poor handwriting and presentation[2]
Boys are better at mathematics[1]	Boys are not keen readers[2]
Boys have better oral skills[1]	Boys do not like writing[1]
Boys have a better general knowledge	Boys are more likely to have special educational needs[1]
Boys are better at construction	Boys like to say they aren't keen readers
Boys are good at investigations	Boys are often struggling readers
Boys can write good poetry	Boys are more likely to underachieve
When you capture their imagination, boys can be keen	Boys are more likely to be disaffected with literacy
Boys in my class will get As	Boys let other things interfere with school work
Boys may write less but it is more incisive	
Boys think more about content than presentation	
Behaviour	
Boys are confident[1]	Boys cannot sit still[1]
Boys ask questions	Boys are disruptive[1]
Boys are leaders	Boys need guidance[1]
Boys are physical	Boys need clear instructions[1]
Boys need challenging	Boys need pushing[1]
Boys are more together and aware	Boys are immature[1]
Boys are into everything	Boys can make a class more difficult[1]
Boys have a sense of humour	Boys are scruffy[1]
Boys have a wider perspective	Boys have weaker concentration skills
Boys are more spontaneous	Boys are less able to work independently
Boys are more enthusiastic	Boys are noisier
Boys are more inquisitive	Boys can be aggressive
Boys will experiment	Boys are more physical
	Boys are not so keen to please
	Boys are too single minded
	Boys do not take on the school ethos
	Boys do not take education seriously
	Boys do not talk about their feelings
	Boys do not like to be seen to be keen
	Boys are lazy
	Boys have lower aspirations
	Boys have lower self-esteem
	Boys only compete if they can win
	Boys are less tolerant

1 Comments made by more than one respondent.
2 Comments made by more than four respondents.
3 Comments made by more than eight respondents.

■ **Table 16.3** Teacher's comments about the achievement and behaviour of girls

Positive statements about girls	Negative statements about girls
Achievement	
Girls are better writers[3]	Girls need a bit more prompting
Girls are more expressive[2]	Girls rely too much on presentation
Girls read more[2]	Girls say 'I don't know what to do'
Girls are neat[2]	Girls tend to waffle
Girls are more likely to do homework[1]	
Girls like writing	
Girls are better at spelling and grammar	
Girls have better English skills	
Girls are quicker to grasp the learning objective	
Girls get better marks	
Behaviour	
Girls settle and get on with it[2]	Girls are less inclined to take risks[1]
Girls want to please[1]	Girls allow boys to dominate[1]
Girls have a stronger work ethic[1]	Girls take a back seat [1]
Girls are more thoughtful[1]	Girls get upset easily
Girls are more keen and enthusiastic	Girls chat a lot
Girls are easier to motivate	Girls change friends a lot
Girls apply themselves	Girls can be more hurtful
Girls are quieter	Girls can be fearful of new things
Girls are more efficient	Girls are more conventional
Girls are smarter (dress)	Girls can have more social and relational problems
Girls are more sensible	Girls are better one to one than in groups
Girls are more willing	Girls hang on to grievances
Girls are concerned about friendships	Girls are more passive
Girls talk yet keep on task	Girls can be sullen
Girls are more aware	
Girls are more 'together' socially	
Girls have gained in confidence, they are now more feisty	
Girls join in	
Girls put up with more	

1 Comments made by more than one respondent.
2 Comments made by more than four respondents.
3 Comments made by more than eight respondents.

environment as they choose to 'play the classroom game'. Conversely, the language relating to boys' behaviour is active: they are 'outgoing', 'needing a challenge' or 'disruptive'.

Teachers' responses to the request to consider whether there was such a thing as a typical boy or a typical girl, and if so, whether the focus children could be viewed as such, underlines further the construction of an inherent relationship between gender and achievement. Although a small minority of teachers were resistant to the notion of gender typicality, the dominant response was to suggest that the high-achieving girl is a typical girl, and the underachieving boy is a typical boy. The high-achieving boys are the only group viewed by the majority of those who commented as atypical of their gender.

While some teachers did not refer to the focus children as either typical or atypical, many made statements about their general perceptions of typical boys and girls. Teacher B comments that:

> Jack is an atypical boy, because he's actually very keen to work, he's very keen to produce, he certainly doesn't under-achieve, he's a leader at a table rather than a follower which boys tend to be, but he doesn't usually engage in silliness.

Teacher X views Greg as atypical because 'he's different in the way he behaves, in that he's very articulate, very well spoken'. Similarly, Teacher T does not see Andrew as typical, because 'he's more articulate . . . he has good manners and that's quite unusual for a boy of his age and he has respect for authority and he has a work ethic'. Teacher P's comment, 'the heavy weight of boys in the class makes a difference, but there are quite a few bright boys. I could have chosen three or four for you, and they're all "real boys" that are into everything', presents a picture of boys in which being bright and being a 'real boy' are somehow incompatible. Teacher U suggests that Justin, a high achiever, is a typical boy; not because he is bright, but because 'he can be silly'. By contrast, under-achieving boys in general were viewed as typical boys. Teacher K spoke of boys as physical and therefore as badly suited to the classroom, where concentration and application are required: 'And therefore I think that Craig [the underachiever] is fairly typical and Darren [the high achiever] is not very typical'.

Comments about high-achieving girls tended to say that they were typical. Teacher F describes Megan as a typical girl because she is sensible, adding 'The girls are, it's really down to behaviour, the girls, I'm sorry to say are more sensible'. Teacher E describes Ellie as 'the typical good girl'. Teacher A describes Alice as typical of bright girls because she is not very forthcoming and needs prompting. From these statements, a picture emerges of the able girl who is hard-working, diligent, quiet, reliable and an unchallenging member of the class. Some of the high-achieving girls are represented as girls who take academic compliance to the limit; for example, teacher X describes Natasha as 'a girl who does more than is required'. None of the boys was described in this way, but teachers occasionally saw their high-achieving girls as being too hard on themselves. Teacher W describes Olivia as a perfectionist who 'sometimes pushes herself too far'. Teacher V speaks of girls in her class that are 'overachieving'. Girls, it seems, are more likely to feel the strain. Perhaps there is still a lingering suggestion that, whereas boys might aspire to effortless achievement, girls' achievements come through diligence and at a cost to themselves.

Teachers, then, reveal a contradictory set of attitudes and assumptions: they speak of boys and girls having equal academic potential, yet give voice to a deficit model of male achievement, whereby expectations informed by pupils' gender are seen to disadvantage boys. The underachieving boy appears to be viewed as the norm for boys, while the high-achieving girl is the norm for girls. The representation of boys as active rather than passive, and as challenging rather than accepting, is seen to contribute to their underachievement. It is possible, however, to imagine that precisely the same set of characteristics – being active, challenging and questioning – could equally well be offered as an explanation for why boys do well, while being passive and accepting could be offered as explanation for why girls underachieve. Just as assumed gender characteristics may not describe nor account for the behaviour of all boys and all girls, it is also the case that these character-istics may not inevitably lead to given patterns of educational performance. The teachers' perceptions, while contradictory, use the language of gender to provide explanations for underachievement.

The classroom observation data, however, do not support either the notion of girls' compliance or of boys' active engagement: instead, the data highlight how participation in the classroom is more strongly linked to achievement levels than to gender. A fuller report of the observation data is given in Myhill (2002), but it is worth drawing attention here to the discrepancy between teachers' perceptions of boys' poor behaviour and girls' compliance, and what the observation data revealed. One element of the observation schedule recorded the degree of task attention displayed by the four focus pupils. A low rank (1) means on-task or working independently, and a high rank (4) means off-task or not working. These ranks were totalled to give a score for each group; thus the higher the score, the greater the incidence of being off-task or not working.

Table 16.4 presents the ranked involvement of the four groups. In general, as with all the classroom observation data, the significant differences are between achievement groups, with relatively smaller differences between gender groups. Underachievers are more likely to be off-task than high achievers, in both whole class activities and when working independently or in a group. The high-achieving girl stands out as being the least likely to be off-task. Across all year groups, high achievers worked more independently than underachievers, and there was little evidence of a gender difference.

Another element of the classroom observation recorded how often each of the focus children was invited to answer a question. As each lesson included some thirty children, no child was invited to respond very often, on average less than twice in a lesson. What does emerge from this observation, however, is that the underachieving girl is consistently

Table 16.4 The ranked involvement of the four groups

	High-achieving girl	High-achieving boy	Under-achieving girl	Under-achieving boy
Off-task rate (whole class)	104	112	145	162
Off-task rate (working at a task or activity)	37	90	125	132
Working independently	120	139	165	182

The statistical significance of the data was tested using a univariate analysis of variance against the two variables of gender and achievement. For all figures quoted, statistical significance with $p < 0.001$ was found for the influence of achievement.

less likely, or the least likely, to be invited to answer a question, and the underachieving boy is consistently more likely, or the most likely, to be invited to respond. Myhill (2002), reporting on this, observes a significant change in the behaviour of the high-achieving boy such that, up to Year 5, he is the most responsive and the most likely to volunteer, but becomes the most reluctant participant by Year 8. By Year 8, it is also the case that the teacher becomes increasingly less likely to invite the high-achieving boy to answer a question. The high-achieving boy has stopped putting up his hand, and the teacher has stopped inviting him to participate. Teachers may not feel the same need to draw in high-achieving boys as a disciplinary strategy, as they feel for underachieving boys. If patterns of inclusion are informed either by the engagement levels of the child or by the teachers' need to keep children on task, it may be that the underachieving girl is overlooked, both because she is less engaged and because the teacher feels less need to include girls as a disciplinary strategy.

Viewing the observation data across the three phases, the groups whose patterns of behaviour and participation were the most consistent were the high-achieving girl and the underachieving boy, being consistently the most and the least engaged, respectively. Conversely, the high-achieving boy and the underachieving girl revealed patterns of behaviour that changed across the three phases, with both groups becoming less engaged as they got older. There is some support here for the teachers' perceptions of boys as more troublesome and girls as more compliant; however, these perceptions appear to be shaped, not by the behaviour of boys and girls in general, but by the behaviour of the underachieving boy and the high-achieving girl.

DISCUSSION

The responses given by teachers in their interviews suggest that perceptions shaped by constructions of gender are confirming and reinforcing the conceptualization of underachievement as an issue about boys. Teachers articulate a deficit model of male achievement: boys are more likely to be chosen as underachievers (Jones, 2003), and the underachieving boy is more likely to be viewed as a typical boy than the high-achieving boy. Correspondingly, the high-achieving boy is often viewed as atypical. The high-achieving girl and the underachieving boy, both viewed as typical of their gender, are described as conforming to gender norms. It might be argued that the underachieving boy is seen as an underachiever, in part, because he is a boy, and the high-achieving girl is seen as a high achiever, in part, because she is a girl.

The evidence from the observation data, however, suggests that achievement levels are a more significant predictor of behaviour and interaction in the classroom than gender. While persistent, sometimes quiet, disengagement might be the most common character-istic of underachievers (Jones, 2003), this is not to deny the huge variety of behaviours, personalities and attitudes that made up both groups of underachievers. Arguably, the most homogeneous group across all three phases was the high-achieving girl, whose perceived characteristics have influenced teachers' perceptions of *all* girls.

Of the four groups, the two groups whose identity stands out as being the most clearly defined in the minds of the teacher are the high-achieving girl and the underachieving boy. Talking to teachers about how and why they had selected the children for inclusion in Project JUDE, several teachers commented that they had trouble finding underachieving girls, and in the first schools some had said that they had no really high-achieving boys in their class. Thus, the two groups who were observed to display the most consistent pattern of behaviour and interaction across the three phases (the high-achieving girl and the underachieving boy) were also the groups who were perceived to be most typical of their gender. The two focus groups whose pattern of behaviour and interaction shows the most fluctuation over the three phases were the high-achieving boy, who is perceived as an atypical boy, and the underachieving girl, whose identity is the least distinct of the four focus groups.

Both the high-achieving boy and the underachieving girl could be said to challenge gender norms. Indeed, it is the high-achieving boy within Years 9 and 10 who is most likely to articulate a challenge to the stereotypical masculine gender identity and speak of himself as somehow bucking the trend (Jones, 2003). This compares with evidence from Year 8 that reveals the high-achieving boy as becoming increasingly disengaged and less likely to be involved in the classroom (Myhill, 2002). Martino (1999) identifies a group of middle-class, able boys who speak of the need to 'act dumb' in order to preserve an appropriate masculine identity. In our sample, by Year 8, the high-achieving boy more closely resembles the underachieving boy in observable behaviour traits than he does the high-achieving girl, with whom he had previously had most in common. It is possible to interpret this as a picture of change whereby the high-achieving boy negotiates his male identity, moving from enthusiastic engagement, to self-conscious and deliberate disengagement, to an increased tendency to challenge gender norms and the impact they might have upon him. Jackson and Salisbury (1996) speak of boys who struggle and resist in the process of becoming masculine, arguing that boys are not merely passive victims of gender socialization. By contrast to the high-achieving boy, the pattern of interaction for the under-achieving boy shows a more constant picture of lower engagement across the three phases than is true for the other three groups. It may be that the underachieving boy is less likely to resist the pressures of gender socialization than the high-achieving boy.

The underachieving girl moves from being engaged in Year 1 to being increasingly less engaged by the end of the middle school, and often disruptively disengaged by the secondary school, and yet the behaviour of girls is rarely referred to by teachers as an issue. The changing identity of the underachieving girl was noted in the field notes of the researchers. The increasing numbers of stroppy, uncooperative, monosyllabic respondents among the underachieving girls in the high school was a point of discussion in research team meetings. It would have been hard to describe several of the girl underachievers as passive and accepting; indeed, their resistance to school values and expectations was acutely expressed. Catherine (Year 4) had no desire to be clever because 'you have to do harder work if you're clever'; and Carla in Year 8, when asked what she liked to write about, subvocalized her resistance by saying she would like to write about 'headmasters getting killed'. Cherie (Year 8) is no compliant girl, already explicitly conscious of her choices regarding behaviour: 'If I don't like a teacher, I won't behave for them', while Janice (Year 9) complains 'I'd still get bad marks because at the start of term I wasn't good and didn't just sit there being quiet.' All of these girls were closer to the picture that teachers painted of underachieving boys, being in varying degrees confrontational, disruptive and challenging of the school ethos. Recognition that such a group of girls existed was more likely to come from the children than from the teachers. Several pupils commented on how girls' behaviour had changed as they got older, and how the poor behaviour of girls went unnoticed by teachers. Teachers, in contrast, have little to say about underachieving girls – the cause of their underachievement is principally seen as caused by lack of confidence, and little is said about poor behaviour or a disaffected atti-tude. Stereotypical gender identities persist, in spite of individuals who clearly do not conform to gender expectations. Teachers have formed a strong set of concepts and opinions in relation to the underachieving boy. The underachieving girl, however, is less clearly defined.

CONCLUSION

Underachieving boys may be different from underachieving girls principally because teachers perceive them to be so. Not only do teachers see boy underachievers as being different from girl underachievers, but much of what they describe as typical boy behaviour has also become the epitome of underachieving behaviour. Teachers know what underachievement looks like; it looks like a boy who is bright, but bored. Girls, by contrast, are not bored: they are keen and hardworking; they will succeed without any special strategies; they will knuckle down and make the best of all school experiences because they make the effort. Underachieving boys have been the focus of attention in the underachievement debate so persistently and for so long that they have taken on an identity, a set of teaching strategies and a whole branch of research all to themselves. By contrast, the underachieving girl remains a shadowy, vague figure, almost invisible. Yet when the focus of attention includes the underachieving girl as well as the underachieving boy, they are not essentially that dissimilar. Both groups of underachievers include those who disengage persistently, possibly quietly, and those who are loud, disruptive and attention-seeking: underachievers often have more in common with each other than with those with whom they share a gender. The teachers' perceptions suggest that their constructions of gender identity are heavily influenced by the two 'norms' of the underachieving boy and the high-achieving girl, and this may influence their expectations of boys' and girls' achievement, in spite of espoused beliefs in equality of outcome. The apparent tendency to associate *all* boys with underachievement and *all* girls with high achievement does little service to the complex needs of individuals, not least the troublesome girls and the compliant boys.

REFERENCES

Arnot, M. and Gubb, J. (2001) *Adding value to boys' and girls' education: a gender and achievement project in West Sussex, Crawley*, Crawley: West Sussex County Council.

Bousted, M. (1989) 'Who talks?', *English in Education,* Vol. 23, No. 3: 41–51.

Collins, C., Kenway, J. and Mcleod, J. (2000) *Factors influencing the educational performance of males and females in school and their initial destinations after leaving school*, Canberra: Department of Education, Training and Youth Affairs, Canberra, AGPS.

DfES (2003) *Aiming high: raising the achievement of minority ethnic pupil*, London: DfES.

Dweck, C., Davidson, W., Nelson, S. and Enna, B. (1978) 'Sex differences and learned helplessness', *Journal of Personality and Social Psychology,* Vol. 36: 457–462.

Floud, J.H., Halsey, A.H. and Martin, F.M. (1957) *Social class and educational opportunity*, London: Heinemann.

Gillborn, D. and Mirza, H.S. (2000) *Educational inequality. Mapping race, class and gender*, London, Ofsted; available online at www.ofsted.gov.uk.

Gorman, T., White, J., Brooks, G., Maclure, M. and Kispal, A. (1988) *Language performance in schools: review of APU language monitoring 1979–1983*, London: HMSO.

Griffin, C. (1982) *Typical girls?*, London: Routledge.

Halsey, A.H., Heath, A.F. and Ridge, J.M. (1980) *Origins and destinations*, London: Clarendon.

Hannan, G. (1996) *Improving boys' performance – INSET materials*, Much Welcome, private publication.

Jackson, D. and Salisbury, J. (1996) 'Why should secondary schools take working with boys seriously?', *Gender and Education,* Vol. 8, No. 1: 103–115.

Jones, S. (2003) 'How does the underachieving boy differ, if at all, from the underachieving girl?'. Unpublished Ph.D. thesis, Exeter University.

Leder, G. (1980) 'Bright girls, mathematics and fear of success', *Education Studies in Mathematics,* Vol. 11, No. 4: 411–422.

Mac an Ghaill, M. (1994) *The making of men: masculinities, sexualities and schooling,* Buckingham: Open University Press.

Martino, W. (1999) ' "Cool boys", "party animals", "squids" and "poofters": interrogating the dynamics and politics of adolescent masculinities in school', *British Journal of Sociology of Education,* Vol. 20, No. 2: 239–263.

Millard, E. (1997) *Differently literate: boys, girls and the schooling of literacy,* London: Falmer.

Myhill, D.A. (2002) 'Bad boys and good girls? Patterns of interaction and response in whole class teaching', *British Educational Research Journal,* Vol. 28, No. 3: 339–352.

Ofsted (2003a) *Yes he can – schools where boys write well,* London: Ofsted (HMI 505).

Ofsted (2003b) *Boys' achievement in secondary schools,* London: Ofsted (HMI).

Osler, A., Street, C., Lall, M. and Vincent, K. (2002) *Not a problem? Girls and school exclusion,* London: Joseph Rowntree Foundation.

Osmont, P. and Davies, J. (1987) *Stop, look and listen: an account of girls' and boys' achievement in reading and maths in the primary school,* London: ILEA.

Platten, J. (1999) 'Raising boys' achievement', *Curriculum,* Vol. 20, No. 1: 2–6.

Plummer, G. (2000) *Failing working class girls,* Stoke-on-Trent: Trentham.

Reay, D. (1999) 'Sugar and spice and all things nice? Gender discourses and girls' cultures in the primary classroom'. Paper presented at *Voices in Gender and Education Conference,* University of Warwick.

Swann, J. and Graddol, D. (1988) 'Gender inequalities in classroom talk', *English in Education,* Vol. 22, No. 1: 48–65.

Walkerdine, V. (1989) *Counting girls out,* London: Virago.

Weinar, B. (1971) *Perceiving the causes of success and failure,* New York: General Learning Press.

Weiner, G. (1985) *Just a bunch of girls,* Milton Keynes: Open University Press.

IT'S NOT WHICH SCHOOL BUT WHICH SET YOU'RE IN THAT MATTERS

The influence of ability grouping practices on student progress in mathematics

Dylan Wiliam and
Hannah Bartholomew

A NOTE FROM THE EDITORS

This reading compared the performances of pupils in different sets in schools that favour whole-class teaching with schools that adopt small-group and individualised teaching.

This reading links with Units 4.1, 6.1 and 6.2 of the 5th edition of *Learning to teach in the secondary school*.

QUESTIONS TO CONSIDER

Are schools overly concerned with squeezing pupils into convenient boxes for teaching, such as 'well behaved' or 'highly motivated' or 'level of achievement', in the belief that this strategy makes for more effective and efficient education and makes teaching easier?

1   Does this process lead to framing teacher expectations of how pupils, or groups of pupils, respond to teaching and how teachers teach?

2   Does this process mean that later pupil achievement is then determined by the way in which they are placed in groups at the earlier stage?

3   Many teachers have particular styles of teaching and favour particular strategies with which they are comfortable. If this is true, can teachers be helped to work outside their comfort zone and adopt a flexible approach to meet the needs of individual pupils; that is, can teachers take on board personalized learning without further professional development?

This reading was first published as: Wiliam, D. and Bartholomew, H. (2004) 'It's not which school but which set you're in that matters: the influence of ability grouping practices on student progress in mathematics', *British Educational Research Journal*, Vol. 30: 279–293.

ABSTRACT

The mathematics achievement of a cohort of 955 students in 42 classes in six schools in London was followed over a 4-year period, until they took their General Certificate of Secondary Education examinations (GCSEs) in the summer of 2000. All six schools were regarded by the Office for Standards in Education (Ofsted) as providing a good standard of education, and all were involved in teacher training partnerships with universities. Matched data on Key Stage 3 test scores and GCSE grades were available for 709 students, and these data were analysed in terms of the progress from Key Stage 3 test scores to GCSE grades. Although there were wide differences between schools in terms of overall GCSE grades, the average progress made by students was similar in all six schools. However, within each school, the progress made during Key Stage 4 varied greatly from set to set. Comparing students with the same Key Stage 3 scores, students placed in top sets averaged nearly half a GCSE grade higher than those in the other upper sets, who in turn averaged a third of a grade higher than those in lower sets, who in turn averaged around a third of a grade higher than those students placed in bottom sets. In the four schools that used formal whole-class teaching, the difference in GCSE grades between top and bottom sets, taking Key Stage 3 scores into account, ranged from just over one grade at GCSE to nearly three grades. At the schools using small-group and individualized teaching, the differences in value-added between sets were not significant. In two of the schools, a significant proportion of working-class students were placed into lower sets than would be indicated by their Key Stage 3 test scores.

BACKGROUND

Reforming education is, as many politicians have discovered, a tricky business. Because the day-to-day practice of a teacher is so intimately linked to the teacher's personality, many aspects of teachers' practice are difficult to change. Furthermore, because what teachers actually do in classrooms is so weakly theorized, attempts at reform have tended to concentrate on administrative aspects of practice, such as the number of episodes into which an hour's instruction ought to be segmented, rather than addressing what, exactly, should be happening in each episode. It is hardly surprising, therefore, that the issue of how cohorts of students should be organized in schools has been hotly debated for many years, and has been a key 'policy lever' that politicians have tried to use to change practice.

The physical arrangement of most schools dictates that students need to be organized into groups of between twenty-five and forty – most of the rooms in schools are not big enough to take more than forty students, and there are not enough rooms to have much fewer than twenty-five in each group. In very small schools (i.e. where there are fewer than twenty students in each year-group), constraints of funding require that students are taught in mixed-age groups (i.e. a group in which the difference in age between the youngest and oldest students is, by design rather than owing to retention or acceleration of individual students, more than one year). However, where resourcing is sufficient to provide one teacher per year-group, this almost invariably results in one class per year-group. Although the range of achievement in a mixed-age class is often not much more than in a single-age cohort (Wiliam, 1992), there appears to be a great reluctance in schools in the UK to adopt mixed-age classes unless absolutely necessary.

In this context it is important to note that, unlike many other countries, schools in the UK have made little, if any, use of grade retention (i.e. requiring students to repeat a year of schooling until they have attained the necessary level of achievement for promotion to the next year). Data from the Third International Mathematics and Science Study (TIMSS) (Beaton *et al.* 1996a, b) suggest that less than 1 per cent of students in England are taught 'out of age', while approximately 25 per cent of students in France and Germany have had to repeat at least one year before the age of 14. The use of grade retention (and acceleration) is intended to reduce the range of achievement in a year-cohort, and, where such strategies are not used, other ways of dealing with the range in student achievement are often felt to be necessary (although whether they are, of course, is another matter).

Because of the reluctance to create mixed-age classes, UK schools with one or two teachers per age cohort have tended to focus on within-class grouping, while, in schools with larger cohorts, between-class grouping has been more important. Since the primary aim has been to reduce the range of attainment in a class, because it is believed that this makes teaching easier, both within-class and between-class grouping strategies have focused on grouping students on the basis of assumptions about ability, achievement, attainment or, in some cases, motivation. Such grouping systems are usually referred to by schools as 'grouping by ability' or 'ability grouping', even though what is meant by ability (and in particular whether this is some fixed notion of ability, or just what a student is able to do at a particular time) is rarely made clear. For the remainder of this article, we will continue to refer to 'ability grouping' and 'mixed-ability' classes simply because that is how schools describe the practice, and this provides a convenient label. However, we would wish to make it plain that we believe that such notions of ability are not in any way well founded and are of dubious validity as predictors of potential.

The advantages and disadvantages of grouping students by ability in schools have been debated for many years. For the first half of the last century, the idea of 'streaming' children – allocating them to teaching groups according to some measure of general ability (usually 'intelligence' tests) – was so natural as to be unremarkable. Almost all secondary schools arranged students into 'streams', so that a student would be taught in the same 'stream' for most or all of their subjects, and many of the larger primary schools did the same. Beginning in the 1960s, however, associated with the interest in child-centred education, there was increasing concern about the effects of streaming in primary schools

(Jackson, 1964), and the use of between-class ability grouping declined in primary schools during the 1970s and 1980s.

In secondary schools, while streaming may have reduced the range of achievement within a teaching group, the range of achievement was still very wide, and, in most secondary schools, subject-specific ability grouping or 'setting' was superimposed on streaming, especially in mathematics and modern languages.

In the 1960s and 1970s, a number of reports highlighted the problems of disaffection from school experienced by students in lower streams in secondary schools (e.g. Hargreaves, 1967; Lacey, 1970), and the Banbury inquiry found little evidence that streaming improved academic achievement (Newbold, 1977; Postlethwaite and Denton, 1978). The result was a general move away from between-class grouping of students on the basis of general ability. However, as streaming was abandoned, between-class grouping of students by ability for particular subjects, particularly mathematics and modern foreign languages, was retained, and although precise figures are impossible to establish, it seems likely that the proportion of secondary schools grouping students by ability for at least one subject (usually mathematics) has never dropped below 90 per cent.

More recently, government pronouncements have proposed that 'setting should be the norm in secondary schools' (Department for Education and Employment, 1997: 38), and increasing numbers of primary schools are also making use of between-class ability grouping because they believe that this will help improve scores on National Curriculum tests (Office for Standards in Education (Ofsted), 1998).

Reviews of research on the effects of ability grouping (Hallam and Toutounji, 1996; Harlen and Malcolm, 1997; Sukhnandan and Lee, 1998) have found little evidence that between-class ability grouping does, in fact, increase attainment. However, many studies have found aptitude–treatment interactions in the effects of ability grouping – in other words, that the effects of ability grouping are not the same for all students. For example, several studies have found that the use of between-class ability grouping increases the achievement of the highest attainers, at the expense of lower attainers, particularly in mathematics (e.g. Hoffer, 1992; Kerckhoff, 1986; Linchevski and Kutscher, 1998), and Boaler (1997) found a third-order effect in that girls were disadvantaged by placement in top sets.

In the most comprehensive study of between-class ability-grouping conducted in the UK in recent years, Ireson and Hallam (Ireson and Hallam, 2001; Ireson, et al., 2002) have investigated the impact of ability-grouping on attainment in English, mathematics and science in forty-five secondary schools in the UK. They found that the amount of setting experienced by students in Key Stage 3 (that is, how many years they were taught in setted, as opposed to mixed-ability, groups) improved performance slightly in mathematics, but not in science. However, in Key Stage 4, they found that the amount of setting experienced had no impact in mathematics or English, but had a slight positive impact on achievement in science. Across both key stages combined, the amount of setting experienced by students had no overall impact in any subject, but Ireson and Hallam did find that set placement (i.e. high, middle or low sets) influenced progress, both in Key Stage 3 and in Key Stage 4. For example, compared with students in middle groups, students in low groups achieved on average approximately one quarter of a grade less, and students in high sets achieved one quarter of a grade more in General Certificate of Secondary Education (GCSE) examinations.

The fragility of these effects suggests that between-class ability grouping cannot be understood as a simple phenomenon with predictable results. Rather, the practices of ability grouping are likely to vary from school to school, and if we are to understand how ability grouping impacts on attainment and influences attitudes, it is necessary to look in detail at how setting is put into practice in schools.

THE SAMPLE

Between 1996 and 2000, we followed a cohort of 955 students, in six secondary schools in the Greater London area, as they moved from Year 8 in 1996–97 to Year 11 in 1999–2000. All the students in the six schools were taught mathematics in mixed-ability groups in Year 7, but by Year 11, all the students were being taught in subject-specific ability groups or 'sets'. The six schools were chosen to provide a range of learning environments and contexts. During the period of data collection, each of the schools was inspected by the Office of Her Majesty's Chief Inspector of Schools (Ofsted), and each was regarded as providing a satisfactory or good standard of education; in addition, all were partner schools with higher education institutions for initial teacher training. The schools were located in five different local education authorities. Some of the school populations were mainly white, others mainly Asian, while others included students from a wide range of ethnic and cultural backgrounds. Table 17.1 provides information about the cohort of students followed, including the GCSE results, the number of students starting Year 10, the number for whom Key Stage 3 scores were available, and the number in each school actually taking GCSE, together with a brief description of the intake (note that percentages have been rounded to prevent identification of schools).

We collected data on the entire cohort of students via questionnaires administered in Years 8–11, conducted interviews with over 100 students, individually and in pairs, conducted over 150 lesson observations, and collected data on performance in the National Curriculum tests at the end of Year 9, and on the GCSE examinations at the end of Year 11.

In an earlier article (Boaler et al., 2000a), we showed that teachers changed their style of teaching when faced with classes of students who had been grouped by ability. In contrast to what had been found by Bennett et al. (1984) for within-class grouping in primary schools, we found that teachers overestimated the capability of students in the top set, giving them work that was often too demanding, and expecting them to be able to do it quickly, while they underestimated the capability of those in the bottom set. Subsequent articles have described the ways in which setting serves to structure and constrain opportunities for students (Bartholomew, 1999, 2000, 2001). In this article we report specifically on the impact of setting arrangements on the progress of students between Key Stage 3 and GCSE, and draw out implications for current government policy on ability grouping in schools.

From Table 17.1, it can be seen that the proportion of students enrolled at the beginning of Year 10 who take GCSE at the school varies from well over 90 per cent (153 out of 165) at Alder school to under two thirds (112 out of 176) at Cedar. Although some of this appears to be the result of 'drop-out' (i.e. students who leave and do not go on to take GCSE elsewhere), our discussions with staff at the schools lead us to conclude that the majority of cases are the result of 'turnover' (that is, students leaving for other schools). However, it has not been possible to trace these students. For the purpose of this article, the data consist of the 709 students who took both the Key Stage 3 tests and their GCSE examinations in the same school.

Of course, we cannot assume that the missing data are representative of the data that are present. In fact, those without Key Stage 3 scores average nearly a whole grade lower

■ **Table 17.1** Details of the schools involved in the study

School	Name	Type	Percent 5 A*-C	Starting Y10	KS3 score?	Taking GCSE	Description of intake
A	Alder	Mixed	45	165	163	153	Mainly white, middle and working class
B	Cedar	Girls	30	176	143	112	Mainly Asian and working class
C	Firtree	Mixed	65	183	167	167	Mainly white and middle class
D	Hazel	Mixed	35	168	161	142	Ethnically diverse, middle and working class
E	Redwood	Mixed	20	153	107	116	Ethnically diverse, mainly working class
F	Willow	Mixed	45	110	104	89	Mainly Asian and African-Caribbean, Middle and working class
Totals				955	845	779	

Note: In an earlier article (Boaler *et al.* 2000a) the schools were referred to by letter (A–F). Here, consistent with other related articles (e.g. Boaler *et al.*, 2000b), pseudonyms are used.

at GCSE than those for whom Key Stage 3 scores are available, and those who did not take GCSE at the six schools scored just over half a level lower at Key Stage 3 than those who did take GCSE at the six schools. This suggests that the students excluded from this analysis are significantly different from the students included, and so some caution must be exercised when interpreting the results. However, since the main thrust of this article is the relationship *between* Key Stage 3 scores and GCSE grades in different sets, the missing data are likely to reduce the numbers in the lower sets, but this is not likely to have a significant impact on the relationship between Key Stage 3 scores and GCSE grades within those sets.

RESULTS AT KEY STAGE 3

In order to be able to compare the results of the six schools, and in order to compare the performance of students within the same school when they took different tiers of the Key Stage 3 mathematics tests, the tiers of the mathematics tests were equated using the level thresholds published by the Qualifications and Curriculum Authority. This allowed all students to be placed on a single mark scale, from 0 to 150. The results of the six schools are shown in Figure 17.1.[1]

As can be seen, the results of four of the schools are broadly comparable, with Cedar's scores significantly lower, and those at Firtree significantly higher (the shaded areas around the median in each of the box and whisker plots in Figure 17.1 represent 95 per cent confidence intervals for pairs of plots, so that if the shaded regions do not overlap, the two medians are significantly different). Analysis of variance revealed no statistically significant gender differences in Key Stage 3 scores at any of the schools, although the girls at Redwood did average 12 marks (approximately half a level) higher than the boys, which was close to statistical significance ($p = 0.06$).

We collected data on parental occupation from each student during the administration of the questionnaires while the students were in year 9.[2] These were coded using the 7-point Office of Population Censuses and Surveys classification, and for the purpose of analysis reported here, these codes were further condensed to a simple dichotomy (i.e. middle class/working class).

In four of the six schools, there was no significant difference between the scores of students from working-class and middle-class backgrounds. At Hazel School, middle-class students outscored working-class students by 7 marks, but at Alder school, working-class students outscored middle-class students by 8 marks.

SETTING IN KEY STAGE 4

All six schools taught mathematics to mixed-ability groups when students were in Year 7 (age 11). One of the schools (Alder) allocated students to 'setted' ability groups for mathematics at the beginning of Year 8 (age 12), three others (Firtree, Redwood and Willow) 'set' the students at the beginning of Year 9 (age 13), and the other two schools set students at the beginning of Year 10.

Three of the schools, Alder, Redwood and Willow, operated 'traditional' setting arrangements, with the students being grouped into five (Redwood and Willow) or six (Alder) strictly hierarchical sets. At two schools (Cedar and Hazel), the age cohort was divided into roughly parallel blocks, with setting within each block (at Cedar, the two blocks were of unequal size, and were divided into three and four sets, respectively;

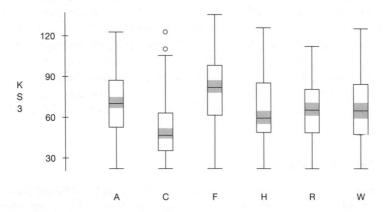

■ **Figure 17.1** Key Stage 3 results.

■ **Table 17.2** Allocation of students to sets

	Bottom	Lower	Upper	Top	Total
Alder	11	71	53	30	165
Cedar	21	50	51	54	176
Firtree	6	49	49	79	183
Hazel	21	81	28	38	168
Redwood	19	70	32	32	153
Willow	8	30	41	31	110
Total	86	351	254	264	955

at Hazel, each block was divided into five sets). At Firtree School, there were three parallel 'top' sets (so that over 40 per cent of the age cohort at Firtree school was nominally in a 'top set' in Year 10), two parallel set 2s, two parallel set 3s, and then a set 4 and a set 5. In Year 11 at Firtree, students in the three top sets were distributed into two top sets and a set 2 (so that the set 2s became set 3s and so on). Table 17.2 shows the distribution of students into the different sets at the six schools at the beginning of Year 10.

It is important to note that setting takes different forms in different schools. In most of the schools, setting was clearly based on some measure of attainment in mathematics. However, in Willow School, the sets described as sets 4 and 5 (out of 5) on the timetable were frequently referred to by teachers as the 'behaviour' group and the 'language' group, respectively. The strategy had apparently been, at one time, to concentrate students with challenging behaviour in one class, and those with language problems in another. However, many of the students with the most challenging behaviour had subsequently been permanently excluded from the school, with the result that the 'behaviour' group was a rather small group, with few challenging students. Similarly, while the 'language' group did have some students for whom English was not their mother tongue, there were also students who spoke only English, and when asked about the constitution of the group, the teacher said that he did not know the basis on which students had been allocated to his class.

In fact, in four of the schools (Cedar, Firtree, Hazel and Willow), we found that the nature of the setting arrangements was not transparent, so that students (and in some cases, teachers) were not aware of how one set related to the others. At Alder and, to a lesser extent, Hazel, sets were referred to by their rank, so that students knew that they were in, for example, set 4. The complexity of these arrangements and the fact that, in some schools, neither the teachers nor the students understood the basis of the grouping arrangements suggest that great caution is needed in drawing conclusions about what is going on in schools from what is reported as happening.

We found no significant differences in the Key Stage 3 scores of boys and girls in any set at any of the six schools (although see section on 'Gender and social class differences' below). However, by using set number as a *dependent* variable in a general linear model, with Key Stage 3 score and social class as *independent* variables, we did find evidence that working-class students were placed in lower sets than middle-class students with comparable Key Stage 3 scores at Alder and Firtree ($p = .03$ at Alder,

$p < 0.01$ at Firtree). This effect was particularly strong at Firtree school, where approximately half the working-class students were in a lower set than would be indicated by their Key Stage 3 scores.

Because of the complexity of the setting arrangements, the number of the set itself conveys little about the experience of the students. For example, set 3 at Cedar might be a bottom set (depending on which block it was in), while, at Alder, set 3 would be a middle set. Ireson and Hallam (2001) used a threefold classification of set into 'higher', 'middle' and 'lower'. However, given what we had learned about the particular circumstances operating in top and bottom sets, reported in Boaler *et al.* (2000a), we decided on a fourfold classification of set. The highest set (or sets if there were two parallel top sets) at each school was classified as 'top', and the lowest set at each school was classed as 'bottom'. The intervening sets were classified as either 'upper' and 'lower', and since lower sets tend to be smaller than upper sets, middle sets were classified as 'lower'. Thus, with five sets, set 2 would be classed as 'upper', and sets 3 and 4 would be classed as 'lower', while, for six sets, sets 2 and 3 would be classed as 'upper', and sets 4 and 5 would be classed as 'lower'.

GCSE RESULTS

The GCSE results obtained by the schools are shown in Table 17.3. As might be expected, there is a tendency for the schools with the highest Key Stage 3 scores to have better GCSE grades, although the distribution of grades is complex. For example, while Firtree has more than twice as many students achieving grades A and B as Alder, the proportion of students achieving at least a grade 'E' at the two schools is the same (86 per cent).

A scatterplot of the GCSE score (converted to a uniform mark scale to take into account the different tiers) against the Key Stage 3 score shows that the relationship is linear, although the distribution of both variables is slightly platykurtic (this plot is not included here owing to limitations of space). Plotting the relationship between Key Stage 3 scores and GCSE score separately for each school shows that the relationship between Key Stage 3 score and GCSE score is not the same at each school. The most successful school in terms of raw GCSE scores (Firtree) is actually no better than average in terms of value added from Key Stage 3 to Key Stage 4 (in fact, if anything, the value added here is worse than average, although this is not statistically significant).

Table 17.4 gives the relative value added (in terms of GCSE grades) for each of the six schools, from Key Stage 3 to GCSE, in comparison with the other five. As can be seen, for four of the six schools, the relative value added is not significantly different from zero, but in two of the schools, this difference is significant – at Cedar, students achieve on average 0.28 grades higher than would be expected given their Key Stage 3 scores and, at Redwood, are achieving 0.27 grades lower than would be expected. However, it is worth noting that these differences are actually quite small in terms of the achievement of the students. For example, at Redwood, students achieve on average slightly over one quarter of a grade lower than would be expected from their Key Stage 3 scores. This is equivalent to one student in four achieving one grade lower than expected in mathematics – a very small effect and almost negligible in comparison with the effect of prior attainment (i.e. Key Stage 3 score). Put another way, the progress made in mathematics in Key Stage 4 by a student at Redwood School is hardly any different from that made by a student at Firtree School, which is regarded as a highly successful school.

■ **Table 17.3** Reverse cumulative frequency of GCSE grades achieved (%)

	Entries	A*	A	B	C	D	E	F	G
Alder	153	0	7	21	46	71	86	97	99
Codar	112	1	4	10	25	45	65	83	96
Firtree	167	4	19	44	63	74	86	94	99
Hazel	142	2	9	25	45	65	85	95	100
Redwood	116	0	1	13	29	55	73	91	97
Willow	89	2	12	28	54	62	78	92	97

■ **Table 17.4** Relative value-added in terms of GCSE grades

School	Relative value-added	p-value
Alder	−0.12	0.06
Cedar	0.28	<0.01
Firtree	−0.09	0.18
Hazel	0.05	0.47
Redwood	−0.27	<0.01
Willow	0.15	0.07

THE EFFECTS OF SETTING

In order to investigate the effects of setting, the relationship between Key Stage 3 score and GCSE score was calculated separately for top, upper, lower and bottom sets in each school, and, where the relationship differed from set to set, this was tested for significance using analysis of covariance. The relationship across the six schools and for individual schools is shown in Table 17.5.

Overall, students in top sets achieve over half a grade (i.e. 0.58 grades) higher at GCSE than would be expected from their Key Stage 3 scores, while those in the bottom sets score just over half a grade (0.51 grades) lower than would be expected from their Key Stage 3 scores. Furthermore, in four of the six schools, these effects are absolutely consistent, with top sets doing better than upper sets, who in turn do better than lower sets, who do better than bottom sets. At Redwood, lower sets do slightly better than upper sets (although this is not significant) and at Cedar, the bottom sets do best of all.

Although the trend for higher sets to do better, even when prior attainment is taken into account, is consistent across five of the six schools, the size of the effect varies markedly. At Hazel School, being placed in the top set, rather than the bottom, would improve your GCSE score by about half a grade, while, at Redwood, the improvement would be just over three quarters of a grade. At Alder, it would be well over a grade, over two grades at Firtree, and nearly three grades at Willow. At Cedar, in contrast, it would actually make your GCSE grade worse! The differential performance by set explains some of the differences in overall GCSE performance found in Table 17.3 above.

■ **Table 17.5** Relative value-added in terms of GCSE grades by set

Set	Relative value-added (measured in GCSE grades)						
	Alder	Cedar	Firtree	Hazel	Redwood	Willow	Overall
Top	0.64	*0.05*	1.12	*0.22*	*0.44*	1.43	0.58
Upper	0.22(–)	*0.05*	0.34	*0.02*	*–0.17*	0.83	0.16(–)
Lower	–0.16	–0.37	–0.47	0.02	0.14	–0.72	–0.22
Bottom	–0.72	*0.27*	–0.99	–0.25	*–0.41*	–1.54	–0.51

1 Differences in italics are not significant ($p > 0.05$).

2 (–) indicates a significant interaction between Key Stage 3 score and set in favour of lower attainers.

3 Scheffe post hoc comparisons show that all the overall differences except those between lower sets and bottom sets are statistically significant ($p < 0.01$).

Of course, these comparisons are merely for illustration – given the extent of curricular differentiation that we found in our earlier article, a student moved from a bottom set to a top set would find that they had missed out a great deal of work, and would almost certainly struggle to catch up. But it does show that the set to which you are allocated – an allocation over which students have little, if any, influence at any of the six schools – makes a huge difference to how well you do, and much more of a difference than which school you go to.

What is, perhaps, most interesting is that the schools where these differences are least marked are Cedar and Hazel, which are both above average in terms of value added in Key Stage 4. These are schools that delayed the introduction of setting until the beginning of Year 10 and are the schools where teachers continued to make extensive use of small-group and individualized work in Key Stage 4. Echoing the results of our earlier article (Boaler *et al.*, 2000a), it appears that the most pernicious effects of setting may not be necessary consequences of grouping students by ability, but appear when teachers use traditional, teacher-directed, whole-class teaching.

GENDER AND SOCIAL CLASS DIFFERENCES

Overall, in the six schools, boys outperformed girls at both Key Stage 3 and at GCSE. At Key Stage 3, the boys outperformed the girls by nearly half a level (girls' average level: 4.56; boys' average level: 5.03) and by almost half a grade at GCSE (using the standard GCSE points scores, girls averaged 4.95 and boys 5.37). Because Key Stage 3 levels and GCSE grades are not measured on the same scale, we cannot compare them directly, but we can convert the differences between males and females to standardized effect sizes by dividing the difference between the scores of males and females by the (pooled) standard deviation of the scores (Willingham and Cole, 1997). This procedure yields a standardized difference of $d = 0.35$ in favour of boys at Key Stage 3 and of $d = 0.24$ at GCSE. Girls therefore do, in fact, 'close the gap' somewhat on boys during Key Stage 4. However, in looking at these data, it is important to bear in mind that the allocation of students to sets in the six schools is not representative. In particular, girls are underrepresented in the top, lower and bottom sets, and overrepresented in the upper sets. A general linear model of GCSE scores, with

Key Stage 3 scores and gender as independent variables, shows that, while the relationship between Key Stage 3 scores and GCSE scores is relatively similar for boys and girls in lower, upper and top sets, there is, in bottom sets, a considerable (and statistically significant) interaction between gender and Key Stage 3 score ($p < 0.01$). In fact, higher-attaining boys in bottom sets achieve up to a whole grade lower at GCSE than girls with similar Key Stage 3 scores. The effect of this is to depress the attainment of low-attaining boys even further.

Middle-class students outperformed working-class students by more than a whole grade at GCSE, but this effect is already mostly present at the end of Key Stage 3. Adding social class to the general linear model for GCSE scores showed that working-class students do make less progress in Key Stage 4 than middle-class students ($p < 0.01$), and the size of the effect (just under one tenth of a grade at GCSE) is consistent with it being caused by the overrepresentation of working-class students in lower sets referred to earlier.

DISCUSSION

The relationship between Key Stage 3 scores and GCSE grades will be subject to a number of influences. For example, while all schools are, presumably, trying to maximize their GCSE scores, the same may not be true at Key Stage 3 (although the recent imposition of targets for schools for achievement at Key Stage 3 as well as for GCSE may change this). The relationship between Key Stage 3 scores and GCSE scores may not, therefore, be a valid measure of comparison *between* schools, although of course, it will be a better measure *within* each of the six schools.

A more serious objection to the conclusion that set placement does affect progress in Key Stage 4 is that schools allocate students to sets on criteria other than just the Key Stage 3 test results (and, in this regard, it is certain that the overlap in Key Stage 3 scores between sets is substantial). The lower 'value added' in Key Stage 4 for lower sets may not be related to set placement at all, but could be because schools place students into particular sets based on notions of 'educability'. If teachers are indeed able to identify students who are capable of getting good GCSE grades despite a modest performance in the Key Stage 3 tests, then we would expect to find that the apparent value added during Key Stage 4 would be highest in the upper sets, and lower in the lower sets, which is what we found in most of the schools. However, if this is the reason for the effect, then we should expect Key Stage 3 scores to predict GCSE scores least well in schools where set placement makes most difference, because set placement is not being based on Key Stage 3 scores. In fact, we find the reverse: there is a modest (and of course, with only six schools, non-significant) but positive correlation of 0.29 between the proportion of variance in GCSE scores accounted for by Key Stage 3 scores and the size of the difference (in GCSE grades) that set placement makes. This, combined with our observations of the teaching in different sets reported in our earlier articles (Bartholomew, 2000, 2001; Boaler *et al.*, 2000a), leads us to believe that the effects we report are attributable to the process of setting and the kinds of teaching that result. In brief, teachers teaching bottom sets were generally the least well qualified to teach mathematics, had lower expectations of their students, frequently set work that was undemanding (often just copying off the chalkboard), used a narrower range of teaching approaches and hardly ever responded to students' frequent requests for more demanding work. In contrast, top sets tended to be allocated well-qualified teachers, who tended to go too fast for many students (particularly girls). Most importantly, teachers teaching setted classes tended to treat the whole class as being of identical 'ability' and made little or no provision for differentiation. The same teachers, when teaching mixed-ability classes, used a wider range of approaches, took greater account of individual differences and were, in our admittedly subjective view, better teachers, even though they disliked teaching mixed-ability groups.

The data reported here provide further evidence that ability grouping does not raise average levels of achievement and, if anything, tends to depress achievement slightly, which is entirely consistent with results from studies conducted in the 1960s and 1970s in the UK, and with the more recent studies conducted in the USA.

More importantly, this study replicates a key finding from earlier studies (e.g. Hoffer, 1992; Kerchkoff, 1986; Linchevski and Kutscher, 1998) that, while ability grouping in mathematics has little overall effect on achievement, it does produce gains in attainment for higher-achieving students at the expense of losses for lower-attaining students (see also Venkatakrishnan and Wiliam, 2003). This produces an increase in the spread of achievement within the age cohort. In this context, it is worth noting that every country that outperforms England in mathematics makes less use of ability grouping. Indeed, one of the key findings from international comparisons is that the greater the difference of achievement *between* classes of the same age, the worse that country's overall levels of achievement in mathematics are likely to be (Bursten, 1992) – again consistent with the pattern found here.

The research reported here suggests that, in terms of mathematics attainment, it doesn't really matter very much which school you go to. However, it matters very much which set you get put into. The irony is that current government policy is to allow parents choice as to which school their children attend, which makes little difference in terms of the results their children are likely to achieve. At the same time, by presuming that setting should be the norm in secondary schools, the Government is denying parents the choice that really matters – being able to send one's children to a school that does not set for mathematics. Of course, as we know from studies of school choice (see, for example, Gewirtz *et al.*, 1995), setting is valued by middle-class parents who presumably assume that their children will be in the top sets, but, given the disadvantages that setting produces for those who are not placed in the higher sets, we should question whether the parents of higher-attaining children should be allowed to secure advantages for their (already advantaged) children in this way.

However, abolishing setting overnight is not the answer. Time is needed to develop strategies for teachers to work effectively with mixed-ability groups, but the evidence, from both the UK and from abroad (see, especially, Linchevski and Kutscher, 1998), is that teachers can develop strategies for working with mixed-ability groups.

The current government claims to be interested in developing educational practice that is informed by research evidence. And yet, it continues to advocate the adoption of setting in all secondary schools, despite the accumulating evidence that setting does not improve overall standards of achievement (and, in fact, probably lowers them), while also contributing to social exclusion by polarizing achievement and in particular by disadvantaging students from working-class backgrounds. One is led, inescapably, to the conclusion that the government's support for ability grouping is not based on evidence at all, but on political grounds. Setting is presumably believed to be popular with (some) voters. But surely a government elected to a second term, with nearly two thirds of the seats in Parliament, could begin to think about what might actually improve achievement in our schools, rather than what is politically expedient.

NOTES

1   In a box and whisker plot, the box represents the attainment of the middle half of the data, with the line indicating the value of the median. The whiskers extend far enough to include most of the remaining data (specifically, the whiskers extend far enough to encompass 99.5 per cent of normally distributed data).

2   Our experience has been that it is difficult to collect reliable data on parental occupation without actually visiting classrooms and collecting the data ourselves. We asked students to provide information on the jobs done by parents or guardians, or, if they were out of work, what job they did when they last worked. An indication of the problematic nature of the data is provided by one incident when we collected information at Redwood School. A girl asked one of us (Dylan Wiliam) for help as she didn't know what to put for her father's job. When asked, 'What does your father do?', the girl replied, 'He's a waiter, but when we were in Iran, he was a professor of history'.

REFERENCES

Bartholomew, H. (1999) 'Setting in stone? How ability-grouping practices structure and con-strain achievement in mathematics'. Paper presented at the *British Educational Research Association 25th Annual Conference*, September, University of Sussex.

Bartholomew, H. (2000 September) 'Negotiating identity in the community of the mathematics classroom'. Paper presented at the *British Educational Research Association 26th Annual Conference*, September, Cardiff University.

Bartholomew, H. (2001) 'Positioning students in setted mathematics groups'. Paper presented at the *British Educational Research Association 27th Annual Conference*, September, University of Leeds.

Beaton, A.E., Martin, M.O., Mullis, I.V.S., Gonzalez, E.J., Smith, T.A. and Kelly, D.L. (1996a) *Science achievement in the middle school years: IEA's third international mathematics and science study*, Chestnut Hill, MA: Boston College.

Beaton, A.E., Mullis, I.V.S., Martin, M.O., Gonzalez, E.J., Kelly, D.L. and Smith, T.A. (1996b) *Mathematics achievement in the middle school years*, Boston, MA: Boston College.

Bennett, N., Desforges, C., Cockburn, A. and Wilkinson, B. (1984) *The quality of pupil learning experiences*, London: Lawrence Erlbaum Associates.

Boaler, J. (1997) *Experiencing school mathematics: teaching styles, sex and setting*, Buckingham: Open University Press.

Boaler, J., Wiliam, D. and Brown, M.L. (2000a) 'Students' experiences of ability grouping – disaffection, polarisation and the construction of failure', *British Educational Research Journal*, Vol. 27, No. 5: 631–648.

Boaler, J., Wiliam, D. and Zevenbergen, R. (2000b) 'The construction of identity in secondary mathematics education', in Matos, J.F. and Santos, M. (eds) *Proceedings of Mathematics Education and Society Conference*, Montechoro, Portugal: Centro de Investigação em Educação da Faculdade de Ciências Universidade de Lisboa: 192–202.

Bursten, L. (ed.) (1992) *The IEA study of mathematics III: student growth and classroom processes*, Oxford: Pergamon.

Department for Education and Employment (1997) *Excellence in schools*, London: HMSO.

Gewirtz, S., Ball, S.J. and Bowe, R. (1995) *Markets, choice and equity in education*, Buckingham: Open University Press.

Hallam, S. and Toutounji, I. (1996) *What do we know about the grouping of pupils by ability? A research review*, London: University of London Institute of Education.

Hargreaves, D.H. (1967) *Social relations in a secondary school*, London: Routledge & Kegan Paul.

Harlen, W. and Malcolm, H. (1997) *Setting and streaming: a research review*, Edinburgh: Scottish Council for Research in Education.

Hoffer, T.B. (1992) 'Middle school ability grouping and student achievement in science and mathematics', *Educational Evaluation and Policy Analysis*, Vol. 14, No. 3: 205–227.

Ireson, J. and Hallam, S. (2001) *Ability grouping in education*, London: Paul Chapman.

Ireson, J., Hallam, S. and Hurley, C. (2002) 'Ability grouping in the secondary school: effects on GCSE attainment in English, mathematics and science'. Paper presented at the *British Educational Research Association 28th Annual Conference*, September, University of Exeter.

Jackson, B. (1964) *Streaming: an education system in miniature*, London: Routledge & Kegan Paul.

Kerckhoff, A.C. (1986) 'Effects of ability grouping in British secondary schools', *American Sociological Review*, Vol. 51, No. 6: 842–858.

Lacey, C. (1970) *Hightown Grammar: the school as a social system*, Manchester: Manchester University Press.

Linchevski, L. and Kutscher, B. (1998) 'Tell me with whom you're learning and I'll tell you how much you've learned: mixed ability versus same-ability grouping in mathematics', *Journal for Research in Mathematics Education*, Vol. 29, No. 5: 533–554.

Newbold, D. (1977) *Ability grouping: the Banbury enquiry*, Windsor: National Foundation for Educational Research.

Ofsted (1998) *Setting in primary schools: a report from the Office of Her Majesty's Chief Inspector of Schools*, London: Office for Standards in Education.

Postlethwaite, K. and Denton, C. (1978) *Streams for the future? The long-term effects of early streaming and non-streaming – the final report of the Banbury enquiry*, Banbury: Pubansco.

Sukhnandan, L. and Lee, B. (1998) *Streaming, setting and grouping by ability: a review of the literature*, Slough: National Foundation for Educational Research.

Venkatakrishnan, H. and Wiliam, D. (2003) 'Tracking and mixed-ability grouping in secondary school mathematics classrooms: a case study', *British Educational Research Journal*, Vol. 29, No. 2: 189–204.

Wiliam, D. (1992) 'Special needs and the distribution of attainment in the national curriculum', *British Journal of Educational Psychology*, Vol. 62: 397–403.

Willingham, W.S. and Cole, N.S. (eds) (1997) *Gender and fair assessment*, Mahwah, NJ: Lawrence Erlbaum Associates.

THE SCHOOL, CURRICULUM AND SOCIETY

INTRODUCTION

Reading 3 in this book talked about 'a growing belief in the importance of schooling for the civilised quality of societies and for the success of national economies' (Hagger and McIntyre, 2008: 1). Had you considered, in becoming a teacher, that this expectation would be placed on you, as well as an expectation that you will be an expert in the subject content knowledge for your specialist area? Schooling is a key mechanism open to society to shape the society of the future and to pass on the values and beliefs that have created the society of today.

To help you appreciate the different decisions different countries take about the core elements of the school curriculum for their young people, we include units on the curricula for Scotland, Wales, Northern Ireland and England (Capel, Leask and Turner, 2009). We recommend you read these together and consider the differences in the aims of education between the four countries. What might be the impact of these differences on what young people in each country experience in their schooling?

READINGS IN THIS SECTION ARE:

Reading 18
Rethinking the school curriculum
John White

The first reading in this section, White (2004), focuses on the aims of education and the role of the subject within the general aims to educate young people to play their role in society. White's position is that 'The question "What should be the aims of education?" is fundamental to any system' (White, 2004: 1). White also addresses the way the aims of the school curriculum may be expressed to reflect the values of society. He defines the ideal pupil that the aims of the English national curriculum are intended to create as follows:

> Broadly speaking the ideal pupil is an informed, caring citizen of a liberal democratic society. He or she is an enterprising, independent-minded, contributor to the national community and all its members, respectful of differences

---

in culture and belief, aware of transnational and global concerns and with an understanding of the major human achievements in different fields.

(White, 2004: 4)

The remainder of the White textbook is devoted to the aims for particular subjects. You may find it useful to look at the readings relevant to you and consider the arguments for including your subject in the school curriculum.

Reading 19
Value-added is of little value
Stephen Gorard

The second reading in this section, Gorard (2006), introduces you to some of the controversies about how to hold schools and teachers accountable for the achievement of their pupils.

Gorard is a statistician who has taken the government data for schools in England and re-analysed them to check their interpretation. His findings challenge the value of the data and the validity of the interpretations of the data. This way of measuring schools has been abandoned in Wales and is not undertaken in Scotland either. That the 'league tables' of schools' results in national tests are published in England but not in Wales or Scotland reflects different values in these societies and different relationships between government and teachers. Gorard challenges the notion of the league tables:

> these lists were labelled 'school performance' tables incorrectly, because there is a very high correlation between the nature of the pupil intake . . . and their subsequent public test scores . . . this means that the majority of the difference between school outcomes . . . is directly attributable to their intakes and thence to the socio-economic characteristics of the intake rather than to the work of each school itself.
>
> (Gorard, 2006: 236)

An earlier reading, Connolly (2004), included in Section 4, makes the same claim. If you are teaching in England, you may find that your school's position in the 'league tables' matters to the school and may drive certain practices in the school, e.g. a focus on pupils whose grades are borderline. The uncertainty over the accuracy and value of league tables is a serious issue because of the high stakes for the school related to its position on the league tables.

FURTHER READING

Brighouse, T. (2009) *Education without failure: is it an impossible dream?* The 21st Century Learning Alliance; available online at www.21stcenturylearningalliance.com/generic. asp?cref=GP1133565.

This paper takes up the theme of aims and purposes of education and happiness of young people. Brighouse quotes from those who influenced the 1944 Education Act in England, and an extract of the text is reproduced here. You may wish to consider what your attitude is to 'failure' of your pupils. What does it mean? How will you manage your relationships with your pupils with respect to success and failure?

The moral argument for trying to minimise failure and optimise individual educational success was well expressed by William Temple whose words powerfully affected R.A. Butler in the production of the 1944 Education Act:

> 'Are you going to treat a man as he is with many of his tastes warped, with his powers largely crushed or as he might become with his faculties fully developed? Are you going to treat a man as he is or as he might be? Morality requires that you should treat him as he might be, as he has it in him to become; business on the other hand requires that you should treat him as he is. Raising what he is to what he might be is the work of education.
>
> 'And so you can have no justice at the basis of your social life until education has done its full work . . . and you cannot have political freedom anymore than you can have moral freedom until people's powers have been developed. Nor can there be individual freedom, for the simple reason that over and over again we find men with a cause which is just (who) are unable to state it in a way which might enable it to prevail . . . there exists a mental form of slavery quite as real as any economic form. We are pledged to destroy It . . . if you want human liberty you must have educated people.'

To this moral Imperative for successful education (which is not emphasised as much now as it was then in the optimism of the post-war period of reconstruction), can be added an economic one. Not merely does education add to the individual's chances of financial advantage, there is a general political consensus that ever higher standards of education and training are now necessary for countries to thrive and survive in a rapidly changing and technologically driven world. For any individual to lead a fulfilling life as a contributing citizen it is arguable that he/she needs to succeed sufficiently in either the Temple sense of being able to tighten an argument and/or to hone a skill which will bring them financial and other reward. (Both have prospects that are economic and if you succeed at only one then you at least need the skill to seek the help of someone who has the skill, rather in the way that the philosopher and the plumber need to respect each other and their mutual interdependence.)

Thirdly in addition to these two *moral* and *economic* imperatives, there is a *cultural* one, at the level both of the individual and of a society collectively. We owe it to our future citizens to ensure they are initiated into the essential culture of a society and are capable of shaping its development. Finally, society expects of its schools that they will re-enforce those values, such as honesty and truth which are the bedrock of most societies' moral norms.

It is really against these three purposes, the moral, economic and cultural, that we should measure educational success or failure.

(Brighouse, 2009: 1)

The above further reading links with Chapter 7 of the 5th edition of *Learning to teach in the secondary school*.

Haydon, I. (1997) 'Values education: teachers as transmitters?', in Haydon, G. (1997) *Teaching about values: a new approach* (Cassell Studies in Pastoral Care and Personal and Social Education), London: Cassell: Chapter 11: 121–133.

The chapter specifically addresses the role of the teacher in conveying the values of society. The extract from the Brighouse article above sets out a whole range of expectations society may have of teachers, and implicit in these expectations is that a higher standard of conduct is expected of teachers than of many others in society.

We recommend you consider carefully your philosophical stance about what it means to be a teacher and what your responsibilities are with respect to society. Do you see yourself as a transmitter of values as Haydon proposes?

The above further reading links with Unit 7.1 of the 5th edition of *Learning to teach in the secondary school*.

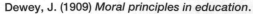

Dewey, J. (1909) *Moral principles in education*.

A blueprint for how to teach moral education in the context of whole-school experience. An old, but not dated, text of importance today. Can be downloaded free of charge at www.gutenberg.org/files/25172/25172-h/25172-h.htm.

Dewey argues that moral education must be related to the life of the pupil and the society in which the pupil lives. Moral education is explained as a social phenomenon, to be taught through socialisation and seeing the relevance of everything taught to life, now and in the future. Dewey's proposal was 'education for change', perhaps implying that moral values may also change over time.

The above further reading links with Chapter 7 of the 5th edition of *Learning to teach in the secondary school*.

Whitty, G. (2006) 'Education(al) research and education policy making: is conflict inevitable?', *British Educational Research Journal*, Vol. 32, No. 2, April: 159–176.

The relationship between research and policy and practice in education is a long-standing issue in many countries. Focusing on the UK government, this paper looks at criticisms of education research that have been made in recent years by government and other public bodies and stakeholders. Specific examples are given of the use that has/has not been made of research in developing policy. The paper emphasises the realities of the policy-making process and the difficulties in establishing, consistently and exclusively, evidence-based policy. At the same time, it argues that researchers should beware of allowing their work to be shaped entirely by the government's call for research that is directly useful to policy by always prioritising applied or practice-based approaches.

RETHINKING THE SCHOOL CURRICULUM

John White

A NOTE FROM THE EDITORS

This reading presents different statistical approaches to the analysis of school data that result in different interpretations of the effectiveness of the school and hence result in controversies about the government approach to using data to make judgements about the effectiveness of individual schools.

This reading links with Chapter 7 (especially Units 7.1 and 7.2) of the 5th edition of *Learning to teach in the secondary school*.

QUESTIONS TO CONSIDER

1   Read the Haydon (1997) article from the further reading and, taking his views on the aims and purposes of education and White's definition of the ideal pupil, consider whether you agree with the definition of the 'ideal pupil', or how you might amend this definition for the pupils you teach.
Consider how the way you teach your subject and your subject content might contribute to the shaping of pupils' understanding of their role in society. See also the Grossman *et al.* (1989) article in the further reading for Section 1.

2   Consider the aims for education expressed in White's reading and in the Scotland, Ireland, Wales and England curriculum units in Capel, Leask and Turner (2009) and draw up aims for your subject. Are these aims for your subject convincing enough to warrant the inclusion of your subject in a national curriculum?

This reading was first published as: White, J. (2004) *Rethinking the school curriculum*, London: Routledge.

INTRODUCTION

The year 2000 was revolutionary for education in England. For the first time in the country's history all state schools were given a common framework of curricular aims. This book looks at the implications of this revolution for the school curriculum itself – not least for the subjects that make it up. Nearly all of these were part of the curriculum before 2000. At that time they were not directed by a national framework because there was no such framework. How closely have the new overall aims matched the aims of the subjects? How far should the latter now evolve so as to improve the match? How far indeed should the curriculum be planned on a subject basis at all? School subjects are, after all, only vehicles to achieve certain ends: they are not self-justifying entities. Now that we have a set of overarching aims, could these be realised by other kinds of curricular vehicle?

Further questions arise about the validity of the new aims themselves. However close the fit may be between subjects and overall aims, nothing is gained if the aims themselves are faulty. One of the topics this book covers is the adequacy of the post-2000 aims. Another, just heralded, is the extent to which subjects or other vehicles are the best way of trying to meet these aims. But its main thrust is an examination of the current school subjects, the adequacy of their objectives and *modi operandi* in the light of the new aims framework.

Although the book is about recent developments in England specifically, its theme is far from parochial. The question 'What should be the aims of school education?' is fundamental to any system. So are the questions 'By what means may aims be best realised?' and 'How good is the match between system-wide aims and the specifics of different curriculum subjects?'. Many, if not most, countries have official statements of aims. Many, if not most, also build their curriculum around a familiar set of subjects, including native language and literature, mathematics, science, history, geography, one or more foreign languages, music, art, physical education. What links are there between recommendations about general aims on the one hand and requirements in the different subjects on the other? Are the latter explicitly derived from, and justified by, the former? Or are the overall aims more like high-sounding national mission statements, which can be ignored in practice? Are the familiar subjects included because it is *taken as read* that these are what the school curriculum must consist of?

At one level, the book concentrates on fundamental issues of this sort. At another, it is intended as a contribution to the next stage of curriculum reform in England. Global and national themes interconnect and illuminate each other throughout its length. England is unusual among countries due to its belated adoption of overall aims. This means that its recent and continuing experience of curriculum reform allows globally important issues to be raised in unusual starkness.

THE NEW AIMS FOR THE SCHOOL CURRICULUM

Before 1988, maintained schools in England were responsible for their own curricula and the aims underlying them. That year saw the introduction of the National Curriculum. This was based on ten foundation subjects – English, mathematics, science, technology, history, geography, a modern foreign language, music, art, physical education.

It is hard to say for certain why these were chosen, since no rationale was provided for them. Richard Aldrich has drawn attention to the very close similarity between the 1988 list and the subjects prescribed for the newly introduced state secondary (later grammar) schools in 1904 (Aldrich, 1988: 22). The National Curriculum gives every appearance of having been lifted from what was originally traditional grammar school practice.

Whatever its origin, it was *not* derived from a set of underlying aims. Not that it was entirely bereft of aims. After 1988 it had two:

■   [to] promote the spiritual, moral, cultural, mental and physical development of pupils at the school and of society;

■   [and to] prepare such pupils for the opportunities, responsibilities and experiences of adult life.

Uncharitable commentators may find these a trifle on the thin side. Certainly, it is impossible to read into these bland truisms anything like a justifying rationale for the ten foundation subjects. In the late 1990s, pressure grew for the purposes of the National Curriculum to be more clearly spelt out. The discussions that the Qualifications and Curriculum Authority (QCA) had around this time with teachers, teaching organisations, local authorities and researchers showed that many believed that current statutory arrangements, including the National Curriculum, lacked a clear vision of what the parts, individually and collectively, were designed to achieve. This reinforced the QCA's view, and that of its predecessor, the School Curriculum and Assessment Authority (SCAA), that there needed to be 'a much clearer statement about the aims and priorities of the school curriculum' (SCAA, 1997).

This statement materialised in the opening pages of the *Handbook* for teachers on the National Curriculum post-2000. This comes in two volumes, one for primary teachers, the other secondary. I shall call these HPT and HST, respectively). The main section is called 'The school curriculum and the National Curriculum: values, aims and purposes'.

VALUES, AIMS AND PURPOSES

Values and purposes underpinning the school curriculum

Education influences and reflects the values of society, and the kind of society we want to be. It is important, therefore, to recognise a broad set of common values and purposes that underpin the school curriculum and the work of schools.

Foremost is a belief in education, at home and at school, as a route to the spiritual, moral, social, cultural, physical and mental development, and thus the well-being, of the individual. Education is also a route to equality of opportunity for all, a healthy and just democracy, a productive economy, and sustainable development. Education should reflect the enduring values that contribute to these ends. These include valuing ourselves, our families and other relationships, the wider groups to which we belong, the diversity in our society and the environment in which we live. Education should also reaffirm our commitment to the virtues of truth, justice, honesty, trust and a sense of duty.

At the same time, education must enable us to respond positively to the opportunities and challenges of the rapidly changing world in which we live and work. In particular, we need to be prepared to engage as individuals, parents, workers and citizens with economic, social and cultural change, including the continued globalisation of the economy and society, with new work and leisure patterns and with the rapid expansion of communication technologies.

Aims for the school curriculum

If schools are to respond effectively to these values and purposes, they need to work in collaboration with families and the local community, including church and voluntary groups, local agencies and business, in seeking to achieve two broad aims through the curriculum. These aims provide an essential context within which schools develop their own curriculum.

Aim 1: the school curriculum should aim to provide opportunities for all pupils to learn and to achieve

The school curriculum should develop enjoyment of, and commitment to, learning as a means of encouraging and stimulating the best possible progress and the highest attainment for all pupils. It should build on pupils' strengths, interests and experiences and develop their confidence in their capacity to learn and work independently and collaboratively. It should equip them with the essential learning skills of literacy, numeracy, and information and communication technology, and promote an enquiring mind and capacity to think rationally. The school curriculum should contribute to the development of pupils' sense of identity through knowledge and understanding of the spiritual, moral, social and cultural heritages of Britain's diverse society and of the local, national, European, Commonwealth and global dimensions of their lives. It should encourage pupils to appreciate human aspirations and achievements in aesthetic, scientific, technological and social fields, and prompt a personal response to a range of experiences and ideas.

By providing rich and varied contexts for pupils to acquire, develop and apply a broad range of knowledge, understanding and skills, the curriculum should enable pupils to think creatively and critically, to solve problems and to make a difference for the better. It should give them the opportunity to become creative, innovative, enterprising and capable of leadership to equip them for their future lives as workers and citizens. It should also develop their physical skills and encourage them to recognise the importance of pursuing a healthy lifestyle and keeping themselves and others safe.

Aim 2: the school curriculum should aim to promote pupils' spiritual, moral, social and cultural development and prepare all pupils for the opportunities, responsibilities and experiences of life

The school curriculum should promote pupils' spiritual, moral, social and cultural development and, in particular, develop principles for distinguishing between right and wrong. It should develop their knowledge, understanding and appreciation of their own and different beliefs and cultures, and how these influence individuals and societies. The school curriculum should pass on enduring values, develop pupils' integrity and autonomy and help them to be responsible and caring citizens capable of contributing to the development of a just society. It should promote equal opportunities and enable pupils to challenge discrimination and stereotyping. It should develop their awareness and understanding of, and respect for, the environments in which they live, and secure their commitment to sustainable development at a personal, local, national and global level. It should also equip pupils as consumers to make informed judgements and independent decisions and to understand their responsibilities and rights.

The school curriculum should promote pupils' self-esteem and emotional well-being and help them to form and maintain worthwhile and satisfying relationships, based on respect for themselves and for others, at home, school, work and in the community. It should develop their ability to relate to others and work for the common good. It should enable pupils to respond positively to opportunities, challenges and responsibilities, to manage risk and to cope with change and adversity. It should prepare pupils for the next steps in their education, training and employment and equip them to make informed choices at school and throughout their lives, enabling them to appreciate the relevance of their achievements to life and society outside school, including leisure, community engagement and employment.

The interdependence of the two aims

These two aims reinforce each other. The personal development of pupils, spiritually, morally, socially and culturally, plays a significant part in their ability to learn and to achieve. Development in both areas is essential to raising standards of attainment for all pupils.

(DfEE/QCA, 1999: 10–12)

It should be apparent from this how much more determinate are these aims than the platitudinous ones of 1988. True, some of the 2000 aims need further precision, but overall they do present a picture of the kind of pupil that the school curriculum can ideally help to foster. They draw attention to the personal qualities pupils require, as well as intellectual equipment in the shape of knowledge and skills. Broadly speaking, the ideal pupil is an informed, caring citizen of a liberal democratic society. He or she is an enterprising, independent-minded contributor to the well-being of the national community and all its members, respectful of differences of culture and belief, aware of transnational and global concerns and with an understanding of major human achievements in different fields.

Some 60 per cent of the specific aims mentioned are about the pupil's personal qualities, as distinct from skills or types of knowledge or understanding. The detailed items in these three categories are:

■ *personal qualities*: valuing ourselves, our families and other relationships, the wider groups to which we belong, the diversity in our society and the environment in which we live; the virtues of truth, justice, honesty, trust and a sense of duty; enjoyment of and commitment to learning; confidence in one's capacity to learn; an enquiring mind; capacity to think rationally; sense of identity; appreciation of human aspirations and achievements; thinking creatively and critically; being innovative and enterprising; integrity and autonomy; responsible and caring citizens; challenging discrimination; respect for the environment; commitment to sustainable development; making informed judgements as consumers; self-esteem; emotional well-being; respect for oneself; respect for others; being able to relate to others; being able to manage risk, cope with change and adversity; making informed choices at school and throughout pupils' lives; having the will to achieve; curiosity about themselves and their place in the world; attitudes needed to foster the inner life; willingness to participate, work with others for the common good; financial capability; qualities associated with enterprise education (confidence, self-reliance, learning from mistakes); entrepreneurial characteristics of tenacity, independence.

- *skills*: essential learning skills of literacy, numeracy and ICT; physical skills; six key skills; five thinking skills.
- *knowledge and understanding*: knowledge and understanding of the spiritual, moral, social and cultural heritages of Britain's diverse society and of the local, national, European, Commonwealth and global dimensions of pupils' lives; acquiring a broad range of knowledge and understanding (so as to enable pupils to think creatively and critically); knowledge and understanding of pupils' own beliefs and cultures; recognising the importance of pursuing a healthy lifestyle; understanding the environments within which one lives; self-understanding; understanding necessary to making moral judgements; understanding relevant to making financial decisions, running mini-enterprises, sustainable development.

It should not be surprising that personal qualities are so prominent in this scheme. Since the view of education in the document is about promoting a certain kind of society, it is understandable that it should concentrate on cultivating citizens of an appropriate sort. This means delineating the type of people these citizens will be.

The skills, knowledge and understanding these citizens will need is a further matter. To some extent these can be derived from the personal qualities themselves. One example in the document is the claim that developing a sense of identity requires one to have knowledge and understanding of diverse cultural heritages. Another, not explicitly mentioned in the document, but in line with it, is that autonomy, which has to do with making informed choices about important goals in one's life, requires knowledge and understanding of the various options among which one is to choose.

One further preliminary point: the section on 'Values, aims and purposes' at the beginning of the *Handbook* is not the only place in it where overall aims are mentioned. They also appear a few pages further on in the section called 'Learning across the National Curriculum' (DfEE/QCA, 1999:19–23 (HPT); 21–25 (HST)). This consists of a hetero-geneous collection of general objectives that the different curriculum subjects are intended to serve. Here is an indication in note form of the aims covered in these four pages: growth of a sense of self; curiosity about oneself and one's place in the world; fostering the inner life; concern for others; making responsible moral decisions; responsibilities and rights of being members of families and communities; making an active contribution to the demo-cratic process; understanding and respecting cultural traditions, one's own and others'; appreciating and responding to a variety of aesthetic experiences; acquiring 'key skills' of communication, application of number, information technology, working with others, improving own learning and performance, problem solving; acquiring 'thinking skills' of information-processing, reasoning, enquiry, creative thinking, evaluation; learning to make sensible choices about managing money; in the context of enterprise education, developing confidence, self-reliance and willingness to embrace change; acquiring the understanding, skills and attitudes required to participate in decisions to do with sustainable development.

A fuller discussion of the overall aims comes in White (2004: Chapter 2). As has been made clear, the aims are set out in lists of items. No rationale for these is given. In the next chapter we explore how well the items hang together in a coherent pattern and whether any adequate justification can be provided for them. For the moment they will be taken as read. This is not a wholly arbitrary decision. Intuitively at least, they appear to be on the right lines, at least if one is working within a broad liberal democratic compass. Although we have to go beyond intuitions into more rigorous assessment, the aims as stated will be taken as baseline for the rest of this article.

FROM AIMS TO CURRICULUM

Having discussed the aims themselves, I now turn to how schools are to realise them. Here it is crucial to hold on to the fact that the aims are for the whole school curriculum, not just the National Curriculum. The *Handbook* states that 'the school curriculum comprises all learning and other experiences that each school plans for its pupils' (DfEE/QCA, 1999: 10). As far as school subjects are concerned, this covers work in religious education as well as in the National Curriculum areas (religious education has been a compulsory subject in state schools since 1944). The *Handbook* definition also transcends the time-tabled curriculum. It can cover what a school plans through the way it structures its 'ethos': its encouragement, for instance, of respect for others in the classroom and in the play-ground. In sum we can distinguish between general aims and the school curriculum (in this wide sense) as the vehicle intended to realise them. Curriculum planning cannot sensibly start with the curriculum. Given that the curriculum is a vehicle, or collection of vehicles, intended to reach a certain set of destinations, we have to begin with the destinations themselves. Once we have these, we have at some point to work out what kinds of vehicle are best to help us attain them in particular circumstances.

Suppose, as suggested, we take as read the overall aims. How is it best to try to realise them? Can we go straight to the curriculum in its broad sense? The curriculum consists of *experiences*, the planned pupil experiences intended to realise the aims. Possible examples of these – generated both via timetabled activities and via whole-school processes (school ethos) – are as follows: Pupils are encouraged to:

■ listen to things (stories, instructions, others' views);
■ look at things (diagrams in books, writing on the board, videos);
■ reason things out (how to solve a problem in maths);
■ consider how to create more interest in the School Council;
■ imagine things (what it is like to be in someone else's shoes);
■ contemplate things (poems, paintings, aesthetic features of the school environment);
■ feel various emotions (compassion, suspense, delight, imagination-mediated fear);
■ try to remember things (past feelings, geographical facts);
■ exercise their bodies.

These and other types of experience constitute the school curriculum as the *Handbook* defines it. What connection is there between things like these and the overall aims? Well, why do we want students to look at things, think about things, feel things and so on? Sometimes these have a partly intrinsic justification: the delight that young children feel in listening to a story is an end in itself. But teachers also have intentions for their pupils that go beyond immediate experience. They are interested in more long-lasting mental states: they want the children to come to believe, know and understand things; to acquire mental or physical skills, such as reasoning historically or climbing ropes; to acquire or deepen dispositions or habitual ways of behaving, such as controlling fears or resentments, being cautious in their thinking, having an appropriate kind of confidence or self-esteem.

This brings out the fact that there are two importantly different kinds of ingredient in the mental life of the child (or, indeed, of anyone) (see also White, 2002: Chapter 1). On the one hand, there are conscious occurrences (experiences of listening, thinking, moving one's limbs); and on the other, continuing mental states (understanding, knowing how to swim, being kind). The continuing mental states exist even when there are no present conscious occurrences. A child can understand fractions without having anything to do with fractions at the moment. He or she still understands them when he/she is having his/her tea, perhaps even when he/she is asleep. The same goes for skills and for personal qualities. A child can know how to dive without actually diving; and is still a kind person when he/she is alone and there is no one around to be kind to.

The experiences – the conscious occurrences – that constitute the school curriculum are vehicles intended to bring about continuing mental states such as knowledge and understanding, skills and dispositions (personal qualities). These are the curriculum's aims. Indeed, as we have already seen, the overall aims in the *Handbook* fall under these headings. General aims take more and more determinate forms the closer one gets to the pupil's experience. At the experiential end they are maximally determinate. Take the class of young children delightedly listening to a story. What does their teacher plan that they learn, over and above, that is, intending them to have an experience enjoyable in itself? One of the things the teacher wants is for them to enjoy experiences *of this sort*, that is to get into the habit of wanting to hear simple stories like this. We can call this an 'immediate' aim – the aim a teacher (or whole school) has in engaging learners in a particular activity. Behind the immediate aim lie aims of increasing generality. He/she wants them to enjoy simple stories of this sort, not only through hearing them, but also through reading them. He/she wants them to enjoy literature in general. He/she wants them to develop a deeper understanding of human nature or a more refined aesthetic sense. Of course, he/she is also likely to have other aims in reading the story – to do, for instance, with sharing enjoyable experiences with others or introducing more advanced vocabulary. These aims also fit in a range from immediate to very general. In addition, all the aims mentioned interconnect and are inextricable from each other in practice.

At the more general end of the continuum, we reach the kind of overall aim that we find in the *Handbook* or similar documents. In between the highly general aims and the teacher's immediate aims are aims of varying levels of generality or specificity. Curriculum planning consists in mapping out, and relating to each other, aims across the whole range, from the most general to the most immediate. At the immediate end, the teacher's, it also includes working out experiences – specific forms of listening, looking, thinking and so on – designed to realise these aims.

Curriculum planning, therefore, is a collaborative enterprise at different levels. As is often the case, not least in post-1988 England, governments lay down overall aims (e.g. developing self-understanding). They also lay down aims at the next levels of specificity, aims for and within particular curriculum areas (e.g. understanding aspects of one's own society's history which help one to understand oneself; more specifically again, under-standing the significance of the rapid rise in the population since the late eighteenth century). Teachers specify these further at the level of the school and the classroom.

In Chapter 2, I will be saying more about curriculum planning, both in general and in relation to developments in England. As well as looking more closely at the justification of overall aims, I will go further into ways in which they may be realised, concentrating especially on what can and should be done via whole school processes and, within timetabled activities, what can be done without using school subjects as a framework.

MATCHING SCHOOL SUBJECTS TO OVERALL AIMS

I now narrow the focus on to the curriculum subjects themselves, specifically the subjects of the English National Curriculum plus religious education (RE).

The *Handbook* on the National Curriculum, separate booklets on all the National Curriculum subjects (which cover most of the same ground as the *Handbook*) and a booklet on the RE curriculum are constructed on a subject basis. As we have seen, the overall aims at the beginning of the *Handbook* in principle cover non-subject-based learning. In actuality, however, virtually the whole of the government documentation just mentioned is about the aims of the different *subjects*, their programmes of study, their contribution to learning across the curriculum and their attainment targets.

The explanation for this is obvious enough. When the *Handbook* appeared in 1999, nearly all the curriculum subjects with which it deals (with the exception of personal, social and health education (PSHE) and citizenship) had already been compulsory elements since 1988. The government had to work with what was already in place.

This is understandable, but it does give rise to a question. The *Handbook* introduced a set of overall curricular aims. Presumably, some coherence is intended between these new aims and the documentation on the aims, programmes and attainment targets of the various subjects. Presumably these latter features are seen as ways in which the overall aims are to be made more determinate, in the way described in Section 3. The question is

■ **Table 18.1** Compulsory subjects of the English school curriculum, including the National Curriculum, from 2003

	Key Stage 1	Key Stage 2	Key Stage 3	Key Stage 4
Age	5–7	7–11	11–14	14–16
Year groups	1–2	3–6	7–9	10–11
National Curriculum subjects				
Core subjects				
English	■	■	■	■
Mathematics	■	■	■	■
Science	■	■	■	■
Other subjects				
Design and technology	■	■	■	
Information and communication technology	■	■	■	■
History	■	■	■	
Geography	■	■	■	
Modern foreign languages			■	
Art and design	■	■	■	
Music	■	■	■	
Physical education	■	■	■	■
Citizenship			■	■
Religious education	■	■	■	■

whether these presumptions are justified. To what extent do we find a good match between the overall aims and the specific requirements laid down for the different subjects?

I explored this question in detail in a project, so far unpublished, undertaken in 2001 for a national educational agency. I took all thirteen current subjects, including RE and the two newcomers, PSHE and citizenship, looked at their aims, programmes of study, attainment targets and contribution to learning across the curriculum and tried to establish how far there is a match or mismatch between these specific items and the overall aims. To what extent are the subjects, as officially conceived, suitable instruments for realising the general aims?

The short answer is that the results are patchy. Very broadly speaking, the best match tends to be found in subjects only recently introduced into the curriculum: design and technology, ICT, citizenship and PSHE. Many longer-established subjects tend to be problematic in various ways. These include art and design, English, geography, history, mathematics, modern foreign languages, music, physical education, RE, science.

There is not space to run through all the results, but below are some examples. In citizenship there is a good match. Its aims are stated as follows:

> **Citizenship** gives pupils the knowledge, skills and understanding to play an effective role in society at local, national and international levels. It helps them to become informed, thoughtful and responsible citizens who are aware of their duties and rights. It promotes their spiritual, moral, social and cultural development, making them more self-confident and responsible both in and beyond the classroom. It encourages pupils to play a helpful part in the life of their schools, neighbourhoods and communities and the wider world. It also teaches them about our economy and democratic institutions and values; encourages respect for different national, religious and ethnic identities; and develops pupils' ability to reflect on issues and take part in discussions.
>
> (DfEE/QCA, 1999: 183 (HST))

If we compare these with the overall aims, we see close links between them. There is the same concern with personal qualities such as self-confidence, responsiveness to others' needs, civic involvement, respect for cultural differences, reflectiveness, as well as with the knowledge and skills needed to sustain them. The programme of study for citizenship is also in sync. It is not difficult to see how the overall aims map on to such randomly selected items as learning about the criminal justice system or the significance of the media in society, learning to 'negotiate, decide and take part responsibly in both school and community-based activities' (KS 3 *Handbook* for Secondary Teachers, 1999: 184–185 (HST)). The whole tone of the citizenship documentation is pupil-centred, in that, like the overall aims, it keeps firmly in mind the ideal of a certain kind of person and the skills and understanding that such a person must have.

The same is true of design and technology. As with citizenship its own aims look outwards, beyond its own confines, towards wider personal and social horizons picked out in the overall aims:

> Design and technology prepares pupils to participate in tomorrow's rapidly changing technologies. They learn to think and intervene creatively to improve quality of life. The subject calls for pupils to become autonomous and creative problem solvers, as individuals and members of a team. They must look for needs, wants and

opportunities and respond to them by developing a range of ideas and making products and systems. They combine practical skills with an understanding of aesthetics, social and environmental issues, function and industrial practices. As they do so, they reflect on and evaluate present and past design and technology, its uses and effects. Through design and technology, all pupils can become discriminating and informed users of products, and become innovators.

(DfEE/QCA, 1999: 90 (HPT); 134 (HST))

Further specification is given to these aims in the programme of study. This includes such items as learning 'to generate ideas for products after thinking about who will use them and what they will be used for' (KS2, DfEE/QCA, 1999: 94 (HPT)); learning 'to select appropriate tools and techniques for making their product' (KS2, DfEE/QCA, 1999: 94 (HPT)), learning 'to identify and use criteria to judge the quality of other people's products' (KS3, DfEE/QCA, 1999: 136–137 (HST)).

GAPS IN MATCHING

With most of the longer-established subjects, there is much less room for confidence about a good match with the overall aims. Subjects where the match is – to different degrees – problematic include art and design, English, geography, history, mathematics, modern foreign languages, music, physical education, RE, science. These problems are discussed below.

Art and design

Similar points, *mutatis mutandis*, could be made about art and design, except that there is more weight here on pupils' making works of art (the musical equivalent being composition). The justification of both subjects in terms of larger aims is unclear both from the documentation and more generally. Both subjects have appeared in curricula for maintained schools since the late nineteenth century. Music grew out of 'singing', and art and design out of 'drawing', the latter included originally for 'the great mass of our working population' as 'likely to be useful to them in their future occupations as workmen and artisans' (Selleck, 1968: 121). Today they are both multifaceted, sophisticated subjects, assured of a place in the curriculum, but unclear as to their overarching purposes.

English

One of the overall aims states that the school curriculum: 'should encourage pupils to appreciate human aspirations and achievements in aesthetic, and . . . social fields, and prompt a personal response to a range of experiences and ideas' (DfEE/QCA, 1999: 11). This would suggest, among other things, acquaintance with literature on a human scale, not necessarily literature written in English. There is no need to dwell on the extraordinary richness of world literature, which nearly all of us access only in translation. It is not only absorbing for its own sake, but affords us the best insights we often have into other cultures and countries.

Yet, because the school subject responsible for literature is called 'English', it has traditionally been taken as read that the texts it studies are those written originally in English. This tradition has come through to the 2000 curriculum, with its long statutory and non-statutory lists of works to be read at Key Stages 3 and 4. All these are texts written originally in English.

If, as seems sensible, we need to create room for world literature in schools, how should this be done? Should we stretch the label 'English' to cover it? Or should the title of the subject be changed to 'language and literature'?

Film is among the most important forms of dramatic art of the twentieth century. There is no clear place for it in the school curriculum, although it is mentioned in odd places under English. It is a visual art, but not included with other visual arts under art and design. All this may reflect the fact that the categories under which education in the arts is delivered – art and design, English and music – date back to the nineteenth century and so do not well reflect twentieth-century developments.

Geography

Unlike some other subjects, most of geography's aims closely match overall aims statements; for instance, geography:

> prepares pupils for adult life and employment. It is a focus within the curriculum for understanding and resolving issues about the environment and sustainable development. It links the natural and social sciences. Through geography pupils encounter different societies and cultures. This helps them realise how nations rely on each other. Geography can inspire them to think about their own place in the world, their values, rights and responsibilities to others and the environment.
>
> (DfEE/QCA, 1999: 108 (HPT); 154 (HST))

But with the exception of work on the environment and sustainable development, the programmes of study and attainment targets tend to focus largely on intra-subject material to do with geographical enquiry and skills. There is less than might have been expected about cultural matters; but much about repeatable features found across different countries, in other words, about subject matter approached scientifically and in abstraction from the child's own perspective.

History

So many of the overall aims are about pupils' roles as national and global citizens in rapidly changing cultural, political, economic, technological and social conditions. This requires a background of understanding of recent and contemporary history. Yet the history curriculum contains very little work on the twentieth century.

Mathematics

The first reason given for mathematics' importance is that it equips pupils with powerful tools of logical reasoning and problem-solving (DfEE/QCA, 1999: 60 (HPT); 57 (HST)). This is an ancient argument for the subject, and it assumes the existence of general thinking skills. However, there are problems about this – akin to problems raised, incidentally, more than a hundred years ago when faculty psychology provided a rationalising theory for the elementary school curriculum (Selleck, 1968: 45–58). For instance, the reasoning and enquiring acquired in history classes seem very different from the reasoning and enquiring involved in planning a family holiday. There *may* be general skills that cover widely diverse fields, but it should not be assumed that they exist before evidence – at present non-existent – is provided for this.

Statutory requirements in mathematics are laid down in great detail. Fourteen pages are devoted to its programmes of study, compared with an average of four pages for all subjects. From the standpoint of the overall aims, just how important are all these statutorily required items? Students at Key Stage 3 have to recall the essential properties of quadrilaterals such as the trapezium and rhombus. When was the last occasion that any reader of this book made use of these notions?

Modern foreign languages

The importance of MFL is said to lie in helping pupils to understand and appreciate different cultures and countries and to think of themselves as citizens of the world (DfEE/QCA, 1999: 162 (HST)). These are goals wholly in line with the overall aims. Yet virtually all the material in the attainment targets and programmes of study has to do with learning linguistic skills. No attempt is made to show why the latter should be thought an especially good means of attaining the goals just mentioned. If promoting the understanding of other cultures is what one is after, other vehicles look much better bets for the non-specialist: accounts of them in English, literature in translation, foreign films with subtitles or dubbing.

Music

The attainment targets and programmes of study are inward-looking. They provide structured progression in acquiring the various sub-skills and forms of understanding and appreciation found within the subject – i.e. as performers, composers, listeners and judges. Pupils are thus led into the foothills of various related specialisms, yet the overall point of this for those children who will not become specialist musicians is not clear.

Physical education

For most people, good physical health is a basic need for whatever activities they wish to undertake. The overall aims acknowledge this in their reference to encouraging pupils to 'recognise the importance of pursuing a healthy lifestyle'. Sub-aims covered by this may be taken to refer to understanding how the body works, diet, sensible habits of eating and drinking, work on body image, the need for adequate exercise, care in avoiding damage to one's body, drugs education and aspects of sex education. School dinner policy can play a part in this, along with timetabled classes in various areas.

In addition some children have a more specialised interest in developing their physical skills in some more particular direction – through dance, gymnastics, games, swimming, athletics. Physical education as a curriculum subject is almost totally orientated towards such specialisms. Its contribution to more general health aims is not well worked out.

Religious education

This subject presents a quite different matching problem. No problem here of links between the aims of RE and overarching aims. The RE material is full of statements such as: 'Pupils learn about religious and ethical teaching, enabling them to make reasoned and informed judgements on religious, moral and social issues' (QCA, 2000, inside front cover).

The most natural way of taking such comments is that RE deals with ethical and moral issues as part of children's general moral education. This is in line with the tradition of religious education in this country. There was a tight link between religious instruction and moral instruction in the elementary schools of the late nineteenth century (Selleck, 1968: 59). Closer to home, the introduction of RE as the only compulsory subject in maintained schools after 1944 had much to do with the belief that Britain needed to 'revive the spiritual and personal values in our society and in our national tradition' (Niblett, 1966: 15).

The civic significance of RE may well have dwindled between 1944 and 2000, but the more general association between religious and moral education has persisted more tenaciously. Until 2000, RE was seen in many quarters as *the* locus for moral education in the curriculum. In 2000, PSHE and citizenship were added to the National Curriculum subjects. In addition to these two new subjects in the ethical/moral/civic field, *every* subject has now to declare – in its *Learning across the National Curriculum* statement – how it contributes to learning in this area.

There are thus two sources of ethical and moral education now flowing into the new curriculum, one associated with religion, the other not. How far may this lead to a confusion in pupils' minds at odds with the insistence on clear, rational thinking prominent among the new overall aims? Recent statistics suggest that Britain is now a country where organised religions play little or no part in the great majority (perhaps 80 per cent) of people's lives. If present trends continue, this majority can be expected to increase (HMSO, 2000: 13.19, 13.20).

The points just made suggest that the whole area of how ethical/moral/civic aims are to be delivered calls out for review. In particular, it needs to be asked if this area of learning should now fall outside RE's remit altogether.

Science

The documentation on this rightly makes much of such aims as understanding the impact of science on industry and the quality of life, and discussing science-based issues that may affect the future of the world. But these are not reflected in the attainment targets. Virtually all the level statements here are about mastering specific areas of knowledge and techniques of enquiry within science.

Jenner, Lavoisier and Darwin are the only names of scientists mentioned, and their theories appear only as non-statutory examples to illustrate more general points. There is next to no work on the great turning points in the history of science, e.g. the impact of Copernicus and Galileo, the scientific revolution and the enlightenment, the impact of geology and evolution theory on views about man's place in the universe, the harnessing of science in the last two hundred plus years to industrial production, military affairs, medicine, social improvement etc. There is nothing about the impact of science on religion over the past five hundred years. There is no reference to any of the human sciences.

Inward-looking tendencies

Judging by the documentation, all the subjects we have considered, with the partial exception of English and RE, have an intra-subject orientation. In other words, their main preoccupation is with helping pupils to acquire knowledge, understanding and skills in their specialised area. Thus history aims at equipping pupils with a degree of historical knowledge and understanding, as well as reasoning and enquiry skills pertinent to the discipline. The same is true, *mutatis mutandum*, for other intellectual subjects, i.e. mathematics, geography and science. In MFL, art, music and PE, the emphasis is more on skills of performance and production, informed by relevant knowledge and understanding.

Learning in these subjects has to do with inducting novices into their *modi operandi*. The model at work seems to be something like apprenticeship in acquiring the rudiments of competence as a geographer, historian, mathematician, scientist, musician, visual artist, linguist.

It would be quite unfair to say that these subjects profess no links with overall aims. Geography, for instance, mentions its contribution to understanding other societies and sustainable development; mathematics its application to everyday life; science its role in understanding technological aspects of industrial and social life. Despite this, the attainment targets, programmes of study and aims statements show a marked intra-subject emphasis.

Does this matter? It may seem odd to upbraid these subjects for concentrating on their own special ways of thinking, their own special skills and facts. What could be wrong with that? In another context – specialist courses at university, perhaps – this might be unremarkable. But in the new school curriculum, overall aims come first, subjects second. Schools' first duty is not in the preparation of specialists, but with providing a sound general education in line with subject-transcending aims.

That does not necessarily mean that an intra-subject orientation is wholly to be ruled out. Among the new overall aims we find 'developing . . . pupils' autonomy' and 'equipping them to make informed choices at school and throughout their lives'. There is a powerful argument that, in order to choose options, which include science-based or music-based careers, or indeed science or music pursued as ends in themselves, pupils have to have an appropriate understanding of the nature of science or music. The knotty question then becomes: what counts as *appropriate* understanding? How much acquaintance with science or music does one need as a basis for choice, and of what kind? Is the apprenticeship model adequate for this, or should one look for one with wider horizons? This kind of justification in terms of equipment for choice is scarcely, if at all, found in the new *Handbook*.

The most striking finding from the survey I carried out was the intra-subject orientation of so many curriculum subjects. However, in the light of the history of school subjects, this is perhaps not so surprising. The intra-orientated subjects have been statutory elements in the National Curriculum since 1988, that is more than a decade before the new aims appeared on the scene. As noted earlier, the list of subjects included in 1988 is remarkably similar to the list included in the secondary regulations of 1904. In those eighty-four years, the internal strength of these subjects increased and was consolidated via their statutory – and later non-statutory but by then entrenched – place in the school curriculum, via their subject-associations and via their links with higher education. Most of them originated as school subjects in the late nineteenth century and were not then taught in universities. Promoters of these subjects sought to enhance their status by emphasising their academic rigour. This process developed further in the twentieth century via links between secondary school teachers, university teachers, subject associations and examining boards (Goodson and Marsh, 1996: an overview drawing on subject-specific works by Ball, S., Jenkins, E., Layton, D. and others). Over the years, subjects that had a lowly place or no place in the 1904 curriculum joined the others on the escalator of respectability and professionalism: as mentioned already, 'drawing' was elevated into 'art and design', while music, absent in 1904 but common in elementary schools as 'singing', grew into the sophisticated, many-sided subject we know today. Achieving the status of a 'foundation' or 'core' subject in 1988 strengthened still further the power of these subjects and of their institutional links.

In 1993, Duncan Graham, the first Chairman and Chief Executive of the National Curriculum Council, which preceded QCA, wrote: 'Do subjects exist to enable learning or as a vehicle for vested interests, lobbies, and departmental baronies?' (Graham and Tytler, 1993: 120). The inward-looking nature of many of the subjects, their attachment to the apprenticeship model and the demands of specialisation raise questions about how far they should be allowed to continue in their present form. The arrival of the new overall aims has given us a touchstone, previously lacking, for assessing their suitability, as presently constituted, for delivering the pupil- and civic-centred education now required.

THE STRUCTURE OF THE BOOK

Most of this book is a subject-by-subject discussion of issues raised in previous sections. Among other things, Chapters 3 to 13 can be seen as putting to the test the conclusions of the project conducted for the national agency. They cover all the pre-1988 subjects now contained in the National Curriculum, as well as religious education. A chapter on design and technology has also been included in the light of the comments made about it above. The post-2000 entrants to the National Curriculum, PSHE and citizenship have not been selected, and neither has ICT. The chapters on subjects are preceded, in Chapter 2, by a discussion of some key questions in general curriculum planning.

Chapter 3 looks at *Art and Design*. With notable dispassion, John Steers sees the subject as marked by a 'prevailing orthodoxy' of approach. He interprets its historical development since the eighteenth century as a process of adding elements thought to reflect 'good practice' at different times, and so generating the less than coherent and fragmented curriculum we have today. Positively, he would like to see art and design recognise the shortcomings of 'school art', which has largely lost touch with wider contemporary developments in the professional field, in favour of more flexible arrangements that bring home to both teachers and pupils that art and design 'can actually *matter* in their lives'. This involves re-addressing the balance within the subject – moving 'fine art' from its privileged position and offering older students more opportunities for choice of working in a range of media and technologies, in design and craft activities as well as in fine art. It also demands more authentic forms of assessment that go far beyond the monitoring of orthodoxy.

Richard Kimbell's discussion of *Design and Technology* in Chapter 4 is distinctly upbeat. The only curriculum newcomer in 1988 (under the title technology), it grew out of former craft subjects (e.g. woodwork and needlework) and areas of technology (e.g. electronics), drawn together and given focus through processes of designing. As an area encompassing both art and science, D&T is by its nature interdisciplinary. Despite continuing problems in the spread of good practice in the teaching of the subject, it makes procedures of values-sensitive planning and making, rather than knowledge content, central to its activity. This means that it conforms more closely than most other subjects to the new generic aims of the curriculum. Unlike other subjects, its attainment target is expressed wholly procedurally, in terms of how tasks are tackled. Kimbell agrees with David Hargeaves that D&T 'is moving from the periphery of the school curriculum to its heart'.

Bethan Marshall shows in Chapter 5 how current debates about the content and purpose of *English* cannot be understood without tracing the historical lineage of competing positions. The view that locates the subject among the liberal arts originated with Matthew Arnold and was developed further by Leavis. The conception of English as a vehicle of critical dissent has even older, religious, roots, but has now become secularised, while contemporary conservatives, influenced by Eliot, often associate the subject with the preservation of English culture and hold that only via adhering to a canon of national literature can its decline be prevented. Marshall goes on to link the 'Gradgrindian' nature of current policy with the anti-utilitarian critiques of Arnold and others. She favours a position that does justice both to the aesthetic aspects of the liberal arts position and to elements of the tradition of dissent, dissociating herself to a large extent from the fashionable tendency in English teaching circles to see print literacy as giving way to a more multi-modal future.

In Chapter 6, David Lambert gives a frank account of the 'identity crisis' that besets *Geography* and of its proponents' keenness to defend the 'place in the sun' which it won in the 1988 settlement against incursions from competitors in curriculum 'turf wars'. He regrets the way National Curriculum requirements have steered teachers towards conformity, noting the role of widely used textbooks in this process. He would like there to be much more thought about the *purposes* of teaching geography, so that the subject can recover a sense of direction. Potentially, geography has a huge amount to contribute to the realisation of the new overall aims of the curriculum, not least because of its interdisciplinary nature. Its future should lie in a greater responsiveness to children's needs as independent thinkers and as citizens; and in a willingness to subordinate the integrity of the subject, where appropriate, to new forms of cooperation and intermingling with other curriculum areas.

This brings us to Terry Haydn's Chapter 7 on *History*. This echoes the theme in the geography chapter about a current lack of consensus on why the subject is important. Traditionally, its purpose has been moral and civic, with a focus on the lives of great men and women. More recently, others have argued for it as a logically distinct form of knowledge. These aims have been held in uneasy tension since 1988, with political pressures in subsequent years towards the former. The current history curriculum fails to appeal to many ordinary children, is too intent on 'coverage', makes too few connections with contemporary affairs, and invites teaching to the test. The way forward lies in reversing these tendencies, and in putting more weight on differences in interpretation and revitalising the history teaching community. The gap between the generic aims and current arrangements is wide and will only be reduced once more freedom is granted to teachers.

Peter Gill begins his Chapter 8 on *Mathematics* with a dismissal of three of the most prominent arguments for the subject's being so extensively taught – its utility (beyond basic numeracy), its role in training thinking skills and its intrinsic interest. His examination of how well it fits the overall aims also reaches largely negative conclusions. As with history, there has historically been a tension between ways of conceiving the subject, in the case of mathematics between those who see it as preparation for further work in higher education and those for whom it is a part of a child's personal development, the former being more influential. Once again, assessment arrangements come under fire as inadequate vehicles for revealing depth of understanding. Peter Gill suggests a radical overhaul of practices and regulations within the field, advocating that those who have not progressed well in the subject by the end of Key Stage 3 should be allowed to opt out.

Chapter 9 is on *Modern Foreign Languages*. Kevin Williams begins, like Gill, with a rejection of familiar vocational and other utilitarian arguments for compulsory provision. He then focuses on several valid arguments for learning a foreign language that are *not* uppermost in official justifications of the subject but that *are* closely in line with generic aims of the whole curriculum. Arguments of an experiential kind are: to provide pleasure, to form a basis for further learning and to engender cultural decentring. Arguments connected with ethical development have to do with promoting openness to others at an individual level and, in a symbolic way, at the national. Williams holds that these arguments together justify giving all students the opportunity to learn a foreign language, perhaps more intensively and at an earlier age than usual, but that, seeing that not all students have an interest in or aptitude for the subject, they do not justify compulsory provision for more than one year.

Music is a prominent ingredient of contemporary culture. Yet, as Charles Plummeridge and Keith Swanwick argue in Chapter 10, its vitality and many-sidedness is not well reflected in school music. The National Curriculum has reinforced the traditional dominance of class teaching (which has its origins in choral singing in church), with a lesser role for instrumental tuition and extracurricular activities. Training in musicianship has been, and still is, the central rationale for the subject, rather than a more general induction into the discourse of music. The music curriculum needs to be more closely linked with the wider musical world and to build on contemporary local initiatives based on outreach programmes and other activities. This calls for a much more flexible music curriculum, reflecting the multiplicity of forms of musical experience and offering more options to secondary students. The changes would bring musical provision much closer to the new overall aims.

In *Physical Education*, too, according to Dawn Penney's analysis in Chapter 11, the National Curriculum has given further legitimation to long-standing practice. Traditionally, the subject has been conceived as a collection of discrete forms of activity, most often connected with sport. This conception originated in élite public (i.e. independent) schools in the nineteenth century, élitist connotations continuing in the privileging of preparation for high-order sporting performance among the aims of the subject as practised. The original National Curriculum order for PE had wider purposes than performance, but political involvement in the early 1990s narrowed these in the direction of the tradition. The curriculum is now built firmly around performance in dance, games, gymnastics, athletics, outdoor and adventure activities, and swimming. Dawn Penney questions the rationale for this structure and favours a radical refocus on a more flexible, interconnected and inclusive curriculum geared to children's current and future lives and with greater opportunities for choice given to schools and pupils.

Religious Education is not a part of the National Curriculum but has been compulsory since 1944. In Chapter 12, Michael Hand begins by looking at the original rationale for RE at that time. He locates this in the wartime desire, given totalitarian threats, to found British democracy on firm ethical foundations, Christian-based RE being the vehicle. After the war, with the decline of confessional RE and the coming of a multi-cultural society, this purpose gradually gave way to two other roles for the subject – moral education of a non-confessional sort and the promotion of understanding and respect for a variety of faiths (although, after 1988, Christianity regained something of its traditional privileged status). Hand argues that neither of these current rationales is strong enough to justify compulsory RE for all. But there is a *third* and more defensible rationale, yet not prominent in the documentation: pupils should be equipped to make informed judgements on the truth or falsity of religious beliefs.

Like many other subjects, *Science* is still imprisoned by its past. Edgar Jenkins shows, in Chapter 13, the class-divided nature of the subject for most of the twentieth century. Science was first taught in nineteenth-century public schools and then in secondary grammar schools. Courses were based on the fundamentals of chemistry and physics and, later, biology, and on extensive practical work in specialised laboratories. The legacy is that most children did little or no science until more recent times; only in 1989 did it become an established part of the standard primary curriculum. In addition, since that date, the élite tradition, with its specialist, university-oriented outlook and ritualised emphasis on laboratory activity, has become further entrenched at the secondary level, leaving school science increasingly divorced from the role that science has come to play in the modern world. However, he cautions that framers of a more inclusive science curriculum should look warily on demands for science to be taught through its technological and civic applications and argues that attention should be given to developing the pedagogical and other strategies needed to introduce students to the key features of how scientists currently understand the world.

As will be apparent from this résumé of the chapters, there are many parallels across the subjects in historical development, the tenacity of custom, the focus on specialist training, social class differences in provision, disagreements about aims, the impact of the National Curriculum, the constraints of its assessment system, a desire for a reshaped curriculum that is more inclusive and in tune with the new overall aims. Chapter 14 picks out a number of these common themes and discusses lessons that can be learnt from them which may be used to formulate more adequate National Curriculum policies.

REFERENCES

Aldrich, R. (1988) 'The national curriculum: an historical perspective', in Lawton, D. and Chitty, C. (eds) *The National Curriculum*, Bedford Way Paper 33, London: Institute of Education University of London.

DfEE/QCA (1999) *The National Curriculum Handbook for Primary/Secondary Teachers in England*.

Goodson, I.F. and Marsh, C.J. (eds) (1996) *Studying school subjects: a guide*, London: Falmer.

Graham, D. and Tytler, D. (1993) *A lesson for us all*, London and New York: Routledge.

HMSO (2000) *Social Trends 30*, London: HMSO.

Niblett, W.R. (1966) 'The Religious Education clauses of the 1944 Act: aims, hopes and fulfilment', in Wedderspoon, A.G. (ed.) *Religious Education 1944–1984*, London: Allen & Unwin.

QCA (2000) *Religious Education: Non-statutory guidance on RE*, London: Qualifications and Curriculum Authority.

SCAA (1997) *Second annual report on monitoring the school curriculum 1996–7*, London: School Curriculum and Assessment Authority.

Selleck, R.J.W. (1968) *The new education: the English background 1870–1914*, Melbourne: Pitman.

White, J. (2002) *The child's mind*, London: RoutledgeFalmer.

VALUE-ADDED IS OF LITTLE VALUE

Stephen Gorard

A NOTE FROM THE EDITORS

This reading introduces debates about the aims of education and considers the educational aims for a range of subject areas.

This reading links with Chapter 7 (especially Units 7.1 and 7.2) of the 5th edition of *Learning to teach in the secondary school*.

QUESTIONS TO CONSIDER

1   Having studied the Gorard and Connolly readings referred to above, what are your views of their arguments that the 'league tables' do not report what they claim to report? What are your views about the role national league tables play in holding schools and teachers to account?

2   What particular provision might a school make, based on the findings that Gorard reports, to maximize the chances of all pupils to achieve their potential in public tests?

3   It is said that looked-after children (or children in care) in England achieve at levels below those of other pupils and have poorer life outcomes. Examine the data on the educational outcomes of looked-after children in the school and local authority in which you are learning to teach and explore the achievement of these pupils in the school in which you are on school placement. Consider what your responsibilities are as a teacher with respect to these pupils.

This reading was first published as: Gorard, S. (2006) 'Value-added is of little value', *Journal of Education Policy*, Vol. 21: 235–243.

ABSTRACT

Published indicators of school 'performance', such as those shown annually in league tables in England, have been controversial since their inception. Raw-score figures for school outcomes are heavily dependent on the prior attainment and family background of the students. Policy-makers in Wales have reacted to this fundamental flaw by withdrawing the publication of school results. In England, on the other hand, they have reacted by asking for more information to be added to tables, in the form of student context such as the percentage with a special educational need, and 'value-added' figures. In 2004, the Department for Education and Skills (DfES) value-added figures for England were based on student progress from Key Stage 2 at the end of primary education to GCSE at the end of compulsory secondary education. For 2005, at time of writing, the DfES plan to use context information in their model as well. This paper re-analyses the 2004 value-added figures and shows that they contain the same flaw as the original raw-score tables. The purported value-added scores turn out to be a proxy for the overall level of attainment in the school, and almost entirely independent of any differential progress made by the students. The paper concludes by considering the implications of these findings, if accepted, for policies based on identifying schools that are clearly more or less effective, and for the field of school effectiveness and improvement research.

INTRODUCTION TO VALUE-ADDED COMPARISONS

This paper reminds readers of some of the flaws in previous attempts to measure the performance of schools, and of how such measurement is currently being attempted by the Department for Education and Skills (DfES) for secondary schools in England. The paper then re-analyses the figures from 2004 and shows that league tables still suffer from what was identified some time ago as 'the politician's error' (Gorard, 1999). This is where differences between two sets of figures are considered in isolation from the scale of the original figures. The enormity of the problem, once accepted, for policy-making, the local reputation of schools, and for studies of school effectiveness would be difficult to over-emphasize.

League tables of school examination outcomes have been controversial since their introduction in England and Wales in the early 1990s. In their simplest form, the tables list the schools in each local education authority (LEA) area, the number of students in a relevant age cohort, and the percentage of those students attaining a relevant qualification or its equivalent. In the printed press, these tables have been presented in descending order of percentage attainment by schools. This information was intended to help parents make judgements about the quality of their local schools, especially in an era of increased parental choice of schools after the 1988 Education Reform Act.

However, these lists were labelled school 'performance' tables incorrectly, because there is a very high correlation between the nature of the student intake to any school and their subsequent public test scores (Gorard and Smith, 2004). This correlation can be expressed in several ways, including in terms of prior attainment or indicators of socio-economic disadvantage. For example, the figures for all secondary schools in England in 2004 are shown in Figure 19.1. The correlation is + 0.87 between each school's intake in KS2 points and its subsequent outcomes in percentage obtaining five or more GCSE grade A*–C. This means that the majority of the difference between school outcomes (76 per cent) is directly attributable to the prior attainment of their intake, and thence to the socio-economic characteristics of the intake, rather than to the work of each school itself (Gorard, 2000). There are no schools with high KS2 intake scores that have low GCSE outcome scores, or vice versa. There are threshold effects at or near 100 per cent, but otherwise there is, as expected, a well-defined linear relationship between input and output. It is, therefore, not at all clear how effective each school had been in producing the outcomes other than in attracting high-attaining students in the first place. In theory, it is possible that some low-scoring schools are more effective at dealing with equivalent students than high-scoring ones, but that this is not reflected in the raw-score tables.

In any study of school effects, typically between 0 and 25 per cent of the variation between school outcomes remains to be explained once the school intake is accounted for, as here. This residual of 0–25 per cent includes a very important error component (Gorard, 2006). This major finding of work in the school effectiveness genre has been quite consistent over time. The larger the study, the more variables available for each student, the more reliable the measures are, and the better conducted the study, the stronger is this link between school intake and outcomes. This strong link makes the work of school improvers difficult, since the most obvious way for any school to produce higher outcome scores is to improve the intake scores, or exclude students with low intake scores before the age 15+. This would be 'sleight-of-hand' school improvement and, of course, a zero-sum process by correspondingly reducing the intake scores to neighbouring schools. However, school effectiveness and school improvement (SESI) advocates try to guard against being misled by not using raw-scores outcomes and using value-added models instead. These models are intended to take the prior attainment of each student into account, and so to produce scores that are 'a measure of the progress students make between different stages of education' (DfES, 2005a).

In response to such problems, general information about school performance is no longer made publicly available in Wales (or Scotland), largely because of its potential to mislead. In England, the alternative response has been to try and maintain the freedom of this information while remedying its defects. One such remedy has been termed

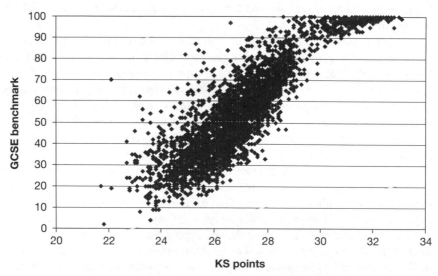

■ Figure 19.1 The link between KS2 points and GCSE benchmark, all secondary schools in England, 2004.

'value-added' analysis. In this, the prior attainment of each student is taken into account, such that the published performance figures reflect, not the intake to the school, but the average progress made by students while in the school. The DfES value-added scores for the average student progress from Key Stage 2 (KS2, the prior attainment of the student at primary school) to Key Stage 4 (examinations, such as the GCSE, at the end of compulsory schooling) in each secondary school are calculated as follows (full details available at DfES, 2005a). For the 2004 figures, all students in a school were included who were aged 15 or more on 31 August 2003, still on the school roll in January 2004, and with at least one matched KS2 score. The KS2 levels achieved by each student for each core subject (English, maths, science) were converted to point scores and then averaged across the three (or fewer) subjects. KS4 points were calculated as a sum of the scores for the best eight GCSE results (or their 'equivalent'). Nationally, it is possible to calculate a median value for progress from any KS2 score to KS4, such that half of the students make less progress and half make more. The median value for 21 points at KS2 ('equivalent' to an average of level three in each subject) was 202 KS4 points (roughly 'equivalent' to five GCSEs at grade C), for example. The value-added score for each student is the difference between their actual KS4 score and the median calculated from their prior KS2 score. The value-added score for each school is the average of the value-added scores for all students meeting the definition above (with 1,000 added to this average to eliminate negative values). The results generally range from 900 to 1,100, but are not uniformly distributed.

A SURPRISING CORRELATION

This paper uses the GCSE (KS4) results for mainstream secondary schools in England in 2004, their KS3 results for 2002, the KS2 scores of their intake in 2000 and the published DfES value-added scores for the same schools in 2004 (DfES, 2005b).[1] Results are presented in scatterplot form, or as Pearson R correlation co-efficients – which can be squared to give an 'effect' size.

The re-analysis presented starts with the 124 schools with complete information in York, Leeds, East Riding of Yorkshire and North Yorkshire. These are used as illustrations of the wider pattern. For the 124 mainstream secondary schools in the four Yorkshire LEAs, Table 19.1 shows a number of unsurprising correlations between indicators of attainment. The link between school outcomes at KS3 and KS4 is + 0.93, which means that over 86 per cent of the variance in school outcomes at KS4 is potentially explicable by prior school outcomes at KS3. In general, we may assume that students who do well at KS3 tend also to do well at KS4, and vice versa. This kind of correlation is one basis for the complaints about raw-score league tables (see above). Table 19.1 also shows a correlation of + 0.81 between the DfES value-added figures for student progress from KS2 to KS3 and from KS2 to KS4. This is also unsurprising because the two measures overlap, with the former subsumed by the latter. The correlation suggests that schools that add value to students' progress up until KS3 add similar value to progress up until KS4. This could mean that the bulk of students' progress occurs by KS3, or that schools tend to be equivalently effective for both phases of secondary education, or a combination of these explanations. In fact, however, neither explanation is necessary, because of the implications of the other correlations in Table 19.1.

There are unexpectedly high correlations between each indicator of overall school attainment and the value-added figures from each phase. The highest (+ 0.96) is between

■ **Table 19.1** Correlations between attainment and value-added

	KS3	KS4	VA KS2–3	VA KS 2–4
KS3	–	+ 0.93	+ 0.91	+ 0.87
KS4	+ 0.93	–	+ 0.81	+ 0.96
VA KS2-3	+ 0.91	+ 0.81	–	+ 0.81
VA KS2–4	+ 0.87	+ 0.96	+ 0.81	–

the KS4 absolute score for each school and the purported 'value-added' score for student progress from KS2 to KS4. These figures for each school are cross-plotted in Figure 19.2, which shows quite clearly that schools with high outcome scores have high value-added figures, and vice versa. In fact, we could predict the value-added figure for any school extremely well just from their absolute level of final attainment.

How can we explain this surprising correlation? It could, of course, be the case that the progress made by students in all schools is truly in direct proportion to their school's average outcomes. *Ceteris paribus*, one would expect schools that helped students to make considerable progress also to have higher outcomes, in general, than those that did not. Perhaps Figure 19.2 merely reflects this? There are several reasons why this cannot account for all, or even much, of the story. The pattern is too good.[3] There are no low- to mid-attaining schools with high value-added scores. All of the schools with a GCSE benchmark of 40 per cent or less are deemed negative value-added. Similarly there are no high- to mid-attaining schools with low value-added scores. All of the schools with a GCSE benchmark of 80 per cent or more are deemed positive value-added. The remaining schools, with 'average' GCSE benchmarks, are mostly very close to zero value-added. It would be possible to argue that the residual variation (i.e. the 'width' of the line) represents differential effectiveness, but the combined error term in assessing, measuring, aggregating and analysing the data is a more plausible explanation for these relatively minor differences. It is also important to note that a similarly high correlation appears

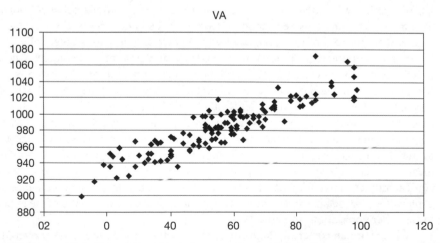

■ **Figure 19.2** The relationship between value-added and absolute attainment, 2004.

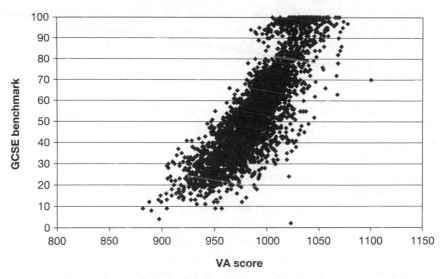

■ **Figure 19.3** The link between GCSE benchmark and KS2 to GCSE value-added, all secondary schools in England, 2004.

between the KS4 value-added score and the prior KS3 results. Given that the assessment system in England is not wholly reliable, and that no data collection, transcription, aggregation or analysis process is wholly accurate, the correlation of + 0.96 means that the DfES value-added figures and the raw-scores for absolute attainment are actually measuring the same thing (like Centigrade and Fahrenheit, they merely use different scales to portray the same underlying variable). It would, therefore, be much simpler to use the raw-score values than to bother with the computation of 'value-added' figures that tell exactly the same story. But these raw-score values have already been rejected by most commentators as being unrelated to school performance. This means, ironically, that the value-added scores have to be rejected on the same grounds.

For the same set of secondary schools as in Figure 19.1, for England in 2004, the DfES value-added school 'performance' figures have a correlation of + 0.84 with the raw-score outcomes they are intended to replace, which themselves have a + 0.87 correlation with the prior KS2 scores. This means that 71 per cent of the variation in school value-added scores is explicable in terms of their raw-scores alone. Figure 19.3 shows that, again ignoring the threshold effects, there is a clear pattern of low-attaining schools having low VA, and high-attaining schools having low VA. Value-added scores are no *more* independent of raw-score levels of attainment than outcomes are independent of intakes.

SOME IMPLICATIONS

School effectiveness and school improvement (SESI) forms an entire field of research and policy endeavour. It is based on the dual premise that schools are differentially effective with equivalent students, and that it is possible to transfer good practice from the more successful schools to the less successful ones. The emphasis is on the rather narrow view of schools as producers of examination and test scores. The Academies programme is one example stemming from this idea, and its questionable initial success has already been attributed to visionary school leadership, curriculum change and a range of other

SESI-type factors (Gorard, 2005). In order to show that a good school is differentially effective, we have to establish that exactly equivalent students would achieve lower test scores after education at another school. In order to show that a school has improved, we have to establish that there has been an improvement in test scores that cannot be explained by a change in the nature of the school intake. Otherwise, SESI is 'sleight-of-hand'.

If accepted, the analysis above shows that the published 'value-added' results for secondary schools are nothing of the sort, because they are not independent of absolute level of attainment at KS2, KS3 or KS4. Value-added scores are no *more* independent of raw-score levels of attainment than outcomes are independent of intakes. The value-added figures are actually the transformed *equivalent* of raw-scores and, therefore, suffer from precisely the same defects as raw-scores, of being largely predictable from prior attainment and/or student background. The rather lengthy procedures described by the DfES (2005a) to produce scores that are 'a measure of the progress students make between different stages of education' have been shown to be pointless. This may explain the otherwise rather perplexing finding from simulated models that value-added figures are no more accurate than raw-score figures as a predictor of school performance (Hoyle and Robinson, 2003). In 2005, at time of writing, the DfES plans to use context information in its model as well. This may mask, but will not solve, the problem described here.

In fact, the value-added calculations are rather worse than pointless because their apparent precision and technical sophistication may have misled analysts, observers and commentators into believing that they had succeeded, or that a greater range of variables or a more complex analytical model would somehow solve the outstanding problems. They make it harder for many commentators to understand fully what the figures mean, and what their limitations are. Some commentators will, therefore, become like the idealized 'villain' described at the start of Gorard (2003a), who is not appropriately sceptical of statistical analysis, and is overly impressed by technicalities at the expense of coherence and transparency. One recent suggestion has been that multi-level modelling is the way forward here, but techniques such as this are already over-used, and inappropriate for population data such as the DfES school performance figures. They create such a distance between the data and the analyst that they appear to encourage simple errors such as mistaking what the numbers involved represent (Gorard, 2003b, 2004).

If accepted, this reconsideration suggests that school improvement policies, at least in this narrow sense, are likely to be ineffective. Policies concerning schools, and judgements about the relative effectiveness of different schools and types of school, will have been misled where they have been based on the government's value-added analyses (or indeed any value-added analysis that does not correct for the politician's error). Families may have been misled about the relative effectiveness of their local schools, with the schools in poorer areas and with academically weaker intakes suffering the most from this misguided comparison dressed up as a 'fair test'. School improvers and school improvement researchers, relying on value-added analyses, will have been misled in their explanations and in making recommendations for practice. The implications of this simple mistake are legion.

The majority of the variation in school examination outcomes can be explained by the intake to the school (prior attainment, socio-economic background and educational need). However, this undisputed finding has led to two very different conclusions. For one group of commentators, it seems obvious that the finding minimizes the role of the school and alerts us to seek improvements in equity otherwise. School improvement is, therefore, seen as 'sleight-of-hand' in generally being explicable by changes in school intakes. Any unexplained variation could be attributed to errors in measuring attainment and bias caused by missing data. For another group of commentators, the fact that at least *some* variation in school outcomes is not explained by school intakes is evidence that schools must have important differential effects on outcomes. This position lies behind the creation of value-added league tables. In light of the foregoing, such a position seems less tenable than ever before.

NOTES ON CONTRIBUTOR

Stephen Gorard holds the Anniversary Chair in Educational Studies at the University of York, and leads the Centre for Research into Equity and Impact. He is currently researching distance learning (*Adult learning in the digital age*, 2005, Routledge), widening participation in HE ('Widening participation for whom?', 2004, *HE Quarterly*), school diversity (*Schools, markets and choice policies*, 2003, Routledge), assessment ('They don't give us our marks', 2005, *Assessment in Education*), justice in schools ('Pupils' views of equity in education', 2005, *Compare*), teacher supply ('Crisis, what crisis?', 2004, *Cambridge Journal of Education*) and school effects ('Is there a school mix effect', 2006, *Educational Review*). He is also interested in the process and quality of research (*Combining methods in educational and social research*, 2004, Open University Press).

NOTES

1   I would like to acknowledge here the help of the DfES for providing the figures and subsequent discussion of the findings.

2   Intriguingly, the fact that the national average for value-added was 988.1 after adding 1000 suggests that the average effect on student progress of all of the secondary schools in England is negative! Of course, this cannot be so because the value is based on the cohort itself, and all 'effects' are relative to the median. However, the scale of this spurious negative average gives us an alarming indication of the level of slippage in the process as a whole.

3   The slight scatter at the 100 per cent end of the x-axis in Figures 19.1–19.3 could be explained by the lack of freedom to vary at this ceiling. The schools at or near 100 per cent on the GCSE benchmark figure have some variation on the y-axis that is unrelated to the x-axis because that is the only kind of variation possible (compare the concept of regression towards the mean).

REFERENCES

DfES (2005a) *Performance tables*, available online at www.dfes.gov.uk/performancetables/schools_04/sec3b.shtml; accessed 25 February 2005.

DfES (2005b) *Performance tables*, available online at www.dfes.gov.uk/performancetables; accessed 25 February 2005.

Gorard, S. (1999) 'Keeping a sense of proportion: the 'politician's error' in analysing school outcomes', *British Journal of Educational Studies*, Vol. 47, No. 3: 235–246.

Gorard, S. (2000) *Education and social justice*, Cardiff: University of Wales Press.

Gorard, S. (2003a) *Quantitative methods in social science*, London: Continuum.

Gorard, S. (2003b) 'Understanding probabilities and re-considering traditional research methods training', *Sociological Research Online*, Vol. 8, No. 1; available online at www.socresonline.org.uk/8/1gorard.html.

Gorard, S. (2004) 'Comments on modeling segregation', *Oxford Review of Education*, Vol. 30, No. 3: 435–440.

Gorard, S. (2005) 'Academies as the "future of schooling": is this an evidence-based policy?', *Journal of Education Policy*, Vol. 20, No. 3: 369–377.

Gorard, S. (2006) 'Is there a school mix effect?', *Educational Review*, Vol. 58, No. 1: 87–94.

Gorard, S. and Smith, E. (2004) 'What is "underachievement" at school?', *School Leadership and Management*, Vol. 24, No. 2: 205–225.

Hoyle, R. and Robinson, J. (2003) 'League tables and school effectiveness: a mathematical model', *Proceedings of the Royal Society of London B*, Vol. 270: 113–199.

YOUR PROFESSIONAL DEVELOPMENT

INTRODUCTION

This section focuses on life beyond your ITE course. Your immediate concern is with getting your first job, then making the transition from student to newly qualified teacher, that is starting your first post, your first year in teaching and then your continuing professional development. There are many opportunities available to you in relation to your professional development; it is your responsibility to take those opportunities.

THE READING IN THIS SECTION IS:

Reading 20
The role of teacher research in continuing professional development
Margaret Kirkwood and Donald Christie

There is one reading in this section, by Kirkwood and Christie (2006), which examines the role of teacher research and enquiry in teachers' professional development. It considers the extent to which continuing professional development activities arising from the Chartered Teacher Programme in Scotland (designed to enhance the status and working conditions of teachers) encourage teachers to value research, equip them to become research-minded and support them to engage in research and enquiry in their own professional contexts. As well as reviewing the literature on continuing professional development and models of teacher research and enquiry, the paper provides examples of professional development and teacher research drawn from one optional module delivered in the Chartered Teacher Programme. Results suggest that the success of this module demonstrates 'how favourable conditions can be created for networks of teachers as researching professionals to develop, and that a successful start can be made to initiating teachers into research as conceived by Stenhouse (1975, 1983), thus enhancing their professional practice and leading to, 'more intelligent and sensitive ways of effective learning' (Kirk *et al.*, 2003: 30).

FURTHER READING

Hammond, M. (2002) 'Why teach? A case study investigating the decision to train to teach ICT', *Journal of Education for Teaching*, Vol. 28, No. 2: 135–148.

This paper investigates the motivations of a cohort of fifteen student teachers on a PGCE course to teach information and communication technology (ICT). Student teachers frequently drew on their own past experience of teaching, mentoring or helping a learner when deciding to train as a teacher. They were influenced by their interest in ICT and generalised from their own experiences to believe that pupils would find ICT an interesting and valuable subject. Although these student teachers were not motivated by material rewards, they did look for salary and career progression. This study confirms findings from several other studies on teacher recruitment. However, it suggests that experiences of taking part in 'teaching-like' activities are more salient than experiences of being a learner when reaching a decision to learn to teach.

The above further reading links with Unit 8.1 of the 5th edition of *Learning to teach in the secondary school*.

Priyadharshini, E. and Robinson-Pant, A. (2003) 'The attractions of teaching: an investigation into why people change careers to teach', *Journal of Education for Teaching*, Vol. 29, No. 2: 95–112.

This paper examines questions related to motivation of student teachers who have changed careers to learn to teach; perceptions held by recruits that led them to choose teaching; and factors that may deter student teachers from remaining in the profession.

The above further reading links with Unit 8.1 of the 5th edition of *Learning to teach in the secondary school*.

See, B.H. (2004) 'Determinants of teaching as a career in the UK', *Evaluation and Research in Education*, Vol. 18, No. 4: 213–242.

As part of an ESRC-funded project, this study gathers data from 1,845 student teachers from four institutions to explore the key social and economic determinants of the choice of teaching as a career in the UK.

The above further reading links with Unit 8.1 of the 5th edition of *Learning to teach in the secondary school*.

See, B.H., Gorard, S. and White, P. (2004) 'Teacher demand: crisis, what crisis?', *Cambridge Journal of Education*, Vol. 34, No. 1: 103–123.

As part of two studies funded by the General Teaching Council for Wales and the ESRC, this study uses official statistics from a range of secondary sources to examine the issue of teacher vacancies, including regional and subject-specific factors in recruitment to teaching.

The above further reading links with Unit 8.1 of the 5th edition of *Learning to teach in the secondary school*.

Yandell, J. and Turvey, A. (2007) 'Standards or communities of practice? Competing models of workplace learning and development', *British Educational Research Journal*, Vol. 33, No. 4: 533–550.

Drawing on interview data derived from two case studies of teachers in their first year in the profession, this article examines the difficulties that confront new teachers as they move from a PGCE course into their first teaching post. It questions the value of discursive practices that construct teaching as a set of discrete competences or standards, and argues that Lave and Wenger's (1991) concepts of legitimate peripheral participation and communities of practice are useful tools with which to analyse the sociocultural complexity of the new teachers' experiences.

The above further reading links with Unit 8.2 of the 5th edition of *Learning to teach in the secondary school*.

THE ROLE OF TEACHER RESEARCH IN CONTINUING PROFESSIONAL DEVELOPMENT

Margaret Kirkwood and Donald Christie

A NOTE FROM THE EDITORS

This reading is a case study that examines the role of teacher research and enquiry in teachers' professional development in one optional module delivered in the Chartered Teacher programme in Scotland.

This reading links with Unit 8.2 of the 5th edition of *Learning to teach in the secondary school*.

QUESTIONS TO CONSIDER

1   Stenhouse (1975) viewed the 'teacher as researcher'; what did he mean by this? What other models of teacher as researcher are there? What models of reflective practice are there, and what do these mean for the practice of teachers?

2   What relationship is there between the teacher as researcher and the teacher as reflective practitioner?

3   The reading gives one example of favourable conditions created for networks of teachers as researching professionals to develop, thus enhancing their professional practice. What examples are there of other such initiatives which might support your own continuing professional practice?

This reading was first published as: Kirkwood, M. and Christie, D. (2006) 'The role of teacher research in continuing professional development', *British Journal of Educational Studies*, Vol. 54: 429–448.

ABSTRACT

This article sets out to examine the role of teacher research and enquiry in the professional development of teachers. The context derives from the initiative of the Scottish Executive to enhance the status and working conditions of teachers. We consider the extent to which continuing professional development activities arising out of the Chartered Teacher Programme encourage teachers to value research, equip them to become research-minded and support them to engage in research and enquiry in their own professional contexts.

INTRODUCTION

Lawrence Stenhouse, an eloquent exponent of the concept of the teacher as a researcher, viewed the nature of educational research as 'systematic enquiry made public' (Stenhouse, 1975: 142) and its object as being to develop thoughtful reflection in order to strengthen the professional judgement of teachers (Stenhouse, 1983: 192). He asserted that curriculum research and development ought to belong to the teacher: 'It is not enough that teachers' work should be studied: they need to study it themselves' (Stenhouse, 1975: 143). When considering the conditions necessary to achieve his vision, however, Stenhouse conceded:

> that it will require a generation of work, and if the majority of teachers – rather than only the enthusiastic few – are to possess this field of research, that the teacher's professional self-image and conditions of work will have to change.
>
> (Stenhouse, 1975: 142)

A generation later, the present article sets out to examine the role of teacher research and enquiry in the professional development of teachers. The context for the present study is the recent initiative by the Scottish Executive Education Department (SEED) to enhance the status and working conditions of Scottish teachers (SEED, 2001). We shall make no attempt to assess whether or not teachers' working conditions have indeed improved over the past three decades. However, we shall consider whether current developments in Scotland are encouraging and supporting teachers to engage in professional research and enquiry, and whether Stenhouse's emancipatory ideals can be applied to a new Scottish model of continuing professional development (CPD).

There is no doubt that the concepts of research and enquiry have entered the discourse of teacher professionalism. As part of the new framework of professional standards for teachers in Scotland, the Standard for Chartered Teacher (SCT) seeks to describe the knowledge, attributes, values and professional action associated with accomplished teaching and which are to be expected of those aspiring to the status of Chartered Teacher (CT) (SEED, 2002a). The significance of research for the teaching profession is signalled within the SCT, in the clear expectation that the CT should demonstrate the capacity to:

> . . . ensure that teaching is informed by reading and research. For example, by:
>
> ■ engaging in professional enquiry and action research, and applying findings
> ■ reflecting critically on research evidence and modifying practice as appropriate
> ■ testing whether a particular theoretical perspective actually applies in practice
> ■ interpreting changes to education policy and practice and contributing and responding to such changes.
>
> (SEED, 2002a)

Kirk comments:

> There has been a tendency for teachers to be the objects and consumers of research rather than its generators. The Standard encourages teachers to be more active in originating research, to apply research findings to their own context, as well as to subject their work to critical analysis using research tools of various kinds.
>
> (Kirk, 2004: 14)

Furthermore, as the CT Programme develops and impacts on education in Scotland, Kirk (2004) envisages networks of teachers as researching professionals becoming established and supporting each other, thus strengthening our understanding of the nature of teaching and learning.

However, it is reasonable to ask whether such expectations are appropriate or realistic. Past efforts by the Scottish Council for Research in Education and the Scottish Educational Research Association to establish networks of teachers as researching professionals have tended to attract only a few members who have then drifted away. The present article aims to answer this question by exploring relevant theoretical perspectives and by relating these to the experiences of a cohort of teachers involved in the pilot study of an option module which forms part of the CT Programme. Before looking in more detail at this particular attempt to implement the SCT, it is important to consider the conceptual framework which informs alternative models of professional development and teacher research.

TEACHERS' CONTINUING PROFESSIONAL DEVELOPMENT

Teachers' CPD can be seen as having quite different purposes, depending on the conceptions of teacher professionalism which are held. Day (1999), for example, argues that teachers' professional development should be an intrinsically motivated process of personal growth. On the other hand, with the apparent emphasis on accountability and performativity by government agencies in many parts of the world, including the UK, the purpose of CPD may become instrumental, measured in terms of increased effectiveness in delivering specified learning outcomes for the consumers of the education being provided, rather than the intrinsic enhancement of professional knowledge and understanding. Knight (2002) distinguishes between the traditional, formal, event-delivery model and non-formal learning opportunities which arise out of the interplay of professional lives in real professional contexts. The formal approach entails individual engagement, with structured programmes often provided by external bodies. The non-formal approach is characterised by collaborative, 'mutual engagement' in what Wenger (1998) would describe as 'communities of practice'. Here, the emphasis is upon learning through social interaction. Wenger (1998) proposes three dimensions of communities of practice, which entail participants being involved in, 'evolving forms of mutual engagement; understanding and tuning their (joint) enterprise; and developing their repertoire, styles and discourses' (p. 95). It may be helpful to attempt to apply these dimensions of professional learning to the idea of teacher research and posit the notion of a community of enquiry as a model for schools aspiring to be effective, evidence-informed professional learning communities of the kind described by Stoll *et al.* (2003).

Humes (2001) discusses ways in which approaches to professional development have changed over the last 30 years, to reflect changed conditions and evolving views of what comprises professional expertise. Traditionally, expertise was identified with professional knowledge involving a high theoretical content, regardless of whether this was ever applied in the professional context. However, recent approaches seem to assume that expertise depends mainly on experience. In this, Humes (2001: 12) recognises a direct challenge to develop new forms of professional development which would lead to, 'a better understanding (and use) of the relation between abstract theoretical knowledge, expressed at a high level of generality, and situated, experiential knowledge, derived from particular contexts'. Humes claims this would certainly involve teachers in subjecting their own practice to rational reflection and critical scrutiny, informed by writing and research. Among other things, it could involve teachers in identifying areas of investigation and looking for evidence that might cast light on situations.

There are features of the new CT Programme in Scotland which reflect the various models described above. In a sense, the contrasting purposes of CPD are captured in the fact that it is defined as both a contractual obligation and a professional entitlement (SEED, 2002b). Teachers' accountability for standards in schools is explicitly stated in terms of the expectation that the CT is capable of demonstrating enhancements in pupils' learning (Kirk, 2004: 14). At the same time, new opportunities for career progression and promotion have been added through a structured CPD programme leading to the status of CT (SEED, 2001, 2002a, b; Purdon, 2003). A formal, modular programme at Masters level has been introduced, but the SCT against which teachers' progress through the programme is to be assessed includes within it the explicit expectations of mutual collaboration and influence, echoing the forms of engagement entailed by communities of practice. And, of course, the components of the Standard itself encompass both theoretical and experiential knowledge as well as professional values and commitments. Having considered different perspectives on CPD, we need now to explore models of teacher research and enquiry, before examining whether the context being created in Scotland is conducive to research as a form of CPD for teachers.

MODELS OF TEACHER RESEARCH AND ENQUIRY

In the preamble to a British Educational Research Association (BERA) guide to issues and principles in educational research for teachers, Campbell *et al.* (2003: 1) identify how the use and conduct of research by teachers have developed within a profession strongly influenced by policy, and that frequent references to teaching aspiring to be an 'evidence based profession' suggest an important and close link between research and classroom practice. However, the term 'evidence based profession' does not make clear whether teachers should make use of existing research knowledge or whether they are able to become researchers themselves. Campbell *et al.*'s position on this is clear: both aspects should be encompassed, although it is recognised that the value placed on teacher research in terms of its impact on professional development and the potential improvement of practice has yet to be fully realised (Campbell *et al.*, 2003: 2). For such research to be worthwhile, its conduct (as with the conduct of any research) must be irreproachable, no matter which set of techniques or procedures is used. Furthermore:

> Teachers need to know about the basics of good research, whether or not they ever conduct their own research. They need to be able to analyse critically the research evidence that they read as part of their professional role, and to judge its findings and conclusions from a well-informed point of view.
>
> (Campbell *et al.*, 2003: 4)

Cochran-Smith and Lytle (1993) define teacher research as, 'systematic and intentional inquiry about teaching, learning and schooling carried out by teachers in their own school and classroom settings' (p. 27). They include both empirical and conceptual inquiry in their definition and suggest that teacher research may generate both local knowledge and public knowledge: local knowledge informing their own practice and potentially benefiting the immediate community of teachers, and public knowledge informing the wider 'community of educators' (p. 42). Stenhouse (1975) envisaged an educational science, 'in which each classroom is a laboratory, each teacher a member of the scientific community' (p. 142). However, he questioned the adequacy of the positivist, nomothetic perspective traditionally associated with the scientific method and advocated a more idiographic approach in order to take into account the practical complexity and uniqueness of every educational setting.

Eisner (2002) has picked up this theme, analysing the shift in prevailing views about knowledge in the sphere of education and in particular about teachers' professional knowledge. The dominance of positivist conceptions of true and certain knowledge, known to the Greek philosophers as *episteme,* has waned, Eisner (2002) argues, with increasing acceptance of a more appropriate pluralist and constructivist epistemology with its emphasis on reasoning in the more uncertain practical domain – *phronesis.* However, a further step is required according to Eisner (2002). He suggests we should describe teaching in terms not confined to practical knowledge but encompassing productive artistry. Eisner offers us the metaphor of the classroom as studio together with the idea of teaching as a craft or art rather than as a science. Here the emphasis is on opening up the practice of teaching as a public performance which can be scrutinised, shared and discussed with colleagues. It is worth noting that the idea of teaching as an art is not new, as can be seen from Stenhouse's (1980) argument that the basis of the development of the curriculum and the improvement of practice is teachers being in a uniquely powerful position to develop '[their] art under the impulse of ideas' and to express in curricular form and subsequently test their 'ideas about knowledge or about teaching' (p. 251).

The collaborative dimension of professional practice in general, and of teacher research in particular, is a recurring theme in the literature. This dimension is not always reflected in current formal postgraduate programmes of study or in higher research degrees. Campbell *et al.* (2003: 3) discuss the importance of collaborative groups and networks to help sustain and embed research in educational settings. They also discuss how research collaboration can provide a useful means for addressing problems of practice in teaching, as follows:

> Through engaging in discussion and joint exploration, a range of perspectives can be brought to bear on a problem, leading perhaps to an enriched understanding of the issues. Also there will be a range of expertise that can be called into play in pursuit of a solution, bringing the possibility for the members of the group to learn new skills. The potential for cross-fertilization of ideas and shared planning and development may lead to greater creativity and productivity.
>
> (Campbell *et al.*, 2003: 7)

In a similar vein, Loughran (2003) suggests that teacher research will thrive where it is a genuinely collaborative, problem-solving activity, where the context is one in which the teacher has the confidence to deal with both success and failure, and where it is possible to communicate the findings of the research to others in a meaningful and effective way.

King (2002) argues that professional enquiry should be seen as most usefully operating as a school-wide collective, collaborative activity. In contrast, Kirkwood (2001) describes how secondary computing-studies teachers from across a large education authority engaged together with a university-based researcher in collaborative enquiry focused on enhancing learning and teaching. In order to develop solutions to problems of practice, they began to routinely adopt a research perspective on their classrooms and formed informal support networks, reaching beyond the boundaries of their own establishments.

Zeichner and Noffke (2001) identify a range of different purposes for practitioner research in education, including: improving practice; enhancing professional understanding of specific aspects of practice, or of practice in general; and influencing the social conditions of practice (pp. 306–307). Pring (2000) acknowledges the potential importance of the idea of the teacher as researcher as being, 'crucial to the growth of professional knowledge' (p. 138). However, Pring sets high standards for teacher research to achieve. Like all research it must be open to proper scrutiny and criticism. Here again we see that professional enquiry is more than an individual activity; it entails collaborative engagement with the wider professional community. Furthermore, Pring (2000) argues that, when comparing teacher research with other forms of educational research within social science traditions, we should avoid false dualisms. It should not be assumed that such research has to ignore the subtlety and uniqueness of situations in order to achieve the social science standard of generalisability. Nor should teacher research focus exclusively on the uniqueness of the situation at the expense of ignoring important broader insights from larger-scale research. Pring (2000) concludes succinctly that research should be the servant of professional judgement, not its master (p. 139), thus echoing Stenhouse's view that the purpose of educational research is to strengthen the professional judgement of teachers. Will the CT Programme in Scotland foster collaborative teacher research which is capable of meeting Stenhouse's purpose and Pring's demanding criteria? This question should also be set in the context of the realities of classroom life. While the framework of professional standards now operating in Scotland calls upon teachers to engage in research and enquiry, it should be acknowledged that the intrinsic demands of the job of the teacher, coupled with the constraints within which teachers carry out their professional responsibilities, may make it difficult for them to engage in research activity. Even for those teachers who could, in Day's (2004) terms, be described as having a 'passion for teaching', any expectation that they should be engaged in original empirical research studies could be construed as unreasonable. On the other hand, collaborative forms of enquiry deeply embedded in the context and ways of working of schools may offer transformational and enhancing opportunities for professional development and school improvement (Day, 2004: 122).

THE IMPACT OF CONTEXTUAL CONDITIONS

The contextual conditions shaping the education system in most countries are undergoing rapid change. Conway (2001) has identified enquiry and reflection as key considerations in the redefinition of teacher professionalism taking place in many countries. In Scotland, a range of government agencies and professional bodies has given impetus to the concept of teacher research by providing financial and other forms of assistance to teachers. The General Teaching Council for Scotland (GTCS) has a modest Teacher Research Programme, enabling teachers working in educational establishments in Scotland to apply to undertake a piece of research related to one of the research priorities identified by the Council each year.

Lack of time has been reported by teachers as a significant obstacle to their actual engagement in classroom action research, even where they might be positively disposed toward the idea (Christenson *et al.*, 2002). GTCS is attempting to address this problem by providing for the cost of staffing cover to release a teacher researcher from classroom duties in order to engage in research. However, this may imply a slightly different model of practitioner researcher from one in which research is intimately embedded in classroom practice.

OECD (2002), reporting on their review of educational research and development in England, commended the government agencies responsible for their efforts to alter the balance between 'pure basic' research and 'pure applied' research by placing greater emphasis on 'use-inspired basic' research. One of the OECD recommendations was to create more networks of university-based researchers and practitioners, focused on core problems of practice. As discussed in the Introduction, the CT Programme is intended to be a stimulus and an appropriate framework within which networks of teachers as researching professionals can develop. In future this could involve partnerships with university-based researchers, and perhaps a greater emphasis on 'use-inspired basic' research, in which the development of theory and practice go hand-in-hand, as envisaged by Humes (2001). The OECD report raises the interesting questions of which (if any) types of networks and partnerships, and which research paradigms, may emerge from the CT developments.

THE STANDARD FOR CHARTERED TEACHER

One distinguishing feature of the Standard for Chartered Teacher is the fact that it was derived by means of a thorough and well-grounded empirical process (see Christie, 2003; Kirk *et al.*, 2003). Essentially, the exercise involved the following sources of evidence: an international literature review; two rounds of focus group interviews involving more than 500 teachers and other key stakeholders, including parents and children as well as policy makers; in-depth interviews conducted with accomplished teachers; and two national consultation surveys of the Scottish teaching profession. Careful content analysis of the collated information from all these sources yielded a standard which could be claimed genuinely to reflect views expressed by Scottish teachers and the wider educational community. The four components of the Standard emerged as:

- professional values and personal commitments;
- professional knowledge and understanding;
- personal and professional attributes;
- professional action.

These components are seen as interdependent:

> the possession of knowledge without the capacity to effect professional actions of various kinds is pointless; professional action that is not informed by relevant knowledge is haphazard; and knowledge or skills that are not subjected to self-criticism constitute a recipe for professional complacency and ineffectiveness.
>
> (Kirk, 2004: 12)

It can therefore be argued that the resulting Standard is no restrictive set of behavioural objectives imposed by an external agency, but is genuinely consensual and 'owned' by the profession. Nor is it a set of unconnected ideas or a mere listing of practical skills.

Against these potential criticisms Kirk *et al.* (2003) rejoin:

> It encompasses values and wide-ranging professional commitments; it expects teachers to ground their work in reading and reflection; it urges them to be self-critical; it enjoins teachers to seek to have an impact on the work of colleagues; and much else besides.

> (Kirk *et al.*, 2003: 30)

Furthermore, Kirk *et al.* (2003: 30) argue that the CT, far from being a mere technician, is expected to be committed to change and development and the improvement of professional performance, and to search for more intelligent and sensitive ways of effecting learning. It is interesting to note that, in their comparative analysis of the CT programme in Scotland and the arrangements for performance threshold payments in England, Menter *et al.* (2004) highlight the distinctive emphasis in Scotland on professional development through personal study in the work context and a prevailing climate which balances accountability with trust.

AN EXAMPLE OF PROFESSIONAL DEVELOPMENT AND TEACHER RESEARCH DRAWN FROM THE CT PROGRAMME

Following national consultation, a modular programme was devised consisting of four core modules, four option modules and project(s) equivalent to four further modules, leading to the award of a university Masters degree as well as the professional status of 'Chartered Teacher' at the end of a period of study and professional development lasting up to six years (accompanied by significant increases in salary during the duration of study). During 2002/2003, a nationally co-ordinated pilot study was conducted of the four 'core' modules and, following this, an invitation to tender for contracts to develop and pilot a number of option modules was issued. A range of delivery modes – university-based, education authority-based and distance-learning – was experimented with. The pilot study was designed to address key questions, such as: Could the whole initiative be made to work in practice? Could the balance of theory and professional practice be achieved? Could the programme be academically sound while remaining relevant to the classroom work of teachers? (Kirk *et al.*, 2003: 63). Evaluations of the core modules indicate that they were positively regarded, with participants saying that they were up-to-date and reflective of real teaching and learning practices (Kirk *et al.*, 2003: 65).

The module to be considered here was Learning to Think and Thinking to Learn, one of the seven option modules. Designed for teachers from across stages and subject specialisms, the module focused on four generic themes: learning to think; learning for understanding; learning how to learn; and the social and affective dimensions of learning and thinking. Learning outcomes were cross-referenced to the relevant competence(s) in the SCT, and included the effective demonstration of a critical understanding of current approaches and research, and the capacity to reflect critically on, and evaluate, classroom and school practice, and inform teaching by personal reflection, discussion, relevant reading and research.

Learning and teaching approaches were wide-ranging. Summative assessment required the compilation of a portfolio designed to demonstrate reflective engagement in module activities leading to successful classroom applications, and an oral presentation with brief accompanying report on classroom-based research.

Since there were many more applicants than the twenty places, it was possible to form the cohort to reflect the overall gender balance (80 per cent female) and the proportion of applicants from different sectors (a random selection was then made within each category), resulting in nursery, primary, secondary and special needs sectors all being represented. Reasons given for studying the module were varied: personal interest in the topic, wanting to develop as a teacher, and wanting to develop pupils' skills were most frequently cited. Interestingly, only three participants explicitly mentioned a desire to become a CT. One participant did not take up her place, four withdrew during the module for personal reasons, three opted out of being assessed, and, of the remaining twelve, eleven passed the module.

A detailed, formal evaluation was conducted (see Kirkwood and MacKay, 2003). Some key findings, which will inform the conclusions to this article – from summative assessment, detailed questionnaires to the twelve participants who completed the module and open-ended written returns from those who did not, and focus group interviews with a sample of four participants nine months afterwards – are summarised below. It is wise at this point to inject a note of caution in respect of the interpretation of this evidence. Teachers' self-reports of their activities cannot be taken at face value as a direct reflection of what actually transpired. Furthermore, in the context of being assessed, some teachers may be tempted to relate a better account of events, one that will please tutors, perhaps by selective use of the evidence or by not expressing an honest opinion. In order to counter these factors (in so far as this is possible), there was considerable emphasis on teachers applying rigorous but nevertheless appropriate research methodologies when gathering and analysing the evidence that they would use to inform their judgements about the efficacy of their own practice. Thus, for example, it was expected that teachers would triangulate their evidence (their own opinions would not suffice) and use a range of reliable sources, such as more experienced peers in the role of critical observer or evidence of pupils' work and attainment analysed in relation to identified learning goals.

The assessed portfolios contained rich and varied evidence on the impact of the module, such as:

■ documented reports on successful lessons using a 'thinking skills' approach, incorporating teaching resources developed by the participant and analysis of a range of evidence drawn from pupils and school colleagues;
■ accounts of how new approaches were being embedded into departmental or school practices and/or of collaborative work with colleagues;
■ reflective study diaries;
■ detailed critiques of published articles, and a personal stance on the issues raised within them;
■ screenshots of contributions to online discussions with other module participants.

Very positive findings emerged from analysis of responses to questionnaires, among which were: module activities had facilitated interchange of opinions and sharing experiences; the content was stimulating, challenging, and reflected current thinking and research; module activities had enabled respondents to be more creative when planning lessons and teaching, and to apply ideas from research to their own teaching; and the assessment approach was ideal. For some participants, the module had the effect of injecting a feeling of renewed enthusiasm and confidence:

> This module has given me an enthusiasm for teaching which I have lost over the last few years. Teachers have not been allowed to think in the present climate and this module gave [me] the confidence to use the skills and experience I have gained over the years to promote better thinking and learning in my class.
>
> (Teacher A)

Focus group discussions provided further evidence of the positive impact on professional practice, which had continued beyond the duration of the module. There are, for example, accounts of successful attempts to link theory and practice resulting in significant shifts in practice, and of respondents adopting a research perspective on their own teaching. The following two vignettes should serve to illustrate the nature of this evidence.

Adopting a research perspective:

> we've done this big school initiative with structured play . . . quite a few teachers, we all met after school and we looked very deeply at what we were doing and there was a lot of work went into it, and eventually the outcome of that was a leaflet . . . on what exactly went on in our school through the different stages from nursery right up to Primary 5. . . . And then at the end of it we actually wrote up a report of everything that we had done and all our evidence and all the different stages we'd gone through to get to this leaflet . . . Yes, I think you're now very aware of keeping evidence. When I was saying that we were making up the leaflets and doing all those things as a school I was keeping everything, so it was just like a folio I was keeping . . . so that in the future if I want to write it up I've got everything there.
>
> (Teacher A)

Significant shifts in practice, informed by reading and research:

> I always make the point of putting some time [aside] at the end to say, 'Well, could you tell us what you've been doing?' . . . and, 'What do you think you've learned today?' I always do that now, and it clarifies for me exactly what's going on. And very often the other ones [pupils] will say, 'Oh, that was interesting', . . . it is a lot of cross-fertilization which I really didn't do before. So that's very useful . . . I think young people really appreciate the amount of consultation they receive. I always did have dialogue with them, but I think even with those simple questions, 'What have you learned?', things like that, I think more about them [my pupils] as well, they really respond very well to that, and I would say that the relationship between us all has grown stronger as a result.
>
> (Teacher B)

A further development indicating the sustainability of their professional and personal commitment was the involvement of nine former module participants within a collaborative learning community in which various forms of enquiry on teaching thinking were pursued (see Kirkwood, 2005). A flavour of the group's activities and how these have stimulated classroom activities is conveyed by the following vignette (again, from focus group discussions):

Well, a few people in the group have actually given talks which I've found very interesting. Ideas, I've taken quite a few ideas from that and used them in my classroom . . . And it's just nice to get together and you know, talk to people who are interested in the same thing. We have a library there and quite a few interesting books on thinking skills and poems and stories, . . . I've used them with my class . . . I found it very useful.

(Teacher C)

DISCUSSION AND CONCLUSIONS

The purposes behind the presentation of key findings are to illuminate issues arising from different perspectives on teachers' CPD and teacher research and enquiry in general, and to examine the early influence of the CT Programme on the development and direction of teacher research and enquiry in Scotland in particular. The option module is closely modelled on the SCT and is genuinely in the spirit of the CT Programme, and therefore it serves as an early and appropriate example to use. The profile of the cohort, in terms of gender balance, age and sector, matches closely that of the core modules during the piloting phase (Kirk *et al.*, 2003: 65). However, the motivations of participants for studying a pilot module may not match those of teachers who have later embarked on the Programme 'for real', for whom there is a longer-term and financial commitment towards continuing study. It is reasonable to assume that participants now registered on the Programme would be at least equally committed to their professional development as the cohort for whom the key findings are presented above. Also, the way that participants experience any particular module may be entirely different from the way that the Programme is experienced overall. Up to six years of study, changing personal and/or professional circumstances, and the possibility of having uneven experiences across different modules and tutors could all have a marked impact on how participants finally come to view the Programme. However, since the purpose of this analysis is not to evaluate the overall experiences of teachers who have completed the Programme, it is sufficient to take note of the above differences. It would seem reasonable to recommend that further national funded research is devoted to examining the overall experiences of teachers completing the Programme and the subsequent impact they are having in their schools. By spring 2006, around 7,000 teachers had gained certificates indicating that they were eligible to embark on the Programme, 3,000 were registered, and 229 had completed, amounting to around 30 per cent of those teachers who were eligible (GTC Scotland). Thus, within a few years, there will be sufficient numbers of teachers who have completed the Programme to merit further investigation of its impact.

Is the object of educational research, according to Stenhouse, realised?

This article began by relating Stenhouse's (1983: 192) view of the object of educational research as being to develop thoughtful reflection in order to strengthen the professional judgement of teachers. This view seems to reflect quite accurately participants' orientations towards research. The presence of thoughtful reflection is captured well in the evidence from Teacher B, and similarly the perception of strengthened professional judgement is captured well in the statement from Teacher A: 'this module gave [me] the confidence to use the skills and experience I have gained over the years'. The evidence overall (see Kirkwood and MacKay, 2003) provides ample support for our assertion here that this purpose has been achieved, and from this it can be concluded that Stenhouse's emancipatory ideals can indeed be applied to a new Scottish model of CPD. However, against this should be placed the many constraints facing teachers – lack of time; limited scope; a prescribed syllabus and teaching plan and/or a school development plan which is fixed and dictated by the national policy agenda and which cannot accommodate any additional developments; a general lack of individual teacher autonomy; hostile or indifferent reactions from some colleagues; school management too busy to provide practical support for research – all of these factors were cited by respondents. In order to lessen these constraints, longer-term systemic changes are needed, for which the CT Programme may provide a strong impetus if it is taken up widely in the profession, particularly by the new generation of teachers now emerging from initial training.

Does the Programme successfully combine a range of CPD purposes?

Earlier, a range of potentially competing purposes and forms of CPD was explored in relation to the features of the CT Standard and format of the Programme. A question which can be posed is whether the contrasting features of the Programme can operate in synergy, or whether instead the Programme represents a classic compromise which is doomed to failure. The evidence indicates that participants welcomed the opportunity provided by the module to engage with theory and to reflect on powerful ideas and perspectives. They also valued the opportunity to develop their situated, experiential knowledge through the exchange of evaluative accounts of their professional experiences with colleagues. It would appear that the balance between these two components provided a context conducive to professional learning, as did the combination of formal aspects of the delivery of the module with the more informal learning opportunities which arose from the interrogation of practice in their own professional contexts.

Engagement in research and commitment to change and development

Kirk (2004: 14) asks, has the CT Standard encouraged teachers to be more active in originating research, applying research findings to their own context, and subjecting their work to critical analysis using research tools of various kinds in order to bring about improvement in professional practice through the search for more intelligent and sensitive ways of effecting learning? Participants' evaluative accounts of their experiences and changing practices offer some evidence that their involvement in this module has made them more 'research-minded', but it is not yet possible to judge the longer-term impact of their avowed commitment to change and development. Participants' research has tended towards the modest integration of theory and application of theory to classroom practice using action research. In relation to the OECD's advocation of 'use-inspired basic' research, the small scale of each individual teacher's enquiry restricts opportunities for pursuit of 'basic' research. Nevertheless, the grounding of the participants' research in theoretical ideas and frameworks should provide a sound basis for any subsequent collaborative developments of 'use-inspired basic' research.

Collaboration and the emergence of communities of enquiry

Are networks of researching teachers or communities of enquiry becoming established, and are these providing the necessary infrastructure to facilitate worthwhile research activity and professional learning? Campbell *et al.* (2003: 3) argue that collaborative groups and networks can indeed help sustain and embed research in educational settings. Lieberman and Miller (1999) posit, as one of their fundamentals of school improvement, the idea of 'building collaboration and cooperation [. . .] people doing things together, talking together, sharing concerns and building group norms over time' (p. 83). More detailed study of the patterns of engagement among participants in the CT Programme would be necessary in order to judge whether it would be appropriate to ascribe evolving forms of mutual engagement as being consistent with Lieberman and Miller's (1999) ideas and Wenger's (1998) concept of community of practice. An element worthy of consideration here is the extent to which participants were able to interact and communicate as members of a distributed, and hence 'virtual', community. There were signs of participants beginning to acquire a shared language derived from the field of thinking skills research. However, there was perhaps less in the way of evidence of shared purpose in the sense of participants' 'understanding and tuning their [joint] enterprise' (Wenger, 1998: 95). This was understandable since the precise purpose or focus of enquiry of each of the participating teachers was specific to their own professional context, and it would primarily be in this context of collaborative working with school colleagues that this understanding and tuning would have gone on. Nevertheless, the adoption by the module of powerful ideas about thinking skills from the literature offered the opportunity to develop a 'shared repertoire' (Wenger, 1998: 95) of approaches among the group. The desire of a significant proportion of the cohort to continue to meet as a group, however, indicates the apparent importance of actual, as opposed to, or at least as a supplement to, virtual meetings for such a community to flourish. Another key question raised which is worthy of further detailed study, also highlighted by Stoll *et al.* (2003), concerns the role of the tutor or facilitator of such a putative community of enquiry.

Are teachers becoming more knowledgeable about the basics of good research?

According to Campbell *et al.* (2003), teachers need to know about the basics of good research, whether or not they ever conduct their own research, so that they are able to analyse critically the research evidence that they read as part of their professional role, and to judge its findings and conclusions from a well-informed point of view. There was good evidence of enhanced 'research literacy' in the work submitted for assessment by participating teachers, reflecting the emphasis on a systematic and planned approach to conducting research in the module delivery. Many of their evaluative comments indicated that they were more confident in their ability to read and appraise research sources critically.

Particularly for those participants who will continue with their studies on the CT programme, the module has provided a grounding in basic research concepts which they should be able to draw on consistently, such as the importance of wider reading in order to inform oneself of relevant theories and research, and the systematic gathering and interrogation of evidence from a range of sources and perspectives as a basis for forming sound professional judgements.

Are teachers prepared to make their practice and research open to public scrutiny and can teacher research also benefit the wider community of researchers?

Eisner (2002) emphasises opening up the practice of teaching as a public performance which can be scrutinised, shared and discussed with colleagues. Pring (2000) expects teacher research, like all research, to be open to proper scrutiny and criticism. Of course, we should ask whether the kinds of professional enquiry fostered by participation in this part of the CT Programme square with Stenhouse's definition of research as 'systematic enquiry made public'. The assessment enabled a judgement to be reached by tutors on whether the evidence counted as 'systematic enquiry'. Pring (2000) reminds us that, in any attempt to realise the potential of this kind of teacher research, not only as an important form of continuing professional development activity, but also as a valid form of educational research which is capable of contributing to our understanding of educational phenomena, we must seek to avoid 'false dualisms'. Teacher research conducted in the context of CPD should seek to capture the uniqueness of the practitioner's particular professional context, but not at the expense of ignoring important broader insights from larger-scale research. One can discern clearly from the assessment evidence, and from participants' positive dispositions towards the prescribed reading materials, that broader insights from larger-scale research have indeed impacted on their thinking and ensuing practical actions.

There was a degree of public scrutiny arising out of the requirement upon participants to present their work to an audience of their peers, and evaluative comments confirmed that this was seen as a welcome part of the learning experience. Indeed, in keeping with the expectations of Cochran-Smith and Lytle (1993) that teacher research should generate both local and public knowledge and hence benefit the wider community of educators as well as the individual teacher and immediate colleagues, there is here scope for the wider dissemination of the results of these enquiries to professional colleagues with similar interests in schools and other professional contexts further afield.

Therefore, we are able to conclude that the success of this module within the CT programme in Scotland provides one effective demonstration of how favourable conditions can be created for networks of teachers as researching professionals to develop, and that a successful start can be made to initiating teachers into research as conceived by Stenhouse (1975, 1983), thus enhancing their professional practice and leading to, 'more intelligent and sensitive ways of effecting learning' (Kirk *et al.*, 2003: 30). Specific design features of the CT Programme and Standard, and of the option module itself, have combined to create these conditions, in the ways that are analysed above. The experiences of participants in this module can be seen as illustrative of the emphasis on professional development in the Scottish policy context, which Menter *et al.* (2004) have contrasted with the prevailing performance management culture in England.

Since the CT Programme is designed for experienced teachers, it would be worthwhile to investigate, in the context of initial teacher education and other CPD provision, the scope for enabling and encouraging teachers at earlier stages of their career development to become part of a research network. We identify as an important implication the need for further research into favourable conditions for sustaining networks of teachers as researchers. Such conditions may arise out of broad national developments in CPD (such as the CT Programme) or specific features of teachers' working environments.

REFERENCES

Campbell, A., Freedman, E., Boulter, C. and Kirkwood, M. (2003) *Issues and principles in educational research for teachers*, Southwell: British Educational Research Association.

Christensen, M., Slutsky, R., Bendau, S., Covert, J., Dyer, J., Risko, G. and Johnston, M. (2002) 'The rocky road of teachers becoming action researchers', *Teaching and Teacher Education*, Vol. 18: 259–272.

Christie, D. (2003) 'Competences, benchmarks and standards in teaching', in Bryce, T. and Humes, W. (eds) *Scottish education: second edition, post-devolution*, Edinburgh: EUP.

Cochran-Smith, M. and Lytle, S.L. (1993) *Inside outside: teacher research and knowledge*, New York: Teachers College Press.

Conway, P.F. (2001) 'Anticipatory reflection while learning to teach: from a temporally truncated to a temporally distributed model of reflection in teacher education', *Teaching and Teacher Education*, Vol. 17, No. 1: 89–106.

Day, C. (1999) *Developing teachers: the challenges of lifelong learning*, London: Falmer.

Day, C. (2004) *A passion for teaching*, London: RoutledgeFalmer.

Eisner, E. (2002) 'From episteme to phronesis to artistry in the study and improvement of teaching', *Teaching and Teacher Education*, Vol. 18: 375–385.

Humes, W. (2001) 'Conditions for professional development', *Scottish Educational Review*, Vol. 33, No. 1: 6–17.

King, M.B. (2002) 'Professional development to promote schoolwide inquiry', *Teaching and Teacher Education*, Vol. 18: 243–257.

Kirk, G. (2004) 'The Chartered Teacher: a challenge to the profession in Scotland', *Education in the North*, Vol. 11: 10–17.

Kirk, G., Beveridge, W. and Smith, I. (2003) *Policy and practice in education: the Chartered Teacher*, Edinburgh: Dunedin Academic Press.

Kirkwood, M. (2001) 'The contribution of curriculum development to teachers' professional development: a Scottish case study', *Journal of Curriculum and Supervision*, Vol. 17: 5–28.

Kirkwood, M. (2005) 'Fostering an inquiry approach to teachers' professional development on teaching thinking skills'. Paper presented at ESRC Conference Seminar, February, University of Newcastle.

Kirkwood, M. and MacKay, E. (2003) *Evaluation of Learning to Think and Thinking to Learn: a pilot study of an option module for the Scottish Chartered Teacher Programme*, Glasgow: University of Strathclyde.

Knight, P. (2002) 'A systemic approach to professional development: learning as practice', *Teaching and Teacher Education*, Vol. 18, No. 3: 229–241.

Lieberman, A. and Miller, L. (1999) *Teachers – transforming their world and their work*, New York: Teachers College Press.

Lipman, M. (2003) *Thinking in education* (2nd edition), Cambridge: Cambridge University Press.

Loughran, J. (2003) 'Exploring the nature of teacher research', in Clarke, A. and Erickson, G. (eds) *Teacher inquiry: living the research in everyday practice*, London: Routledge Falmer.

Menter, I., Mahony, P. and Hextall, I. (2004) 'Ne'er the twain shall meet? Modernizing the teaching profession in Scotland and England', *Journal of Education Policy*, Vol. 19, No. 2: 195–214.

OECD (2002) *Educational research and development in England: examiners' report*, Paris: OECD; available at www.oecd.org/dataoecd/17/56/1837550.pdf; accessed 5 May 2005.

Pring, R. (2000) *Philosophy of educational research*, London: Continuum.

Purdon, A. (2003) 'A national framework of CPD: continuing professional development or continuing policy dominance?', *Journal of Educational Policy*, Vol. 18, No. 4: 423–437.

Scottish Executive Education Department (2001) *A teaching profession for the 21st century: agreement reached following recommendations made in the McCrone Report*, Edinburgh: SEED.

Scottish Executive Education Department (2002a) *The Standard for Chartered Teacher*, Edinburgh: SEED; available at: www.teachinginscotland.com.

Scottish Executive Education Department (2002b) *Continuing Professional Development*, Edinburgh: SEED; available at www.teachinginscotland.com.

Stenhouse, L. (1975) *An introduction to curriculum research and development*, London: Heinemann Education.

Stenhouse, L. (1980) 'Reflections', in Stenhouse, L. (ed.) *Curriculum research and development*, London: Heinemann Education.

Stenhouse, L. (1983) 'Curriculum, research and the art of the teacher', in Stenhouse, L. (ed.) *Authority, education and emancipation: a collection of papers*, London: Heinemann Education.

Stoll, L., Wallace, M., Bolam, R., McMahon, A., Thomas, S., Hawkey, K., Smith, M. and Greenwood, A. (2003) *Creating and sustaining effective professional learning communities: DfES research brief*, London: DfES; available at www.dfes.gov.uk/research/data/uploadfiles/RBX12–03.pdf; accessed 27 May 2005.

Wenger, E. (1998) *Communities of practice learning, meaning and identity*, Cambridge: Cambridge University Press.

Zeichner, K.M. and Noffke, S.E. (2001) 'Practitioner research', in Richardson, V. (ed.) *Handbook of research on teaching*, Washington: AERA.

INDEX